MW00488960

LUCKY MUD
& OTHER FOMA

CHRISTINA
JARVIS

LUCKY
MUD
& OTHER FOMA

A FIELD GUIDE TO KURT VONNEGUT'S ENVIRONMENTALISM AND PLANETARY CITIZENSHIP

SEVEN STORIES PRESS

New York • Oakland • London

A SEVEN STORIES PRESS FIRST EDITION

SEVEN STORIES PRESS
140 Watts Street
New York, NY 10013
www.sevenstories.com

College professors and high school and middle school teachers
may order free examination copies of Seven Stories Press titles.
Visit https://www.sevenstories.com/pg/resources-academics
or email academics@sevenstories.com..

Library of Congress Cataloging-in-Publication Data
Names: Jarvis, Christina S., author.
Title: Lucky mud & other foma : a field guide to Vonnegut's planetary
citizenship / Christina S. Jarvis.
Description: New York : Seven Stories Press, [2022] | Includes
bibliographical references and index.
Identifiers: LCCN 2022022916 | ISBN 9781644212257 (hardcover) | ISBN
9781644212264 (ebook)
Subjects: LCSH: Vonnegut, Kurt--Criticism and interpretation. | Vonnegut,
Kurt--Political and social views. | Environmentalism in literature. |
World citizenship in literature. | American fiction--20th
century--History and criticism.
Classification: LCC PS3572.O5 Z735 2022 | DDC 813/.54--dc23/eng/20220720
LC record available at https://lccn.loc.gov/2022022916

Printed in the USA.

9 8 7 6 5 4 3 2 1

FOR MY EXTENDED FAMILIES,
REAL AND ARTIFICIAL,
BUT ESPECIALLY FOR TOM,
CHRISTOPHER, CALDER,
AND THE LATE PATRICIA JARVIS

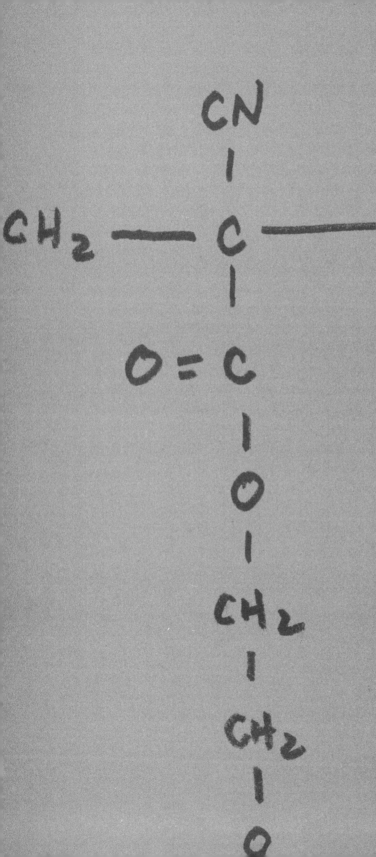

Contents

Illustrations

INTRODUCTION

So how did we get from that humility before life's precariousness to Branson's game of planet beach ball? One person who saw it all coming was the irascible American novelist Kurt Vonnegut.

—NAOMI KLEIN, *This Changes Everything: Capitalism vs. The Climate*

I think one thing that's really loony is that people would be perfectly content and think we've stolen something if life goes on for another hundred years. . . . I think that it's reasonable to suspect that the world is ending and to propose ways of preventing this.

—KURT VONNEGUT, Library of Congress Address, February 1, 1971

SOPPY PILLOWS AND SAINTS

When Kurt Vonnegut took the stage in New York City's Bryant Park for the 1970 Earth Day rally, the crowd was jubilant.[1] It was an auspicious day for the beginning of the environmental movement. The sun beamed down on the marchers on Fifth Avenue, peaceful demonstrators sang and carried daffodils, and a brass ensemble played fanfares on the steps of the New York Public Library near the speaker platform. Noting the joyous mood, Vonnegut opened his speech with a joke: "It is unusual for a total pessimist to be speaking at a spring celebration. Anyway, here we all are." He wasted no time getting to his central point: that the Earth Day demonstrators needed to get President Nixon's attention, because "he has our money and he has our power." Responding to Nixon's decision to sit out the events, Vonnegut wondered "which sporting event the president was watching. . . . Perhaps a boxing match by satellite" television.

This jab at Nixon was personal for Vonnegut, who had participated in the Washington, DC, Vietnam Moratorium march the previous November while Nixon watched college football, deliberately ignoring the crowd. Critiquing the administration's decision to prioritize military spending over environmental protection, Vonnegut soberly declared that Nixon's worries over being the "first American president to lose" a war were misplaced. "He may be the first American president to lose an entire planet," Vonnegut declared. Like the thousands of other Earth Day speakers, who called for science-based, ecological perspectives, Vonnegut leveled his most urgent critique of Nixon at his profession: "I am sorry he's a lawyer; I wish to God that he was a biologist."

From the grand scale of national policy change and planetary survival, Vonnegut shifted to the small actions that nearby marchers were making while the Vietnam War continued—"picking up trash missed by the Sanitation Department." These efforts, Vonnegut feared, would be no match for the pollution masked by "great advertising campaigns," the Nixon Administration's inattention, and an economic model where "polluters are looked upon as ordinary Joes just doing their job." Vonnegut predicted, "In the future [polluters] will be looked upon as swine," and he had final, comforting words for his audience: "Those who try their best to save the planet will find a loose, cheerful, sexy brass band waiting to honor them right outside the Pearly Gates. What will the band be playing? 'When the Saints Come Marching In.'"

When the *Village Voice* published coverage of its April 21 interview with Vonnegut and his Bryant Park speech, Anna Mayo reported that of all the speakers, "he was the gloomiest." While responding to his opening comment and pessimistic take on the Nixon administration, Mayo also highlighted Vonnegut's claim that the environmental movement was "a big soppy pillow." Vonnegut bestowed the label because he predicted, "Nobody's going to *do* anything." Vonnegut, of course, was famously wrong. Earth Day helped create the first "green generation" in US history, the Environmental Protection Agency (EPA), bans on DDT and leaded gasoline, the Clean Water Act (1972), the Endangered Species Act (1973), and other landmark legislation.[2] Perhaps it was because of Vonnegut's failure of vision that the *Village Voice* retitled Mayo's piece "Kurt Vonnegut Tries to Spoil Earth Day" when it republished it forty years later. Or perhaps the retitling was inspired by Vonnegut's dire late-life predictions about climate change or early posthumous portraits of the author as a "congenitally gloomy" chain-smoking prophet of the apocalypse.[3] What all these characterizations miss is that beneath Vonnegut's surface pessimism lay deeply held beliefs in planetary citizenship and engagement. They also miss the fact that much of Vonnegut's writings was richly conversant with, and sometimes ahead of, environmental approaches throughout his career.

Read in the context of the more than fifty speeches collected by Environmental Action, the group coordinating Earth Day, Vonnegut's speech seems neither out of place nor particularly gloomy. Nixon got off light in Vonnegut's remarks compared to the scathing critiques leveled at the president by politicians Adlai Stevenson, Gaylord Nelson, Richard Ottinger, and Frank Moss. Vonnegut's criticisms of anti-litter campaigns and corporate greenwashing, meanwhile, were in line with those of key Earth Day organizers, including national coordinator Denis Hayes. Environmental Action flatly refused all corporate funding, and Hayes condemned the politicians and business leaders who tried to "turn the environmental movement into a massive anti-litter campaign."[4] Vonnegut also immediately contradicted his claim that no one was going to *do* anything about environmental change. He donated his speech to Environmental Action, which used the royalties from sales of *Earth Day—The Beginning* to fund an explicitly political agenda aimed at unseating congressional leaders with the worst environmental records as well as implementing widespread legislative, social, and cultural change. He also gave the Wave Hill Center for Environmental Studies permission to use his May 1970 Bennington address in its new "Earth Kit," a free collection of "the finest available" environmental readings, for use in New York City schools.[5]

The main way Vonnegut responded to the urgent environmental issues he addressed on Earth Day was through writing. In the months following his Bryant Park speech, he revised his off-Broadway play *Happy Birthday, Wanda June* to include more didactic environmental messages, strengthened his critiques of America's polluting car culture in working drafts of *Breakfast of Champions*, and irreverently went after hypermasculine technological fixes to Great Lakes pollution, invasive species, and human population issues in his final short story, "The Big Space Fuck." In fact, he was so deeply affected by Isaac Asimov's predictions about global warming and his own responsibilities to the nation's youth that he abruptly cut short his speech at the Library of Congress on February 1, 1971, and cancelled all speaking engagements for six months. Vonnegut, who could joke about virtually everything, wept later that evening and, according to his longtime friend and agent Don Farber, was troubled by the event for the rest of his life.[6]

Both as a writer and as a New York City resident, Vonnegut frequently returned to the site of his Earth Day speech. In *Slapstick*, Wilbur Daffodil-11 Swain explains his campaign to end American loneliness via artificial extended families on those same steps. In *Jailbird*, Walter Starbuck spends hours admiring springtime flowers in Bryant Park on April 22. And in *Timequake*, police officers pick up Kilgore Trout at the New York Public Library and transport him uptown, where his creed would do "as much to save life on Earth as Einstein's *E equals mc squared* had done to end it two generations earlier."[7] By the time Vonnegut completed his final novel, he was still worrying about the possibility of a "dying" planet, but he had come up with kinder words to describe the Fifth-Avenue-litter-collecting saints. As he explained in *Timequake*, he defined a saint "as a person who behaves decently in an indecent society." Fittingly, thirty-seven years to the day after he described the burgeoning environmental movement as a "big soppy pillow" in his interview at the Algonquin Hotel, Kurt Vonnegut's memorial service was held there, with a brass jazz trio led by trumpeter Tatum Greenblatt.[8] The trio played "Back Home in Indiana" and New Orleans–style renditions of "Amazing Grace" and "Fly Away." If only they had played "When the Saints Come Marching In."

PECULIAR TRAVEL SUGGESTIONS

This book tells the story of Vonnegut's planetary citizenship. It discovers the origins of his environmental stewardship in lessons from Vonnegut's Orchard School teacher Hillis Howie and the ethics and political ideals forged during his teenage Western adventures. It also explores Vonnegut's deep attachments to place and the profound ways his biology, chemistry, and anthropology studies shaped his planetary thinking. Primarily, I investigate Vonnegut's planetary citizenship in his novels, short stories, plays, speeches, and essays.

Vonnegut saw writing itself as an act of good citizenship, as a way of "poisoning" the minds of young people "with humanity . . . to encourage them to make a better world."[9] Often, that literary activism meant addressing real social and environmental poisonings—polluted water, soil, and air; the plasticization of cultures and lives; racial and economic injustice; isolating and dehumanizing technologies; and lives and landscapes desolated by war. Vonnegut's remedies for addressing these spiritual and physical poisonings took many forms, from the redemptive power of the arts to artificial extended families to vital communities and engaged democracies. Reminding us of our shared connections as humans, as Earthlings, as stardust, Vonnegut's writings offer whole Earth, interstellar, and species-level perspectives, and challenge readers to think, create, and love beyond national boundaries. Although Vonnegut was quintessentially an American writer who responded to his time, paradoxically, it may be his willingness to be "a man without a country," a planetary citizen, that makes his work "so urgently needed in our time."[10] If the devastating impacts of climate change, systemic racism, hypercapitalism, militaristic nationalism, pollution, the COVID-19 pandemic, and digital tribalism haven't confirmed the need for planetary citizenship, I don't know what will.

While Vonnegut often used the term "planetary citizens" to refer to artists and cosmopolitan thinkers whose work exceeded national boundaries, I consider Vonnegut's planetary citizenship in broad environmental and social justice terms. Like his father, Kurt Sr., the "first planetary citizen" of his life, Vonnegut knew that "beauty could be found or created anywhere on this planet."[11] He also recognized that threats to this beauty and the planet's life-supporting systems could happen anywhere. Telling the story of Vonnegut's planetary citizenship means looking at both his global and local perspectives, at his warnings about climate change, species extinction, and planetary apocalypses, as well as at his quiet meditations about places, communities, and everyday interactions.

You can probably see where all this is going. I didn't at first, and this is not the book I had planned to write. Although I have (more or less) stuck with my plan to explore Vonnegut's planetary citizenship by viewing his life and writings through an environmental lens, many of my initial assumptions and approaches changed when I started working with his papers at the Lilly Library. Manuscript drafts for some of his key environmental novels, *Galápagos* and *Slapstick*, were missing, but other works and scores of unpublished pieces offered unexpected ecological engagements. And although Vonnegut's statements about his creative process were largely true, they omitted much of the complexity of, and intense struggles behind, certain texts. He *generally* "bashed" away, retyping introductory pages and chapters over and over again until he got them right. However, Vonnegut also "swooped" at times and would switch from fiction to poetry to drama to television scripts if an idea beguiled him in a new direction. His beautifully messy creative process burst forth in different ways—from epically long scrolls collaged together with tape, staples, and paper clips to drafts that included as many drawings and handwritten notes as they did typed pages. Even the gestation processes of works were much longer than I had imagined, and I found sections of novels spread out in multiple collections, under various titles, and in different genres. I quickly realized that I would need to return again and again and again to appreciate the tales behind Vonnegut's publications and planetary citizenship. So I did.

My initial two-week research trip to the Lilly Library not only prompted four subsequent visits to study Vonnegut's papers, but also led to a host of "peculiar travel suggestions," which, as any good Bokononist or fan of *Cat's Cradle* knows, are "dancing lessons from God." To place Vonnegut's own papers in context, I scoured other archival collections, ranging from business, publishing, marketing, editorial, and agent records to unpublished letters, historical society holdings, and the files of other scholars, writers, and Vonnegut family members. Research trips also allowed me to explore places that shaped Vonnegut's life and writings: the shores of Lake Maxinkuckee, Indiana, and sacred sites in Indianapolis; the industrial environs of Schenectady and Alplaus, New York; Barnstable, Massachusetts, and Cape Cod's outer beaches; and New York City.

Locating Vonnegut's writings within the contexts of US environmental history and his own ecologically minded frameworks presented its own intellectual adventures. To tell the story of Vonnegut's planetary citizenship, I've drawn on a wide range of fields, including environmental science, history, sustainability, religious studies, cultural anthropology, and literary studies. Through biographies, documentaries, interviews, memoirs, published letters, posthumous collections, and his own autobiographical collages, an increasingly complex portrait of Kurt Vonnegut continues to emerge. Central to that portrait are analyses of his World War II experiences, post-war trauma, and pacifism; apprenticeship, struggles, and tremendous popularity as a writer; roles as a counterculture icon, public intellectual, secular humanist, and champion of writers' freedoms worldwide; grappling with depression, marriage problems, and complicated family relationships; and creative crossovers into drawing, painting, printmaking, and collaborative musical compositions.

My aim in exploring Vonnegut's planetary citizenship through his published works and manuscripts is twofold. First, I hope to give fans fresh reasons to revisit beloved texts and provide scholars with an archival road map to exciting new terrain. Second, I want to unfreeze some of the more prescient moments of Vonnegut's planetary citizenship for all of us, human and nonhuman, trying to make just, humane, and useful lives on our "once salubrious blue-green orb."[12] Although Kurt is up in heaven now, his critiques of isolating, dehumanizing, and environmentally destructive technologies and his frameworks for planetary thinking and vibrant communities still offer useful wisdom. Our spaceship Earth continues to get hotter, less hospitable, and rife with global economic, racial, and social injustices. And whether or not the Anthropocene becomes an official epoch, it's clear that human beings are altering Earth's living systems at the scale of geological forces and are ushering in our own existential threat through climate change.[13] Restoring the health of our air, soil, water, and human cultures will require unprecedented global cooperation and seismic shifts in action and imagination. This tough planetary moment calls for the wisdom of a writer who loved humankind "completely and unromantically." As interviewer J. Rentilly said of the late Hoosier icon, "Vonnegut saw us for who we really are, and loved us anyway."[14]

A BRIEF PRIMER FOR NON-BOKONONISTS

While devout Bokononists and adventurous readers may not need directions for the pages ahead, some might wish to know what the title means. Both "foma," a harmless untruth, and the idea of humans as "lucky mud" that "got to sit up and look around" come from Bokononism, Vonnegut's invented religion in *Cat's Cradle*. In the novel, Bokononism is created as an instrument of hope because its founder is unable to offer any real economic, social, or other material improvements. More than just a "useful delusion," Bokononism is also a tool for Vonnegut to deepen critiques of blind faith in science and Cold War conflicts in *Cat's Cradle*.[15] It's that tension between providing hope, comfort, imagination, and agency for humanity and nakedly telling the truth about all the ways we are damaging the planet, ourselves, and other life forms that makes Vonnegut's planetary citizenship so vital. Perhaps in this field guide you'll find some Vonnegutian "foma" that will help make you and the planet healthy, brave, just, and kind.

PART ONE

FOUNDATIONS

CHAPTER 1

BECOMING A
PLANETARY CITIZEN

The value system under which I operate
relative to animals and plants and the
earth and persons with cultures different from mine is one I learned from him.
There are thousands of us who were lucky
to come under his influence, and my guess
is that we are more at home on this planet,
and more respectful of it, than most of
our neighbors are.
  —KURT VONNEGUT, on teacher, mentor,
    naturalist Hillis Howie

The only way I'll ever be happy will be out
there under the stars . . . Damn but that's
wonderful!
  —KURT VONNEGUT, "The Rover Boys in
    the American Southwest"

EARLY MENTORS AND A FATEFUL BARGAIN

Expecting their third child, Kurt and Edith Vonnegut gathered with
other Northside Indianapolis parents at the All Souls Unitarian
Church on Alabama Street in early July 1922. Although Kurt Sr.
had designed the building, he wasn't there to inspect his architectural work or to make a polite Freethinker's nod toward religion.
The Vonneguts came to hear Marietta Johnson, the founder of
the Organic School, share her ideas for a revolutionary new way

of educating young children. In contrast to traditional schools, which Johnson saw as extensions of the industrial factory system, Johnson's school in Fairhope, Alabama, had no desks, standard textbooks, report cards, graded projects, or examinations.[16] And although instruction in reading and writing was delayed until the children were developmentally ready, older students tackled Latin, French, physics, chemistry, botany, biology, and history, all the while exploring nature, art, and folk dancing. Breaking with his grandfather Clemens Vonnegut's long-standing enthusiastic support for Indianapolis's public schools, Kurt Sr. and his wife, Edith, joined other Northside parents in planning a new private school based on Johnson's teaching philosophies.

Just three months after the July parents' meeting, the first young Orchard School students arrived at the Carey family's large frame house at 5050 North Meridian Street for an experiment in student-led learning. Named for the lush apple and pear tree orchard that occupied much of the five- to six-acre property, the school quickly developed a reputation for excellence, and many of the Northside's affluent families began sending their children there. Kurt Vonnegut Jr.'s older siblings, fifth-grader Bernard (Bernie) and kindergartener Alice (Allie), were among this early cohort. Like their peers, Bernie and Allie came to have their talents nurtured by the Orchard School's innovative pedagogies as they studied drawing, painting, geography, science, mathematics, foreign languages, drama, nature study, sculpture, history, and folk dancing.

As the number of students neared seventy, it became clear that the school would need to move to a new location. An established architect from a prominent family of Indianapolis businessmen, artists, civic leaders, and Freethinkers, Kurt Sr. quickly stepped in to help with the move. Along with two other fathers, "Doc," as he was affectionately known to family and friends, managed the purchase of the new property on West Forty-Third Street and then spent much of the summer of 1926 remodeling the main classroom building. It was to this more spacious, generously wooded campus that young Kurt came for kindergarten in the fall of 1927.[17]

Just nine blocks away from his house on North Illinois Street, the Orchard School gave Vonnegut a chance to develop his creativity, his imagination, and a sense of wonder in the natural world. By both historical or contemporary standards, the school adopted an innovative approach to connecting children with their local environments. The students helped grow their own food by planting and maintaining school gardens, and tapped fifty-three sugar maples on the property each spring to make their own syrup.[18] An early adopter of farm-to-table principles, the school had an on-site cook prepare for the students healthy lunches that featured fresh country milk, eggs, butter, and local produce. The children also explored nearby streams, sailed boats on the campus pond, and, during their third-grade year, cared for one of the school's animals, Billy the goat. Amid this nurturing, creative, soul-growing environment, Vonnegut also met some key members of his karass—his future wife Jane Cox and mother-in-law Riah Cox, his future best man Ben Hitz, and lifelong friends and Owl Club members Victor Jose and William "Skip" Failey.[19]

Later in life, Vonnegut acknowledged his debts to his former Orchard School teacher Hillis Howie by dedicating his most explicitly environmental novel, *Galápagos*, to him. In interviews, Vonnegut mentioned Howie's influence on the 1985 novel and praised him as a "truly great person" and "great naturalist."[20] But his most poignant tribute appears in a June 7, 1982, letter to the newly widowed Elizabeth Howie: "The value system under which I try to operate relative to animals and plants and the earth and persons with cultures different from mine is one I learned from him. There are thousands of us who were lucky to come under his influence, and my guess is that we are more at home on this planet, and more respectful of it, than most of our neighbors are."[21] The value system that so profoundly influenced young Kurt became the foundation of Vonnegut's own planetary citizenship.

Hillis Howie came to the Orchard School in the spring of 1925. A recent graduate of Butler University and a seven-year veteran counselor of the Culver Summer School of Woodcraft, Howie arrived with extensive outdoor education and camping experience, the burning curiosity of a lifelong learner, and a firm belief in empowering children to become self-reliant, respectful observers of the natural world.[22] While still in college at Wesleyan and Butler Universities, Howie became an adult leader and then scoutmaster of Troop #18 of Indianapolis, where he distinguished himself as an extraordinary conservationist and teacher.[23] Under Howie's leadership, his scouts patrolled state parks during spring bird migrations to protect endangered species and prevent nest robbing. They distributed game law pamphlets, established bird sanctuaries at Boy Scout camps, built birdhouses, and conducted bird censuses over multiple nesting seasons. Howie also led students at Culver and Camp Chank-Tan-Un-Gi in fieldwork, gave bird talks to more than 750 students at various Indianapolis public schools, and published pieces on Indianapolis's bird counts. For these and other efforts, famed conservationist William Hornaday awarded Howie one of three gold badge awards from the Permanent Wild Life Protection Fund in 1924, and Howie received special recognition at the National Boy Scout Court of Honor that year.

As he did with his scouts, the twenty-two-year-old nature and shop teacher inspired his Orchard School students to embrace conservation through "learning by doing," creative problem solving, and countless hours observing and playing in nature.[24] Under Howie's gentle guidance, Orchard School students became adept at naming birds, investigating swamps, and learning about all the plant and animal communities that shared the grounds with them. He also snuck in lessons in science and math as students built and launched boats, measured the grounds, and even figured out how to remove a boulder in the path of a proposed sports field. Beyond this local, place-based education, Howie also took students on field trips and overnight camping expeditions to state parks, and he fostered strong

Mr. Howie, director of the expedition. *(Bretzman.)*

1.1 ✳ This portrait of Hillis Howie, Kurt Vonnegut's naturalist men–
tor and Orchard School teacher, ca. 1930, comes from a scrapbook
documenting the accomplishments of early Prairie Trek expeditions.
Courtesy of Indiana Historical Society, BV2692.

ties between the school and other educational institutions—especially the Indianapolis Children's Museum. His students even helped the Children's Museum launch one of its first traveling exhibits by collecting, curating, and arranging natural objects.

Impressed by the traveling exhibit and Howie's teaching at the Orchard School, Kurt Sr. began to turn to Howie for help with other projects at the museum, and these ties blossomed into a warm friendship. As a founding board member, respected architect, and father, Kurt Sr. was charged with designing the museum's logo and organizing a junior board of local schoolchildren to help plan exhibits.[25] Drawing on children's love of fairy tales, Doc created a simple, crest-like emblem for the museum featuring a seahorse and the letters *C* and *M*. To make the seahorse come to life as a mascot for young visitors, he visited Howie in the school's portable shop building. Within a few hours, Howie carved an exquisite seahorse statue for the museum. A few years later, Doc offered to enlarge Howie's portable science and shop building at the Forty-Third Street campus, and, starting in 1930, Howie had his summer prairie trek participants collect specimens for the Children's Museum.[26]

Although Kurt had to leave the Orchard School after third grade because his family, hard-hit by the Depression, could no longer afford the tuition, Doc continued to nurture his son's naturalist interests. As Vonnegut recalled in *Fates Worse Than Death*, his father was "the first planetary citizen" his public-school friends had ever met. Through simple acts, such as appreciating the beauty of a moth, a clarinet, or a chess set, Kurt Sr. shared his sense of wonder as well as a more global vision of the arts. His father was "no more a respecter of politics and national boundaries than . . . a unicorn." Vonnegut continued: "Beauty could be found or created anywhere on this planet, and that was that." While providing a model of artistic planetary citizenship, Doc also encouraged his son's identity as a "citizen of the Earth" by sharing his love of gardening and the outdoors—especially through fishing trips and summer outings at the family cottage at Lake Maxinkuckee.[27]

Inspired by these outings and his father's involvement, Vonnegut became a school representative on the Children's Museum junior board, where he helped curate nature exhibits and joined the world of serious birding. Young Kurt faithfully rode his bike to the museum for Saturday morning meetings, but one day confessed to his father that the board "seemed incomprehensibly preoccupied with birds instead of general museum operations." Doc quickly corrected the mistake, and his son began attending meetings for the junior board instead of the bird club—but not before the seeds had been planted for a lifelong love of birds that would surface frequently in his fiction.[28] Vonnegut and his father's involvement with the Children's Museum was also pivotal in the younger Kurt's reunion with Hillis Howie in the summer of 1937. When Howie discovered an opportunity to acquire cabins for the Prairie Trek's base camp in Cottonwood Gulch, he turned to Kurt Sr. for new design and remodeling ideas. In exchange for creating architectural drawings and plans for reconstructing and retrofitting the cabins, Kurt Sr. asked Howie to let his fourteen-year-old son join the 1937 twelfth annual Prairie Trek, which took fifteen teenage boys and three adult leaders on a two-month, six-thousand-mile journey through the American Southwest.[29] Alternating between caravan camping and stays in a base camp near Thoreau, New Mexico, the expedition's sights were pure high adventure. The participants traveled to remote ruins in Mesa Verde National Park and Chaco Culture National Historical Park, explored deserted mining towns in Colorado, witnessed spectacular sunsets in Canyon de Chelly and Monument Valley, and hiked from Bright Angel Point to Roaring Springs at the north rim of the Grand Canyon. The trekkers experienced extraordinary Native American events as well, from an unplanned visit to a Navajo rodeo to a Hopi Snake Dance to the famous Gallup Inter-tribal Indian Ceremonial. As in previous treks, the junior scientists gathered specimens for the Indianapolis Children's

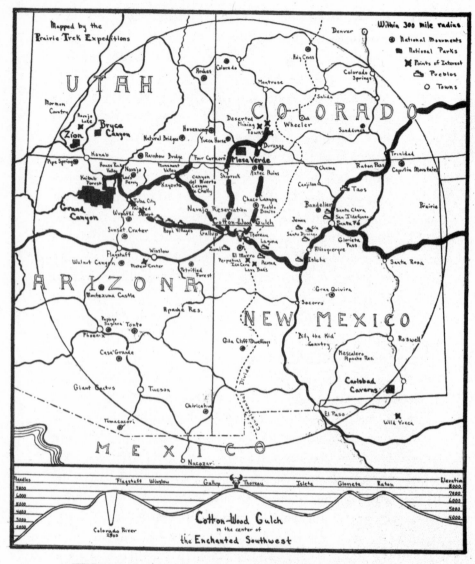

THIS MAP SHOWS THE ROUTE OF THE 1937 EXPEDITION.

I.2 ☀ This map highlights many of the national parks, towns, and Indigenous cultural sites Kurt Vonnegut visited during the Southwestern portion of the 1937 Prairie Trek. Courtesy of Indiana Historical Society, M0390.

Museum, but this time they had a special mission—to collect small mammals for the American Museum of Natural History in New York.

TAWNY DEER MOUSE AND TARZAN YELLS

The 1937 Prairie Trek played a vital role in shaping Vonnegut's planetary citizenship, but it also likely influenced his career-long calls for puberty ceremonies. The adventures through the American Southwest took adolescent boys away from their families and returned them to their communities two months later as young men, brimming with confidence from the independence, self-reliance, and advanced scientific skills learned on the trek. The appeal of the Prairie Trek and its counterpart for adolescent girls, the Turquoise Trail, is so enduring that Cottonwood Gulch continues to offer these expeditions. For Vonnegut, the trek offered that timeless journey into young adulthood and broadened the maps of his future fictional cosmos. Along the way, he also learned from Howie important lessons about nature, civics, and social justice, rooted in rugged environmentalism and American history.

Started by Hillis Howie in 1926, the prairie treks embodied the sometimes contradictory ideals that shaped nature-based tourism and conservation efforts in the 1920s and 1930s. Relying on Ford station wagons and trucks to support camping, the expeditions coincided with the rapid increase in automobile tourism to America's national parks, monuments, and wilderness areas—a trend that democratized Americans' access to protected landscapes but also increased the commercialization and management of these locations. From the numerous brochures, posters, and magazine articles he collected, Howie was intimately familiar with other adventure travel operations and "See America First" campaigns that beguiled automobile tourists to the country's natural wonders. Unlike family vacations and commercial trips that stuck to paved routes and carefully produced nature experiences, the prairie treks often left the highways, sometimes traveling hundreds of miles from the nearest town.[30] These departures from "civilization" also fueled the "Wild West" adventure elements of the trip, which appealed to boys growing up during a time of national nostalgia for the closed frontier of the West. As Howie explained in a 1941 *Regional Review* article about the treks, they "sought out the remote and generally unknown wilderness regions" and sometimes "pretended that we were the first white men to penetrate these wilds."[31]

Vonnegut's *Galápagos* dedication reveals that some of these "American Wild West" elements remained fixed in his imagination nearly fifty years later—learning to ride horses, meeting "real Indians," and hearing "a real wildcat" scream. Like *Galápagos's* animated biology teacher Mary Hepburn, Howie understood that embracing the frontier myth and re-creating the paths and practices of nineteenth-century pioneers and cowboys was the perfect hook for reeling in participants. Howie had the boys lead "a simple life" where they "did [their] own cooking, gathered fire-wood, sagebrush or buffalo chips for fuel and slept under the stars almost every night." While at Cottonwood Gulch, the 440-acre base camp near Thoreau, New Mexico, they further embraced the spirit of Western adventure. The boys borrowed horses from the neighboring E4 Ranch to ride through the Zuñi Mountains and Cibola National Forest, participated in the trek's third annual rodeo, learned campfire songs, pitched horseshoes and quoits, and even had a knife-flipping tournament.

Howie also understood that the journey should be fun, and he gave the boys space to discover their own identities, interests, and talents. Vonnegut found his own "wild" voice during the expedition, becoming the trek's official "Tarzan yell man." The comedic third child of his family, Vonnegut also slipped into comfortable roles as "stock company comedian" and "famous clarinet player" for the trek's first-ever swing band. Bonding with other performers, Vonnegut helped "entertainment at the Gulch hit a new all-time high" by adding the swing band and an hour-long Follies production to the annual rodeo.

1.3 * In this photograph of the 1937 Prairie Trek Members at Cottonwood Gulch, Kurt Vonnegut appears in the first row, third from the left. Courtesy of Indiana Historical Society, M0390.

As much as he enjoyed showing off his comedic, musical, and playwriting skills, Vonnegut was equally enthralled with the ecology, social justice, and early anthropology lessons he learned on the trek. The real tribute to Howie isn't the *Galápagos* dedication, but Vonnegut's solid engagements with evolutionary theory, ecology, and environmental and social justice in the novel. The further we delve into Howie's own writings and the history of the treks, the more we can see why Vonnegut felt so indebted to his mentor.

Howie used the "Wild West" adventure elements to attract expedition members, but, at their core, the treks were serious scientific endeavors. To be selected as a participant or "junior staff member" as they were called, the boys had to fill out an application outlining their special naturalist interests, trek goals, and previous summer experiences. Upon completing a successful interview with staff leaders, each boy chose at least one role that would aid the trek's particular natural history research. They could be archaeologists, entomologists, ethnologists, mammalogists, ornithologists, herpetologists, and geologists, as well as photographers and newspaper correspondents. To give them a foundation in these fields, Howie brought forty books (selected from the 118-title permanent collection) and scores of academic journal articles in the trek's library chest.

Under the guidance of experienced leaders and veteran trekkers, the boys blossomed as junior scientists, fulfilling the trek's commissions and producing impressive individual and collective reports. Ben Hitz, Vonnegut's tent mate and future best man at his wedding, identified 221 different species of insects that summer. Ultimately, Hitz and his fellow entomologists cataloged a total of 337 species from eight different orders, carefully recording each insect's common and scientific names along with notes about the sightings. While most of the collecting was done via lists and photography, some of the Indianapolis boys used jars to preserve specimens for their zoology teacher at Shortridge High School.[32]

Because the 1937 trek was five boys short of the usual twenty junior staff members, Vonnegut and his peers took on multiple roles.

With the special charge from the American Museum of Natural History to collect specimens for its North American mammals exhibits, four boys, including Vonnegut, worked as mammalogists. Given the trek's length and limited storage capacity, the boys had to learn to trap, skin, and mount the mammals sent to the museum. George Goodwin, assistant curator of the museum's mammalogy department, identified at least fifteen species collected by the boys, including a Jemez Mountains Pika, a Zuni Prairie Dog, a Chuska Mountains Wood Rat, and a Dark-brown Grasshopper Mouse. In a November 3, 1937, letter to Howie, Goodwin praised the "splendid work" done by the junior mammalogists and thanked Howie for the new acquisitions to the museum. Goodwin was so impressed by their efforts that he encouraged Howie to devote more time to "the study of mammalian life in the regions visited" by the treks.[33] Nearly fifty years later, Vonnegut was still proud of his role as a mammalogist, which had earned him an honorable mention for scientific achievement. In a 1987 interview with Hank Nuwer, he reminisced about putting "trap lines out every night" and personally catching "a subspecies of the tawny whitefoot mouse which had not been seen before." Vonnegut mentioned that he had bragged years earlier in the Army about his scientific discovery, and a fellow soldier jokingly renamed the mouse "Meesis Vonnegeesis."[34]

Had Howie's lessons been merely scientific or just superficial "Wild West" adventure, they probably would not have influenced Vonnegut so profoundly. What resonated with Vonnegut and took him decades to appreciate was the way Howie taught conservation and ecology alongside lessons about human relationships, social justice, citizenship, and common decency. As Howie explained in articles about the trek, the "Wild West" elements were a way to instill a deeper "spirit of adventure and exploration" of the natural world. Like other conservation advocates of the 1930s, Howie tried to empower "nature leaders" to counter the "pathetic depletion" of America's natural resources. Despite embracing some of the lore and practices of pioneers and cowboys, Howie recognized that these

Euro-American "pioneer forefathers" were also "empire builders" who "conquered the wilderness and converted the resources into more immediate forms of wealth."[35]

But Howie didn't preach to the boys. Instead, he used deserted mining towns and Dust Bowl farms as laboratories to explore complex conservation, economic, and social justice issues. On the 1937 trek, Howie led the boys through a twenty-mile stretch of abandoned, dust-encased farms and houses, where they had conversations about "annual precipitation, surface waters, underground water tables, wind velocity, soil types, native grasses, public land policy, speculation, ownership and tenure." While learning many of the lessons taught by the Civilian Conservation Corps and Soil Conservation agency, the boys began to reflect on a broader web of ecological relationships that included burrowing owls, rattlesnakes, prairie dogs and other animals affected by Dust Bowl conditions. Drawing on Aldo Leopold's 1933 landmark speech "The Conservation Ethic," Howie taught the boys that civilization was not "the enslavement of a stable and constant earth."[36] Like Leopold, he wanted them to work toward "a state of mutual interdependent cooperation between human animals, other animals, plants, and the soils, which may be disrupted at any moment by the failure of any of them."[37] That meant becoming nature leaders and engaged citizens who realized that environmental and other land-use issues were important topics for democratic debate. As Howie developed his own land ethic and thinking about sustainable, long-term use of resources, the treks gathered fewer and fewer specimens, shifting the focus instead to people and cultural relationships.

This transition was apparent in 1937, surely influenced by Hillis and Elizabeth Howie's deepening friendships with the Henio, Silversmith, and other Navajo families near Cottonwood Gulch. While it's impossible to guess how much the trek's emphasis on human relationships and Indigenous cultures influenced Vonnegut's decision to study anthropology after the war, the expedition exposed young Kurt to Pueblo archaeology and Indigenous Southwestern rituals, reservation conditions, and economic realities. Far more than simply introducing the boys to "real Indians," the trek included visits to Hopi, Navajo, and intertribal events as well as to markets and trading posts in Taos, Santa Fe, Cochiti, and other places throughout the Southwest. There the junior staff members purchased Navajo buttons, kachina dolls, and woven baskets for the Indianapolis Children's Museum, recording the locations and circumstances of the acquisitions.

Given his own deep respect for and dependence on his Navajo neighbors, Howie wanted the boys to have more than touristic or merely commercial experiences. Eighty percent of the boys worked as archaeologists on the Gulch's own property, excavating potsherds and walls of old pueblo ruins, and all trek members visited dozens of intact cliff dwellings and pueblos in Mesa Verde, Chaco Canyon, and Canyon de Chelly, going well beyond more famous and accessible sites. They learned the science of tree ring chronology to estimate the dates of pueblo construction, drought periods, and migrations, and made a special visit to Canyon del Muerto, where approximately 115 Navajo warriors were killed by Spanish forces in 1805.

The boys also witnessed living history during a Navajo Ye-bet-chi dance, a Hopi Snake Dance ritual, and many other performances at the Gallup Inter-tribal Indian Ceremonial events. Howie helped contextualize the dances by having trek participants read from the library chest's titles devoted to Navajo lore, ethnology, and archaeology, but he also wanted the boys to understand social justice dimensions of reservation life. Like the conservation and land ethics, these lessons come through in the boys' dispatches and final reports. As junior ethnologist Haskell Torrence documented Navajo carding, spinning, dyeing, and weaving practices, he also calculated the five- to six-cents-an-hour wage Navajo weavers would make on their finished rugs at then-current market prices.[38] Howie himself bemoaned "the mortgaged wealth" of Navajo silver lost to traders and the huge losses incurred when some forty-five thousand Navajo horses were sold "to dog meat canners for the average price of $1.75 per head as a phase of the range improvement."[39]

These powerful lessons in social justice and respectful cultural exchange coupled with training in conservation, ecology, and citizenship made the 1937 trek expedition a watershed event in Kurt's life—and a crucial foundation of his early planetary citizenship. Vonnegut was so inspired by the trip that he began planning his own expedition for the following summer as soon as he returned to Indianapolis. With his family unable to afford the trek's $425 tuition, Vonnegut recruited two close friends, George Jeffrey and Bryant "Bud" Gillespie, to join him for a monthlong tour of national parks, Indigenous cultural sites, and other Western adventures. Despite their route planning, saving, and inquiries to various parks and campsites, the trio was unable to take the trip in 1938 as they had originally planned. Vonnegut, who was "more eager" for camping and treks than most boys in Indianapolis, was able to quench some of his thirst for outdoor adventure with a spring 1939 camping expedition to Florida.[40] But Vonnegut and his friends were determined, and on July 31, 1939, at 5:40 a.m., they left Indianapolis and headed due west for a monthlong, 4,500-mile adventure.

THE ROVER BOYS

Already imagining himself as a serious writer, Vonnegut chronicled the journey through dispatches he sent home, which he revised into a thirty-eight-page, single-spaced typed manuscript, "The Rover Boys in the American Southwest." As biographer Ginger Strand notes, "The Rover Boys" is a true archival gem that "foreshadows Vonnegut's mature style." The rambling episodic narrative, short sections, "simultaneously ironic and heartfelt" tone, Strand observes, create a text that is signature Vonnegut: "Characters move in and out of the action, sketched with quick strokes that highlight their oddball qualities. His sentences are nimble and his paragraphs frequently conclude with one- or two-word interjections like 'Golly!'" Strand also recognizes that "The Rover Boys" is "the urtext" of so many journeys in Vonnegut's fiction—from Kilgore Trout's road trip in

Go West! These Three on Way—Almost

Times Photo.

Kurt Vonnegut, Bud Gillespie and George Jeffrey (left to right) practicing on how to set up their gasoline stove which will cook their meals on a month's journey.

1.4 ✳ Taken shortly before their "Rover Boys" Southwestern adventure, this photograph of Kurt Vonnegut, Bryant "Bud" Gillespie, and George Jeffrey, accompanied an article about the trip in the July 22, 1939, issue of the *Indianapolis Times*. Courtesy of Hoosier State Chronicles, Indiana State Library.

Breakfast of Champions to the narrator's peculiar travel suggestions in *Cat's Cradle* to the Shah's state tour in *Player Piano*. Vonnegut's "picaresque ramble through Depression America" not only shaped his views about people, politics, and culture, but also added to the tapestry of places that would become enshrined in his fiction.[41]

"The Rover Boys" *is* a wonderful road trip text, filled with many poignant moments worth freezing in amber—Kurt's early self-awareness as a writer, the "Oklahoma Eden" that protected him from the start of World War II, the priceless teenage slippage between innocence and experience, and bona fide high adventure.[42] Beneath the entertaining characters, well-told adventure tales, and overt social commentary, "The Rover Boys" has another signature Vonnegutian element: the serious intellectual engagement that informs his planetary citizenship and his writing as a whole. What's remarkable is not that Vonnegut delighted in driving down the hairpin turns on Pike's Peak or that he talked about sex and infinity with his friends beneath the stars or that he glamorized his border crossing into Juárez, Mexico. What's remarkable is that a sixteen-year-old boy with complete freedom to roam the "Wild West" sought out remote landscapes and attended lectures on the place of women in cliff-dwelling societies. While full of humor and entertaining sketches, "The Rover Boys" also reveals Vonnegut's self-directed environmental, artistic, anthropological, and political interests and viewpoints. The travelogue captures Kurt's early planetary citizenship through the sights, ethics, and habits he chose as he shaped his own adventures.

Even at the time, the local press thought the scientific nature of the journey was newsworthy. Both the *Indianapolis Times* and *Indianapolis Star* printed photos of the trio and previewed their botanical, geological, and archaeological expedition, noting their specific commission from the Indianapolis Children's Museum. Amidst this modest media fanfare, the trip was launched with the support of their families. Mr. Jeffrey supplied the camping equipment, Mr. Gillespie loaned them his Packard Coupe, and Doc

Vonnegut, a well-known gun collector, outfitted them with rifles and formal letters explaining the Children's Museum commission.[43]

Bringing guns ran counter to Howie's philosophies. Howie specifically forbade firearms on prairie treks, noting that boys did not "need firearms to identify, collect and study the geology, fauna and flora of the regions in which we camp."[44] While Vonnegut's wartime experiences would later inspire his pacifism and strong anti-weapons position, the sixteen-year-old Kurt was still developing his ethics and perspectives. On the one hand, he embraced the glamour of guns, drawing a pistol on the manuscript's cover, but later decided to omit another gun drawing after treading dangerously close to real violence among striking miners. With that major exception, the trio heeded most of the guidelines Howie sent out to trek junior staff members. They brought their cameras, rolls of Verichrome film, paper and postage for daily reports to family members, carefully packed duffels, limited spending money, sleeping bags, a library box, and camping and fieldwork supplies. They also followed the caravan camping rules of shared cooking, rotating responsibilities, careful campsite cleanup, and sleeping under the stars whenever possible.

As with the guns, the boys added their own rules and new destinations, but large portions of their route and itinerary re-created stretches of the 1937 trek. In his descriptions of Mesa Verde, for instance, Vonnegut delighted in returning to ruins he visited with Howie and recorded the special awe the ancient cliff dwellings inspired in him. "I feel that these ruins are of far more interest than those of Italy and the Mediterranean," Vonnegut reflected, noting the "mystery and unanswered questions" scattered throughout the "wonderful buildings."[45] He was so enamored of Mesa Verde that he convinced his friends to obtain a permit to visit remote unexcavated ruins in the park. After a four-mile canyon hike, the trio climbed to "Spring House," where Vonnegut lamented that the ruins "had been fairly well worked over by unscrupulous tourists and 'pot hunters.'" With George resting from foot pain,

Kurt and Bud pressed on, climbing a long ladder and crawling "along a narrow sandstone ledge" to reach the "inaccessible and hence untouched" "twenty-one and a half house." Because of his trek experience, Vonnegut was able to help Bud when his nerves failed and to strike up lengthy conversations with park rangers about archaeology and natural history.

Re-creating other trek experiences, the boys visited specific deserted mining towns and trading posts in Colorado and New Mexico, the Gallup Inter-tribal Indian Ceremonial, and the base camp at Cottonwood Gulch. The return to the Gulch was a high point for Vonnegut, and the pride he took in earning Howie's respect shines through in "The Rover Boys." "Mr. Howie gave my hand a warm shake," Vonnegut wrote, adding that he "seemed really interested in the venture." At the Gulch, Vonnegut reunited with four other former trek-mates, and the trio basked in the campfire glow as they told their most exciting adventure stories—breakdowns, car chases, and a run-in with disgruntled miners. Even better than stories was Kurt's fire pit, where he cooked corn between the coals, producing ears "done better than the Chief's." Although proud that his "reputation was made," Vonnegut ended his August 16 entry on a modest, grateful note: "We set the tent beneath a mammoth pine—and so to sleep. The gleams of light from the nifty little cabins by Vonnegut of Vonnegut & Bohn, make our plight seem most humble."

While Vonnegut relished in returning to Mesa Verde, Gallup, Santa Fe, and other trek sites, his decision to visit new public lands— Rocky Mountain National Park, the Black Canyon of the Gunnison, Carlsbad Caverns, and Elephant Butte Lake State Park—highlights his continued love affair with big sky, spectacular peaks, mesas, deep canyons, and endless caverns.[46] Time and again Vonnegut's preference for the parks and "unspoiled" lands shows through in his travel diary. Whether bemoaning the "tourist infested" nature of Manitou Springs at the base of Pikes Peak or the fact that they ran into George's ex-girlfriend in Gallup, Vonnegut longed to get to the "real West."

He found it in the sweeping vistas and untrammeled wilderness of the Black Canyon of the Gunnison, remarking, "The Canyon has just recently been opened and promised to be untouched and devoid of the more obnoxious type of tourist." Not surprisingly, the Black Canyon of the Gunnison, with its lack of trails, sheer cliffs and 2,800-foot drop to the river below, became one of the most "outstanding" events of the trip for everyone. Vonnegut himself "was far more impressed by this little known wonder than by the Grand Canyon." He marveled at its barely explored "45 miles of torrents, wilderness, and desolation" and carefully recorded the local wildlife. After noting the deer and wild horses that came within a few feet of their camp, Vonnegut cataloged "mountain goats, wildcats, ringtailed cats, marmots, bull snakes, bald and golden eagles, prairie chickens, grouse, pheasant, and quail—no open season!" Moved by the park's sublime scenery and wildlife, Vonnegut even rose early for his own private expedition to the bottom of the canyon to bathe in the Gunnison River. It's clear from Vonnegut's sense of wonder, independence, and careful observation of the natural world that Howie's attitudes toward the land had entered Kurt's mind and heart.

Although a relatively small portion of "The Rover Boys," Vonnegut's accounts of the trio's archaeology work and museum commission highlight other key principles instilled by Howie. Respecting the protection of ancient ruins outlined in the 1906 Antiquities Act, the boys secured permission to camp and to dig on private land outside of Cortez, New Mexico. Although they failed to find any Folsom points—one of the specific charges from the museum—the boys alternated between digging and surface collection work. They gathered an arrowhead, turquoise, an axe-head, various potsherds, and several metates that were too heavy to bring home. The weight of history and previous civilizations inspired Vonnegut to record the "thrill" of finding representative and "outstanding" artifacts "from a civilization at least 600 years past." During their archaeology work, they also embraced Howie's preference for recording but not collecting wildlife specimens. They released the snakes and toads they caught, and only took animal skeletons with permission on private lands.

"The Rover Boys" also reveals Vonnegut's deep respect for Indigenous cultures, learned on the 1937 trek. Despite lamenting the flocks of tourists, Vonnegut mentions that the Gallup Inter-tribal Indian Ceremonial dances held them "mute for the evening" and that the event "was one of the best evenings of the whole adventure." While interactions with Navajo, Hopi, Laguna, Acoma, and other Southwestern Indigenous cultures later influenced Vonnegut's graduate anthropology study, they also made him intensely aware of restrictive cultural stereotypes. Throughout the narrative, Vonnegut routinely and humorously critiqued Bud's desire to play cowboy and was embarrassed by his friend's "pretty silly questions about the ferocity of Indians." Bud's quests to purchase a ten-gallon cowboy hat, belt buckle, and other "Wild West" items become a running joke throughout "The Rover Boys," emphasizing the contrast between Vonnegut and his traveling companion. More than a humorous flourish, that contrast offers a glimpse into the solemnity with which Vonnegut viewed other cultures while sharply critiquing his own—a perspective that would become a hallmark of his fiction and broader literary planetary citizenship.

"The Rover Boys" also captures Vonnegut's emerging leftist political views and firsthand experiences of Great Depression hardships.[47] While some of Vonnegut's political views were firmly in place before the trip, his time with Civilian Conservation Corps (CCC) youth, itinerant workers, and farmers ruined by the Dust Bowl exposed him to new economic justice issues. At their camp near Elephant Butte, Vonnegut visited a CCC camp and welcomed some "swell" CCC boys to the trio's campfire, leading him to declare that the agency seemed "to be a very fine thing." His admiration for New Deal programs, however, wasn't shared by his friends. Earlier in the narrative Vonnegut complained, "George is a fatalist and refuses to acknowledge any good democrats — anywhere! On these two points we argue incessantly." Nonetheless, all three boys realize their good fortune after hearing about eight years of crop failures in Moxie, Kansas, or meeting a "friendly laborer" in the Black Canyon of the Gunnison. They cringe and nod when the man tells them of a life of ceaseless work from age twelve on and declares his disgust for "damned sissies" who leave within a week after performing hard labor in the park.

Despite their own tight budget, evident in recording every lunch bill, ten-cent quart of milk, and three-cent toll, Vonnegut often noted his good fortune on the trip. Whether exalting in the momentous occasion of receiving a dollar from home or splurging on a full thirty-cent breakfast, Vonnegut had already learned from his uncle Alex the importance of appreciating nice moments in life and saying thank you. In a long private note to his family on August 13, he acknowledged his "entirely unselfish parents," who, despite their economic troubles, strove "to finance a most expensive education" for Bernard, aided Alice in her marriage prospects, and sent "a son who most selfishly planned an expensive vacation for himself alone, out West when the purse was lightest." Vonnegut's gratitude was not restricted to his parents' financial support. Vonnegut praised his "talented" and affectionate family, noting, "The beautiful relationship between Allie, Bernie, and myself, is such a wonderful relief from the squabbling, jealous genre one finds so often."[48]

The destitute families, farmers with sick children, and tramps they encountered all along their route helped Vonnegut to appreciate a lot more than just his family and middle-class comforts. Depression hardships made their final adventure at Phillips's Woolaroc Ranch and estate seem uncomfortably lavish at times. When the trio arrived at Woolaroc, the opulent Oklahoma ranch owned by Frank Phillips, founder of Phillips 66 and friend of the Gillespie family, they noticed how the trip had transformed them. After nearly a full month of camping, they looked like "three dirty, open-mouthed, thugs" with "shameful luggage." Despite careful scrubbing, primping, and wearing good clothes saved for the occasion, the boys still found themselves underdressed compared to the servants, who outnumbered them three to one. Vonnegut was awestruck by the estate's affluence as he noted the enormity and splendor of the buildings, the eight-car garage, a six-door icebox, an overstocked lake, and a bathhouse with "ten shower stalls (just the men's side)."

In the end, the boys struck a balance between enjoying their time riding horses, swimming, and relaxing and being astounded by the estate's grandeur. But Vonnegut, despite growing up with Doc's hunting, never seemed at ease with Woolaroc's ostentatious displays of big game trophies. Upon entering the property, Vonnegut was "awe-stricken at the sight of the lodge," which "was a massive structure with horns, skulls, heads, and antlers of all types covering every available inch of wall surface—inside and out!" He went on to describe the fifty animal heads that lined the walls of the living room, cataloging "a giraffe, elephant, camel, lion, tiger, moose, gnu, water buffalo, yak, mountain sheep, antelope, elk, alligator, crocodile, zebra, etc." But it's not just the sheer quantity of animal trophies that astounded Vonnegut. He noted a "spread eagle with extended talons" that slowly turns overhead from ceiling fan drafts and a "mounted Texas Longhorn head" that "lights up [in] the eyes and blows smoke from the nose and mouth!"

Although it would be decades until Vonnegut critiqued this type of trophy taking in his plays *Penelope* (1960) and *Happy Birthday, Wanda June* (1970–71), it's clear that the sixteen-year-old Vonnegut associated the animal heads with a type of violence. Shortly after the descriptions of the living room Vonnegut noted the "Weapons, planes, relics . . . Machine Gun (St. Valentine's)" of the Phillips' museum and commented on the "pelt-paved boudoir of Mrs. Phillips." The former museum junior board member, however, found enjoyment among the living animals on the ranch. In the dining room, he discovered "one gorgeous cockatoo (whose repertoire consisted of 'Hello' and 'Goodbye'), two parrots (one was dumb, the other laughed uproariously), and about ten parrakeets [*sic*]." Strikingly, it's only when Vonnegut leaves the ranch for "a moonlight ride" with Bud in the wild environs of the estate that he "felt quite at peace with the world."

A few days after that moonlit ride, the boys ended their Western adventure, arriving home around midnight on August 31. For Vonnegut, the expedition offered unprecedented independence, a chance to become "more world-wise and self-reliant." In applying the skills and philosophies from the 1937 trek, he deepened his appreciation of wilderness and sense of wonder in the natural world. The final lines of "The Rover Boys" capture this sentiment: "The only way I'll ever be happy will be out there under the stars. . . . Damn but that's wonderful!"

THOREAU, NEW MEXICO, TO THOREAU'S *WALDEN*

On September 14, 1941, Kurt Vonnegut presented Jane Marie Cox with a 1940 edition of *The Works of Henry D. Thoreau* to mark their first engagement. With the full text of *Walden, Cape Cod, A Week on the Concord and Merrimack Rivers, The Maine Woods*, and an introduction by Ralph Waldo Emerson, the book was a fitting, romantic gift for a Swarthmore English major. The edition was also a suitable love token for a couple that would one day put down roots on Cape Cod and raise planetary-minded children.[49] In the first part of the inscription, Kurt promised to love Jane all his life, and then imagined they would show the volume "to our children when they begin to wonder what things are most important in this world."[50] Without Jane's letters, it's impossible to know which of Thoreau's ideas they deemed "most important" or what specifically comprised the shared "admiration for Thoreau" Kurt mentioned on January 3, 1942. From the inscription, selected letters, and Kurt's own writings, we can see that Thoreau's writings influenced the relationship most crucial to launching his literary career and helped shape his planetary citizenship and identity as a writer. Vonnegut looked to Thoreau for ideals of self-reliance and deliberate living, critiques of emergent technologies and injustice, and even stylistic conventions.

Before he fell passionately in love with Jane in college, Vonnegut read *Walden* and continued his environmental education as a student at Shortridge High School. In addition to introducing him to classics such as *Moby Dick, Life on the Mississippi*, and *The Red Badge of Courage*, Vonnegut's eight semesters of English exposed him to other environmentalists and naturalist writers, including John Muir, Ralph Waldo Emerson, Theodore Roosevelt, and John Burroughs.[51] The school's courtyard gardens, greenhouse, botany department, land acquisitions, and zoology field trips also gave Shortridge students multiple ways to experience the natural world. Vonnegut's own *Shortridge Daily Echo* columns chronicle his participation in two zoology trips to Florida and early environmental advocacy as he argued to preserve the natural features of the school's grounds.[52] So it's not surprising that Vonnegut would be attracted to Thoreau's *Walden*, a landmark in American environmental literature. What's noteworthy is the depth of his appreciation for Thoreau's lessons.[53]

During his five semesters at Cornell, Vonnegut expressed his admiration for Thoreau publicly and privately. Although enrolled as a biochemistry major, Vonnegut made English 2, the university's required freshman course in literature and composition, the subject of one of his *Cornell Daily Sun* columns on February 19, 1942. In the piece, Vonnegut critiqued the course's "befuddled curriculum" and missed opportunities to hear lectures by the university's top literature professors, but made it clear that he and his fellow students "approve[d] of the Bible and Thoreau." His college love letters to Jane, meanwhile, revealed that Thoreau's philosophies affected his worldview and played a key role in the couple's courtship. Whether mentioning elements of Thoreau-inspired practicality on September 18, 1941, or remarking on the lack of "ostentation" and materialism in his room in an undated letter, Kurt took many of Thoreau's ideas in *Walden* to heart and saw in Jane enough of a Thoreauvian kindred spirit to share allusions to Thoreau's bean-eating woodchuck and other aspects of life near Walden Pond. And as he dreamed of their future home, complete with a courtyard, thick oak tree, and writing studio on January 3, 1942, Vonnegut identified Thoreauvian notions of simplicity, deliberate living, and self-reliance, along with a desire "to cure an ailing world" as "things which are really important in life."

Although World War II and other relationships upended their lives and courtship, Kurt and Jane eventually married on September 1, 1945. Sadly, Jane's own literary aspirations were sacrificed as she worked tirelessly to help launch Kurt's writing career. It's both romantic and fitting, though, that Vonnegut dedicated his first novel, *Player Piano*, to Jane and paid homage to Thoreau in the 1952 work. *Player Piano*'s reference to "Civil Disobedience," Thoreau's essay about his arrest for refusing to pay his poll tax in 1845, occurs at a critical moment in the novel; in chapter 14, Ed Finnerty uses the story of Thoreau's protests against the Mexican-American war and slavery to inspire Paul Proteus to rebel against Ilium Works and the larger automated national system. While critical to the novel's plot, the references to "Civil Disobedience" also set up key ideas about citizenship and technology that would pervade Vonnegut's entire writing career. For Thoreau, true citizens "serve the state with their consciences," which sometimes calls for rebellion and revolution.[54] In the essay, Thoreau also likens people who unquestioningly follow laws to machines: "The mass of men serve the state thus, not as men mainly, but as machines, with their bodies." *Player Piano* examines how people have become "machines" in the Thoreauvian sense— uncritical supporters of the government-run, technology-based system. But the novel also examines the spiritual emptiness and human obsolescence that accompanies an increasingly automated society in which human beings have little purpose other than as consumers. Thus, Thoreau's call for a "counter-friction to stop the machine" has a double meaning in *Player Piano*; it's an appeal for conscience and consciousness. It's both a directive for the novel's protagonist, Paul Proteus, and, as we'll see in chapter 6, a specific wake-up call for Vonnegut's postwar readers.

Vonnegut also looked to Thoreau as he envisioned himself as a writer and paid tribute to his predecessor via epigraphs for two collections. The first, the line "Beware of all enterprises that require new clothes," framed Vonnegut's 1968 short story collection, *Welcome to the Monkey House*. The quotation from the "Economy" section of *Walden* was so important that Vonnegut transcribed it onto art objects and furniture, and kept it near his writing desk. As his daughter Nanette Vonnegut explains, one such object was even created in a very Thoreauvian manner:

> When my father did leave the house, it was usually a trip to the dump, where he salvaged beautiful old planks of wood and slabs of marble. Into one plank he carved these words: "'Beware of All Enterprises That Require New Clothes,' Thoreau," and turned it into a six-foot coffee table.[55]

The full quotation, which warns readers to "beware of all enterprises that require new clothes, and not rather a new wearer of clothes," explores the metaphorical nature of clothes.[56] Likening our layers of garments to the growth of exogenous plants, Thoreau suggests that as we get caught up in materialistic pursuits, we lose our true selves under all the layers. For Vonnegut, a writer who struggled for nearly two decades to balance the financial pressures of writing for the marketplace and his conscience as a social critic, the passage must have been a salient reminder to remain true to his artistic voice and vision. It's especially symbolic, then, that *Welcome to the Monkey House* was the first book delivered to his new publisher, Seymour Lawrence, who gave him the three-book contract that allowed him to finish *Slaughterhouse-Five* and embark on a new phase of his career.[57]

Vonnegut likewise turned to Thoreau for the epigraph to *Wampeters, Foma & Granfalloons* in 1974. This time, Vonnegut chose the line "I have traveled extensively in Concord"[58] from the third paragraph in *Walden* to frame his first collection of (mostly) nonfiction essays. Once again, Vonnegut drew on Thoreau's ideas about perspective and writing. Rather than telling of "the Chinese and Sandwich Islanders," Thoreau chose to write about his hometown, Concord, Massachusetts. As Thoreau explained in a September 1851 journal entry, "It is worth the while to see your native village thus sometimes, as if you were a traveller passing through it, commenting on your neighbors as strangers." Like Thoreau, Vonnegut wanted "to tell the truth nakedly" about his own society, in this case about America more broadly.[59] In both *Palm Sunday* and a 1987 interview with William Rodney Allen and Paul Smith, Vonnegut also mentioned trying to emulate Thoreau's clear, direct voice and childlike wonder, crediting much of his own success as a writer to Thoreauvian accessibility and marvel.[60] And although Vonnegut attributed his lean, tight prose to his training in journalism, he likely applauded Thoreau's rejections of ornamentation and celebration of self-taught endeavors in *Walden*.[61]

Vonnegut also honored Thoreau's environmental and literary legacies by contributing to *Heaven Is Under Our Feet*, a 1991 essay collection published to raise money for the Walden Woods Project. Co-edited by recording artist Don Henley and author and music critic Dave Marsh, the sixty-essay volume contains a somewhat odd mixture of reflections by celebrities, ranging from Senators Edward Kennedy and John Kerry to actors Tom Cruise and Whoopi Goldberg to writers E. L. Doctorow and Louise Erdrich. Vonnegut's essay, "To Hell With Marriage," at first seems like a comical, breezy reflection, but its heartfelt appreciation of Thoreau is as thoughtful as the pieces by environmental writer and activist Bill McKibben or Edmund Schofield, president of the Thoreau Society.

In signature Vonnegut style, "To Hell With Marriage" blends comedic storytelling with serious study of an important American figure and topic. The essay begins with a story about Vonnegut's conflicts with his freshman-year English Composition and Literature professor at Cornell and the "make-or-break assignment" that would determine whether he passed the required course: an essay on Henry David Thoreau. Vonnegut hooks his readers with the anecdote and humorous details, such as his overly confident freshman self tumbling down the stairs after turning in the essay. Then he quickly links past and present, explaining that what he wrote about then is "what I have to say about him right now: that [Thoreau] was a sensualist, a voluptuary, and a debauchee."[62] This claim skillfully makes his readers pause. Even if they don't remember that Thoreau built his cabin for $28.12 5 and lived for eight months on $8.74 worth of food, anyone vaguely familiar with *Walden* knows that Thoreau reduced his food, clothing, and shelter to the barest necessities. Vonnegut explains, though, that Thoreau derived intense pleasure not from material things but from nature and solitude. Drawing on quotations from the "Solitude" and "The Village" sections of *Walden*, Vonnegut suggests that Thoreau was able to become "the greatest exemplar of total self sufficiency" because he rejected marriage, family, and other social obligations. Thoreau's ability to find solace in his own thoughts and in the flora, fauna, and other elements of "Dame Nature" at Walden Pond, Vonnegut implies, also helped him become "a witty moralist," "a playful and cunning naturalist," and "perhaps our most accurate and direct user of the English language so far."

Having already made a comic figure of himself via his opening story, Vonnegut further humbles himself before Thoreau in his conclusion. Commenting on Thoreau and the many people inspired by him able to live sparingly and with little human contact, Vonnegut writes, "I envy and admire them, and deeply regret that my own mind is not the perfect companion that theirs must be." Considering Vonnegut's remarkable publication record and enormous popularity, his tribute to Thoreau is especially gracious. But it's also telling that Vonnegut chose to separate himself from Thoreau, the writer who had captured for him and Jane what was "most important" in life, on the topic of human community. As a proponent of extended families and strong communities, Vonnegut needed and would continue to require additional models for his planetary citizenship.

Some of these models would come from Vonnegut's graduate coursework in anthropology at the University of Chicago. After witnessing firsthand the inhumanity of our species during the war, Vonnegut decided that "man was the thing to study."[63] Embedded in that study were key lessons about human cultures and interactions and how civilizations affected and were shaped by their environments. While Howie's ethics, his naturalist expeditions, and Thoreau's writings fostered largely localized environmentalism, Vonnegut's time at Chicago would add global dimensions to his planetary citizenship.

A SECRET INGREDIENT FROM CHICAGO

Vonnegut's papers at the Lilly Library contain some frustrating gaps—missing speeches, pages, letters, and the complete absence of drafts for his novels *Slapstick* and *Galápagos*. Not so with Vonnegut's anthropology course materials.[64] Vonnegut saved everything, and I mean *everything*. He kept his blue book exam answers, seminar papers, course syllabi, lecture notes, copies of lectures, journal articles filled with marginalia, registration cards, bibliographies, homework assignments, and his own hand-drawn maps, charts of oceanic linguistic groups, and diagrams of trait distribution across Micronesia and Polynesia. From extensive notes on varying puberty rites, totems, marriage and family customs, ancestor worship, religion, and magic to large, fold-out maps noting global dominant economies, language groups, and early village culture sites to his own doodles, reflections, poems, and thesis drafts, Vonnegut saved it all—and long after he finally received his master's degree in 1971 for the anthropological elements of *Cat's Cradle*.

Vonnegut's decision to include his anthropology materials in his papers while excluding his other academic coursework should come as no surprise. Although he was self-deprecating about his biochemistry major at Cornell, he often spoke proudly of his anthropology studies and frequently noted how vital the concepts of folk societies and cultural relativity were to his writings and worldview. In his 1971 "Address to the National Institute of Arts and Letters," he cited his admission to Chicago's program as "the happiest day of my life so far" and noted that Dr. Robert Redfield was "the most satisfying teacher in my life." Vonnegut was so enamored of Redfield's concept of folk societies that he quoted his former professor's 1947 *American Journal of Sociology* article on the topic and highlighted the close-knit, personal, sacred, nature-minded aspects of these pre-literate peasant societies in the speech. And in a 1995 interview with Molly McQuade, Vonnegut stated, "Anthropology made me a cultural relativist, which is what everybody ought to be" and mentioned that his "ironic distance as a novelist" stemmed from his coursework at Chicago. Vonnegut even traced the "secret ingredient" in his fiction—his lack of villains—to the idea of cultural relativity, which helped him realize that culture "was a gadget, and that one culture is as arbitrary as another."

Vonnegut scholars Peter Reed, Jerome Klinkowitz, and Todd Davis are spot-on in linking Vonnegut's unique voice and perspective to the interdisciplinary connections between his background in journalism, biochemistry, and anthropology.[65] But Vonnegut was correct in claiming that anthropological elements were the "secret ingredient" in his writings. When you examine his manuscript drafts, it's only after he added the Shah of Bratpuhr sections to *Player Piano*, the Bokononist elements to *Cat's Cradle*, and Salo's views of Earth to *The Sirens of Titan* that those novels truly find their Vonnegutian zest. Can we even imagine those novels without the ethnographic insights of a cultural outsider or the playful commentary in their invented religions? Would we want to?

Beyond adding a "secret ingredient" to his fiction, Vonnegut's anthropology studies refined his criticisms of weapons technologies and the new global, planetary-minded worldview unleashed by the nuclear age. His time at Chicago helped him to ask the really big questions that are a hallmark of his writings: Where have we come from? What does it mean to be human? What's "sacred" in human cultures? What type of species *are* we? At the risk of wearing my Vonnegut geekdom and ORD (obsessive research disorder) on my sleeve, I'd like to dive in to Vonnegut's extensive anthropology materials and program at Chicago. His essays, notes, and reflections are like beads of amber, freezing his insights and journey as a writer and planetary citizen. Why wouldn't we want to know more about that "secret ingredient"?

Accepted to Chicago's anthropology program in October 1945, Vonnegut began his master's coursework in the 1946 winter quarter with support from the GI Bill. He was part of a program undergoing dramatic revisions as it accommodated an influx of returning veterans and addressed new realities of the postwar world.[66] Already a Rockefeller Foundation Center of Excellence, Chicago's program continued to be one of the top graduate anthropology departments in the country, with scholars engaged in innovative research topics and approaches. When Vonnegut began his four-quarter series of Anthropology 220 and 230 courses in January 1946, he was one of the first students to experience the newly redesigned introductory sequence organized by social-cultural anthropologist Sol Tax, physical anthropologist Wilton Krogman, and archaeologist Robert Braidman. The courses were a guide to studying human origins, and they provided extended introductions to the program's five distinctive subfields: physical anthropology, archaeology, "primitive" linguistics, ethnology, and social anthropology.[67]

The rich range of pedagogical experiences and cutting-edge scholarly materials that Tax, Krogman, and Braidman incorporated made for an impressive curriculum. The sixty-five-page Anthropology 220 syllabus, for instance, included lectures or round-table presentations by twenty-six scholars—half from Chicago's anthropology department and half from other fields and programs, including Melville Herskovits, who founded the first African Studies program in the United States. The students also participated in four Saturday visits to Chicago's Field Museum of Natural

History, regular two-hour discussion groups and laboratories, student-led and scholar-led roundtables, and debates.

Anthropology 220's required reading list was likewise ambitious, with ten key texts to be read in their entirety, seventeen in part, and seventy-five shorter selections. The students also had to use newly created large-format maps to analyze topics such as distributions of language groups, natural vegetation, dominant economies, agricultural production systems, North and South American Indigenous groups, and key early village culture sites from the Aegean to the Indies. Within the broader sequence, Anthropology 220 focused on the differences in "social and cultural phenomena" around the world while Anthropology 230 explored shared characteristics of humankind. Ultimately, the four-part sequence gave Vonnegut a strong foundation in cross-cultural analyses of cultures and societies, holistic thinking, and multiple anthropological methods and subfields.

Although his interest in puberty ceremonies, kinship patterns, religions, totems, and cultural symbols nudged him toward social-cultural anthropology, Vonnegut learned to view human beings scientifically from Krogman and his physical anthropology professors. The introductory sequence emphasized that *Homo sapiens* was merely one species among many, subject to the same evolutionary rules as other animals. And like the cultural portions, the sequence adhered to Franz Boas's challenges to ideas of racial hierarchies and white superiority.[68] Krogman's lecturers strongly emphasized shared human traits and placed a special focus on common primate evolutionary paths and varieties of hominids. As Vonnegut's own handwritten notes on these lectures reveal, he began to ask questions that would be central to his writings and planetary citizenship, such as "What is a species?" Vonnegut concluded, "A species is what any zoologist defines it as—to hell with arbitrary definitions" and "What applies in zoo[logy] applies to man."[69] As the lectures went on, Vonnegut continued to put modern human beings in their evolutionary place, writing, "Man is not as highly specialized and demarcated from anthropoids as he would like to think."

As he studied the human species with humility, he also examined our collective and unique cultural impacts on the planet through the key anthropological concept of adaptation—the way various cultures adjust to and shape their environments. In Anthropology 220 and 230, he explored multiple models of geographic determinism and made numerous cross-cultural comparisons of environmental adaptations. Vonnegut seemed particularly interested in these concepts, and chose to write an eleven-page paper on "The Toda and the Chinese Cultures in Relation to their Respective Environments."[70] The paper, which received excellent marks and a thoughtful, laudatory end-comment, raised pointed environmental concerns about forest clear-cutting and population growth in China.

As a World War II veteran, Vonnegut did not need coursework to teach him about the devastation human technologies could do to environments—and all the life within. During his time as a prisoner of war in Dresden, he had seen bodies charred like matchsticks, schoolgirls boiled alive, and whole city blocks reduced to rubble like the surface of the moon. And after the war, he pondered news of Hiroshima with his physicist brother Bernie, who grasped the full horror of an atomic age where entire cities could be wiped from the map with a single bomb.[71] Then his postwar studies at Chicago gave him many opportunities to reflect on the destructive paths Western civilizations seemed to be taking, and he could ponder those paths alongside equally concerned students and professors. At Chicago and across the country, anthropologists were rethinking the discipline as a whole in light of the bombings of Hiroshima and Nagasaki.

Two of Vonnegut's biggest mentors, Robert Redfield and Sol Tax, were particularly affected by the use of atomic weapons. On August 19, 1945, Redfield wrote to his daughter Lisa to share their concerns and explain the bomb's influence on Chicago's newly redesigned 220-230 sequence:

What does one think of now but the new world, with its fears, and the hope that grows large out of the very bigness

of the fear? One muses, and wonders why this crisis in the
world, this immense leap in the preposterous acceleration of
man's technology, this threat, greater than all other threats,
to man's existence ... should come when you and I are alive,
just now, in this generation. Sol Tax was working, at the
beginning of this month, on some charts to show the rate
of acceleration of technological advance in human history
from flint handaxe to—whatever was the latest up to the
atom bomb. He was doing this for some new courses he
and I are working on.... His interpretation was that this
is where we get off. Another nova, another sun—the first
made by man—and the cycle begins again somewhere.[72]

Further discussing Tax's desire to respond to atomic weapons
technology not just in Chicago's courses, but also on a broader international scale, Redfield returned to the imagery linking technology
and the sun's power. He continued, "Sol wants Prometheus to put
the fire back. He wants to get the physicists to admit that utter
destruction is a possibility, and with this admission to compel an
international agreement to make atomic research everywhere illegal."

Although Sol Tax avoided using Anthropology 220 and 230 as
a soapbox for proposing a ban on atomic research, he and other
professors wove the moral implications of atomic weapons into the
fabric of the courses. Historian Rushton Coulborn, for instance,
traced a pattern of civilizational collapse from volcanic eruptions at
Knossos to droughts in the Indus valley to modern-day possibilities
of human extinction by atomic force. Redfield, meanwhile, incorporated links between technology and moral order in civilizations
into his lectures, leading Vonnegut to conclude in his handwritten
May 3, 1946, notes, "Technology is cumulative—moral and aesthetic
order has a revolving, dissolving, returning motion."

Vonnegut's short discussion papers and poetic responses reveal
more specific reflections on nuclear technology and human extinction.
In a response paper on the ways resources shaped specialized trade

in various cultures, Vonnegut contemplated what would happen to "seal hunters, industrial workers, rice farmers, fishermen, acorn gathers and so on" if these environments were destroyed. He postulated:

> And if the seals are exterminated, the factories bombed flat, the soil exhausted, the fish sterilized by Atom bomb tests, and the oaks killed by oak blight, then considerable disorganization will be felt by those subsisting on the various affected economies, and society and its culture will face—as did the dinosaurs—extinction.[73]

While apocalyptic landscapes and futures would become a staple element of his novels, Vonnegut turned to poetry as he contemplated the new realities of an atomic age. Mixed in with his 220 notes and papers is a two-stanza, twenty-two-line poem about humankind's "new Holy Trinity" of energy, matter, and time. Strikingly, it foreshadows Vonnegut's 2005 poem "Requiem," which he would publish nearly four decades later in response to the global environmental threats of climate change. In the spring of 1946, though, it was the atomic bomb that would usher in an "Oblivion, / To be shared by all." Like "Requiem," the untitled poem demonstrates concern not with human extinction but with larger planetary destruction. Vonnegut offers this vision in the second stanza:

> Man, thou art but dust:
> To dust return.
> And wonder not what followed
> For no living thing remains on Earth;
> Not a bird now bursts its breasts with melody
> Nor are there forests, nor shy forest creatures

While the inspiration for the poem is unclear, its placement alongside studies of civilizations, adaptation, environmental resources, morality, and technology highlights the anthropological roots of his planetary citizenship. The poem also helps us understand why Vonnegut was so enchanted by the folk societies he learned about in Redfield's spring 1946 lectures. Who wouldn't prefer close-knit, small human communities to a postwar world with unprecedented weapons of mass destruction? From his foundational 220-230 sequence, Vonnegut chose courses that would add more of that "secret ingredient" to his writings: a special topics seminar with James Sidney Slotkin (ANTH 369), a course on the Individual and Society (ANTH 390), an advanced class on Magic and Religion (ANTH 499), and other social and cultural anthropology classes.[74] He would also go on to start two different master's theses in the spring and summer of 1947: a comparison between leadership of the Ghost Dance and Cubist movements, and a study of Native American revitalization movements and spiritual practices that emerged in relation to colonization, titled "Mythologies of North American Indian Nativistic Cults." Despite completing extensive research and generating more than 150 pages of notes, Vonnegut only drafted seven pages of "Mythologies." As he mentioned in his 1995 interview with Molly McQuade, the pressure of providing for his young family prevented him from doing fieldwork and focusing on the project. With his first child, Mark, born in May, Vonnegut could no longer count on his job at Chicago's City News Bureau to pay the bills. In late August, he received an offer to work in General Electric's News Bureau and left Chicago in late September without completing his thesis or his master's degree.[75]

Vonnegut's work on the Ghost Dance movements, however, would later make its way into *Player Piano*, and his examination of revolutionary social movements, mythological structures, and religious belief systems undoubtedly influenced other novels—from invented religions in *Sirens of Titan*, *Cat's Cradle*, and *Slapstick* to allusions to prophet figures and creation myths in numerous works. His interest in revitalization and oppositional social change movements also nurtured his planetary citizenship and other forms of activism. As Vonnegut explained to McQuade, his master's

Matter can neither be created nor destroyed.
Energy can neither be created nor destroyed.
Matter is Energy
Energy is Matter.
There we begin our dismal story,
When Man lay aside his crucifix
    For the new Holy Trinity:
Matter,
Energy
and Time;
When mass suicide was made possible —
The Grand Ideal, Oblivion,
To be shared by all,
No longer to be inhibited
By the faint heart
Nor by the minority will to live.

Man, thou art but dust:
To dust return.
And wonder not what followed
For no living thing remains on Earth;
Not a bird now bursts its breast with melody.
Nor are there forests, nor shy forest creatures

1.5 * As this untitled 1946 poem in Vonnegut's Anthropology 220
notes reveals, nuclear weapon technologies added global dimensions
to his planetary thinking while studying at the University of Chicago.
Archival image by Kurt Vonnegut, courtesy of the Lilly Library, Indiana University, Bloomington. Copyright © Kurt Vonnegut LLC, used
by permission of The Wylie Agency LLC.

thesis allowed him to study "what it takes to effect radical cultural change." And although Vonnegut questioned a novelist's ability to spark large-scale change, he admitted that he was still trying to infect "people with humane ideas before they're able to defend themselves." "Society can be a villain," Vonnegut told McQuade, "yet it seems to me that it's no more trouble to be virtuous than to be vicious. I'm critical, but not a pessimist. Look at all that humans can do! They're versatile. They can ride a unicycle. They can play the harp. They can, apparently, do *anything*."[76]

CHAPTER 2

VIEWS FROM TITAN, TRALFAMADORE, AND THE BLUE TUNNEL
Writing for a "Salubrious Blue-green Orb"

When I write, I don't want to write a story about a man, a love affair, or a trial. I want to write about the whole damned planet.
—KURT VONNEGUT, March 1972 *Chicago Tribune Magazine* interview

To learn to work on planet-wide problems, we must become planetary thinkers. We must learn how to be humans aware of our natures, our Earthly context and the systems which make up the planet of which we are a part.
—ALEX STEFFEN, "What Does Planetary Thinking Mean?"

SALO'S "GREETINGS"[77]

Kurt Vonnegut often described his second novel, *Sirens of Titan,* as a "favorite child" because it was "delivered by natural childbirth."[78] As he explained to Richard Todd in a January 1971 *New York Times Magazine* interview, Vonnegut made up the idea for the novel while talking to an editor at a party. "I had no idea at all for a book," Vonnegut told Todd, "but I started talking and told him the story for

Sirens of Titan." Vonnegut's notes, outlines, charts, and scroll drafts reveal a relatively easy compositional process for Kurt—especially compared to his decades-long struggle with *Slaughterhouse-Five.* What's missing from *Sirens of Titan's* birth story is its midwife, Jane Vonnegut, who not only saved crucial key scenes, but also rescued one of the novel's central components of planetary citizenship. As she did with many of Kurt's early stories, Jane copyedited drafts and offered five pages of handwritten suggestions. When Kurt considered scrapping some of the Titan scenes, Jane instructed him to keep Salo's planetary views in the novel. She advised him, "Don't leave out about Salo watching people on Earth in memorable poses & making the statues. His creative process. The Eye in the sky. Put all that back in."[79] Kurt was wise enough to listen to Jane and was able to finish the masterful interstellar novel, a key work within his literary planetary citizenship.

Selected for the Great American Read in 2018, Vonnegut's 1959 novel has long been a fan favorite for its wildly imaginative explorations of space and time that encourage philosophical questions about free will and the place of human beings in the universe. *Sirens of Titan* tells the story of Malachi Constant, the richest, luckiest man in America, who embarks on a free-fall journey of repeated losses and humbling interstellar adventures before discovering peace and purpose on one of Saturn's moons. Beyond these philosophical wanderings and parodies of the science fiction space-opera subgenre, *Sirens of Titan* also offers important environmental planetary visions as characters contemplate tiny, fragile Earth and its place in the vast universe. Anticipating key 1960s environmental metaphors of "Spaceship Earth" and the Earth as an interconnected "global village," the novel inspires planetary thinking by emphasizing humanity's shared problems and by presenting "an opportunity to think about your native planet from a fresh and beautifully detached viewpoint."[80]

Read within this framework, *Sirens of Titan* simultaneously presents humans as important biological agents, altering their own and other planets through weapons technology, and as one humble species among many in the cosmos. It defamiliarizes Earth and its inhabitants through the perspective of alien others while also drinking from the well of "deep time" to put human history in scale with the far older existence of the cosmos. Like the science fiction Vonnegut draws on and parodies, *Sirens of Titan* is ultimately about social, political, and environmental issues on our planet. As Vonnegut later explained in a 1972 interview, "every time I write about another planet, it is deliberately so unrealistic that people can't really believe in it. In a way it makes our own planet more important, more real."[81]

The unrealistic but clever device that makes the plot and insights of *Sirens of Titan* possible is a chrono-synclastic infundibulum, a funnel-shaped space-time conduit between Mars and Earth that turns all entities passing through it into wave phenomena "pulsing in a distorted spiral" between the Sun and Betelgeuse. Drawing on his anthropology background, Vonnegut links the chrono-synclastic infundibulum to cultural relativity or the concept of multiple correct perspectives. The device also sets in motion the literal and metaphorical journeys of the novel's central characters, Winston Niles Rumfoord, Malachi Constant, Beatrice Rumfoord, and Chrono. Bending our earthbound laws of physics, the chrono-synclastic infundibulum enables Rumfoord and his dog Kazak to exist in multiple space-time coordinates and to use his materializations on Earth every fifty-nine days to mastermind a colony on Mars, a Martian invasion, and the founding of his own religion, the Church of God the Utterly Indifferent. The playful reconceptions of time and space enabled by the chrono-synclastic infundibulum also highlight Vonnegut's debts to science and science fiction as well as his key literary strategies for encouraging planetary thinking.

True to its space opera roots, *Sirens of Titan* takes readers on an intergalactic journey, primarily exploring Mars, the caves of Mercury, Saturn's moon Titan, and Earth.[82] While these explorations entertain and offer fodder for social critique, the most moving and enlightening views comes from the robot Salo, an eleven-million-year-old messenger from the planet Tralfamadore sent on a peaceful ambassadorial mission "from One Rim of the Universe to the Other." While stranded on Titan, awaiting a part for his broken spaceship, Salo watches Earth and various paths of evolution and human civilization that take place from "the Earthling year 203,117 B.C." to the present. To amuse himself, he sculpts "two million life-sized statues of human beings," capturing the range of emotions, behaviors, and dramas that he sees via the monitor screen of his broken-down spaceship. Working within geological and evolutionary timescales, Salo's statues and his "human" behavior in resisting his machine origins help pose the question "What kind of species are we?" Salo's technology-enabled "eye in the sky" offers a view of human civilization that is both moving and humbling.

Although he imagined other worlds and alien species in his short stories years before he wrote *Sirens of Titan*, the novel is a good starting place to explore the key literary techniques Vonnegut would use to encourage planetary thinking and citizenship throughout his career. Born out of concerns about global annihilation via nuclear war, nurtured by his ecological awareness and the environmental movement, and heightened through his engagements with globalization and climate change, Vonnegut's writings call for careful stewardship of the Earth's life-supporting systems. Despite this persistent focus, Vonnegut was wildly creative and varied in the ways he tried to inspire a sense of planetary citizenship in his readers. He used his own signature blend of anthropological, scientific, and science-fiction-inspired approaches to imagine creative shifts in space, scale, and time. From Titan to Tralfamadore, from viewpoints of atoms to microbes, from brief moments of frozen time to eons of deep geological time, Vonnegut tenaciously reinvented new perspectives to address environmental issues.

KILGORE TROUT,
THE MOON LANDING, AND A RARE EARTH

Vonnegut scholars and fans alike have long recognized Kilgore Trout as Vonnegut's alter ego and most distinctive character.[83] Modeled in part after real-life science fiction writer Theodore Sturgeon, Trout is, for Vonnegut, "a combination of a self-mocking parody of himself, an embodiment of his worst fears of becoming a denigrated science fiction writer, and a voice for some of his most impish and inventive ideas."[84] These "impish and inventive ideas," however, are one of the consistent ways Vonnegut encourages planetary thinking. Perhaps the original flash-fiction artist, Trout peppers Vonnegut's novels and, occasionally, nonfiction works with snippets of science fiction stories that quickly transport the reader to different worlds and times. As Vonnegut scholar Peter Reed notes, Trout's stories serve many functions—injecting slapstick humor, vitality, and pace into the text—but their ultimate role is as "parables that offer wisdom and insight into our condition."[85] Because Trout is a prolific science fiction writer, his parables often involve intergalactic travel, switching rapidly between fictional worlds and different time-space coordinates to present readers with a fresh view of Earth and its environmental conditions. They are, in effect, like the iconic "Earth Rise" and "Blue Marble" photos used by the US environmental movement to show the Earth's fragility and global connectedness; however, the views from Trout's universes rarely presents a peaceful, beautiful globe.

Since Trout's stories figure so prominently in Vonnegut's writing, it's worth returning to the character's debut in *God Bless You, Mr. Rosewater* (1965). From the start, Vonnegut established a close relationship between himself and Trout, crediting his alter ego not only with the short story "2BRO2B," which Vonnegut had published in January 1962 in *Worlds of If,* but also with the central question from *Player Piano,* "What in hell are people *for?*"[86] Vonnegut likewise set up the close relationship between Trout and his most consistent fan and benefactor, Eliot Rosewater. It is through Eliot's appreciative eyes that Vonnegut readers first view Trout and his brand of science fiction. A failed lawyer turned philanthropist and part-time volunteer fireman, Rosewater praises science fiction generally and Trout specifically in a drunken speech at a writers' conference. Explaining that science fiction is the only genre worth reading, Rosewater proclaims, "You're the only ones who'll talk about the *really* terrific changes going on, the only ones crazy enough to know that life is a space voyage . . . that will last for billions of years." After further praising science fiction writers for *really* caring about the future and the impact of machines and wars, Rosewater concludes that they "were more sensitive to important changes than anybody who was writing well." With a boozy flourish, Rosewater exclaims, "The hell with the talented sparrowfarts who write delicately of one small piece of one mere lifetime, when the issues are galaxies, eons, and trillions of souls yet to be born."

Rosewater's speech not only captures many of Vonnegut's own priorities and preferences as a writer, but also outlines Trout's fictional agenda in *God Bless You, Mr. Rosewater* and elsewhere. From "2BRO2B" to *Venus on the Half-Shell* to *Oh Say Can You Smell?* and *Pan-Galactic Three-Day Pass*, Trout's stories traverse the universe, introducing fictional planets such as Shaltoon, Tralfamadore, and Glinko X-3 to comment on rampant population growth, postwar technologies, and military logic.[87] Trout's *Pan-Galactic Three-Day Pass* plays a special role in the novel, juxtaposing the fictional destruction of the Milky Way with Rosewater's war recollections and his hallucination of Indianapolis being consumed by a firestorm. While drawing on his own experiences surviving the firestorm at Dresden, Vonnegut uses the destruction of an entire galaxy in Trout's story to underscore the potential planetary-level destructive capabilities of nuclear weapons. Although no cause is given for the galaxy's demise, the almost immediate references to Dresden and World War II force readers to contemplate the global potentials of human-caused destruction.[88]

After *God Bless You, Mr. Rosewater*, Kilgore Trout and his dop-pelgangers frequently appeared in novels, speeches, and essays over the next four decades, introducing new worlds and revisiting familiar locales to encourage even greater leaps of imagination. By affording Vonnegut hyperbolic fictional license and limitless potential for shifting perspectives, Trout's stories gave Vonnegut creative places and spaces for encouraging planetary-scale vision and for offering some of his most incisive ecological critiques.

Given his (and Trout's) many interstellar fictional settings and strong background in science, you might think that Vonnegut would have been an avid fan of real space travel. Instead, Vonnegut opposed the immense costs and priorities of NASA so vocally that he was invited to appear on CBS's July 20, 1969, coverage of the moon landing.[89] Someone had to be a wet blanket, and Vonnegut willingly countered the ecstatic pronouncements issued by his fellow panelist and author Arthur C. Clarke.

While Vonnegut's CBS appearance came on the heels of his incred-ible *Slaughterhouse-Five* fame, the network likely featured him because of his *New York Times* essay "Excelsior! We're Going to the Moon!," published on July 13, 1969, just three days before the Apollo 11 mis-sion launch.[90] The essay captures Vonnegut's signature contrarian planetary-minded ethics—an environmentalism partially rooted in visions of the Earth from space but one deeply critical of the tech-nological hubris and governmental spending priorities that enabled those images. The essay itself strings together a series of vignettes, ranging from his brother Bernard watching a rocket launch at Cape Kennedy to his Cape Cod neighbors' reactions to the safe watery landings of Soviet cosmonauts to Vonnegut's own readings of books about space travel. What Vonnegut ultimately suggests is that we don't need space travel to achieve a shared sense of humanity or to discover new frontiers and challenges. Quoting Patricia Lauber's 1967 children's book on stars and planets, Vonnegut instead reminds readers that we are already "flying through space" on Spaceship Earth and that the very same spirit of mastering "new environments with new technologies" fueling the space race has produced centuries of human and environmental exploitation.

Despite its many incisive critiques, Vonnegut briefly pauses three-quarters of the way through the essay to imagine "the first human footprint on the moon as a sacred thing," because "Earthlings have done an unbelievably difficult and beautiful thing." For Vonnegut, however, the most important planetary vision for human beings is an Earth-bound one, and the best way to achieve it is through our flights of imagination.[91] Calling the Apollo and other rocket launches "very expensive show biz" Vonnegut outlines his environmental position: "We have spent something like $33 billion on space so far. We should have spent it on cleaning up our filthy colonies here on earth." Like his fellow activists who would use the iconic "Earth Rise" image to call for local and global environmental action on Earth Day, Vonnegut focuses on the ecological and social justice implications of these NASA pictures. Instead of using the photographs to highlight the Earth's fragility and our connectedness on this small planet in space, he writes, "Earth is such a pretty blue and pink and white pearl in the pictures NASA sent me. It looks so *clean.* You can't see all the hungry, angry Earthlings down there—and the smoke and sewage and trash and sophisticated weaponry." Vonnegut thus turns from a macro view to the individual yet connected pollution problems caused by DDT, massive dumping in the Great Lakes, and the increased levels of carbon dioxide in the atmosphere linked to the Industrial Revolution.

While reminding readers of their planet's interconnected environmental systems, Vonnegut was careful not to use our shared status as Earthlings to gloss over inequalities. He reminds us that this environmental degradation has been caused by specific cultural systems and nations. Reacting to James Webb's *Exploring Space with a Camera*, Vonnegut explicitly connects "the mastery of a new environment" that might accompany space exploration with centuries of Western imperialism, including the Roman empire,

Germany's rocketry program in World War II, slavery in the United States, DDT, and "the Spaniards' mastery of the New World, with several million other Earthlings already here." These examples, Vonnegut suggests, stem not only from superior technologies, but also from a sense of entitlement to any human and environmental resources within the imperial power's reach.

Although Vonnegut continued to oppose funding for US space exploration throughout his career, his most caustic and environmentally focused critiques, appear in his final short story, "The Big Space Fuck."[92] Published in 1972, the story takes place in the very near future, on July 4, 1977—the night of the launch of the *Arthur C. Clarke*. Devoid of a human crew, the US-built spaceship carries eight hundred pounds of freeze-dried sperm, which will be fired at the Andromeda Galaxy in an effort to save the human species. Reinforcing the critiques offered in "Excelsior!" and his CBS moon-landing appearance, Vonnegut unambiguously warns of the dangers of ignoring our problems here on Earth while embracing technological optimism. The space program, the narrator informs us, encouraged people "to believe that there was hospitality out there, and that Earth was just a piece of shit to use as a launching platform. Now Earth really was a piece of shit, and it was beginning to dawn on even dumb people that it might be the only inhabitable planet human beings would ever find."

More than just an attack on the space program, the story lambastes a hypermasculine technological model that disrespects "Mother Nature," pursues a future driven by the military-prison-industrial complex, and can only imagine continuing human life by "fucking" Andromeda. From the phallic, jizzum-loaded rocket to the president's tough language and theatrical staging of the event to a Senate filled with "men wearing codpieces in the shape of rocket ships," the gendered dimensions of this technological paradigm couldn't be clearer.

What likely resonated with 1972 readers were the allusions to landmark events that gave urgency to the 1960s and early 1970s environmental movement. Senator Flem Snopes's "campaign to eliminate the bald eagle as the national bird" because it "hadn't been able to cut the mustard in modern times," for example, invokes Rachel Carson's suggestion in *Silent Spring* that rapidly declining eagle populations "may well make it necessary to find a new national emblem."[93] Vonnegut also chose the shores "of what used to be Lake Erie" for the story's setting, telling the broader story of "the big space fuck" via the small family drama of Dwayne and Grace Hoobler, who are watching the rocket's countdown at home on TV. Evoking the rampant industrial pollution and algae blooms of Lake Erie, which was declared "dead" in spots and received widespread media coverage after the June 1969 Cuyahoga River fire, the setting adds a final layer of irony to the interstellar repopulation plan. Instead of watching the rocket's final countdown, Dwayne, Grace, and the county sheriff are consumed by gigantic "man-eating lampreys," which have found "the Great Lakes too vile and noxious even for *them*" and have taken to land instead. The "cruel Fate" of pollution-nurtured lampreys poised to wipe out humans on what's "supposed to be the most joyful night in the history of mankind" needs no further commentary than what Vonnegut offers as the story's afterword: "And so it goes."

To balance the menacing portrait of the planet's fragility and environmental conquest in "Excelsior!" and "The Big Space Fuck," Vonnegut offered gentler but equally urgent visions of Earth's unique ability to support life in other early 1970s pieces. In the preface to his 1974 collection of nonfiction, *Wampeters, Foma & Granfalloons*, Vonnegut wrote, "The Universe does not teem with life. It is inhabited at only one point by creatures who can examine it and comment on it. That point is planet Earth." "All the twinkles and glints in the night sky," Vonnegut continued, "might as well be sparks from a cowboy's campfire, for all the life or wisdom they contain." His May 1974 commencement address at Hobart and William Smith Colleges, meanwhile, linked Earth's unique life-supporting abilities and human consciousness/conscience to inspire global environmental stewardship. Embracing the spirit of Aldo Leopold's land ethic, which called for a new ecology-minded form of citizenship, Vonnegut put forward the idea of "a modern and simple [planetary] moral code" that rejected "anything which wounds the planet" and embraced "anything which preserves it or heals it." Just as Leopold called for love, respect, and non-economically-driven valuation of the land, Vonnegut suggested that healthy, non-materialistically-driven human communities were critical to halting environmental destruction "in order to have life on the planet go on for a long, long time."[94]

In the 1980s and throughout the rest of Vonnegut's career, his planetary visions shifted from optimistic efforts to inspire global environmental stewardship to more pessimistic portraits of our doomed "Rare Earth." His 1985 address at MIT imagined an expansion of the Hippocratic oath to reinforce earlier notions of a planetary moral code. He asked students to take a graduation pledge to work "for the benefit of all life on this planet, according to [their] own ability and judgment, and not for its hurt or for any wrong." Vonnegut's 1988 piece, "Ladies and Gentlemen of 2088 A.D.," meanwhile, used a futuristic perspective to critique Reagan-era environmental policies.[95] In true contrarian fashion, Vonnegut turned the text for the *Time* magazine ad sponsored by Volkswagen, into an opportunity to lay out six key sustainability principles, urging people to stabilize human population, "stop poisoning the air, the water, and the topsoil," reject war preparations and technological fixes, and learn "how to inhabit a small planet without helping to kill it." Despite—or perhaps because of—the whole-Earth thinking in these calls for stewardship, Vonnegut also returned to gloomy planetary visions as he contemplated the devastating system-wide impacts of human-caused climate change. Vonnegut saw in climate change, "a problem far worse than the rise of another Hitler" that could ultimately mean "the destruction of a life-supporting apparatus of delicate and beautiful complexity." The data, trends, and predicted impacts of climate change were so overwhelming to Vonnegut that he canceled the rest of his spring college speaking tour in 1989. As in his abrupt departure from the stage in his 1971 Library of Congress address, Vonnegut found it too hard to make jokes about "challenges so real and immediate and appalling."[96] While still on the speaking tour, Vonnegut kept returning to a bleak "epitaph for the whole planet, which was 'We could have saved it, but we were too darn cheap and lazy.'"

Despite its gloomy implications, Vonnegut's repeated returns to and creative reimagining of the epitaph highlight the tenacity of his planetary citizenship. Variations of the phrase appear in multiple essays, speeches, versions of the 2005 poem "Requiem," and his 1990 novel *Hocus Pocus*, as well as in his personal correspondence. Vonnegut even began an artistic collaboration with graphic artist and Ragged Edge Press founder Joel Cohen after he learned that Cohen was creating "Rare Earth" stickers for mail art and other social justice projects. The black, white, and red graphic featured an image of the Earth skewered on a spit, roasting over a fire with Vonnegut's famous planetary epitaph below.[97] Vonnegut received several hundred copies of the "Rare Earth" sticker from the socially minded artist, which he used to spread his environmental message through correspondence and gifts to friends and fans.[98]

Vonnegut's long-term collaborations with artist Joe Petro III, meanwhile, offered more public venues to promote planetary thinking. In *A Man Without a Country*, Vonnegut credited Petro with saving his life through their friendship and artistic partnership, Origami Express. While the silk-screen prints they co-created led to exhibits, publications, book illustrations, and a broad range of political engagements, Vonnegut produced several Confetti prints addressing climate change and environmental sustainability in the final years of his life. Created in part to get ideas "off his chest" and to survive the heartache caused by the

Rare Earth

© Ragged Edge Press, NYC

We could have saved it, but we were too darn cheap and lazy. --Kurt Vonnegut

2.1 ✳ This 1993 "Rare Earth" sticker led to several environmental and social justice artistic collaborations between Kurt Vonnegut and Joel Cohen. Drawing by Thomas Kerr, Art Direction by the Sticker Dude, Production by Ragged Edge Press, NYC.

wars and policies of the Bush administration, the direct, largely text-based silk-screen Confetti prints allowed Vonnegut to leave his fans with pearls of wisdom, reprieves of laughter, sobering critiques, and stark reflections.[99]

Just as his various visions of Rare Earth and planetary thinking took a range of forms, his climate-change-related Confetti prints highlight Vonnegut's continued wavering between optimistic calls for change and pessimistic assessments of planetary degradation. An early Confetti print, #7, didactically addressed automobile-related greenhouse-gas emissions by asserting that "Driving a car is so dangerous it ought to be against the law." Other prints, such as #52, offered more humor in their critiques of fossil-fuel consumption, stating, "Dear Future Generations: Please accept our apologies. We were roaring drunk on petroleum. Love, 2006 A.D." Perhaps what Vonnegut ultimately hoped for—planetary, systems-minded, ethical vision—is best conveyed in print #44, which states, "There should have been a secretary of the future," punctuated with an upside-down exclamation point composed of a red dot (a burnt planet?) above a drop of water.

POLYMERS, JOCK ITCH, AND THE EARTH'S IMMUNE SYSTEM

From views of Earth from space to heartfelt moral codes to epitaphs for our Rare Earth, Vonnegut's writings used whole-Earth perspectives to encourage planetary stewardship. But focusing solely on these wildly imaginative views from Titan or his concerns about climate change misses crucial dimensions of Vonnegut's environmental engagements. Like Hillis Howie and the environmental writers he read at Shortridge and beyond, Vonnegut knew that the significance of the whole—whether ecosystems or planetary systems—was dependent on the intricate agents, elements, communities, and layers within those larger systems. To complement those cosmic scales, Vonnegut repeatedly shifted to very small,

DEAR FUTURE
GENERATIONS:
PLEASE ACCEPT
OUR APOLOGIES.
●
WE WERE
ROARING DRUNK
ON PETROLEUM.

LOVE, 2006 A.D.

1/85

2.2 ✳ One of more than two hundred silk-screen confetti prints co-created by Kurt Vonnegut and Joe Petro III, "Dear Future Generations" highlights Vonnegut's late-career climate change activism. Courtesy of Origami Express, kurtvonnegutprints.com. Copyright © Kurt Vonnegut LLC, used by permission of The Wylie Agency LLC.

often microscopic perspectives to demonstrate that we are part of the Earth's living systems and subject to the same laws of Nature that govern life in the currently known universe. From his earliest to his final writings, Vonnegut looked to microscopic and atomic levels of cells, microbes, and chemical elements and molecules to remind us that we are made from stardust and that our bodies contain a teeming universe of human cells, viruses, bacteria, fungi and other living beings.

Vonnegut's insistence in connecting human beings to the eco-systems within us and to the planet's living systems stems from his formal training as a scientist. Although Cornell University's Chemistry Department will probably never include Vonnegut in its list of distinguished former students, he spent five semesters as a biochemistry major from the fall of 1940 until January 1943, when he dropped out of school after a bout of pneumonia to join the Army. In his 1977 *Paris Review* self-interview, Vonnegut freely admitted that he was "flunking everything by the middle of [his] junior year" and that he had "no talent" for his biology and chemistry courses. As he explained, his father and brother "agreed that [he] should study chemistry" because it was a *practical* major and because Bernard had excelled professionally thanks to his training in chemistry and physics at MIT.[100]

Despite complaints about his major choice and his expressed wish to Carl Sagan in 1977 that he'd like to "steal" his Cornell "transcripts and burn them," Vonnegut *did* have talent and interest in chemistry and other natural sciences.[101] He wouldn't have been admitted to Cornell's exceptionally strong program without the A+ and A he earned in two semesters of chemistry and the A+ for his second semester of physics at Shortridge High School.[102] These were not easy classes either. The chair of Shortridge's Chemistry Department, Frank Wade, had such valuable teaching and research expertise that Kurt's brother Bernard bicycled from the private Park School to study chemistry with Wade.[103] Vonnegut brought solid high school preparation to his Cornell

THERE SHOULD HAVE BEEN A SECRETARY OF THE FUTURE.

1/10

lectures and labs on organic chemistry, inorganic chemistry, bio-chemistry, and quantitative analysis. And although he credited his English 2, public speaking, history, and German classes with keeping him academically afloat, Vonnegut's college letters to Jane Cox and select *Cornell Daily Sun* columns show that he was engaging scientific concepts in creative ways.

Vonnegut often stated that he was drawn to anthropology because it was "poetry which *pretends* to be scientific." His college writings reveal that he was also drawn to the *poetry* of science. He could also find a good joke anywhere, and he used his experiences in the chemistry major as material for humorous pieces in the *Cornell Daily Sun*. Vonnegut wrote about an explosion in his inorganic chemistry lab and his academic probation to create laughs at his own expense, but he also enjoyed finding humor in scientific language and relationships.[104] He played with the pun potential of "ethyl" and "Ethel," and, in an early "Innocents Abroad" column, used the heading "Science Cannot Be Stopped" to set up a good joke. In the piece, he invented or perhaps discovered a title for "a paper delivered before the Michigan Academy of Science, Arts and Letters," which read "The Effect of the Histamine Antagonist, Thymozyethyldiethylmaline (929F) on Gastric Secretion."[105] Although a pun involving histamines' regulatory functions in the gut might be a bit uncultured, Vonnegut was at least putting his chemistry studies to use.

His letters to Jane demonstrate more poetic applications of scientific knowledge as well as early examples of examining subjects from micro perspectives. In a letter dated September 18, 1941, he turned to his knowledge of cell physiology to pledge his love to his future wife.[106] Toward the end of the letter he wrote, "I love you, and did you know that you have thirty-five trillion (35,000,000,000,000) red corpuscles in your shapely body, and that laid edge to edge they would extend around the world about three times at the equator?" While the passage is one of Vonnegut's many hyperbolic metaphorical declarations of love, it's worth noting that his calculations and basic understanding of cell diameters and micrometers are sound.[107] He also employed cellular-level thinking to express his disdain for the "dirty little viruses" that made Jane sick in late October 1941 and promised that he'd become "the slickest biochemist ever to dream up a hormone" in another letter. I suspect, though, that it was the intersection of science and language that helped win the heart of his English major fiancée. In an undated letter shortly after their unofficial September 1941 engagement, Vonnegut wrote, "This week will go like a gamete. You are the most desirable specimen of woman with all its overtones and connotations [*sic*] that I have ever known. I guess that's how one chooses one's wife." Drawing on the ancient Greek definition of the word "gamete" as "wife," the passage not only uses the micro-level of human reproduction to highlight Jane's singularity among all potential female human beings, but also expresses the long, slow passage of time until they can meet (presumably forming a new union as a zygote).

While some of Vonnegut's cellular-level imagery came from his summer course in bacteriology at Butler University,[108] he left Cornell with enough background to engage scientists and key scientific concepts throughout his writing career. His preparation at Cornell along with high scores on the Army General Classification Test (AGCT) also earned him admission to the Army's Specialized Training Program (ASTP), which enrolled promising soldiers in college programs to provide high-level technicians and other specialists needed for the war effort. In the summer of 1943, Vonnegut began an eighteen-month program in mechanical engineering at Carnegie Mellon University, where he took general engineering courses.[109] Upon successful completion of this introductory phase, Vonnegut started the advanced sequence of mechanical engineering courses at the University of Tennessee that fall, enrolling in thermodynamics, shop practice, calculus, statistics and dynamics, and mechanical engineering drawing. Although Vonnegut told Walter Miller in a 1981 interview that he was "a perfectly lousy engineer" and at the bottom of his engineering classes, his grades were quite decent.[110] More importantly, the ASTP courses broadened and deepened his background in science and engineering, preparing him to address scientific and technical subjects during his time working at General Electric and throughout his career. As a result, Vonnegut long valued and kept the company of scientists and repeatedly emphasized the importance of studying and writing intelligently about science.

The need for more manpower in Europe and the ASTP's cancellation in spring 1944 cut short Vonnegut's studies in engineering and set the course for his famous war experiences in Germany. Ultimately, Vonnegut's time in the Army provided some of his most important literary subjects—firsthand experiences with mass-killing weapons technologies and human cruelty—as well as additional scientific study that would stimulate his literary imagination and tireless efforts as a pacifist. Within Vonnegut's planetary thinking, many of his most biting critiques focus on the ways in which humans have used science and technology to destroy not just each other, but the living systems around them. In Vonnegut's writings, however, scientific thought and experimentation are never problems by themselves. It's only when science is removed from ethical, humanist, and environmental concerns that disasters unfold.

One of the best showcases of Vonnegut's chemistry training, micro-focused perspectives, and environmental activism working in tandem is his 1973 novel *Breakfast of Champions*. Perhaps most famous for its hand-drawn illustrations, caustic critiques of America's past injustices and cultureless present, and Vonnegut's self-referential presence as author and character, *Breakfast of Champions* is also awash in chemicals and environmental commentary. In his brief preface to the novel, Vonnegut, writing in the persona of Philboyd Studge, remarks, "I tend to think of human beings as huge, rubbery test tubes, too, with chemical reactions seething inside." This statement sets the stage for some of protagonist Dwayne Hoover's bizarre behavior in the novel, stemming from the "bad chemicals" in his brain. While Dwayne's immense power and privilege also influence his behavior in *Breakfast of Champions*, the novel highlights the many ways he and other characters are shaped by chemicals they ingest or by "faulty" chemical reactions in their bodies. In contrast to these characters, Vonnegut presents us with other individuals who knowingly or unknowingly act as chemical agents to alter lives and landscapes, and he uses his background in chemistry and micro-level perspectives to drive home his environmental critique.

Although *Breakfast of Champions* purports to tell the story of two characters meeting "on a planet which was dying fast," it's Vonnegut's shift to molecular levels that makes his ecological concerns so profound. As readers discover about a third of the way into the novel, Sugar Creek, the main body of water running through Midland City, has been "polluted by some sort of industrial waste which formed bubbles as tough as ping-pong balls." The pollution, we later learn, is the by-product of "a new anti-personnel bomb" that scatters "plastic pellets instead of steel pellets." Because the Barrytron plant has subcontracted its waste disposal to the shady Maritimo Brothers, the by-product is dumped directly into Sugar Creek. While the fact and circumstances of the pollution are sobering enough, Vonnegut has the readers confront the plastic molecule directly first through an examination of human impacts and then through a drawing of the polymer itself.[111] The waste's concentration is so high that Kilgore Trout's feet become covered in plastic after wading through the creek.

This somewhat fantastic outcome, however, is not a fiction of Trout's imagination. With the help of physical chemist Walter Stockmayer, Vonnegut offers readers a portrait of a genuine insidious pollutant. According to Great Lakes plastics pollution expert Sherri "Sam" Mason, Vonnegut and Stockmayer created a fairly rare and certainly advanced polymer for 1973. As she explained, the polymer "is one of a class of CTBN (carboxyl-terminated butadiene nitrile) co-polymers. These are generally used to add toughness to adhesive compounds. The $-C=N$ (cyanide/nitrile) group would make this a particularly nasty pollutant."[112] True to his ability to see the poetry of science, Vonnegut looks to the repeating molecular chains of the polymer to grasp its true perniciousness and planetary implications. Focusing on the "etc." used to indicate the polymer's repeating chains, Vonnegut highlights the ways in which humans, as chemical agents, have found ways to pollute and to plasticize our interconnected bodies of water and other living systems.

Moving rapidly from the molecular to the planetary, Vonnegut concludes that the "etc." is a "proper ending for any story about people it seems to me, since life is now a polymer in which the Earth is wrapped so tightly." To reinforce this metaphor, Vonnegut channels one of his (and Jane's) favorite Russian authors: "'It's all like an ocean!' cried Dostoevski. I say it's all like cellophane."[113] Sadly, Vonnegut's ever-extending polymer and predictions about plastic pollution have come true. As science editor Robin McKie reported in a January 23, 2016, *Guardian* article, "Humans have made enough plastic since the second world war to coat the Earth entirely in clingfilm. . . . No part of the planet is free of the scourge of plastic waste." Those five billion tons and counting are one of the many indicators that we have entered a new epoch marked by human impacts as chemical and geological agents: the Anthropocene.

Just as he turned to varying forms of artistic activism and planetary visions to communicate the urgent dangers of climate change, Vonnegut returned to microscopic characters and perspectives in his 1990 novel *Hocus Pocus*, to deliver an even sterner warning about the ways human beings "were killing the planet with the by-products of their ingenuity."[114] Like every Vonnegut novel, *Hocus Pocus* treats a broad range of subjects and institutions, but, like the meandering Sugar Creek in Midland City, it features a central, recurring thread of incisive environmental critique. In *Hocus Pocus*, this thread is the embedded story "The Protocols of the Elders of Tralfamadore," from the fictional *Black Garterbelt* magazine, that was almost certainly penned by Kilgore Trout.[115]

2.4 ✳ Vonnegut's original drawing of the molecule described in *Breakfast of Champions* highlights his use of scientific concepts to raise prescient concerns about plastics pollution. Archival image by Kurt Vonnegut, courtesy of the Lilly Library, Indiana University, Bloomington. Copyright © Kurt Vonnegut LLC, used by permission of The Wylie Agency LLC.

Like *Sirens of Titan*, the story hinges on the notion that human civilization has been in service to the larger aims of Tralfamadorians. Instead of evolving and collectively working to bring Salo a replacement part for his ship, this time human beings serve as a petri dish to help breed germs tough enough to travel through space. According to the story, "intelligent threads of energy trillions of light-years long" want "mortal, self-reproducing forms to spread out through the Universe." The Elders of Tralfamadore look to human beings on Earth as a way to breed microbes tough enough for interstellar travel. In short, "they saw in us a potential for chemical evils on a cosmic scale." Emboldened by ideas of planetary mastery and conquest in their origin myths, people create increasingly deadlier chemicals and weapons until they kill almost all life on Earth, except for some "virtually indestructible spores," lying in wait for a meteor or some other astral body suitable for interstellar hitchhiking.

While this parable of a largely lifeless and sterile Earth wrought by humans' industrial and military adventure was, by 1990, a familiar Vonnegutian theme, "The Protocols of the Elders of Tralfamadore" is testimony to Vonnegut's creativity. Although he revisits views of Earth from imaginary planets to critique species-level patterns of conquest, this time it's microbes that dethrone *Homo sapiens*. It's worth noting, too, that Vonnegut once again interweaves sound scientific ideas into a fantastic tale. As renowned biologist E. O. Wilson has speculated about life on other planets, "One prediction seems unavoidable: whatever the condition of alien life, and whether it flourishes on land and sea or barely hangs on in tiny oases, it will consist largely or entirely of microbes."[116]

The power of "The Protocols of the Elders of Tralfamadore" lies not in its apocalyptic scenario, but rather in its related shifts in perception. While we are used to thinking of germs as external threats, it's sobering to imagine humans as a literal source of disease in the broader web of life on Earth. The story also forces readers to examine the ways in which our metaphors and visions of disease have incredible destructive potential. Moving between science and history, the story specifically references *The Protocols of the Elders of Zion*, an anti-Semitic text that helped promote Nazi racial hygiene theories and Jewish genocide during the Holocaust. Through the chronic tuberculosis-related coughs that punctuate Eugene Debs Hartke's narration of *Hocus Pocus*, Vonnegut creates opportunities to remind readers of the Holocaust and the dangers of subscribing to ideas that see any group of people as a disease on the body politic. Hartke's refusal to view his Athena students, inmates at a racially segregated prison, as "germs" challenges the foundations of this type of racist thinking.

His reflections about his own immune system, meanwhile, ensure that Nazi racial hygiene legacies won't be forgotten. After one of his many coughs, Hartke reflects on the mechanics of his body's immune system this way: "My body, as I understand it, is attempting to contain the TB germs inside me in little shells it builds around them. The shells are calcium, the most common element in the walls of many prisons, including Athena. This place is ringed by barbed wire. So was Auschwitz." Once again shifting levels, Vonnegut takes us inside Hartke's body, using the cellular and atomic examples to explore some of the key connections between mastery, conquest, and extermination in "The Protocols of the Elders of Tralfamadore." Although Hartke struggles with a wide range of issues and sources of guilt, including the legacies of his experiences as a soldier in Vietnam, the final words he shares with readers offer the same moral as *The Black Garterbelt* story: "Just because some of us can read and write and do a little math, that doesn't mean we deserve to conquer the Universe."

This warning against human conquest, whether at the local, national, planetary, or galactic scale, was so central to Vonnegut's beliefs that he continued to revisit it throughout the rest of his career, trying new strategies and shifts in scale to get his message across. In terms of increasingly shrinking micro levels, another one of Kilgore Trout's embedded stories in *Timequake* shows how Vonnegut used chemical elements to raise ethical questions about human agency in the atomic age. Once again, the setting is Tralfamadore, although this time the meeting is run not by the planet's elders or other citizens, but rather by "representatives of all the chemical elements."[117] The purpose of the conference, which takes place September 1, 1945, is "to protest some of their members' having been incorporated into the bodies of big, sloppy, stinky organisms as cruel and stupid as human beings."[118]

In choosing the date Truman announced Japan's official surrender for the story's setting, Vonnegut via Trout can draw on the destruction created by World War II generally while evoking the United States-Japanese conflict specifically. Instead of mentioning Truman's speech or the actual surrender, the story uses chemical shorthand to suggest the nuclear research that enabled the bombings of Hiroshima and Nagasaki. The first chemical element personified in the story is Polonium, the highly radioactive element discovered by Marie and Pierre Curie, who, along with Ytterbium, is "outraged that *any* chemicals should be so misused" despite the fact that neither had ever been "essential parts of human beings." Without having to mention atomic weapons, Vonnegut highlights the "misuse" of uranium, plutonium, and other radioactive elements that ushered in new forms of global destruction during World War II.

The story's focus, though, is on a much broader history of human cruelty and destruction. Vonnegut via Trout uses eight of the ten main elements composing the human body by mass to address these historical events. Oxygen recounts tales "about black African slavery" while Potassium tells "hair-raising stories about the Spanish Inquisition, and Calcium about the Roman Games." To reinforce the specific World War II connections, Nitrogen weeps about "its involuntary servitude as parts of Nazi guards and physicians" in concentration camps. While the story leaves out Hydrogen, the only of the top six elements in the human body by mass not mentioned, it uses atomic-level thinking to raise important species- and planetary-wide concerns. It's no coincidence that Vonnegut chooses Carbon as the first speaker of the conference. Although only the second most common element in the human body by mass, Carbon is one of the most essential building blocks for all life on Earth. To state the obvious: *all* living beings (currently known) on Earth need carbon compounds to exist. Vonnegut not so subtly highlights Carbon's pervasiveness by mentioning that it was "an embarrassed veteran of countless massacres throughout history." However, Vonnegut quickly shifts the level of scale down to the minuscule by focusing on a single, horrific public execution in fifteenth-century England. While providing readers with an easily comprehensible example of human brutality, this turn to the singular at both the human and elemental level forces us once again to consider what type of agents humans have become on the planet.

The conference and the story itself culminate in a bleak course of action strikingly similar to the one developed at the meeting in "The Protocols of the Elders of Tralfamadore." After hearing from its far more prevalent human-body peer elements, Sodium proposes a motion that "all chemicals involved in medical research combine whenever possible to create ever more powerful antibiotics." These super antibiotics, Sodium reasons, would, in turn, "cause disease organisms to evolve new strains that were resistant to them."[119] Trout's story ends with Vonnegut's signature blend of dark humor and profundity: "In no time, Sodium predicted, every human ailment, including acne and jock itch, would not only be incurable but fatal. 'All humans will die,' said Sodium, according to Trout. 'As they were at the birth of the Universe, all elements will be free of sin again.'" While specifically referencing Felix Hoenikker's reaction to the testing of the atomic bomb in *Cat's Cradle* and loosely alluding to J. Robert Oppenheimer's famous quotation from the *Bhagavad Gita*, the line about freeing the elements of "sin" highlights humanity's unique but troubling place in the known universe. Their posthuman existence removes their participation in brutal human practices, but it also separates the elements from the complex and often beautiful cultural systems that produce the concepts and language necessary to communicate ideas of "sin" and innocence.

Trout's story in *Timequake* is a parable to help us realize our connections to living systems on the planet by reminding us that we are made up of the very same elements integral to all life on Earth. While the story foretells an "innocent" universe, cleansed of the dangerous chemical by-products of human ingenuity, even at a scientific level it's human-centered. Despite his shifts to increasingly miniaturized perspectives—bodies to cells to molecules to atoms—Vonnegut's examinations never go below the atomic level. Most likely, it's because the physical (Newtonian) laws of nature are different below the atomic level, and that would take us away from the realities and perceptions that shape human experience. And so Vonnegut's writings take readers through space and time to imaginary planets and microscopic worlds, but ultimately he dwells in the 4.6 percent of the universe composed of atoms because that's where human awareness lies.[120]

It's not surprising, then, that Vonnegut used a very human-centered metaphor in other late-career acts of planetary citizenship. Weaving together insights from Trout's stories, his background in bacteriology, and holistic views of Earth's living systems, Vonnegut returned to the idea of human beings as pathogens challenging their planet's immune system. In 1999, he worked with Joel Cohen and Ragged Edge Press to produce a limited print run of bright green and yellow bumper stickers that said, "YOUR PLANET'S IMMUNE SYSTEM IS TRYING TO GET RID OF YOU." As with the Rare Earth stickers, Vonnegut primarily shared the stickers with close friends and correspondents, but a limited number of them were made available to the public at a nominal charge to advance the press's progressive arts mission. Vonnegut's friends and colleagues, such as William Rodney Allen and Robert Weide, didn't always know what to make of the gift, but he persisted in sharing the bumper stickers as another form of his environmental activism.[121] In 2004, he turned to Joe Petro III to produce another version of the statement in silk-screen Confetti print #29, this time using bold red text to express his particular frustrations over President George W. Bush's war, energy, and environmental policies.[122] Reproduced in gray and white for *A Man Without a Country*, the Confetti reproduction read: "That's the end of good news about anything. Our planet's immune system is trying to get rid of people. This is sure the way to do that."

WHY BURN TIME WHEN YOU CAN WANDER THE EARTH FOR A MILLION YEARS?

As effective and creative as Vonnegut's shifts in physical space and scale were for encouraging environmental engagement, he is probably most famous for imaginative conceptions of time. From Billy Pilgrim's ability to become "unstuck in time" in *Slaughterhouse-Five* to the ten-year "rerun" that forces everyone to repeat everything they have done for nearly a decade in *Timequake*, Vonnegut's fiction creatively bends the laws of physics governing our concepts of time on Earth. These experiments help us see ourselves as geological agents on the planet, as members of a species born of "deep time," and as caretakers of the Earth who must look to future generations if we want to achieve environmental sustainability. While such experiments might not help us write a Beethoven-caliber symphony, they are especially prescient as we witness the tumultuous birth pangs of the Anthropocene Epoch and the dying gasps of the Holocene.

As environmental writers, scholars, and activists have known for decades, human beings' shortsighted views on resource extraction and consumption have led to long-term patterns of environmental destruction and unsustainable use—particularly in the Global North and most profoundly since the Industrial Revolution. While Vonnegut makes this point in many works, his embedded story about the planet Vicuna in *Jailbird* (1979) brilliantly captures this squandering of time and environmental resources. Appearing almost a hundred pages into the generally realistic novels, the story at first seems like a distraction from protagonist Walter Starbuck's storyline. However, it functions as an important connective thread in a novel that tackles American labor history, mid-twentieth-century US political history, and the rise of huge corporate conglomerates like the fictional RAMJAC.

Penned by fictional convict and writer Robert Fender (who uses "Kilgore Trout" as one of his pseudonyms!), the untitled story explores the possibility of souls that can attach to different bodies, chronicling the wanderings of "a former judge on the planet Vicuna, two and a half galaxies from Earth."[123] The Vicuna judge must travel through the "virtually lifeless" universe to Earth for a new body, because his planet "ran out of time." Once again using an alien view to highlight the unique richness of Earth teeming with life, the story cleverly plays with the concept of time by giving it physical dimensions. As Walter Starbuck explains in his summary of the story, "The tragedy of the planet was that its scientists found ways to extract time from topsoil and the oceans and the atmosphere—to heat their homes and power their speedboats and fertilize their crops with it; to eat it; to make clothes out of it; and so on."

The parallels between Vicuna's extracted time and petroleum are unmistakable, and Vonnegut highlights the three-hundred-plus-million years that turned Carboniferous plants and animals into fossil fuels. The story mentions the insatiable demand for oil ushered in by America's post–World War II car and consumer culture, noting "the patriotic bonfires of time" that squandered "a million years of future" in a single celebration. Vonnegut shifts the focus back to time itself by imagining "great rips in reality" and holes in Vicuna's time-space dimensions as the planet approaches the moment when only a few weeks of the future remain. By giving time physical properties and aligning Vicuna's uses with those in mid-twentieth-century America, Vonnegut forces readers to consider the consequences of unsustainable resource use. This small, somewhat outlandish story was so important to Vonnegut that he began several early drafts of *Jailbird* with it, using the narrative perspective of one of many Vicuna souls who had made it to Earth.

In one draft Vonnegut made the lesson of his environmental parable even more explicit. The Vicuna narrator mentions, "We chose Earth because there was a lot of time left here still. The creatures hadn't found out yet how to mine it and package it and sell it and throw it away."[124]

In *Galápagos*, his most explicitly environmental novel, Vonnegut explores these combined fears and hopes for the planet's future not through a short, embedded story but through a large-scale experiment with time. Set in the year 1,001,986 A.D., *Galápagos* examines human and other forms of life in the far distant future, forcing readers to think in terms of deep, evolutionary time instead of the human-centered sweeps of history that normally shape our decisions. Vonnegut employs this macro-view of life on Earth over the course of the novel's three-hundred-plus pages because his subject is so large. *Galápagos* is fundamentally about the human species and the promises and perils of human nature. Although Vonnegut published *Galápagos* fifteen years before scientists Paul Crutzen and Eugene Stoermer first proposed the idea of naming our current geological epoch the Anthropocene, the novel's environmental parables become even more relevant as we experience the effects of humans acting as geological agents on the planet.[125]

Galápagos is able to tackle these topics successfully because it is grounded in science. The novel simultaneously employs Darwin's theories of natural selection with scientific integrity while critiquing social Darwinism. Vonnegut's 1982 trip to the Galápagos Islands, careful study of Darwin's writings, and additional research on evolution, in fact, earned him praise from renowned evolutionary biologist Stephen Jay Gould, who thought the novel was "a wonderful *roman à clef* about evolutionary theory" and study of "how random the selection is."[126] Despite its elements of plausibility, the novel does not attempt to imagine the possible evolutionary paths of multiple species in different parts of the globe. Instead, Vonnegut returns to the site of Darwin's inspiration to explore the fate of the species most profoundly altering the surface of the planet: *Homo sapiens*. As we peer one million years into the future, we discover a dramatically altered, benign form of humankind, evolved from a tiny band of colonists on the fictional island of Santa Rosalia. The "whole rest of the animal world," by contrast, "has done strikingly little to improve its survival tactics in all that time," leaving little doubt that it's our species that needs to contemplate its planetary role.[127]

For Vonnegut, the enormous stretch of time and narrative perspective of the novel presented a far greater challenge than envisioning possible evolutionary paths. After all, how can anatomically modern *Homo sapiens* think within a million-year time frame when we've only existed as a species for about 200,000 years and can only point to approximately 5,500 years of recorded history? Or, to borrow the language of journalist Alan Weisman's famous title, how do we imagine "the world without us"? As historian Dipesh Chakrabarty points out, "we have to insert ourselves into a future 'without us' in order to be able to visualize it."[128] Vonnegut brilliantly solves these problems by creating the ghostly narrator Leon Trout, who can draw on his former human experiences to interpret human and planetary conditions, but who also possesses an omniscient narrative capacity due to his phantom wanderings. Like the residents of Vicuna, Leon Trout can slip into the bodies of humans to explore their thoughts, emotions, and histories. And because his curiosity about the fate of the Santa Rosalia colonists prevents him from crossing over into the "blue tunnel to the afterlife," his one-million-year sentence to wander the Earth allows for the appropriate "deep time" framework.[129] The biological offspring of Kilgore Trout and his far more optimistic mother, Leon can also see the best and worst in humanity and raise important questions about our species.[130]

As a Vietnam veteran and son of Kilgore Trout, Leon is especially well equipped to see the dark side of humanity and the particular environmental problems human beings are causing in November 1986, the pivotal time frame when a series of "lucky" accidents gathers the ten future colonists and send them on their way to Santa

Rosalia. Vonnegut assigns both particular and species-level blame for these widespread ecological woes. Embodying the worst of these behaviors is Andrew MacIntosh, a fifty-five-year-old "American financier and adventurer of great inherited wealth." We learn, for example, of MacIntosh's "mania for claiming as his own property as many of the planet's life-support systems as possible" and of the fact that he "found ensuring the survival of the human race a total bore." MacIntosh's environmental crimes are rendered more sinister as we watch him masquerade as "an ardent conservationist" while his companies act as "notorious damagers of the water or the soil or the atmosphere." Vonnegut underscores the huge economic disparities between MacIntosh, the urban poor, and Indigenous rain forest tribes of Ecuador, but he ultimately emphasizes the broader anthropocentric devastation of Earth.

Leon sets up these collective impacts early in the novel, noting that the worldwide financial crisis in 1986 A.D. "was simply the latest in a series of murderous twentieth-century catastrophes which had originated entirely in human brains." With the broader vision afforded by expanses of time and space, Leon carefully mentions *human* causes for the famines, wars, and environmental damage "to all other living things"—not a scarcity of natural resources. By attributing this damage to people's "oversize brains," he goes beyond the economic policies, national conflicts, and greed immediately underlying the problems, to address one of the most distinctive features of our species. This vision of our big-brained species destroying "the earthling part of the clockwork of the universe" aligns with what biologist E. O. Wilson bemoaned for decades: "Humanity has so far played the role of planetary killer, concerned only with its own short-term survival."[131] As Vonnegut learned in his physical anthropology classes, it was indeed our large brains, along with our bipedalism and dexterous hands, which helped our hominid ancestors develop tools and alter their environments.

True to his career-long pacifism, Vonnegut uses Leon's war experiences as a filter to underscore the ecological damage done by weapons. *Galápagos* is littered with descriptions of destructive twentieth-century military technologies, which, Leon notes, can rival even the mechanisms of evolution. After explaining the origins of new explosives used in the fictional Peruvian-Ecuadoran conflict of November 1986, Leon concludes, "And the Law of Natural Selection was powerless to respond to such new technologies. No female of any species, unless, maybe, she was a rhinoceros, could expect to give birth to a baby who was fireproof, bombproof, or bulletproof." To heighten the bite of this observation, Leon mentions that "the best that the Law of Natural Selection could come up with" was people who weren't "afraid of anything, even though there was so much to fear"—people like Andrew MacIntosh.

Despite all the planetary dangers posed by humans and their large brains, *Galápagos* suggests that although we have become geological agents capable of altering the planet on a large scale, human beings are still governed by the same natural laws and life-supporting systems that affect *all* species. Ultimately, it's not a human-caused catastrophe that wipes out everyone except for the ten Santa Rosalia colonists. It's a microscopic bacterium that destroys human ova in women's ovaries. This "new creature" emerges at the Frankfurt Book Fair and spreads around the globe, reaching every human population but the isolated Santa Rosalia colonists. Comparing the near total extinction of humans to that of "mighty land tortoises," Leon again uses his macro views of time and space to place the pandemic within the broad history of many David-Goliath stories. Leon's dry sense of humor and lack of details about the pandemic minimize the brutal realities of human extinction outside of Santa Rosalia. The biological stakes of Vonnegut's literary experiment, nevertheless, are all too real. As environmental historian Dan Flores reminds us, if we refuse to recognize the "selfishness and short-sightedness" apparently "built into our very evolution" and "stop the steady destruction of the world . . . then externally delivered checks are what we can expect."[132] The Law of Natural Selection, Leon points out, can easily repair the planet's "clockwork," bringing "humanity into harmony with itself and the rest of Nature."

In *Galápagos* that "harmony" comes at the expense of losing virtually all the traits that make *Homo sapiens* "human." In the year 1,001,986 A.D., the descendants of the Santa Rosalia colonists have evolved into amphibious "fisherfolk" with a silky, seal-like pelt, arm flippers, streamlined skulls, and much smaller brains. With adaptations in keeping with the rich marine life surrounding the isolated volcanic islands, these future hominids spend much of their thirty-year life span catching fish or simply frolicking like sea lions on shore. The shorter life span has reduced childhood to nine months, and "people" identify each other by their distinctive odors, since their sense of smell has been dramatically increased.[133] Although Leon contemplates possible evolutionary paths had the Santa Rosalia colonists been composed of the wealthy celebrities originally scheduled for the *Bahía de Darwin*'s maiden voyage, he concludes that the outcome still would have been the same: "In the long run, the survivors would still have been not the most ferocious struggler but the most efficient fisherfolk. That's how things work in the islands here."

Because the novel is fundamentally about modern *Homo sapiens* and our dangers to ourselves and the planet, Vonnegut offers comparatively little narrative space to our species' successors. Rather than provide any detailed portraits of them, Vonnegut instead has his ghostly narrator reveal individual characteristics of these new hominids one at a time over the course of the novel. In another experiment with time, the narrative symbolically simulates evolution on the very human-centered timescale it takes for the reader to finish the novel. The future "fisherfolk" come into focus trait by trait as Leon's tale first sweeps back to 1986 A.D. and then returns to the "present" of a million years beyond that. While this technique forces readers to contemplate the deep time of evolution and geology, Vonnegut's primary purpose is to explore the ways natural selection has put destructive human characteristics in check.[134] As Leon reminds us at the start of his story, "this was a very innocent planet, except for those great big brains."

This innocence is restored as mainland humans are wiped out and as humans lose the features, such as large brains and dexterous hands, that have enabled destructive technologies and institutions. To further emphasize that this evolutionary path has kept humanity's destructive potential in check, Leon notes that their "arms have become flippers in which their hand bones are almost entirely imprisoned and immobilized." As he introduces new information about our descendants, Leon can't resist throwing in a few barbs. Describing a missile strike, for instance, he says, "it is hard to imagine anybody's torturing anybody nowadays. How could you even capture somebody you wanted to torture with just your flippers and your mouth?" As a follow-up, he adds, "Nobody today is nearly smart enough to make the sorts of weapons even the poorest nations had a million years ago."

The evolutionary path that brings humans into harmony with the rest of the planet, however, also leads to the extinction of the best elements of human culture. While Leon reveals new traits and the loss of destructive behaviors, he also offers an unfolding catalog of vanished human skills and characteristics. As his tale moves back and then forward again in time, Leon marks the loss of religious practices, extended families, intelligence, sculpture, music, love, curiosity, and imagination. True to his anthropologist roots, Vonnegut positions Leon as a type of observer-participant who is forced to give up his ethnographic study because virtually all his cultural subjects are gone. No one is left to read his words written in air "with the tip of the index finger of [his] left hand, which is also air." These vanished skills and qualities accumulate in the novel along with the lost words of famous writers, thinkers, and artists quoted by the portable computer Mandarax (before it is tossed into the water by Captain Von Kleist, the genetic patriarch of virtually all future hominids). Not surprisingly love and imagination are two of the last "extinct" human behaviors mentioned, giving them symbolic weight as we discover the key lesson of *Galápagos*'s extended parable.

Ultimately, *Galápagos* is a remarkably optimistic novel. Although Leon looks to the peaceful, untroubled, cooing, laughing descendants of modern humans as an evolutionary improvement, Vonnegut's real hope is that we will heed nature's warnings and adopt the planetary thinking needed to bring about changes on our own. Leon's decision to remain behind and observe the Santa Rosalia colonists and their descendants is more than a simple device to solve the narrative challenges of the book. Leon's rejection of his deeply pessimistic father at the edge of the blue tunnel allows Vonnegut to infuse a hopeful counterbalance into the novel. During the father-son exchange, Kilgore Trout reminds Leon of his mother's favorite quotation, the Anne Frank line that serves as the novel's epigraph: "In spite of everything, I still believe people are really good at heart." Reinforcing this vision of hope within despair, Kilgore tells Leon, "You believe that human beings are good animals, who will eventually solve all their problems and make earth into a Garden of Eden again." Toward the end of his tale, Leon concludes "Mother was right: Even in the darkest times, there really was still hope for mankind." This hope, Vonnegut's cautionary tale suggests, lies in countering our destructive behaviors with regenerative, selfless, and imaginative ones. Perhaps our powers of imagination and love just might help us learn the vital ecological lesson the Santa Rosalia colonists did: "Just in the nick of time they realized that it was their own habitat that they were wrecking—and that they weren't merely visitors."

As his epitaphs and requiems for the Earth suggest, Vonnegut was not always as optimistic about humanity's potential for harmony within itself and the planet. Despite his own Kilgore Trout–style pessimism and genuine heartbreak over our failures to address climate change and other planetary emergencies, Vonnegut persisted. Whether writing letters from the year 2088, leaving apologetic notes for future generations, or imagining "timequakes" born of the universe's crisis of self-confidence, Vonnegut continued to play with shifts in space, scale, and time to investigate our species, planet, and place in the universe. Like Leon Trout, he kept writing even when he feared that there wouldn't be future human beings to one day read his words. However grand (or tiny) his creative visions were, he was also an Earthling deeply connected to and grounded in real places.

PART TWO
PLACE

CHAPTER 3

A HOOSIER'S SYMPHONY OF PLACE

From Fresh Water to Salt Water to Quartz Porcupine Quills

But please don't forget where you came from. I never did.
—KURT VONNEGUT, Address at Butler University, May 11, 1996

What counts as place can be as small as a corner of your kitchen or as big as the planet.
—LAWRENCE BUELL, "Space, Place, and Imagination"

Saddled with two mortgages and desperately trying to break into the world of one-hour television plays, Kurt Vonnegut began drafting *The Hoosier Symphony* in the spring of 1955. The finished version, simply titled *The Hoosiers*, was a satire on the wealthy inhabitants of Indianapolis's northern suburbs, using the visit of Baron Von Gaartz, a young, handsome German suitor, to expose the eccentricities and foibles of the Schaeffer family. The staff at NBC decided to pass on the script they received in late August 1955.[135] Perhaps the comedic scenes involving marital conflict over the unsightliness of a compost pile, a six-man police search for Eileen Schaeffer's "babies" (two pampered Great Danes who had never felt rain), or Annie Schaeffer's snobbery induced by her "grand tour of Europe" weren't quite up to NBC's standards for live television theater. Remarkably, Vonnegut had already stripped the play of its more unusual elements—a Russian composer named Koradubian contemplating defection, a secret-police agent named Tanya posing as Koradubian's wife, an African American servant named Wanda who drinks crème de cocoa with Mr. Schaeffer, and Tanya's farcical vision for a symphony that begins with the sounds of the Indianapolis five-hundred-mile Speedway and ends with the snippets of the Schaeffer's family's conversations picked up via hidden microphones in their heavily bugged "brand-new Hoosier dream house."

At first glance, *The Hoosier Symphony* is just one of Vonnegut's many unpublished works written to bring quick financial reward, with embryonic beginnings of ideas more successfully realized in his novels.[136] More so than *Celeste*, *Jonah*, *Something Borrowed*, the co-written *Emory Beck*, or the other plays that Vonnegut wrote in 1954 and 1955, drafts of *The Hoosier Symphony* highlight Vonnegut's complicated, nested attachments to place.[137] Begun just after his recently expanded family had moved from Osterville to their two-hundred-year-old, twelve-room house in West Barnstable, Massachusetts, the drafts explore family dynamics, family history, place, home, and region. After many years away from his home state, Vonnegut had returned in November 1954 with his daughter Edith to visit Kurt Sr. at his new home in Nashville, Indiana. The visit was a brief one; Vonnegut left after only two days, spending the remainder of the week with old friends in Indianapolis.[138] Yet the pull of Indiana places manifested itself in multiple play drafts even as Vonnegut was physically immersing himself in West Barnstable, exploring the old barn, Hinkleys Pond, dunes, the Great Marsh, and the village that surrounded the new family home.

Early drafts of *The Hoosier Symphony* reveal a complicated and often bittersweet web of connections to Indiana places. An early outline, for instance, included Vonnegut's childhood friend Majie Failey and her mother as characters and drew on details from Vonnegut's family homes on Illinois Street in Indianapolis and in the town of Williams Creek. Those familiar with Vonnegut's boyhood home would recognize distinctive elements in the drafts, such as the wooded lot, his father's garden, the large picture window, and the basement rumpus room. Vonnegut also invoked his high school home by including a character based on the mayor of Williams Creek. Drawing on the recent unsuccessful pheasant hunt with his father, Vonnegut wove in details about a hunt club, tracking dogs, a rifle above the fireplace, and the uniform and pageantry associated with hunting traditions. Despite the fractious nature of his short visit with his father, at the heart of every draft, whether in the character of Clem Schaeffer or that of Baron Kurt Von Gaartz, was a sympathetic and loving portrait of Kurt Sr. As Vonnegut imagined characters clearly based on his father, he highlighted Doc's love of painting, architecture, music, and the broader connections of art that made him a "citizen of the world."[139] The drafts also honored Doc's naturalist interests and influences. By rewarding Clem Schaeffer, originally conceived as "the father," with a compost heap teeming with worms and other bugs, Vonnegut also cast him as a citizen of the earth.

Vonnegut's engagements with place were not restricted to his new home in West Barnstable and his old ones in and near Indianapolis. The short stories and plays he drafted in 1955 transported readers to the desolated post-firebombed streets and shelters of Dresden, a comfortable farm home in Mercer, Ohio, George Helmholtz's band room in the fictional Lincoln High School, and, in "This Son of Mine,"[140] Merle Waggoner's centrifugal pump factory. Like most of his novels, these stories and plays also included passing references to other places significant to Vonnegut's life and prior writings, such as the fictional General Forge and Foundry Company of Ilium, and Cornell University.

Although the short-lived character Koradubian never entered his public, published creative universe, Vonnegut ultimately created his own Hoosier symphony. Instead of limiting himself to the sights and sounds of one specific city, however, Vonnegut adopted a symphonic sense of place—one that layered together a lifetime of nested place experiences both real and imagined. His writings simultaneously draw on the local landscapes and communities where he lived—Indianapolis, Ithaca, Alplaus, Cape Cod, New York City, Sagaponack—while incorporating his memories of and wholly imagined interactions with other places. As we'll see, Vonnegut's own place attachments and experiences also shaped his environmental critiques, notions of stewardship, understanding of communities, and identity as a writer. Because it would be impossible to capture Vonnegut's connections to place in their full symphonic glory, I've selected a few melodic lines from his various movements: his nonfiction essays on Lake Maxinkuckee, Barnstable, and New York City and an unpublished piece on the Cape Cod National Seashore.[141] Examining these nonfiction works will, I hope, inspire us to think with more complexity about place in Vonnegut's writings—whether investigating how Vonnegut's own imagination was shaped by the landscapes where he lived or simply appreciating the layered richness of place in the Vonnegutian fictional cosmos.

"EPTA-MAYAN-HOY" AND *BERALIKUR*

It is only fitting to begin a survey of Vonnegut's explorations of place with his own starting point—the shores of Lake Maxinkuckee. Although Vonnegut had just turned sixty-five when he mailed a copy of "The Lake" to *Architectural Digest* editor Michael Wollaeger, the essay transports Vonnegut back to pivotal childhood experiences when he "made [his] first mental maps of the world."[142] Originally appearing in the June 1988 issue of *Architectural Digest*, "The Lake" is, like the concept of place itself, "associatively thick."[143] The essay is as much about Vonnegut's imaginative maps of the place as it is about Indiana's second-largest freshwater lake and its environs. Lake Maxinkuckee is simply "the lake," we learn, because the actual location, locale, and geographical coordinates no longer matter to Vonnegut. As he discovers while flying over those beloved waters, "That wasn't the real Maxinkuckee down there. The real one is in my head."

When he was a boy, though, the "real" Lake Maxinkuckee mattered very much. The five-mile-long, two-and-a-half-mile-wide lake was where the extended Vonnegut family kept five summer cottages and an orchard for multiple generations, and young Kurt could spend weeks on end immersed in nature. According to Vonnegut, this combined sense of family, home, and nature led Lake Maxinkuckee to become firmly "imprinted on [his] mind." And we can see this imprint in the structure of the essay itself, which mirrors the "closed loop" of the lakeshore, as it winds its way from childhood to adulthood, beginning and ending with notions of home.

Vonnegut opens the essay with the claim that he "can achieve a blank and shining serenity" if he can "reach the very edge of a natural body of water." This serenity, he explains, stems from the early "mental maps" he made as a small child exploring the lake's circumference. As he asks his reader, "Isn't your deepest understanding of time and space and, for that matter, destiny shaped like mine by your earliest experiences with geography, by the rules you learned how to get home again?" Further emphasizing this sense of serenity and security, Vonnegut continues, "What is it that can make you feel, no matter how mistakenly, that you are on the right track, that you will soon be safe and sound at home again?" It's almost as if Vonnegut was culling thoughts from cultural geographer Yi-Fu Tuan, who noted that childhood offers foundational moments for deepening our awareness of place, expanding our geographical horizons, exploring space and the natural environment, and building emotional ties to place.[144]

We can see this deepening sense of place over the next few paragraphs as Vonnegut expands his notion of "home" from his family's own "unheated frame cottage overlooking the lake" to the additional "four adjacent cottages teeming with close relatives." This widening sense of home parallels the essay's broadening sense of childhood place attachments, as he blends his own childhood memories of "a first cousin fishing from a leaky rowboat or a sister reading a book in a hammock" with those of his parents' and grandparents' generations, preserved through the family's calls of "Epta-mayan-hoy" ("Do abbots mow hay?"). Vonnegut also links these German calls, which were "pure nonsense from their childhoods," to earlier families and peoples, noting that the now vanished Vonneguts succeeded the more tragically displaced Potawatomi Indians. The section culminates with Vonnegut's memory of swimming across the lake at its widest part while his brother Bernie and sister Allie cheered him on in the boat named for all three siblings, *Beralikur*. Although the essay weaves through family history, noting Alice's death and Bernard's contemporaneous research in the late 1980s, the lake and that memory remained fixed in time. Vonnegut concludes the section, "Times change, but my lake never will."

Moving from childhood to young adulthood, Vonnegut revisits memories of his honeymoon with Jane, when they stayed in his family's old cottage in September 1945. The cottage had been sold to the concertmaster of the Indianapolis Symphony Orchestra, but the romantic new owner allowed Kurt and Jane to honeymoon there before taking possession of it. The newlyweds spent a week rowing the leaky old family boat, *Beralikur*, observing the Culver Military Academy, and reading *The Brothers Karamazov*. Although he does not incorporate the story of Jane sharing her favorite Dostoyevsky quotation with him, Kurt includes its most salient part: "some good sacred memory from childhood is perhaps the best education."[145]

3.1 ✳ This photograph captures a young Kurt Vonnegut standing on the pier of his family's cottage at Lake Maxinkuckee, when he was first starting to make his "mental maps of the world." Courtesy of the Vonnegut family and Robert Weide. Copyright © Kurt Vonnegut LLC, used by permission of The Wylie Agency LLC.

Embedded in his reminiscences of rowing Jane in *Beralikur* is a second brief account of swimming across Lake Maxinkuckee when he was eleven. As if to further freeze this sacred childhood memory in time, Vonnegut accentuates his memory of Jane in *Beralikur* with a brief paragraph describing a loon's "chilling, piercing, liquid cry of seeming lunacy."[146] Remembering his boyhood cries of delight after traversing the lake, Vonnegut adds, "Only now do I realize that my answer should have been this: "Ya! Epta-mayan-hoy!" Thus, early adulthood and later adulthood become fused as well, capturing Yi-Fu Tuan's insight that "place can acquire deep meaning for the adult through the steady accretion of sentiment over the years."[147]

With his mental navigation of Lake Maxinkuckee complete, Vonnegut transfers his loop of childhood to adult memories to a second home and body of water. The essay jumps in time to Kurt and Jane's Barnstable house and "a very deep puddle made by a glacier and called Coggin's Pond." Building on the layers of place-making, the final portion moves from the portable mental maps his own children have made of Barnstable's harbor, marsh, and pond to the new ones currently being created by his grandchildren. The essay wraps up with the final word of *The Brothers Karamazov*, but it's clear that Vonnegut has envisioned a larger, still unfolding loop of descendants inventing generational nonsense phrases, forming attachments to local bodies of water, and creating sacred mental maps of place that will teach them "how to get safely home before the sun goes down."

Neither a nature essay nor a travel piece, "The Lake" is about the layers of meaning attached to a place that exists through memory instead of immediate lived experience. Vonnegut even equated his memories of Lake Maxinkuckee to mythic representations of a lost paradise. Writing to longtime friend Pete Miller in 1996, Vonnegut explained that the "feelings of an Eden lost evident in my writings and the longings for a folk society, are all about Maxinkuckee."[148] That liquid Eden also helped shape Vonnegut's sense of regional identity. As he explained in his "Coda to My

Career as a Writer for Periodicals," fresh water was the basis of his identity as a Midwesterner.[149] Vonnegut saw in freshwater lakes—especially the Great Lakes—"something distinctive" for all "native Middle Westerners." He wrote, "Get this: When we were born, there had to have been incredible quantities of fresh water all around us, in lakes, and streams and rivers and raindrops and snowdrifts, and no undrinkable salt water anywhere!" For Vonnegut, these connections to freshwater lakes were literally etched onto his tongue: "Even my taste buds are Middle Western on that account. When I swim in the Atlantic or Pacific, the water tastes all wrong to me, even though it is in fact no more nauseating, as long as you don't swallow it, than chicken soup." While giving him a distinctive sense of region, Lake Maxinkuckee also offered Vonnegut transferable place-making skills. He was able to put down roots and to create new mental maps of real and imagined worlds as he settled in Cape Cod—another place rich in water, albeit water that would always seem a bit foreign to Vonnegut's Midwestern freshwater taste buds.

MARSH TROMPS, A SALMON CURTAIN, AND THE OUTER SHORE

Kurt and Jane's decision to move to Cape Cod was strongly tied to their associations of the Cape with writing and the arts. The family's summer stay in Provincetown in 1951 was so artistically nourishing that they instantly narrowed their initial Atlantic coast home search and bought a house in Osterville that fall. Purchasing the rambling old home in West Barnstable three years later signaled that Vonnegut was willing to swap his freshwater pleasures for saltwater ones—especially if they reinforced his status as a full-time writer. Although the economic inconsistencies of his writing career forced him to take on freelance work and other jobs, from school teacher to Saab dealer, it was, ironically, Vonnegut's career as a writer that often made him feel out of place during the two decades that he lived on Cape Cod.

Vonnegut often felt isolated from his neighbors who didn't read, understand, or care for his writings.[150] As both Jane and Mark note in their respective memoirs, this sense of isolation was compounded by other class, political, regional, and cultural differences that set the Vonneguts apart from their Cape Cod peers.[151] Reflecting on these differences, Jane writes that they were "Democrats in a sea of Republicans, liberals in an overwhelmingly conservative area (except for one little patch of Hyannis port), the last people in the village to acquire a television set, and then only to watch the McCarthy hearings." "They didn't go to church. They didn't have a boat," she continues, adding that Kurt "stayed home all day and wrote while the other kids' fathers went off somewhere every day and *worked*."[152]

Despite these differences, or perhaps because of them, Vonnegut developed especially strong connections to the natural features of Cape Cod—biotic communities that included bluefin tuna, striped bass, harp seals, common terns, razorbills, great blue heron, mussels, clams, greenhead flies, bayberry, native cranberry, diamondback terrapins, and scores of other creatures and entities that roamed or grew in the Sandy Neck Dunes, Great Marsh, and the ever-changing contours of the outer shore. As he mentioned in an April 1972 radio interview, one of the things Vonnegut enjoyed most about living on Cape Cod was taking long walks with the family dog, Sandy, along the shores of Barnstable Harbor and on Sandy Neck Beach.[153]

Despite the solace offered by these landscapes, Vonnegut still needed human communities. His distance from his affluent neighbors cemented ties to "the carpenters and plumbers and salesmen whose livelihoods depended on serving Cape's population of moneyed families."[154] These middle- and working-class laborers, critic Jerome Klinkowitz suggests, not only became useful collaborators for Vonnegut's home repair, gardening, and sculpture projects, but also influenced the distinctly accessible, "comfortably familiar and ordinary" voice that became a hallmark of Vonnegut's short stories and personal essays.[155] It's not surprising, then, that the pieces Vonnegut wrote about Cape Cod, "You've Never Been to Barnstable?" (1964) and his unpublished "The Cape Cod National Seashore" (ca. 1966/67), offer richly layered and complicated relationships to place. In both essays, Vonnegut maintains an outside observer's distance while advocating for the preservation of the Cape's natural features with an insider's intimate knowledge of both human and nonhuman communities.

Long before Vonnegut published "You've Never Been to Barnstable?" in October 1964, the particular towns, professions, landmarks, and scenery of Cape Cod had been making their way into his short stories and novels. "The Cruise of the Jolly Roger" (1953) captured some of the Cape's geography with Major Durant's voyage from Martha's Vineyard to Provincetown, while "The Powder-Blue Dragon" (1954) incorporated the smallness of a seaside village and some of the wealth disparities of the Cape. Other early but posthumously published stories, such as "Hello, Red" and "The Honor of a Newsboy," included details that drew on Vonnegut's immediate Barnstable surroundings via Eddie Scudder's name and mention of the Blue Dolphin, a restaurant just blocks away from his house. *Sirens of Titan*, meanwhile, featured the Barnstable First Church of God the Utterly Indifferent, incorporating many of the architectural details of Barnstable's West Parish Church, which was being restored while Vonnegut was drafting the novel.[156] Vonnegut's essay "You've Never Been to Barnstable?" stands apart from these fictional works in its rich detail and explicit investigations of place. The essay is so immediate and locally situated that you can easily pinpoint the essay's key sites or make your own mental maps of Barnstable Village. Tellingly, Vonnegut chose it as the opening piece in *Welcome to the Monkey House*, which he framed with a Thoreauvian epigraph on writing about subjects near home.

Although originally published in travel magazine *Venture*, the essay is not a typical tourism promotion piece. Instead, as his revised title suggests, "Where I Live" offers an intimate exploration of the village that had become another home for Vonnegut.

Despite this personal perspective of Barnstable, Vonnegut never uses the first-person narrative voice that one might expect and that he frequently used in his short stories. Using third-person limited perspective, Vonnegut creates the rhetorical situation of an outsider visiting Barnstable to view the village's people, buildings, natural features, and character through a fresh lens. And while Vonnegut may have chosen this narrative perspective to connect with his original *Venture* audience, it also gave him a way to explore his own complicated relation to Barnstable.

Vonnegut begins the essay, his "tour" of Barnstable, with a description of an encyclopedia salesman visiting "the lovely Sturgis Library," which Vonnegut simply describes as "America's oldest library building."[157] The bookseller senses a potential sale when he discovers that the library's most current reference book was "a 1938 *Britannica*, backstopped by a 1910 *Americana*." Quickly positioning the library and village as sites more rooted in the past than the present, the salesman notes that "many important things had happened since 1938, naming among others, penicillin and Hitler's invasion of Poland." Beneath this seemingly simple frame is a more intimate entry point for Vonnegut to explore his own relationship with Barnstable. While the recollected encyclopedia salesman is sent off to track down some of the library's directors, Vonnegut had a close relationship with the Sturgis Library as a trustee on the library's seven-member board. Vonnegut resigned the position on June 20, 1966, citing his job with the Iowa Writers' Workshop and his inability to keep up with the Sturgis's operations. However, in an August 1970 interview, he revealed a more vexatious relationship with the library, which he called "a clapboard tomb," adding, "if he did not live four blocks down the road, his books would never have been acquired by the Sturgis Library."[158] As critical as he was, Vonnegut also recognized the Sturgis Library's historical and cultural significance. Constructed in 1644 as the home for Barnstable's founding father, Reverend John Lothrop, the Sturgis Library is a logical starting point for a tour. As a trustee, Vonnegut knew that much of the village's maritime, religious, genealogical, and historical documents were housed there.

Having introduced his readers to Barnstable's early colonial, Puritan history, Vonnegut uses the encyclopedia salesman's search for library trustees to explore the village and its environs, and, ultimately, to discover the village's soul. The bookseller's quest first leads to the Barnstable Yacht Club, which has nothing of the grandeur he expected. This fruitless stop for the salesman, though, allows Vonnegut to appreciate Barnstable Harbor. Whereas the bookseller is "insensitive to the barbarous beauty all around him," Vonnegut shows that even with the tide "utterly out" the harbor is teeming with life, activity, and vitality. Above the "bluish-brown glurp of the emptied harbor's floor" soar "clouds of gulls and terns yelling . . . about all the good things in it they were finding to eat." Broadening this view near the Yacht Club, Vonnegut's gaze leads due north and east to incorporate several men "digging clams as fat as partridges from the rim of Sandy Neck, the ten-mile-long sand finger that separates the harbor from the ice-cold bay." After highlighting the natural rhythms and food chains at the interstices of Barnstable Harbor and Cape Cod Bay, Vonnegut shifts his view to the west, including the biotic communities closer to his home on the corner of Scudder Lane and Main Street (Route 6A). The scene now includes herons, geese, ducks, and other waterfowl feasting in the harbor and "in the great salt marsh that bounds the harbor on the west." This salt marsh was especially dear to Kurt and Jane, who led treks across the Great Marsh and its muddy creeks. What began as a "romp for their extended family of eight" in the late 1950s became an annual mud-filled long-distance "marsh tromp" that included dozens of friends and neighbors.[159]

Although Vonnegut doesn't incorporate his detailed knowledge of the Great Marsh here, he calls attention to the difference between locals' understanding of the harbor and outsiders' explorations. In contrast to the smaller, shallow-bottomed Rhodes 18s, Beetle Cats, and Boston Whalers near the Yacht Club's pier, Vonnegut notes that "near the harbor's narrow mouth, a yawl from Marblehead with a six-foot keel lay on her side, waiting for the water to come back in again." The yawl, like the "insensitive" encyclopedia salesman, is out of place in the harbor and its "Ozarks," the ramshackle Yacht Club.

This insensitivity to the village's beauty and centuries-old maritime traditions continues as the salesman returns to downtown Barnstable. After an unsatisfying lunch at the Barnstable News Store, he visits the Customs House, where he is "excruciatingly" bored by exhibits about the village and the harbor's "long-gone days when [it] was used by fair-sized ships, before it filled up with all that bluish brown glurp." Completely uninterested in past maritime laborers and present-day tradespersons, the salesman flees south. Leaving the walkable, quiet village, the bookseller drives "toward the cocktail lounges, motor courts, bowling alleys, gift shoppes, and pizzerias of Hyannis, the commercial heart of Cape Cod." The shift to Hyannis allows Vonnegut to underscore the negative impacts of the tourist boom and Kennedy-related development of the 1950s and early 1960s. Rather than decrying the mass of local and national chain motels, restaurants, and tourist traps popping up all along the Cape's commercial Route 28, Vonnegut focuses his critique on "Playland," a mini golf venue, typical of "the random butchery of the Cape's south shore." The kitschy, artificial miniature golf course, we learn, is not only tied to crass commercialization of the Cape's southern harbors and beaches, but it has defiled a war memorial honoring World War II veterans.

While contrasting the antiquated, static Barnstable with the Cape's rapidly changing central and south-side areas, the salesman's escape to Hyannis also enables Vonnegut to shift from the bookseller's "depressed" view of Barnstable to a more intimate lens. Although Vonnegut retains the third-person perspective, the mid-essay shift allows him to discover the points where the historical "soul of Barnstable" and his own sense of the village's soul overlap. Here Vonnegut moves from local politics to his beloved Barnstable Comedy Club, which he and Jane joined in 1953 before they even moved to the village.[160] Although Vonnegut omits his

3.2 * Anne Bossi, a friend of the Vonnegut family, photographed
Kurt and Jane leading one of their famous treks across the Great
Marsh on Cape Cod in 1965. Courtesy of the Vonnegut family and
Robert Weide. Copyright © Kurt Vonnegut LLC, used by permis-
sion of The Wylie Agency LLC.

extensive service to the club as its president, an officer, an actor, a director, a workshop leader, and a member of the reading committee that selected plays, he weaves in detail rich in personal connections. The conservative treasurer's worries over a "four hundred dollar and some odd cents" balance references the club's 1961 purchase of Village Hall—a sale facilitated by Vonnegut himself as president of the group. The "spoiled salmon" or "ptomaine curtain" purportedly purchased with the club's funds, meanwhile, pays quiet tribute to the new curtain Jane made for the club's production of *The Glass Menagerie* and her many significant roles both in front of and behind the curtain. Lastly, the description of the club's production of *The Caine Mutiny Court-Martial* sentimentally references several firsts— the club's first all-male production and Vonnegut's own debut in a leading role in October 1957.

Moving from this personal grounding of the village's artistic and cultural soul, Vonnegut once again looks to Barnstable's environs. After playfully mocking the fishermen who only "recently" discovered "that tuna were good to eat" and that "mussels can be eaten without causing instant death," Vonnegut returns to Barnstable Harbor, the Great Marsh, and Sandy Neck to further survey their rich biological diversity. This time he fills in his earlier sketch, sharing insights gleaned from his many contemplative walks, fishing trips, and marsh tromps. As an experienced amateur fisherman, Vonnegut offers the directions: "To get bass, one follows the birds, looks for cone-shaped formations of them, casts his lure to the place where the cone points. Bass will be feeding there." This old-fashioned rod fishing and respect for ecological relationships is juxtaposed with the "greedy, tasteless boom" of the Cape's south side. And it's at this point that the negativity associated with Barnstable's antiquity and stodginess at the essay's start fades away. Vonnegut suggests that it's precisely the village's ability to change "as fast as the rules of chess" that might save it from the general "vulgarization" of the Cape.

3.3 ✳ Standing on the dunes in Sandy Neck, Cape Cod, ca. 1963, Kurt Vonnegut surveys the landscape he wanted to see preserved as a public park. Courtesy of the Vonnegut family and Robert Weide. Copyright © Kurt Vonnegut LLC, used by permission of The Wylie Agency LLC.

After praising the year-round "carpenters, salesmen, masons, architects, teachers, writers" and other working residents who keep Barnstable from being a "hollow village," Vonnegut explores the undeveloped expanses of marsh and shoreline he'd like to see preserved. As he explains Barnstable's natural features, his understanding of the Great Marsh's biologically rich, sometimes hazardous 3,500 acres shines. He investigates the natural salt hay that "tempted settlers down from Plymouth in 1639" and describes a marsh "laced by deep cracks that can be explored by small boats . . . goes underwater at every moon tide, and is capable of supporting a man and his dog, and not much more." The "seeming vast green meadow" that maintained Barnstable's livestock and wild biotic communities for centuries, we infer, also supports a writer's and a dog's respective souls.

As fond as Vonnegut is of the "bluish-brown glurp" lining Barnstable Harbor and spread throughout the marsh, his descriptions of Sandy Neck's beach capture the stark beauty of the area. Sandy Neck's "long, slender barrier of spectacular dunes that bounds the harbor on the north," Vonnegut explains, is filled with "grotesque forests of dead trees out there, trees suffocated by sand, then unburied again." Sandy Neck's outer beach, meanwhile, "puts the beach of Acapulco to shame." As a writer seeking quiet spaces for contemplation, Vonnegut registers relief and delight that local village government was purchasing "all of Sandy Neck but the tip" to turn it into "a public park to be kept unimproved forever." The earlier critiques of the village's "anachronistic, mildly xenophobic" character melt away as we learn that "the charming queerness of Barnstable Village" has indeed saved the soul of the place—the quiet, quirky community groups and the historical character that remains even as "outsiders" like the Vonneguts replace old families. With the preservation of the land and its people assured, Vonnegut wraps up the essay by noting that the Sturgis has purchased new encyclopedias. Despite their differences, villagers have discovered an "underlying spiritual unity" in their appreciation of both vast "wild" stretches of nature and small, cultivated slices of paradise such as St. Mary's Church gardens.[161]

Because of its humor, lighthearted tone, and distancing narrative perspective it's easy to underestimate the depth of Vonnegut's commitment to preservation in "You've Never Been to Barnstable?" When it is read alongside his unpublished essay "The Cape Cod National Seashore," Vonnegut's deep commitment to the protection of the Cape's remaining undeveloped shorelines, marshes, salt ponds, dunes, and beaches becomes clearer.[162] With its lengthy quotations from Thoreau's *Cape Cod* and Henry Beston's *The Outermost House* and references to Rachel Carson's *The Edge of the Sea*, Vonnegut's essay on the Cape's outer shore offers some of his most explicit connections to environmental writers and calls for wilderness preservation.

True to Vonnegut's unconventional style, the fourteen-page manuscript veers away from traditional forms of the nature essay or standard political arguments for preservation. Written and revised ca. 1966–67, the piece was composed *after* President John F. Kennedy signed the bill to create the forty-mile Cape Cod National Seashore on August 7, 1961.[163] And with its extensive focus on the builders, chamber of commerce, and other Cape Codders opposed to the park's creation, the essay explores political debates and human foibles more than landscapes, ecosystems, and wildlife. More than anything else, though, the nonfiction piece captures a more mature version of the politically minded planetary citizenship Vonnegut learned from Hillis Howie, merging Vonnegut's love for the Cape's ephemeral shorelines with his literary activism.

While the piece's target audience and specific purpose will most likely remain a mystery, the essay was part of Vonnegut's greater turn toward nonfiction as the short story market further dried up in the mid- to late 1960s. What's striking is the amount of in-depth journalistic research Vonnegut did. Obviously invested in the park's creation, zoning debates, and land-use issues, Vonnegut quotes several times from the 446-page, two-volume Congressional hearings about the park.[164] He also interviewed park superintendent Robert Gibbs and Cape Cod Chamber of Commerce Executive Secretary Norman Cook for the essay. In other hands these elements might lead to bland, straightforward reporting, but Vonnegut uses his signature humor and storytelling skills to create characters from the Chatham, Cotuit, North Truro, Eastham, Wellfleet, and Marstons Mills residents who made statements, sent letters, and attended hearings related to the park's creation.

Even the briefest examination of the Congressional hearings reveals that Vonnegut had to pore over the lengthy discussions of zoning laws, town tax revenue projections, and local political dynamics to pull out the colorful statements he chose. Vonnegut's fruitful search gives him enough material to hook his readers. We hear from a Chatham resident who worried that the park would threaten free enterprise, individual rights, and initiative, sending Cape Cod and the country down a road of self-destruction. Adding to these anxieties, Vonnegut weaves in the concerns of a Cotuit resident who challenges the merits of adding more public recreational areas, stating, "Yet Russia is virtually all public lands, and are the inhabitants any happier?" Vonnegut plays up these Cold War fears by comparing the frigid, rolling Atlantic waves to Russia's Murmansk waters, but also sneaks in his own take on the key issue underlying the debates—that the "26,666-acre park would be cut from the shank of a juicy real estate boom."

Having introduced his human characters and outlined debates about the park, Vonnegut moves to a portrait of the outer shore and his arguments for its protection. Although Vonnegut does not mention Thoreau's *Cape Cod* until later in the essay, the second section contains much of the same appreciation Thoreau expressed in his descriptions of the outer shore. Like Thoreau, Vonnegut praises the wildness and immense power of the ocean: "What gives the National Seashore such an air of gorgeous violence is the fact the Atlantic is tearing it to pieces."[165] Further describing the constantly changing terrain, Vonnegut continues, "The tremendous sand cliffs backing much of the beach are profiles of hills that were well inland not long ago. The cliffs have no strength. There are little avalanches all day and night long. And then the sea comes in to carry the newly fallen land away."

KURT VONNEGUT, JR.
LITTAUER & WILKINSON, INC.
500 FIFTH AVENUE
NEW YORK, N.Y.

THE CAPE COD NATIONAL SEASHORE

BY KURT VONNEGUT, JR.

After some of the most amusing wrangling in the history of the
National Park Service, the Cape Cod National Seashore now exists.
Not only has a blow been struck for conservation, but for literature as well. The Congressional hearings relative to the tremendous land-taking, published by the U.S. Government Printing Office,
deserve to be placed on the same shelf with the works of James
Thurber, Mark Twain, and Finley Peter Dunne.

"The more we destroy individual enterprise and individual
initiative and destroy individual rights," Bertram Courier of Chatham testified, "the farther we are stepping along the road to self-

3.4 * The first page of his unpublished essay "The Cape Cod National Seashore" captures Vonnegut's humor and unconventional
approach to advocating for environmental conservation. Archival
image by Kurt Vonnegut, courtesy of the Lilly Library, Indiana
University, Bloomington. Copyright © Kurt Vonnegut LLC, used
by permission of The Wylie Agency LLC.

To further illustrate these malleable borders, Vonnegut describes the growing sand bars at the shore's end points in Provincetown and Chatham, made as fierce waves and currents "chew the middle" out of the outer shore. Looking first to the predicted erosion of the famous Coast Guard Beach and then to the impermanence of the entire shoreline, Vonnegut informs his readers that "the geological prognosis is gloomy." With ever broadening shifts in time and scale, he concludes, "It was the guess of the late Rachel Carson, that the whole Cape, Chamber of Commerce and all, would be gone within 4000 years—in the wink of an eye." This geological time frame further diminishes the political squabbles mentioned in the first section, as it calls for planetary perspectives and humility in the face of nature's "gorgeous violence." Ending the section, Vonnegut concludes, "Most national parks teach us that God's works are enduring. This newest park teaches us that His works can be ephemeral as well."

Turning away from meditations on the shore itself, the next section examines the underlying economic concerns linked to residents' oppositions to the bill, the benefits of creating the national seashore, and the initial impacts the park has had on tourism. Although the essay remains firmly grounded in continuing debates over the park and in its new realities, Vonnegut's larger purpose seems to be railing against the "vulgarization" of the Cape that has come from development. He makes his position clear at the start of the section, writing, "If the Congressional hearings demonstrated nothing else, they demonstrated that many influential Cape Codders do not know how lovely the Cape is, don't imagine that such loveliness is rare, and do not understand what somebody means when he speaks of beauty's being in danger."

Although a resident as well, Vonnegut distances himself from these "true" Cape Codders. In one telling example, he mentions that the "typical male native never goes to the beach except for clams, doesn't fish or sail or take pleasure walks. . . . If he gets any money, he takes off for his idea of Paradise, which is a Florida hotel." In another section, Vonnegut recounts the story of a former friend, a builder, who was forced "to move his business out of a residential area because of zoning." Vonnegut describes the man as "a real Cape Codder [who] hates beauty that gets in his way," and includes his complaints about people enforcing the zoning restrictions. The builder remarks, "All they do is look out their windows. . . . What's so important about looking out windows?" Through his sarcasm and comment about the rift in friendship, Vonnegut deepens the divide between himself and other Cape Codders, claiming affiliation with the "outsiders" who want to see the outer shore remain undeveloped for the American public and the biotic communities of the heaths, dunes, marshes, and ocean waters.

At this point, Vonnegut's environmental and aesthetic conscience forces him to break from his largely third-person perspective and initial journalistic—albeit pointed—distance. After writing favorably about the nature hikes, lectures, and other outdoor education programs of the park, Vonnegut discovers the common ground that has been created between local businessmen and park officials. With more visitors coming to Cape Cod to appreciate the outer shore's geology, biodiversity, and history, the economic development possibilities for the towns outside the park will grow. As Vonnegut puts it, "Since there is nothing to spend money on inside the park, business in the jazzy hell outside might just improve." Immediately following this statement, reflecting on the possibility of a fourfold increase in the number of tourist visits to the Cape each year, Vonnegut launches into personal reflection:

> I myself won't like it, that multiplying by four. I spend most of my time looking out windows. . . . I am not a native. I am a Hoosier. I work very little with my hands. I have lived here for 15 years. I don't want to see the place grow. I don't want it to become more popular.

Although he undercuts this direct plea with a bit of resignation via the French phrase "*tant pis*" in the next line, the remainder of the essay is distinctly personal and forthright in its preservationist politics.

After reiterating the point that "it will be mainly people from off Cape Cod" who will protect the national seashore "with political action and talk of beauty and peace," Vonnegut paradoxically turns to preservation efforts in Sandy Neck. Despite having just identified himself as a Hoosier outsider, Vonnegut reveals that it is the regular view from his Barnstable window that helped him discover "the marsh is a haven for waterfowl ... and terribly important in many of the life cycles of the sea." Lest he be mistaken for an insider, Vonnegut clarifies that it was the fight over the marsh that led him to terminate his friendship with "Sam" the builder and that it has been "outsiders"—not "true Cape Codders"—who have led the Sandy Neck conservation efforts: "He won't get the marsh. Outsiders who have taken up residence are bringing pressure to have that bought for all mankind, too—and for the birds and the life cycles of the sea."

Despite a return to a seemingly more distanced, journalistic perspective as he reflects on the park's future and name, Vonnegut concludes the essay with personal tributes to environmental writers Henry David Thoreau and Henry Beston. After mentioning efforts to rename Cape Cod National Seashore for President Kennedy after his assassination, Vonnegut suggests that Thoreau and Beston would be more deserving of the honor. Reminding his readers of Thoreau's love for the outer shore and the fact that "there's nothing much named for him anywhere," Vonnegut then includes the first half of the final paragraph in *Cape Cod*'s "Provincetown" chapter. Vonnegut underscores Thoreau's prophetic vision, recognizing that the outer shore has finally become "a place of resort for those New-Englanders who really wish to visit the sea-side."[166] Although the Cape Cod National Seashore has spared the outer shore the "ten-pin alley," "circular railway," and "ocean of mint-julep" Thoreau feared, Vonnegut invokes his beloved predecessor to mourn the "jazzy hell" and other forms of development that have sprung up along the Cape's center and southern roads. Vonnegut writes, "What Thoreau should have abominated, if he wanted to establish himself as a prophet, were automobiles, canned beer, bulldozers, super-highways, neon, hot-top money for the many, and the creation of one rich, teeming, stinking city that runs from Virginia to Maine."

Although he praises Thoreau's prophetic vision, Vonnegut's true homage to Thoreau would be the journeys he took across the Cape to discover the outer shore's dramatic landscapes firsthand. During one such trek in the early 1960s, Vonnegut took his nephew Kurt "Tiger" Adams and Tiger's friend Wink "on a fifty-mile hike along the railroad track to the outer Cape."[167] Drawing on at least one detail from the adventure in the essay, Vonnegut rejoices in the temporary suspension of train service, which made the tracks "turn to rust and punk in the leaf mold." By referencing the conclusion of *Cape Cod*, Vonnegut suggests that it was more than the escape from commercialization and development that made the outer shore so exquisite. Like Thoreau, Vonnegut realizes that the outer shore's beauty resides in its ability to be "made and unmade" each day and to be a place where he can stand "and put all America behind him."[168]

Perhaps it was this image of Thoreau looking from the beach that inspired Vonnegut to end his essay with a tribute to Henry Beston and *The Outermost House*, which chronicled Beston's year living in a small frame cottage he built on the dunes in Nauset/Eastham. Given Beston's influence on the initial proposals to create Cape Cod National Seashore, it's fitting that Vonnegut would turn to the author, veteran, and Thoreau disciple who wrote lyrically about his "year in outer nature" on the Cape. To emphasize this point and offer his own tribute to Beston, Vonnegut briefly describes the October 11, 1964, dedication ceremonies that made Beston's cottage a National Literary Monument. We learn not only of the Park Service Director's praise for Beston's role in "explaining why the beach should be precious to everyone," but also of the fact that "Mr. Beston could say more in a paragraph than we could say in a year." Taking that idea quite literally, Vonnegut ends the essay with his recollection of Beston "reading the last paragraph from *The Outermost House*, raising his unsteady voice above the sounds of the Atlantic" and then the final paragraph of Beston's book.

It's somewhat ironic that Vonnegut would end his own essay with someone else's words at precisely the time when he was working so doggedly to find the first-person narrative voice that opens *Slaughterhouse-Five*. Considering that Beston went to the outer shore in 1926 seeking peace, solitude, and healing from his experiences in the volunteer ambulance corps during World War I, Vonnegut's substitution of Beston's voice for his own makes sense. Perhaps it was Beston's restored spirit so many years after the war and his reflections on humankind's debts to nature that helped make the outer shore more sacred for Vonnegut. Or maybe Beston's final sentence about the "songs of the birds at daybreak, Orion and the Bear, and dawn seen over ocean from the beach" seemed particularly appealing to Vonnegut, who had already associated a bird's "Poo-tee-weet" with the aftermath of the firebombing of Dresden.[169] The nested images of both Thoreau and Beston looking out from the shore were no doubt powerful for Vonnegut. Perhaps in the end what was most precious to Vonnegut about the Cape Cod National Seashore was the shore itself and the perspective it gave him as a writer. As writer Rebecca Solnit reminds us, "The seashore is an edge, perhaps the only true edge in the world whose borders are otherwise mostly political fictions, and it defies the usual idea of borders by being unfixed, fluctuant, and infinitely permeable."[170]

While Lake Maxinkuckee provided safety, security, and extended family as he made his first mental maps of the world, Vonnegut's views from his Barnstable window and the Cape's shorelines gave him the perspectives to make and remake numerous fictional worlds during his two decades on Cape Cod. Ultimately, Barnstable and its layered memories of home, creativity, and multiple generations of extended family exerted enough of a pull on Vonnegut's soul for him to consider making it his final resting place. In a letter to his literary agent Don Farber, dated August 7, 1999, Vonnegut expressed a desire "to be cremated as quickly and cheaply as possible" after his death, and requested that his "ashes should be scattered by family in Barnstable Harbor, not far from the foot of Scudder's Lane."[171]

DIRT AND GUILDS IN
"SKYSCRAPER NATIONAL PARK"

While I don't know where Vonnegut's ashes wound up (and I'd like to imagine them scattered throughout his symphony of places), his memorial and selected final wishes were celebrated in New York City—Vonnegut's "home" for the last thirty-five years or so of his life. Many factors, such as his disintegrating, increasingly fractious marriage to Jane, his turn to professional theater productions, and his newfound celebrity as a writer and public spokesperson, prompted his move, first to apartments on East Fifty-Fourth and East Fifty-First Streets and then to the four-story brownstone at 228 East Forty-Eighth Street, which he shared with his second wife, renowned photographer Jill Krementz.[172] Manhattan provided the artificial extended family of writers he had first encountered at the University of Iowa and had longed for while living on Cape Cod. New York City was also appealing precisely because it could not be reduced to a singular or static place. Like the constantly shifting outer shore on Cape Cod, New York City was always in flux, made and unmade each day via new flows of people, performances, and ideas. In interviews and letters from the early 1970s, Vonnegut explained what excited him about the city was the diverse multitudes of people, the "useful electricity" he was able to draw "from millions of milling strangers around me."[173] As *Detroit News* reporter William Noble described in his June 1972 feature, for Vonnegut New York was "a gigantic, priceless laboratory filled with kooky, serious, snobbish or plain wonderful folks, transplants from Indianapolis or elsewhere living every moment to the fullest."[174]

Without ever invoking *The Death and Life of Great American Cities*, Vonnegut intuitively grasped Jane Jacobs's key insight that human cities were natural, "being one form of nature, as are the colonies of prairie dogs or the beds of oysters."[175] In New York, Vonnegut's anthropology training could merge with his architectural ancestry, allowing him to study masses of humanity in their built environments. Like urban historians and sociologists, Vonnegut also understood that New York is not a singular place but "collections of places fostering utterly and starkly different vantage points on the world."[176] While Vonnegut's various place attachments to and within Manhattan changed over his time there, his writings and final memorial wishes reveal that he had assembled a collection of places that grounded him as he wandered through the city's "priceless laboratory" of people and ideas.

Those final wishes also blended two key aspects of planetary citizenship passed down from Kurt Sr.—Vonnegut's border-defying literary career and connections to nature through gardening. As Mark Vonnegut noted in his May 7, 2007, memorial statement, his father left specific instructions for a brief, intimate memorial service at the Algonquin Hotel, a site steeped in literary tradition and a favorite place long before Kurt moved to Manhattan.[177] In addition to gathering his extended family and friends to celebrate his life, Vonnegut's wishes called for a final act of place making. He asked Mark to collect dirt from his garden and deposit it at "the New York Public Library, the Chrysler Building, Grand Central Station, Times Square, and three places in Central Park—the statue of Balto, the Avenue of Literature, and the Dairy Building." Although Vonnegut had already immortalized most of these sites in *Jailbird* and other New York City–inspired writings, he wanted to combine soil from the private, intimately tended "sacred" site of his garden with a range of public yet deeply personal places.

Somewhere in the multiverse, another version of myself has pondered Vonnegut's choices for his final collection of sacred places in Manhattan. In this universe, we can at least explore Vonnegut's November 1987 essay "Skyscraper National Park," which offers his own explicit reflections on New York City and explains why he made his home on "an island which has a reputation for being less like a Folk Society than anywhere else on Earth." Like "The Lake," "Skyscraper National Park" was originally published in *Architectural Digest* and then reprinted in Vonnegut's second autobiographical collage, *Fates Worse Than Death*. In contrast to his piece on Lake Maxinkuckee, Vonnegut substantially rewrote "Skyscraper National Park," claiming that he had taken the *"filets* cuts" from the earlier piece because it had been poorly written. A close comparison of the two versions suggests that Vonnegut probably revised it to blend more smoothly with other pieces in *Fates Worse Than Death*. The original version actually has more internal coherence and stronger structural arrangement, but the additions and revisions reinforce how vital New York's "guild" of writers and its ever-changing nature were for Vonnegut.

Both versions of the essay begin with a brief description of Robert Redfield's concept of "The Folk Society" and why the idea of small, tightly knit, like-minded groups was so appealing to Vonnegut and his fellow "rootless" World War II veterans. Vonnegut suggests this longing for kinship and connection was not unique to his generation, but rather to a broader yearning manifested in communes and other social experiments of the 1960s and 1980s. Perhaps inspired by his return to "The Lake" in *Fates Worse Than Death*, Vonnegut mentions in the revised version that he still finds himself "daydreaming of an isolated little gang of like-minded people in a temperate climate, in a clearing in a woodland near a lake." Given the deeply felt connections to Lake Maxinkuckee and the foundational mental maps of the world he created there, it's not surprising that Vonnegut returned to this sacred childhood place as he contemplated the idea of folk societies to heighten connections to Manhattan. As Vonnegut explains, it was precisely his "undying fantasy" to join a folk society, his "Holy Grail," that made him "garble" the original essay.

"Skyscraper National Park," however, is far from garbled, and, if anything, it is deeply grounded in anthropological musings about the nature of the companionship offered by folk societies and Vonnegut's own need for such camaraderie. The anthropological distance also allows Vonnegut to explore why he felt like an outsider on Cape Cod and "a member of an army of occupation" at his home in Sagaponack. Returning to Robert Redfield's Chicago lectures, Vonnegut explains that "the thoughtless harmony for which I yearned was hell for any-body with a lively imagination, curiosity, inventiveness or a sense of the ridiculous." As someone who felt politically, artistically, and socially at odds with many residents of his village communities, Vonnegut recognizes the tension between a desire for belonging and a need for physical rootedness in a specific, tight-knit community. Ultimately, the former outweighs the latter, and Vonnegut realizes that it's precisely Manhattan's barriers to rootedness, permanence, and ownership that create a sense of belonging.

Fittingly, this insight comes to Vonnegut through the observations of another outsider, Turkish novelist Yashar Kemal. As he notes, "It took a foreigner with whom I had no language in common to describe for me the peculiar ambience of Manhattan." The revelation, prompted by a letter from Kemal weeks after their literary tour of Manhattan, is this: "I suddenly understood it! The city belonged to me as much as to anybody *as long as I was there!*" Kemal's insight becomes both the literal and figurative center of the essay. From it, Vonnegut offers his own descriptions of Manhattan's mutability, impermanence, and appeal for planetary citizens. He builds on Kemal's observation, stating, "Spiritually speaking, everybody and nobody owns this place." And, after noting the foolishness of attaching personal and corporate names to buildings, Vonnegut remarks, "Manhattan is a stupendous, ongoing event to which the entire planet is contributing." The city's global connections, which make it a hub for transnational flows of people, ideas, art, culture, products, and capital, further add to its refusal to be owned. Invoking the essay's title, Vonnegut suggests that any attempt, even by its richest and most powerful inhabitants, to own portions of the city is "a joke": "They might as well lay claim to the moon or the Grand Canyon or Old Faithful at Yellowstone."

Having rejected the possibility of belonging to a true, provincial folk society, Vonnegut proceeds to describe the nourishing substitute that Manhattan can offer because of its fluid, ever-changing, dynamic nature. He characterizes the island as a city full of guilds. Setting up the final section and arriving at what might be considered the soul of the city, Vonnegut writes:

Those of us lucky enough to have specific skills which are valued by others can sometimes feel themselves part of the clan whose magnetic center is not a place, is not real or imagined kinship, and is not blind faith in this or that. The magnetic center for them is pride in craftsmanship. Such a social organization was called a guild in olden times.

Despite its failure to provide important elements of a folk society, the writers guild to which Vonnegut belongs was so central in providing an artificial extended family that he remained in the city even though it was becoming "an increasingly dark and dangerous" place.

Kurt and Jill's shared Turtle Bay and Sagaponack homes provided ideal sites for Vonnegut's literary planetary citizenship as he connected with local, national, and global writers' guilds. Unlike his earlier homes, these domestic spaces put Vonnegut in close contact with his publishers, editors, critics, hundreds of fellow authors, and the extensive network of literary organizations that he actively participated in, from PEN America to the American Academy of Arts and Letters to the National Endowment for the Humanities and New York Council on the Arts. While these guild networks raised Vonnegut's literary, artistic, and activist profile, they also enabled him to nurture the careers of other planetary citizens.[178] New York also offered Vonnegut artistic rejuvenation through contact with other guilds—from painters and musicians to chefs and fashion designers to rare coin dealers and theater production experts.

Even as "Skyscraper National Park" celebrates the creative, nourishing aspects of Manhattan and revels in the city's mutable character, Vonnegut criticizes New York's disparities in wealth and insatiable appetite for energy and resources. Manhattan can become a "stupendous ongoing" global event, Vonnegut explains, only because "the paper wealth from everywhere is concentrated in a tiny space." In his revised and more overtly political version, Vonnegut explores the negative impacts of this "geological phenomenon." "An enormous fraction of the planet's wealth was concentrated on a little island of solid granite," he notes, causing "crystals to sprout in such profusion that the island when viewed from the air now resembles a quartz porcupine."

With the turn to economic justice issues (and *Slapstick*'s vision of a ruined Manhattan evoked by the title), we realize that the "dark and dangerous" elements of the city aren't ones typically associated with urban settings such as crime, disease, pollution, or gang violence. Instead, what's dangerous for Vonnegut is that "more crystals from overheated capital sprout and grow." In the *Fates Worse Than Death* revision, these symbols of wealth, entitlement, and globalization are not just a symptom of growing social and economic inequalities in New York, but part of the broader "Neo-Conservative" threat to "dark-skinned poor people not just in this country but in many, many other parts of the world."

The revisions to "Skyscraper National Park" in *Fates Worse Than Death* further suggest that Vonnegut's connections to Manhattan were as mutable as his conceptions of his "home" city. As he must have realized in his final memorialization wishes, his critiques of the city's paper wealth, observations of global environmental problems and injustices, and celebrations of Manhattan's irreducibility of place were made possibly by his privileged collection of places from which to observe and write about the world. Although "Skyscraper National Park" had no fixed center for him, Vonnegut needed many public and private places to be a member of its writers' guild—from his study in his Turtle Bay brownstone to the park bench he favored facing the Audrey Hepburn gardens in Dag Hammarskjöld Plaza to the Chrysler Building to the theater district off Times Square.

In the end, New York, with its guilds, rich tapestry of built environments and laboratory of people and ideas, allowed Vonnegut to compose the last movements in his Hoosier symphony of place and gain a global platform for his planetary citizenship. But whether surrounded by fresh water, salt water, or quartz porcupine quills, perhaps the place that mattered most was inside his window, where he could curl over his Smith Corona typewriter, making marks on 8½" x 11" sheets of paper.

CHAPTER 4

APOCALYPTIC LANDSCAPES
Cat's Cradle, Slapstick, and Galápagos

**The real moral and political challenge of
ecology may lie in accepting that the world
is *not* about to end, that human beings are
likely to survive even if Western-style
civilization does not. Only if we imagine
that the planet *has* a future, after all, are
we likely to take responsibility for it.**
—Greg Garrard, *Ecocriticism*

**I think you should devote your lives to cre-
ating something which this planet has never
had. The planet will die, if it doesn't get it
now. You must create an American people.**
—Kurt Vonnegut, Address at SUNY Albany,
   May 20, 1972

In April 1950, Kurt Vonnegut's planetary citizenship took shape in
his worries about radical scientific irresponsibility and the destruction of the entire stream of life. As he worked on notes and outlines
for his first drafts of "Ice-9," the story that eventually evolved into
Cat's Cradle, Vonnegut imagined a possible apocalypse literally born
in our streams and other waterways.[179] In one initial brainstorming

paragraph, Vonnegut explored the source for ice-nine, the crystal that would unleash this environmental apocalypse by freezing all water it comes in contact with. He emphasized its importance by underlining "THE CRYSTAL" and placing ten exclamations points beneath the words. Then he imagined an unnamed scientist, a "research man, interested only in finding truth," who discovers rare, unusual crystals in several old caves that "nucleate water into a stable substance with a melting point near scalding."[180] While Vonnegut had not yet figured out how the crystal would be unleashed, his outline of the resulting apocalypse was clear. He typed, "Power plants fail. Sea life is killed. Animal life, plant life killed. War breaks out around the few waterholes not nucleated." As he fleshed out the story, he developed the scientist's character and central ethical issues by having his protagonist create a synthetic version of ice-nine and give it to a military-backed Caribbean dictator.

Although Vonnegut initially envisioned Cold War military conflicts over deadly technologies being played out on a tiny island in the Caribbean Sea a dozen years before the Cuban Missile Crisis, when *Cat's Cradle* was published on March 18, 1963, just five months after the event, it became a hit with Vonnegut's underground college readers but went largely unnoticed by the public at large.[181] After the publication of *Slaughterhouse-Five* and Vonnegut's meteoric rise to fame, *Cat's Cradle* gained more critical and commercial success—especially as readers drew parallels between a world frozen by ice-nine and nuclear winter, and retrospectively appreciated the timing of the novel's publication. Most critical and pedagogical approaches to the novel still view ice-nine as a stand-in for nuclear weapons and read *Cat's Cradle* chiefly as a warning about destructive atomic technologies. If we return to the novel's origins and another landmark environmental book published near the height of Cold War nuclear tensions, however, *Cat's Cradle*'s far more profound apocalyptic implications emerge.

Published just seventeen days before the start of the Cuban Missile Crisis, *Silent Spring* launched an equally historic and perhaps more revolutionary series of events—the start of the modern American environmental movement. The serialized version of Rachel Carson's landmark book had already sparked heated debates about the dangers of chemical pesticides and incurred the wrath of the chemical industry during the summer of 1962. But the book's publication at the height of the Cold War helped propel *Silent Spring* to the top of the *New York Times* best-seller list, where it remained for thirty-one weeks. While Carson's ability to write accessibly about chemical pollution, food chains, biomagnification, and the chemistry of the human body popularized key ecological concepts, comparisons between the impacts of nuclear fallout and the slow poisoning of the environment via widespread pesticide applications gave *Silent Spring* its urgency. With the threat of an actual nuclear exchange fresh in readers' minds, Carson's apocalyptic opening fable about lifeless streams, a silent spring, "browned and withered vegetation as though swept by fire" and "a white granular powder" falling like snow no doubt seemed like "a stark reality we all shall know."[182]

As with *Cat's Cradle*, *Silent Spring*'s origins more complexly preceded its watershed publication moment.[183] Carson first proposed a story on the environmental impacts of DDT for *Reader's Digest* in 1945, and, throughout the 1950s, grew increasingly alarmed about the hundreds of new, untested toxic chemicals being unleashed into the environment. She worried not just about human health implications, but also about poisoning the "whole stream of life." Given her concerns about the irresponsibility of science and the future health of the entire biota, it's not surprising that Carson dedicated *Silent Spring* "To Albert Schweitzer who said 'Man has lost the capacity to foresee and to forestall. He will end by destroying the earth.'"

At first glance, *Cat's Cradle*, with its science fiction elements, dark humor, postmodern style, and elaborate invented religion, might bear little resemblance to Carson's meticulously researched, sober, best-selling scientific text. Both works were part of the large body of apocalyptic narratives that emerged after World War II and became staple features of 1960s and 1970s environmentalist rhetoric. Beginning in 1948 with William Vogt's *Road to Survival* and Fairfield Osborn's *Our Plundered Planet*, environmentalists began to warn of global environmental catastrophes caused by erosion, overpopulation, and "Man's so-called conquest of nature."[184] As environmental critic Greg Garrard has noted, apocalypse became "the single most powerful master metaphor" that the modern US environmental movement had "at its disposal."[185] Like Carson and other planetary citizens, Vonnegut was profoundly shaped by life in the atomic age, but in Dresden he had also witnessed firsthand the damage science and technology divorced from ethics could do to people and nature. It's no surprise, then, that his writings are filled with apocalyptic scenarios ranging from global catastrophes in *Cat's Cradle* and *Slapstick* to localized destruction of cities in *Slaughterhouse-Five* and *Deadeye Dick* to the personal apocalyptic struggles of characters like Dwayne Hoover in *Breakfast of Champions*.[186]

Like his nonfiction works, his apocalyptic novels contain a rich tapestry of places and capture Vonnegut's responses to key environmental issues. And like other period environmental writings, Vonnegut's major apocalyptic trio—*Cat's Cradle*, *Slapstick*, and *Galápagos*—prompts broad global, national, and species-level thinking about environmental issues via fantastic scenarios. Ultimately, Vonnegut's apocalyptic scenarios are not born of true despair or hopelessness. His stories are in keeping with much of environmental apocalypticism, which "is not about anticipating the end of the world, but about attempting to avert it by persuasive means."[187] Despite their rather bleak imagined futures, Vonnegut's key apocalyptic novels look to human-centered solutions to keep life going on our fragile blue-green orb.

CREATING AN APOCALYPSE:
FROM "ICE-9" TO *CAT'S CRADLE*

Cat's Cradle's gestation time was only half that of *Slaughterhouse-Five*'s. In *Palm Sunday* Vonnegut gave both novels a grade of A+.

Given *Cat's Cradle*'s enormous popularity among Vonnegut fans and scholars, it's safe to say that Vonnegut didn't inflate the novel's grade. In its final, published form, *Cat's Cradle* is exquisitely balanced and elaborately structured despite its accessibility and simple plot, which tells the story of ice-nine's creation and eventual apocalyptic release on the tiny Caribbean nation San Lorenzo. Not only does each short chapter work as its own perfectly contained episode, complete with a well-crafted joke, biting critique, or philosophical insight, but the novel also flawlessly balances its main central threads, which explore the negative consequences of blind faith in *both* science and religion. A postmodern novel par excellence, *Cat's Cradle* loops together an almost endless string of narratives that intertwine to question irresponsible applications of science and technology while exploring a much broader "history of human stupidity." Taking the basic form of a book within a book, Vonnegut weaves together religious, environmental, and literary apocalyptic traditions, shifting between texts and traditions with the whimsy and seeming effortlessness of a game of cat's cradle.[188] Despite the novel's exquisitely crafted structure, it's *Cat's Cradle*'s narrative openness that gives it its profound impact.

The manuscript drafts highlight the extraordinary work that went into Vonnegut's first A+ work and the simple yet profound environmental implications of its apocalyptic vision.[189] Beneath the novel's intricate layers of satire, ethical questions, and meditations on the arts, *Cat's Cradle*, like *Silent Spring*, is ultimately a warning about humanity's potential to destroy the literal stream of life on this planet: water. Although deeply tied to Cold War contexts, Vonnegut's apocalyptic scenario for freezing all the liquid water on Earth, the central chemical compound needed for all cellular life in the known universe, is perhaps even more relevant today, when climate change, ocean acidification, widespread plastic pollution, chemical contamination, water scarcity, and the water wars of the twenty-first century lend *Cat's Cradle*'s warnings about damaging the lifeblood of the planet resonance far beyond its original Cold War nuclear fears.

Cat's Cradle's compositional wanderings also show that the novel's own Cold War origins were far more complicated than Vonnegut ever revealed. As Ginger Strand demonstrates in *The Brothers Vonnegut*, the genesis of ice-nine was more complex than Kurt disclosed in speeches and interviews. Vonnegut repeatedly acknowledged that he "stole" the idea for ice-nine from a story outline Irving Langmuir offered to H. G. Wells and that he based the character Dr. Felix Hoenikker on a caricature of the famous GE Nobel Prize–winning scientist. However, Strand reveals that Kurt's brother Bernard and his GE Project Cirrus colleagues profoundly shaped the science and ethical questions behind ice-nine. Bernard was the one who introduced Kurt to water's unusual behavior under extreme conditions and to the existence of different ice crystals—"a whole series of ice phase variants, ice-1 through ice-6." In explaining ice-2, "an ice crystal that looks like a tetragon, rather than its usual hexagonal shape," Bernard used the image of "cannonballs stacked on a courthouse lawn" to illustrate how "ice crystals could stack up in different configurations."[190] This analogy later appeared in Asa Breed's explanation of ice-nine in *Cat's Cradle*, but, perhaps more crucially, it was the military's interest in Bernard's chemical cloud-seeding research that steered Kurt toward the enormous global implications of weaponizing water.

While Kurt's regular interactions with Bernard influenced the science behind ice-nine crystals, it's somewhat ironic that many of the signature GE-inspired elements in *Cat's Cradle* don't appear at all in the earliest drafts of "Ice-9." Despite the assignments, social gatherings, and News Bureau work that put Vonnegut in direct contact with Irving Langmuir and stories about GE's most famous living scientist, Vonnegut's spring 1950 drafts of "Ice-9" don't include the details about Felix Hoenikker absentmindedly tipping his wife at breakfast, his obsession with turtles, or playful research tangents. In fact, Felix Hoenikker doesn't appear as a character at all.

Instead, the story, which grew out of notes scrawled on Vonnegut's News Bureau memo forms and note pads, focused on the adventures of Dr. Arnold Macon, a tall, thirty-something bachelor who takes a job as president of the Caribbean island's university.[191] With no classes to teach and only ceremonial obligations, Dr. Macon has plenty of time to drink, play chess, and help the island's dictator, General Monzano, manage his "rotten university." Between April 11 and June 11, 1950, Vonnegut crafted two fairly similar versions of the same tale—the story of an American scientist who hands over ice-nine to the dangerous military dictator and then counters his irresponsible action by saving the world from his creation. The fifty-two-page version of "Ice-9" incorporates a romantic subplot between the scientist, David, and his sociologist girlfriend, Marion, while the more elaborate sixty-eight-page draft juxtaposes Dr. Macon with a sociology professor named Dr. Franklin Dale.

While the relationships spin the tales in different directions, the Marion/Franklin sociologist character serves as an important foil for Vonnegut's scientific protagonist. Using virtually identical dialogue in both opening sections of the drafts, Vonnegut leaves little doubt what the scientist's fatal flaw is. As Dr. Macon explains to his former colleague Dr. Dale, "All I'm interested in is finding truth. You can't reproach me for that, can you? I don't give a damn about practical applications. I'm a pure research man. Applications are for engineers to figure out." Vonnegut also utilizes the Marion/ Franklin character to underscore the dire consequences of a scientist divorced from ethics, the arts and humanities, and humanity at large. David barely listens to Marion because "she bored him stiff with what he considered sententious nothings—society . . . culture . . . mass psychology." Unsurprisingly Marion and Franklin deliver the same critique to their partner: "Between us, maybe we'd make a whole human being—your brains and my conscience."

Perhaps the most interesting thing about Vonnegut's early drafts of "Ice-9" is that the apocalypse doesn't happen. In the romantic subplot version, an American destroyer bombards Monzano's sea-facing castle while David heroically uses gasoline and a long fuse to burn Monzano and ice-nine frozen water in a cave adjoining the castle. The novella-length story, meanwhile, ends dramatically with Dr. Macon and Monzano, locked in combat, going over the edge of a parapet toward the sea. The crystal, attached to a chain by Monzano, never falls into the water because it catches on a spike six feet above the tide line. Had Vonnegut's agent Ken Littauer successfully placed the novella for serialization, the more profound and sobering apocalyptic scenario in *Cat's Cradle* probably never would have materialized, and "Ice-9" would have been lost in the sea of mediocre early, fear-inspiring stories of the Cold War.

While these early drafts of "Ice-9" laid the foundation for key elements of *Cat's Cradle*—a scientist blind to ethics and humanity at large, a dangerous scientific invention with destructive capabilities beyond atomic weapons, a power-hungry, colorful dictator, and an island backdrop on which the drama could be played out—another series of drafts primarily set in Cape Cod added new crucial components. Written between the spring of 1953 and May 1954, these unfinished, longer drafts of "Ice-9" are stylistically much closer to *Player Piano* and show how far Vonnegut could "swoop" in order to discover new characters, ideas, and other seeds for a book.[192]

With the shift from the Caribbean setting to Cape Cod and New Paradise, Pennsylvania, the home of General Forge and Foundry, the drafts also switch to first-person narration to explore the character George Hoenikker, who has discovered the deadly crystal. Ranging in length from 70 to 110 to 143 pages, the partial drafts move slowly compared to the action-packed 1950 tale, and it's clear Vonnegut was still working out the plot. In a nutshell, the story, with events put in chronological order, looks something like this: A crystallographer discovers ice-nine and flees to Cape Cod because he's worried about the crystal's deadly potential. While on Cape Cod he befriends his boardinghouse hosts, becomes intrigued with the restless and alluring Elaine Brophy, survives a car accident, takes a job in Harold Brophy's lumberyard, reflects on an old flame named Amy, and is investigated by local police, FBI agents, and

ICE - 9

Scientist denies having any social responsibility as a scientist.

He discovers ice-9.

He reports it in a meeting of a scientific society.

He expects the Nobel Prize for it.

Says now any man can walk on the water.

~~Haxisxattiaeked~~
Culmination of his career.

He is a professor in a university in a Carribean Dictatorship.

He has no political acumen at all, no cognizance of moral rottenness

of the dictator.   He tolerates him, enjoys his hospitality.
        He gives the dictator a sample of ice nine.
The dictator is quite insane.

The dictator is about to be overthrown.

Dictator threatens to destroy the whole world if he is not restored

to power by the major powers.

Professor pushes dictator off parapit. Goes off himself.

The box tumbles, but catches, wedged in the rocks, twenty feet

above the grasp of the sea.

4.1 ✳ In this 1950 outline for "Ice-9," Vonnegut sketched out key elements of the story that evolved into *Cat's Cradle*, but he had not yet imagined an environmental apocalypse or the fictional religion Bokononism. Archival image by Kurt Vonnegut, courtesy of the Lilly Library, Indiana University, Bloomington. Copyright © Kurt Vonnegut LLC, used by permission of The Wylie Agency LLC.

a newspaper reporter named Mr. Chase. Only in the longer 143-page draft does Vonnegut really begin to explore General Forge and Foundry and its critical characters.

With one exception, these drafts begin with an initially unnamed narrator who is in hell for killing himself. Before we learn his name, George Hoenikker, we are introduced to his afterlife void, with "no clouds, no sun, no stars, no moon; no hills, no trees, no shrubs, no grass." We also discover the contents of his pockets: empty cigarette packages and matchbooks, a pen, a railroad ticket to New Paradise, Pennsylvania, and a tiny glass bottle with a light blue ice crystal that won't melt. Although the imprisoned narrator telling the story of his apparent guilt anticipates *Mother Night* and *Hocus Pocus* more than it does *Cat's Cradle*, the drafts introduce posthumous examinations of the "father" of ice-nine. Rather than dwelling on the image of George Hoenikker "on all fours in eternity, with [his] behind in the air," Vonnegut quickly moves his narrator's story to the very earthly setting of a "winter evening, a mile from the sea, in a village on Cape Cod, Massachusetts." With atypically slow pacing, George takes the reader to Christmas Eve in a large, clock-filled, two-hundred-year-old house on Cape Cod owned by Bud and Nancy Price, where we initially learn more about George's hosts than about the doomed scientist.[193]

In terms of anticipating *Cat's Cradle*, the introduction of ice-nine on a snowy Christmas Eve on a house in Cape Cod near the ocean is significant. In "Ice-9" George Hoenikker bids his hosts good night and then retrieves a small glass bottle with "a milky blue needle of ice." He tells the reader, "On the label I had written: 'Danger! Ice-9. Do not bring in contact with water. Destroy in fire.'" As he smokes and waits to fall asleep, he sketches "a tiny skull and crossbones on the label." Vonnegut later developed this kernel from "Ice-9" into chapters 111 and 112 in *Cat's Cradle*, which explain how Angela, Newt, and Frank Hoenikker procure their shards of ice-nine. Vonnegut places the details of the Hoenikkers' Christmas division of the crystal fairly late in the novel, shortly after the first two human deaths from ice-nine, Papa Monzano's and Dr. von Koenigswald's. The Cape Cod setting makes the Hoenikker children's division of the blue-white crystal especially irresponsible. In a cottage right on the beach, having just walked through a strange snow like "orange blossoms," the Hoenikker children don't destroy or place the ice-nine in its carefully marked original glass bottle with its pirate "logo"—the universal symbol of death on the high seas. Instead, they place it in Mason jars and later transfer it to three innocuous Thermos jugs, which they transport over oceans and carry to a home that straddles a waterfall.

In addition to developing the profound environmental implications of the Hoenikker children's Christmas exchange of ice-nine, the longest of the 1953–54 "Ice-9" drafts enabled Vonnegut to return to his scientist's intellectual and ethical blind spots. George's moral shortcomings emerge during a conversation with his wife, Janet, when the scientist mocks Albert Schweitzer, the famed physician, humanitarian, organist, and scholar. When George pretends that he's "dazzled" by Schweitzer, Janet reminds him that he "didn't think much of his 'reverence for life,' and that was the key to the whole thing, the key to all the other things he is." While Janet tries to explain that Schweitzer's universal reverence for life ethic isn't just about *not killing things*, but about *revering everything*, George can only focus on technical questions and continues to privilege human life far above other organisms. Janet, however, grasps Schweitzer's efforts to develop a new ethical philosophy that would fundamentally redirect the destructive course of human civilization.[194] Because the draft ends shortly after George and Janet's exchange, it's impossible to know where Vonnegut was headed with "Ice-9." However, the story's opening absence of all trees, shrubs, grass, and other living entities takes on new weight as we discover George's inability to see humanity's place within the vast stream of life.

In *Cat's Cradle*, Schweitzer appears indirectly via narrator John's interactions with Julian Castle, the "American sugar millionaire" who follows Schweitzer's model of medical humanitarianism in Lambaréné by starting the House of Hope and Mercy, a free hospital in the jungle of San Lorenzo. Vonnegut replaces the serious, direct allusions to Schweitzer's philosophies with a far less saintly Schweitzer figure in Castle. The cigar-smoking Castle, who talks "out of the corners of his mouth like a movie gangster" and says "satanic things" seemingly bears little resemblance to the Alsatian physician who played the organ, studied theology, and wrote his medical dissertation on psychiatric analyses of Jesus.[195] Despite this comic caricature, Julian Castle embodies the humanist dimensions of Schweitzer's teachings. Although knowing that Bokononism is an invented religion founded on bittersweet lies, Castle runs his hospital on "aspirin and *boko-maru*" because they provide comfort and help his patients "feel better about each other and the world."[196]

As versions of "Ice-9" transformed into the earliest draft titled *Cat's Cradle* in May 1954, Vonnegut shifted from firsthand explorations of George Hoenikker to the wider web of ethical decisions that result when ice-nine falls into the hands of the scientist's three sons.[197] When Vonnegut returned to the story in late 1950s and ca. 1960 drafts, he breathed new life into the manuscript via early explorations of Bokononism, the invented humanist-inspired religion practiced throughout San Lorenzo, more careful delineation of the island setting, the creation of the novel's central characters (a.k.a. its karass), and the first glimpses of an actual global ice-nine apocalypse. When we look to the 70-page novel start, the 32-page story/outline "CAT'S CRADLE: A True Science Adventure," or the full 289-page draft he sent to his friend and editor Sam Stewart at Dell Publishing, we see Vonnegut swoop to follow some peculiar plot suggestions and struggle to release ice-nine into the world.[198] Although still different stylistically with its five long chapters and realistic allusions to President Eisenhower and Premier Khrushchev, the 70-page draft has key early elements of the finished novel—an epigraph about *foma* from *The Books of Bokonon*, the core content of John's and Newt's correspondence, a proposed book about the day the United States dropped the atomic bomb on Hiroshima, and the connective threads of a karass (team of people) and cat's cradle string. Instead of John/Jonah as our narrator, a journalist named Kurt Vonnegut Jr. tells the tale, and more heavy-handed Cold War elements abound.

In that draft, the book project is called off in the name of patriotism after the narrator is interviewed by FBI agents, and much of the first three chapters are devoted to explorations of US military and economic aid to San Lorenzo, Ambassador H. Lowe Crosby's views, embassy secretary Philip Castle's reports, and Papa Monzano's larger-than-life personality and corporate holdings (including shares in Pepsi). While Papa Monzano introduces Bokononism as an overhaul of Christianity gone too far, Frank Hoenikker views the religion as "anti-science," as a manifestation of "what people used to be." Frank's fears about Bokononism's anti-progress leanings prove true as a military air show turns into a revolution led by Bokononists, who have also been sabotaging American industrial development of San Lorenzo. From his jail cell near Frank and Newt, the narrator learns more about Bokononism, its invented terms, and then finally about the existence of ice-nine. Although the draft ends just pages after ice-nine is first mentioned, a frozen world doesn't seem likely. We learn that Newt has left his tiny crystal of ice-nine in a bank safe-deposit box and Frank has enclosed his share in a tiny glass jar, cushioned in silicone putty inside an eight-hundred-pound box of steel, lead, and concrete.

Based on his correspondence with Sam Stewart, who arranged for *Cat's Cradle* to be published with Dell, Vonnegut continued to rewrite the novel in July and August 1960. In a letter to Stewart, dated February 11, 1961, Vonnegut confided that he still didn't know how things were going to turn out. He did realize that "two major elements will be Bokonon's new religion and the possession of a superweapon by the three children of the father of the atom bomb." Vonnegut sensed the "inter-play" of the two threads would "yield something good," and he hoped the satire would "show an impressive system of human morality independent of institutions or even knowledge." The connections to the Cuban Revolution, Vonnegut thought, "might interest the sales promotion staff" but they didn't interest him. As he explained to Stewart, he "started tinkering with this idea before Castro got out of law school."

As Vonnegut continued to place these central narrative threads in "dynamic tension," he developed Bokonon's backstory, invented terms like "vouprass" that now only exist in the apocryphal *Books of Bokonon*, shortened the chapters, severed the Mintons from the Crosbys, and added minor characters and Ilium scenes. In a 289-page draft he sent to Stewart, Vonnegut spun a tale remarkably close to the final version of the novel, but once again took a detour after the air show. In this version, Hazel, Newt, and a heroic Philip Castle perish when the fortress wall slides into the sea. However, Frank and his men pull the golden boat containing Papa's ice-nine-solid corpse with a rope, preventing it from sliding into the sea. With this heroic tug, not only is the world saved, but Vonnegut the character and writer also leans toward the triumph of Bokononism. After overseeing the funeral pyre of Papa's and von Koenigswald's frozen corpses beneath the hook, the new president of San Lorenzo, Mr. Vonnegut, sobs in relief before announcing the arrival of the millennium and declaring that Bokonon will marry Mona and rule the country. The draft ends with a strong humanist moral, Julian Castle's warnings about scientific miracles, and Bokonon's predictions, including the future death of Mr. Vonnegut caused by a dog.

Vonnegut must have known that if he wanted to deliver those warnings, he'd need to unleash an environmental apocalypse. Although it's hard to pinpoint when exactly he decided to let ice-nine contaminate the world's water, Vonnegut was ready to play with the idea in a 32-page story outline, "CAT'S CRADLE: A True Science Adventure" that he may have used to pique publishing interest in the novel after he broke his contract with Scribner's.[199] A bridge draft of sorts, the story incorporates the action-packed elements of the earliest "Ice-9" drafts, the Cold War espionage and intrigue elements of the later 1950s drafts, and new ethical questions that stem from the Bokononist elements. It also includes the literary allusions to *Moby Dick* and the playfulness that would become hallmarks of *Cat's Cradle*. While the draft has some noteworthy elements—Lyman Knowles as a CIA agent, several foreign operatives, Frank's "secretive helper" (and lover) Mrs. Mergendeiler,[200] a wild Bokonon hunt and car chase to Mt. McCabe, and multiple kinds of ice crystal (ice-seven, ice-eight, and ice-nine)—its turn to apocalypse is the most significant. Instead of characters merely warning about a frozen world, Vonnegut finally presents it.

In its final form *Cat's Cradle* offers a minimally described ice-nine-induced landscape in chapter 119, noting tornadoes, uniform blue-white solidity, an angry sun, and air that was "hot and dry and deathly still." In "CAT'S CRADLE: A True Science Adventure," Vonnegut imagined the chain reaction of ponds, brooks, bays, rivers, and oceans freezing finally ushering in a "worldwide ice age" that "would abate only if the temperature reached 123.4° Fahrenheit, the melting point for Ice Nine." Whereas the eternal, locked "winter" of *Cat's Cradle* is relatively abstract and experienced locally on San Lorenzo, here Vonnegut has John and Mona listen to world reports on a shortwave radio, discovering that "England and Continental Europe, as observed by a doomed Norwegian pilot, are covered by glaciation."

This global picture quickly shrinks and darkens. Vonnegut writes, "In the next few days Mona and John hear the stations gradually die out one by one as a massive ice sheet covers the earth. Their only hope is the fact that they are probably the only human beings at the equator in such a complete shelter." When they emerge, warmly dressed "like mice," blinded by the glare of "an infinity of ice and snow," they encounter Bokonon, the "great seer and prophet." Bokonon instantly recognizes their status as new Adam and Eve figures. Instead of telling them "Be fruitful! Go forth and multiply!," Bokonon says, "I can hardly tell you to do that today." Vonnegut completes his anti-Eden scenario by calling attention to the rest of the creation already destroyed: "Locked in eternal snow, are the green plants, the brown, red and black trees, the bright birds, the chocolate earth, the houses, buildings, the people—the life of what had once been a tropical island in a warm sea."

As he bashed away at the final drafts of *Cat's Cradle* from the spring to fall of 1962,[201] Vonnegut discovered the perfect tension between the threads of his narrative and further refined the novel's "secret ingredient"—Bokononism. No doubt drawing on his "Magic and Religion" anthropology seminar at Chicago, Vonnegut developed a robustly detailed version of the fictional religion, complete with its own creation story, cosmology, rituals, parables, funeral rites, holy books, prophet figure and holy man, songs (calypsos), and complex terminology.

While earlier versions of Bokononism were linked to anti-science or millennial movements, in its final form the invented religion is designed to provide beauty, community, and comfort in an unpredictable and often harsh world. In *Cat's Cradle*, Lionel Boyd Johnson, the religion's founder and later holy man Bokonon, designs the religion cynically and playfully because he is unable to offer the people of San Lorenzo any real economic, social, or other material improvements. More than just a type of opium for the masses, Bokononism is a tool for Vonnegut to deepen the critiques of blind faith in science and Cold War conflicts that were always at the heart of his stories about ice-nine. In one of his most poignant examples, he introduces the Bokononist term "granfalloon," a false karass or group based on meaningless connections, using the examples of the communist party, DAR, General Electric and "any nation, any time, anywhere." Viewed through this Bokononist concept, the idea of creating nuclear weapons or ice-nine in the name of national defense seems even more foolish and dangerous than in earlier versions.

Vonnegut also uses the Bokononist last rites ritual, which invokes the human creation story, to revisit key moments from the novel's scientific narrative thread. In chapters 98 and 99, Dr. von

Koenigswald, "a very bad scientist [who] will do anything to make a human being feel better," administers Bokononist last rites to the dying Papa Monzano. As they sit sole-to-sole in *boko-maru* reciting the lines, we hear the story of how God "made mud" and then in his lonesomeness invited some of the mud to "sit up" and share the rest of creation—"the hills, the sea, the sky, the stars" with him. In the Bokononist last rites, the dying person reflects, "And I was some of the mud that got to sit up and look around. . . . Lucky me, lucky mud. . . . The only way I can feel the least bit important is to think of all the mud that didn't even get to sit up and look around." After thanking God "for the honor" and recalling good memories and sights, the person recognizes that "Now mud dies again and goes to sleep."

While playfully referencing the first chapters of Genesis and Christian funerary lines, the exchange also reminds us that like all life on Earth we are simply water and other matter. While it's unclear whether the former biochemistry major thought about water's dissolving and transmitting properties at the cellular level, we do know that he thought about the approximately 60 percent of the adult human body that is composed of water. He had Papa Monzano kill himself by ingesting ice-nine shortly after these final rites. The ritual also sparks sobering ethical questions as we remember what inspired Felix Hoenikker to create ice-nine in the first place: he was trying to solve the problem of a Marine general who wanted "to do something about mud."

In the final, published version, Bokononism not only invites *Cat's Cradle* readers to question everything within the novel via its first epigraph, "Nothing in this book is true," but encourages broader skepticism through a religion that forces individuals to create their own meanings. It's blessedly ironic that Vonnegut almost offered a clear moral for *Cat's Cradle* in one of his final drafts. In a very late alternate version of chapter 119, titled "How to Pose," Vonnegut did not make Bokonon a self-preserving cynic who refused to take his own advice of committing suicide by ingesting ice-nine.

Instead, Bokonon's death is his final pose, an important symbol and "form of prayer."[202] As the narrator explains, "Every good Bokononist is expected to strike a self-conscious pose three times a day, to make himself a living statue" for a hundred seconds. *The Books of Bokonon* explains that people should "<u>Pose like a man or a woman or a child doing something that would help make Earth as nice as Paradise.</u>"

Choosing to die alongside all the other San Lorenzans, Bokonon's last pose is as a writer, offering the world a final message. This closing line to *The Books of Bokonon* turns out to be "a blending of Voltaire, Jesus, and Bokonon": "<u>We must love one another, cultivate our gardens, and be very careful what we grow.</u>"[203] The specific allusion to the ending of *Candide*, one of Vonnegut's favorite satirical texts, and to Voltaire more generally, *would* have been an apt moral for *Cat's Cradle*. Vonnegut's colonial history of San Lorenzo, Lionel Boyd Johnson's hazardous journeys, descriptions of torture devices in the castle's oubliette, and the long string of wars and military events that form a "history of human stupidity" are fitting updates to Voltaire's powerful critiques of torture, religious cruelty, and state oppression.

As writer Adam Gopnik reminds us, Voltaire was much more than just a satirist of "the horrors of religious cruelty and the emptiness of religious apologia"; he was a Freethinker, scientist, and human rights advocate who found in exile and gardening "the better place we build by love" and localized, immediate actions.[204] This alternate ending to *The Books of Bokonon*, then, would have beautifully pulled together the humanist aspects of Bokononism, Schweitzer's model of Jesus-inspired loving kindness, and richly layered warnings about the types of crystals we choose to grow in our laboratories. Fortunately, Vonnegut, who played with other alternative endings, decided to leave a certain degree of narrative openness in the final chapters of *Cat's Cradle*. While the text implies that John will climb Mount McCabe for his own final pose holding the "magnificent symbol" of his book, which also incorporates the final lines of *The Books of Bokonon*, Vonnegut leaves the fate of the other survivors undetermined. Readers are the ones who must decide what to do with the "magnificent symbol" in their hands.

The paradox of *Cat's Cradle* is that the more literary, religious, scientific, and philosophical layers and weight Vonnegut added to the story, the "lighter" it became as a text. With its lean sentences, fast pacing, and brief chapters, you can easily read *Cat's Cradle* in a single sitting. However, it's *Cat's Cradle*'s pervasive dark humor, situational irony, puns, whimsy, and pure outlandishness that give the apocalyptic novel its power. As critic Greg Garrard reminds us, environmental problems might seem more solvable if they are "framed by comic apocalyptic narratives that emphasize provisionality of knowledge, free will, and ongoing struggle."[205]

PAST *IS* PROLOGUE: RASPBERRIES, CHIPMUNKS, AND DAFFODILS ON "THE ISLAND OF DEATH"

If comic elements alone were the key to effective environmental apocalyptic narratives, then *Slapstick* should have been Vonnegut's most successful apocalypse novel. Vonnegut's eighth novel draws on the comic form of slapstick in theme and structure as it portrays a disaster-ridden America and tells the story of Wilbur and Eliza Swain, physically grotesque "neanderthaloid" twins who possess a "single genius" together but limited intellects separately. But *Slapstick* had comparatively weak sales and was anything but a critical triumph.[206] It was severely attacked by critics, led most famously by Roger Sale, who accused Vonnegut of "giving up storytelling." In his September 24, 1976, *New York Times* review, Sale claimed that reading the novel was like devouring "a bowl of air." Although many of Vonnegut's fellow writers came to the novel's defense, Vonnegut was "wobbled" by the many harsh, sometimes scathing, reviews and ultimately assigned *Slapstick* a D grade in *Palm Sunday*.[207]

Not all critics were as harsh as Sale or Vonnegut himself, and some appreciated the novel's treatment of artificial extended families or were charmed by Kurt's touching reminiscences of his sister Alice and descriptions of his travels with Bernard in the prologue. Although few scholars rate the novel highly, Jerome Klinkowitz suggests that *Slapstick* is an important bridge novel that looks toward Vonnegut's more developed treatments of "reverse evolution" and "social reordering" in *Galápagos* and *Jailbird*.[208] Indeed, history itself becomes a character in *Slapstick*, as it does in *Jailbird*, and with its vision of humanity rendered less dangerous to itself, Vonnegut's 1976 novel anticipates *Galápagos* in striking ways.

If we look not to *Slapstick*'s lightness but rather to its weight in American history, the novel emerges as a powerful apocalyptic novel. With the distance of more than four decades, we can see the novel is born of the eco-apocalyptic rhetoric and concerns of the 1970s. *Slapstick* is also decidedly a Bicentennial novel, which uses the retrospective framing of Dr. Wilbur Daffodil-11 Swain's autobiography and embedded presidential narrative to engage in a broader cultural conversation about America's past. Unlike other Bicentennial narratives, these retrospective meditations neither explore how the US arrived at its present dark age of democracy and environmental ruin nor long nostalgically for a simpler pastoral past. Instead, *Slapstick* is a plea to revitalize democracy by creating an American people to save both country and planet. Like other planetary citizens of the mid-1970s, Vonnegut saw the interconnections between democratic and ecological renewal as vital—especially in the wake of the Vietnam War, Watergate, and Earth Day.

This hope for democratic and environmental renewal isn't apparent in *Slapstick*'s opening or its catastrophe-sculpted landscape. Like *Cat's Cradle*, *Slapstick*, after its Vonnegutian prologue, begins with a survivor of the apocalypse writing his story on the "Island of Death" (formerly known as Manhattan). Whereas *Cat's Cradle* opens a mere six months or so after the ice-nine apocalypse and focuses primarily on the complex tendrils of human stupidity and irresponsibility that led to that point, *Slapstick*'s "present" begins more than fifty years after the start of globally catastrophic events. Thanks to this longer time span and a more complex web of apocalypse-inducing factors, Wilbur offers some vivid descriptions of a ruined Manhattan and other American cities in his autobiography.

Our "blue-eyed, lantern-jawed" centenarian narrator locates himself at the start of his tale in the back seat of a ruined taxicab, watching "Smoke from a cooking fire on the terrazzo floor of the lobby of the Empire State Building" float out "over the ailanthus jungle which Thirty-fourth Street has become."[209] The deeply cracked pavement of the island's ailanthus jungle has been caused by "frost-heaves and roots," but the far greater structural damage to Manhattan's buildings, bridges, and tunnels took place when gravity "turned mean" and destroyed countless structures all over the globe. Thanks to "The Green Death," a mysterious "plague peculiar to this island," Manhattan is largely unpopulated. Apart from his sixteen-year-old granddaughter and her lover with whom he lives in the Empire State Building, Wilbur's nearest neighbor is one and a half kilometers away. The entire global population has also been greatly diminished via an epidemic of "Albanian Flu," and survivors live under permanent yellow skies, inhabiting a world where the "planet's natural resources [have] come to an end."

While the perennially yellow skies and polluted water affect all organisms on the planet, *Slapstick* offers a future in which human—primarily American—civilization has been destroyed and nature has begun to reclaim vast stretches of the previously conquered continent. In a reversal of setting aside tracts of wilderness, natural scenic wonders, and threatened ecosystems, Manhattan has been dubbed "Skyscraper National Park," and the new tourists and settlers are wildlife, like the turtles that have "in great profusion . . . returned to Turtle Bay." As Wilbur moves through the ruins of Manhattan, he hears mostly animal sounds, like a rooster crowing, the "jittering, squeaking" of bats that "stream out from the subway," and the cry of the whip-poor-will, the nocturnal goatsucker, near an "Army tank with a tree growing out of its turret." The two main human communities that exist within Skyscraper National Park are relatively primitive by twentieth-century American standards. Vera Chipmunk-5 Zappa, whom Wilbur calls "the Thomas Jefferson of modern times," labors alongside her "slaves" to raise chickens, goats, pigs, and cattle and to grow "corn and wheat and vegetables and fruits and grapes along the shores of the East River."[210] Re-creating appropriately Jeffersonian-era technologies, they have constructed "a windmill for grinding grain," a smokehouse, and a brandy still. The Raspberries, the group that inhabits the ruins near the New York Stock Exchange, meanwhile, are "food gatherers," who fish, harvest berries, mine for canned foods, grow their own limited crops, and trap birds, rats, cats, bats, and dogs for meat.

The son and grandson of architects, Vonnegut was enormously attuned to the structures and symbolism of buildings, so it's no surprise that he used iconic Manhattan landmarks and neighborhoods in his social and environmental critique. Although the apocalyptic future in *Slapstick* stems from both human causes and shifts in physical forces, we learn early on that unchecked greed, power, and Gilded Age–style capitalism were responsible for the exhaustion of resources. Noting his Mellon, Vanderbilt, and Rockefeller ancestors, Wilbur explains that his parents "descended from Americans who had all but wrecked the planet with a form of Idiot's Delight—obsessively turning money into power, and then power back into money again, and then money back into power again." But Vonnegut overhauls the class structure and values of the world's most powerful financial city. The Swains' former home in Turtle Bay becomes housing for "slaves" and the Gilded Age structures of Wall Street become a homestead for Raspberries, who value only practical and comforting possessions. While sparing the building itself from the devastating whims of gravity, Vonnegut also takes aim at New York City's most iconic building by playing on its Depression-era nickname, "the Empty State Building" and wreaking havoc on its interior. Instead of taking visitors to the top of what was once the world's tallest building, the elevators are broken, and their shafts are only useful as toilets.

While these images of Skyscraper National Park, a Washington, DC, populated by eight hundred people, and a balkanized America blend into Vonnegut's larger fictional cosmos, they also fit within the broader apocalyptic environmental discourse of the 1970s. Vonnegut's friend and fellow author Kirkpatrick Sale dubbed the seventies "the Doomsday Decade" because a seemingly endless stream of "Cassandras turned out books predicting Armageddon," with titles such as *The Last Days of Mankind, The Death of Tomorrow, The Doomsday Syndrome, The End of Affluence,* and *The Coming Dark Age.*" Following the images and rhetoric of eco-catastrophe that led up to Earth Day, the energy crisis of 1973–74 psychologically "gave credence to the idea that perhaps Western society's collapse was not far off."[211]

From interviews he gave around the time of *Slapstick*'s publication, it's clear Vonnegut thought dismal planetary and species-level futures were on the horizon. In a January 21, 1976, *Australian Women's Weekly* piece, for instance, Vonnegut linked his scheme for creating artificial extended families to population control. Citing the failures of the nuclear family model, Vonnegut asked the interviewer, "Why should everyone produce his own little universe—and overrun the planet in the process?" Later in the interview, Vonnegut stated that he was "also very concerned about the future of life generally." "We are such vulnerable animals," he continued, "We have to eat incessantly, breathe incessantly, and it is so easy to kill us."[212]

In a fall 1976 interview with Charles Reilly, Vonnegut reflected more specifically on the ruined New York City portions of *Slapstick*.[213] After noting the parallel breakdowns in the legal system and the law of gravity, Vonnegut highlighted "the larger issue" at stake: "I think what will finally kill *us* will be God. God will kill us by the millions quite soon, I think—by starvation, with flu, through war, in any number of ways." "He is killing us by the millions right now," Vonnegut maintained, "on the growing margins of the Sahara desert and in places like Bangla Desh [*sic*]." While Vonnegut's mention of God is an anomaly for the self-described freethinking atheist, his concerns about external forces putting our species in check were not.

In *Slapstick*, these outside forces appear in microscopic form via Albanian flu and the Green Death. Described throughout much of the novel as mysterious plagues, these diseases seem to come right out of the pages of Paul Ehrlich's bestselling *The Population Bomb*, which surely would have been familiar to Vonnegut, who had been addressing human population issues since the early 1950s. Ehrlich predicted hundreds of millions of deaths via "war, pestilence, and famine" and devoted special attention to the return of "mankind's old enemies, like bubonic plague and cholera." He also pointed to the likelihood of "a visitation from a 'super flu,' perhaps much more virulent than the famous killer of 1918–1920." Worse yet, Ehrlich suggested that biological warfare agents combined with other factors could result in "1.2 billion deaths—one in every three people."[214] Although Vonnegut's comments about population indicate that he took warnings about exponential human population growth seriously, in *Slapstick* he infuses his plagues with comic absurdity. In the novel's epilogue, an unnamed omniscient narrator informs us that the Albanian super flu germs were "Martians, whose invasion had apparently been repelled by anti-bodies in the systems of the survivors." And thanks to Eliza's otherworldly insights, we learn that "The Green Death . . . was caused by microscopic Chinese, who were peace-loving and meant no one any harm. They were nonetheless invariably fatal to normal-sized human beings when inhaled and ingested."

Channeling Stan Laurel and Oliver Hardy's slapstick humor, which brought him comfort during the Depression and other difficult moments of his life, Vonnegut turns to "grotesque situational poetry" to mitigate these eco-catastrophe fears. While the Martian super flu/invasion threat spoofs Cold War fears of biological agents, the Chinese "Green Death" is a more elaborate joke. Earlier in the novel we learn that the Chinese were "experimenting with making human beings smaller, so they would not need to eat so much and wear such big clothes." An already playful response to Ehrlich's and others' fears about human population and resource scarcity, the miniature "invasion" from China also evokes long-standing American fears of "the Yellow Peril." To make sure readers get the punch line, Vonnegut names the official Chinese emissary Fu Manchu, the grotesquely caricatured villain who starred in many of the films and popular cultural texts that fueled xenophobic fears of invading hordes of Asians.

In a slightly less absurd vein, *Slapstick* also addresses impacts and apocalyptic fears born of the five-month OPEC oil embargo stemming from the Yom Kippur War. The 1973–74 energy crisis not only sent major shock waves through the US economy as the price of oil increased by 400 percent, but was also felt broadly by Americans who had to wait in long lines for rationed gasoline, observe reduced speed limits, forgo their Christmas lights, and adhere to non-wartime conservation efforts.[215] As historian Thomas Wellrock reminds us, the oil and natural gas shortages and related conservation measures were not calmly or cheerfully received by many Americans:

> Panic ensued in the U.S. Motorists held up gas stations so often that attendants carried guns. Children wearing mittens and wool hats shivered in stone-cold classrooms. Tanker trucks were hijacked, and pleasure boats and luxury automobiles, symbols of American affluence went unsold. Those who hoped the crisis might unite the country as the Great Depression had were given pause by the Texas bumper sticker that said of Northerners: "Let the Bastards Freeze in the Dark."[216]

While inspired by 1973–74 events, the fossil-fuel shortages and energy crisis depicted in *Slapstick* unfold over a longer stretch of time. Prior to the gravitational shockwaves, dwindling oil and gas supplies lead to a decline in plastics and other synthetic products, the return of horse-drawn transportation, the appearance of wooden ships in the New York, Boston, and San Francisco harbors, and major declines in industrial and communications technologies. By the time Wilbur becomes President of the United States two decades later, the "fuel shortage [is] so severe" that he has trouble finding "enough electricity to power the computers which would issue the new middle names" for his artificial extended family scheme. The inauguration receives no coverage because the media has been "shut down—for want of fuel," and ultimately the few inhabitants of the White House are forced to "cannibalize" their home, "absent-mindedly, burning furniture and bannisters and paneling and picture frames and so on in the fireplaces to keep warm." Apart from the gallons of "absolutely priceless gasoline" used to power the presidential helicopter that takes Wilbur on his final official state journeys, we learn that the "planet's fossil fuels are completely exhausted."

As the United States encountered a second energy crisis in 1979, Vonnegut moved from visions of fossil-fuel collapse to harsh critiques of America's oil addiction. In an interview with Kevin Bezner, he identified Ford and Rockefeller as "national heroes" who knowingly "sold this massive addiction." "It must have been obvious from the first that these fossil fuel fields were limited," Vonnegut remarked. He further lamented, "With the collusion of this government, we were made a nation of gasoline junkies. And now it's over. We have been made fools of."[217] We can see in *Slapstick* that Vonnegut had already begun criticizing Standard Oil co-founder John D. Rockefeller. Wilbur wears a top hat, tails, and a vest "festooned with a gold watch-chain which had belonged to John D. Rockefeller" when he presides over the dissolution of the United States and delivers some of the strongest environmental critique in the novel. And it's no coincidence that Wilbur changes his original middle name, Rockefeller, to Daffodil-11.

This name change is part of Wilbur and Eliza's efforts to suggest a new direction for America via artificial extended families. The obvious symbolism of replacing Swain family names such as Mellon, Vanderbilt, Rockefeller, DuPont, and Dodge with terms for natural entities and elements highlights one strategy for reversing a course of "planet wrecking." Vonnegut, who initially toyed with other types of new middle names, such as Greek gods and colors, has Wilbur announce and explain his artificial family political platform at the very place where Vonnegut delivered his 1970 Earth Day speech.[218] Designed to provide people with thousands of new siblings and cousins, so they'll be "lonesome no more," the new middle name scheme also connects human beings to the natural world. As Wilbur explains, an individual's new middle name would include a number and "the name of a flower or a fruit or nut or vegetable or legume, or a bird or a reptile or a fish, or a mollusk, or a gem or a mineral or a chemical element."

More than just a strategy to connect humans to their ecological networks and to replace destructive names and systems, the artificial extended family proposal in *Slapstick* is an attempt to restore democracy and heal the planet simultaneously. As Vonnegut suggested in his May 1972 speech at SUNY Albany and in pieces about the 1972 election, restoring American democracy was essential because so much planetary damage had been done through US wars, consumption, technology, trade, and foreign policy. To reverse the "suspicious and prideful and secretive and warlike" course of the last three presidencies, Vonnegut urged his SUNY Albany listeners to devote their "lives to creating something which this planet has never had." "The planet will die," he continued, "if it doesn't get it now. You must create an American people. There never has been one. You must create one now. We must create one now. This is a matter of life or death."[219]

Vonnegut elaborated on the political implications of uniting the American people via extended families in his 1973 *Playboy* interview. If the American people were "lonesome no more," engaged with each other instead of isolated from neighbors, they could become a society again instead of an audience. In *Slapstick*, though, Vonnegut used the retrospective occasion of the Bicentennial to imagine a symbolic fairy-tale journey back to the Republic's origins and to the birth of an American people via artificial extended families. Although the eco-catastrophes plunge the nation and the world into another dark age, *Slapstick* offers both a literal and metaphorical light at the end of the tunnel.

Vonnegut's numerous references to the Bicentennial in reviews, letters, editorials, and speeches reveal that he saw the event not as an opportunity to ponder "blank hokum like the Liberty Bell," but as a way that "we may yet become a nation."[220] In *Slapstick*, we get the story of the nation's dissolution told by the one-hundred-year-old surviving half of a pair of twins. Fittingly, like the Bicentennial, Wilbur's narrative looks to and ends with his birthday. It also includes a colorful account of his time as the last President of the United States. While Wilbur's larger autobiography focuses on his and Eliza's Edenic childhood and painful separation by Dr. Cordiner, the embedded narrative of his presidency offers a slapstick-style "reverse" history.

Appropriately, Vonnegut sets up this loose, often campy look backwards by staging Wilbur's first official action as president at the National Archives as an event where he "posed for photographs beneath the inscription of the façade ... which said this: 'THE PAST IS PROLOGUE.'" To make good on his campaign promise, Wilbur removes Richard Nixon's papers so that they can be used for the official middle name mailings. Vonnegut, who criticized Nixon in his speeches and made the thirty-seventh US president a "minor character" in *Wampeters, Foma & Granfalloons*, wastes no time taking jabs. Explaining his decision to use the Nixon papers, Wilbur tells the small crowd, "He promised to bring us together, but tore us apart instead. . . . Now, hey presto, he will bring us together again after all." Extending the Watergate scandal to a longer history of corruption in American politics, Wilbur then suggests changing the motto on the National Archives' façade: "'So many crimes committed by lonesome people in Government are concealed in this place,' I said, 'that the inscription might well read, "Better a Family of Criminals than No Family at All."'"

This revised motto, which shows that past *is* prologue, serves as a bridge to keep looking backward to other moments and administrations in US history. To compile and publish the family directories, Wilbur mines the National Archives again, this time selecting the papers of Warren Gamaliel Harding and Ulysses Simpson Grant. This glance back to two scandal-ridden administrations complements earlier critiques of the greedy "planet wreckers" by specifically alluding to presidencies later known for the Teapot Dome scandal and numerous corrupt Treasury Department practices during the Gilded Age.

Shifting from Vonnegut's post-Watergate present to the Jazz Age to Reconstruction, the allusions to Grant's presidency, which was also marked by profiteering at Western trading posts, set up the next humorous jump in time. One day, after Wilbur's wife, "the former Sophie Rothschild," leaves him, a frontiersman on horseback arrives at the White House, which has been cannibalized during the cataclysmic social, environmental, and political upheaval. Not knowing whether it was "Halloween or the Fourth of July," Wilbur sees the frontiersman "dressed in buckskins and moccasins and a coon-skin hat," carrying a rifle. He remarks to himself, "You've really gone crazy this time. That's ol' Daniel Boone down there."

Closer to the Daniel Boone of the 1964–70 television series than the real historical figure, the frontiersman Byron Hatfield initiates Wilbur's journey to the Midwest frontiers of the now balkanized America. The frontiersman sends Wilbur forth to Indianapolis, where he receives an invitation, "Napoleonic in tone," to meet with the King of Michigan. In one of his last presidential acts, Wilbur signs over the territory from the 1803 Louisiana Purchase to the king, whose military-tactical and empire-building obsessions echo those of Napoleon Bonaparte. Wilbur's nation-unraveling tale ends with his own one-hundredth birthday celebration, where he receives a thousand candles "made in a colonial candle mold" from Vera Chipmunk-5 Zappa, the "Thomas Jefferson of modern times."

Wilbur's autobiography and this embedded "reverse history" narrative are more than just an irreverent Bicentennial fable calling attention to moments of corruption, greed, and power in US history. By taking the national narrative back to its colonial past and birth via allusions to the "father" of the Declaration of Independence, Vonnegut also sets the stage for remaking the nation via the creation of an American people. After all, as Wilbur remarks to the King of Michigan, "Washington, D.C., runs out of ideas from time to time."

True to Eliza and Wilbur's original idea, extended families become both the soul and the pragmatic, democratic core of the former nation. While far from perfect, extended artificial families provide comfort, basic care, and companionship during the environmental and social disruption of the Albanian flu, gravity disruptions, and resource shortages. They also offer more equitable, more democratic, and less violent paths forward. Although wars have been rendered less deadly because machines have broken down, the key reason for lower casualties and fewer conflicts is that "there's no such thing as a battle between strangers any more." It doesn't matter who fights whom, "everyone will have relatives on the other side." Wilbur sums up this more promising direction for America in his speech to fellow Daffodils in Indianapolis: "Because we're just families, and not a nation any more ... it's much easier to give and receive mercy in war." Given Vonnegut's long-standing critiques of deadly military technologies and warfare, the more humane, less violent future offered via extended families is indeed progress.

The weekly Daffodil-family meeting preceding Wilbur's remarks also offers a glimpse of an American people engaged in democracy. Presided over by "an eleven-year-old black girl named Dorothy

Daffodil-7 Garland," the meeting runs smoothly according to Robert's Rules of Order and effectively addresses issues ranging from selecting Daffodils to serve in the King of Michigan's army to caring for refugees and neglected children. Even the "children and the drunks and the lunatics" participate meaningfully, because Dorothy "kept things moving so briskly and purposefully that she might have been some sort of goddess up there, equipped with an armload of thunderbolts."

This vision of healthy democratic exchange remedies the principal problem Wilbur and Eliza identified with the US Constitution during their childhood moments of collective genius. As Wilbur explains, they recognized that keeping citizens and democracy healthy "depended on the strength of the people themselves—and yet [the Constitution] prescribed no practical machinery which would tend to make the people, as opposed to their elected representatives, strong." This flaw, they argued, stemmed from the fact that "the framers of the Constitution were blind to the beauty of persons who were without wealth or powerful friends or public office, but who were nonetheless genuinely strong." Because *Slapstick*'s primary narrative lens is a retrospective one, Vonnegut provides only a few glimpses into the workings of the extended families that have become the new spiritual and democratic cores of the nation. He leaves the reader to imagine what might have happened if the public spheres of Jeffersonian democracy truly had included *all* the American people—not just white, land-owning men.[221]

As *Slapstick* resets American history, offering new seeds for a robust democracy and a true American people, it also gives clues about the types of political leaders Vonnegut would like to guide the nation forward. It's no accident that Eliza and Wilbur get their idea for changing people's middle names from the "most intelligent of all [their] known ancestors," Professor Elihu Roosevelt Swain, who deliberately changed his middle name from Witherspoon to Roosevelt. Vonnegut's long-standing appreciation of FDR's views on federal government and conservation efforts comes through in

Wilbur's characterization of this key Swain ancestor. Not only is Professor Swain "a citizen of the world" but he is also a citizen of the earth, who chooses to settle among the apple trees in his bucolic Vermont homestead instead of in the wealthy cities of his day.

Slapstick also pays tribute to another aristocratic-born social justice advocate via the character of Dr. Stewart Rawlings Mott, the twins' pediatrician, who urges Wilbur to make the Hippocratic oath the foundation of his medical practice. Dr. Mott's graduation gift to Wilbur is the simple, handwritten note that reads, "'If you can do no good, at least do no harm.' Hippocrates." When Wilbur sets up the relationship between Dr. Mott and his Napoleonic grandson, the King of Michigan, he mentions that the relationship is "a curious footnote in history, and probably a meaningless one." The allusion to the eccentric political activist and philanthropist Stewart Rawlings Mott is far from meaningless. Born in Flint, Michigan, to General Motors' largest individual shareholder, Charles Mott, Stewart Mott was a major supporter of Senator Eugene McCarthy's 1968 campaign and the single biggest contributor to McGovern's 1972 campaign. In addition to starting the "Fund for Constitutional Government to expose and correct corruption in the federal government," Mott fought for civil liberties, arms control, free speech, access to birth control, and other progressive issues, and maintained a small farm with more than 460 plant species atop his Manhattan penthouse.[222] Mott was also included on Richard Nixon's famed "enemies list."

More than a peculiar footnote, Wilbur's reference invokes the memory of Dr. Stewart Rawlings Mott during the most historically minded, self-reflexive portion of his autobiography. The King of Michigan's scribes take down "all this history that was being made" because, as the younger Mott notes, "Those who fail to learn from history are condemned to repeat it." Wilbur's words for the historical record carefully unite *Slapstick*'s twin environmental and political threads, and Vonnegut indicates the apocalyptic future he'd like to see averted. Although veiled with humor, Wilbur's warning is sincere:

If our descendants don't study our times closely, they will
find that they have again exhausted the planet's fossil fuels,
that they have again died by the millions of influenza
and the Green Death, that the sky has again been turned
yellow by the propellants for underarm deodorants.

Wilbur finishes by stating, "History is merely a list of surprises. . . . It can only prepare us to be surprised yet again." These
surprises, Vonnegut suggests, don't have to veer in a fatal direction.

Despite *Slapstick*'s apocalyptic future setting, Vonnegut offers
readers a glimmer of hope that post-Bicentennial America could
surprise itself.[223] By creating a true American people—one that
recognizes our nonhuman relatives along with our human ones—
we can begin to restore both democracy and the planet. Although
Wilbur dies with his narrative unfinished, the epilogue's fairy-tale
story of Melody's "incredible journey eastward" to Skyscraper
National Park suggests that the common decency, kindness, and
sense of interconnectedness needed to create this future is possible.
Melody not only receives guidance, sustenance, and transportation
from her fellow human beings but also encounters other "relatives
everywhere—if not Orioles, then at least birds or living things of
some kind." Ironically, it just might be in the story of the Island of
Death that we can begin to restore the stream of life.

AN ARK, SIX EVES,
AND MARINE-IGUANA SPIT:
GALÁPAGOS'S NEW EDEN

White sand beaches with blue lagoons. Seals and sea lions "lolling
everywhere." A generous and bountiful nature. The "final door
opening on perfect happiness."[224] The landscapes of the Galápagos
Islands and the world at large are not very apocalyptic in the year
1,001,986 A.D.—unless you're a *Homo sapiens*. If you are a modern
human, the future *Galápagos* depicts might seem pretty catastrophic.

Thanks to a microscopic "new creature" that destroys women's ova, virtually all human beings are wiped out over the course of the late twentieth and twenty-first centuries, leaving only a small band of people to evolve into simple but contented seal-like "fisherfolk" in the Galápagos Islands. As we've seen in chapter 2, Vonnegut uses Leon Trout's ghostly narrative to portray a human being as both a planetary agent, dangerously affecting its fragile planet, and as one tiny "earthling part of the clockwork of the universe," subject to the laws of nature and natural selection like everything else on Earth.

Although *Galápagos* clearly puts humanity in check, bringing our species "into harmony with itself and the rest of Nature," the 1985 novel, like its apocalyptic predecessors *Cat's Cradle* and *Slapstick*, also examines then-current anthropogenic threats to the planet's lifeblood. The novel's time line of 1986 events offers a "shadow" apocalyptic thread of threats from advanced weapons technologies, worldwide financial crashes, globalization-related famines and starvation, large-scale pollution, habitat destruction, and other factors. Unlike *Cat's Cradle* and *Slapstick*, *Galápagos* complements its cataclysmic elements with another distinct and powerful environmental trope—the pastoral. Because we've already explored the more apocalyptic aspects of the author's meditations on deep time and a posthuman future in *Galápagos*, we'll focus on its pastoral elements here.

Like *Cat's Cradle* and *Slapstick*, *Galápagos* incorporates allusions to the Eden myth to highlight the gap between our present "fallen," environmentally ravaged world and a more harmonious vision of humans and nature. In *Galápagos*, Vonnegut further complicates the backward-looking narrative by also incorporating the Biblical story of Noah, which, as literary critic Leonard Mustazza notes, "is actually an end-of-the-world/re-creation myth." These two linked tales of creation, regeneration, judgment, and returns to innocence, Mustazza suggests, reinforce the novel's Darwinian explorations of "nature's million-year task of re-creating and morally reforming humanity."[225] More than mere juxtapositions of religious and scientific narrative threads, the stories of human destruction and regeneration in *Galápagos* work together to deliver Vonnegut's most urgent, complex, and hopeful cautionary tale about humanity and the planet. Vonnegut employs "a backward mythic movement," shifting from Noah's story back to "prelapsarian Eden"[226] to provide the ethics and insights that we'll need to become "better planetary citizens" during our own "Era of Hopeful Monsters."

Vonnegut clarified the connections between the Eden myth and planetary citizenship in late-1980s drafts of *Fates Worse Than Death*. In a near final version of his second autobiographical collage, Vonnegut offered a very different opening to chapter XII, which is primarily a reprinting of his 1985 MIT speech. Instead of beginning with the speech itself and then inserting a bit of personal context for the address, the draft picks up the ending sentiment of the previous chapter: "WE PROBABLY COULD HAVE SAVED OURSELVES, BUT WERE TOO DAMN LAZY TO TRY VERY HARD . . . AND TOO DAMN CHEAP."[227] In his explanation of why the "human race will not be saved," Vonnegut writes "I blame God for this mess." He continues, "The Christian writer John Updike says that I am certainly a strange Atheist, since I talk more about God than any seminarian. So be it. And the whole story of life on Earth as God's booby trap for well-meaning people can be found in the Book of Genesis."

In keeping with his freethinking roots, Vonnegut identifies the story of "Adam and Eve and the snake and the apple" as a foundational Western myth that locates the seeds of environmental destruction in human curiosity and overreaching. Even the first person to tell the Eden story, Vonnegut observes, recognized "that we were far too smart for our own good, and could be counted on to wreck a lovely blue-green planet." Channeling his climate doom, Vonnegut continues, "This we have done. The last frontier, except for the finely divided gravel pit of outer space, is the Amazon Rain Forest. We are burning that down on purpose, so that the polar ice caps should be melted in maybe a quarter of a century. How to go."

This cataclysmic vision resembles Leon Trout's initial worries about the "earthling part of the clockwork of the universe," so it's a seamless transition when Vonnegut explains that he's "written a whole book about too much intelligence: *Galápagos.*" Vonnegut goes on to explain that we don't have the million-year time frame of *Galápagos* to bring humanity into planetary harmony: "So the best I can do, when we are on such a short leash survival-wise, is to recommend to simply everyone Free-thinker restraint." "If it might somehow hurt the community, meaning everything on the planet nowadays . . . even a little bit," Vonnegut pleads, people simply "should not do it."

This sort of restraint is at the heart of Vonnegut's MIT speech, delivered the same year he published *Galápagos.* Drawing on the Schweitzer-like ethics that informed drafts of "Ice-9" and *Cat's Cradle* and seminal portions of the Hippocratic oath highlighted in *Slapstick,* the graduation oath he suggests for all MIT students is Vonnegut's own humanist planetary ethic. Instead of focusing solely on humankind, Vonnegut's revised oath reads: "The regimen I adopt shall be for the benefit of all life on this planet, according to my own ability and judgment, and not for its hurt or for any wrong. I will create no deadly substance or device, though it be asked of me, nor will I counsel such."

Although Vonnegut described his MIT speech as a "flop" met with polite, tepid applause, his efforts to enact this humanist planetary ethic in *Galápagos* via imagined human evolution and revisionist mythmaking are far more successful. Vonnegut's evolutionary path disarms humanity both figuratively and literally, taking away its ability to kill entire biomes, species, and planetary systems. However, the choices Vonnegut makes as he returns to and rewrites the Genesis stories are equally steeped in lessons for planetary citizenship. Even though Leon Trout assures his imagined readers that luck, chance, and natural selection alone determine the path of human evolution into our benign successor fisherfolk, Vonnegut carefully decides which characters are delivered to "their Garden of Eden," Santa Rosalia, in the "Second Noah's Ark."

Once again, Vonnegut's MIT speech and its framing in *Fates Worse Than Death* provide clues to understanding his decisions about which characters survive. Considering that Vonnegut singled out Mary Shelley as "the most effective doubter of the benefits of unbridled technological advancement" and suggested that women generally "don't like immoral technology nearly as much as men do" in his MIT speech, it's not surprising that Vonnegut provides clearly gendered critiques of technology in *Galápagos*. Of the original ten colonists on Santa Rosalia, nine are women, with six Eves to one inept Adam/Noah figure. Vonnegut goes to great lengths to introduce and develop key male characters only to kill them off before reaching the ark, the *Bahía de Darwin*, or the Garden of Eden, Santa Rosalia. Murdered within seconds of each other are computer genius Zenji Hiroguchi, whose inventions such as Gokubi and Mandarax help automate workplaces and render people obsolete, and Andrew MacIntosh, American financier and venture capitalist extraordinaire. Boarding the ark but dying at sea, meanwhile, is James Wait, the conniving swindler of widows, whose amassed estate would "encompass the whole universe" if it kept growing to the novel's "present" of 1,001,986 A.D.

Tellingly, all three men, but primarily MacIntosh and Wait, masquerade as good planetary citizens. MacIntosh, the major corporate polluter, so convincingly presents himself as "an ardent conservationist" that he inspires Jackie Onassis and other celebrities to join the "Nature Cruise of the Century"; Hiroguchi poses as "a world famous expert in animal diseases"; Wait, assuming the alias Willard Flemming, pretends to be a windmill engineer who celebrates "clean, free energy" and children as "the planet's greatest natural resource." While these false identities allow them to pursue their other business enterprises, the novel's critiques of the commodification of nature and greenwashing make these additional trespasses especially grievous.

Vonnegut's choice of the bumbling Adolph von Kleist as "latter-day Adam" further reinforces the novel's gendered critiques of technology. Despite his training at the US Naval Academy and position as captain of the *Bahía de Darwin*, von Kleist is completely incompetent in his dual roles as Noah and Adam. As Leon observes, von Kleist "did not know shit from Shinola about navigation, the Galápagos Islands, or the operation and maintenance of a ship that size." Von Kleist's poor navigational skills unwittingly save the passengers by running the "new Noah's ark" aground not on Baltra, the Hood Islands, or "Mount Ararat," where the Biblical Noah lands, but on mythical Santa Rosalia, "their Garden of Eden." Von Kleist's lack of technological skills again preserves life on Santa Rosalia when he is unable to alter the island's main fresh water source. The stripped-down "ark" also aids in the colonists' survival. Leon pointedly observes, "If the Captain had had any decent tools, crowbars and picks and shovels and so on, he surely would have found a way, in the name of science and progress, to clog that spring."

To complete this divesting of technological skills and devices, as the new Adam, von Kleist's "final act was to cast the Apple of Knowledge into the deep blue sea." As if disposing of Mandarax, the apex of computer technology at the time, weren't enough, Vonnegut takes pains to emphasize his extremely limited reproductive role. No more than an unwitting sperm donor, von Kleist passes on none of his culture, heritage, or values to his progeny. His near obsolescence is suggested via Mary's rhetorical question, "If we could have made a baby out of marine-iguana spit, don't you think we would have done that, and not even disturbed your Majesty?"

Vonnegut further underscores the gendered dimensions of planet-harming technologies through his selection of the Kanka-bonos as the "six Eves to Captain von Kleist's Adam." No doubt modeled after the Taromenane and the Tagaeri, the last two isolated Indigenous groups living in Ecuador's Amazon rain forest, the Kanka-bono girls are flown "from the Stone Age to the Electronics Age" after the rest of their families are "killed by insecticides, sprayed from the air." Destined for extinction by environmental "warfare" and remotely descended from escaped African slaves, the Kanka-bonos bear symbolic if not conscious witness to dangerous paths of Western technology that put so many living things in peril. Echoing this idea is the closely linked mention of the source of Akiko's furry skin—her grandmother's exposure to radiation during the bombing of Hiroshima. Vonnegut's revised Eden myth not only restores humanity to innocence via renunciation of masculine technology, but also literally builds a cautionary tale about technological destruction into the genes of humanity's future descendants. In a final gesture of reverse colonization, Kanka-bono jokes, songs, language, religion, and dances completely subsume all remaining cultural traditions, creating "a perfectly cohesive human family" for centuries prior to the evolution into fisherfolk.

Vonnegut completes his gendered revisionist mythmaking by replacing the fatherly god of Genesis with Mary Hepburn, the biology teacher, amateur naturalist, and Hillis Howie figure, who is fittingly nicknamed "Mother Nature Personified." Armed with science, a genuine respect for nature, and the most extensive knowledge of the Galápagos ecosystems of all the colonists, Mary Hepburn acts not as a god but as a secular tinkerer of the Earthling portion of the planet's clockwork. Mary also embraces the "fruity" and "feminine" planetary ethics Vonnegut put forth in his MIT speech. As Leon remarks, "Nothing could keep her from doing all she could to keep life going on and on and on."

Despite Vonnegut's gendered critiques of Western technologies and the literal and symbolic disarming of humanity's descendants, Vonnegut is, as Leonard Mustazza notes, *not* "advocating a return to the Stone Age."[228] Layered into Leon's inventory of all the destructive things future hominids *can't* do is a catalog of all the beautiful, artistic, and sacred human behaviors that have disappeared with smaller brains and a loss of limbs. Like *Cat's Cradle* and *Slapstick*, *Galápagos* draws on the strategies of environmental apocalypse narratives with the hope that we will realize "in the nick of time" that it's our own habitat we're wrecking, that we're not "merely visitors."

As a secular humanist, Vonnegut did not believe that another paradise awaits human beings after they are finished "visiting" on Earth. Whether we look to the vague "blue tunnel into the Afterlife" in *Galápagos* or a "heaven" so boring in *Slapstick* that Eliza can't wait for Wilbur to die so they can fix it together, Vonnegut's writings affirm the idea that life on Earth is both precious and unique in the universe. His turn to the pastoral, to an innocent, Edenic planet, is just as cautionary as his more standard eco-apocalyptic novels. Do we want to become "Nature's way of creating new galaxies" by "blowing the place to smithereens"?[229] Do we really want to imagine a future Earth without human beings? Do we want the larger forces of nature to put our species in check to restore our harmony with the rest of Nature? Or can we achieve Leon's mother's dream of solving our problems and making "earth into a Garden of Eden again"? True to form, Vonnegut does not provide the reader with easy solutions, but like Mary Shelley, Albert Schweitzer, Rachel Carson, and his first naturalist mentor Hillis Howie, he suggests that we need new ways of thinking about technology, scientific responsibility, and our roles as planetary citizens to keep the stream of life flowing.

CHAPTER 5

MIDLAND CITY
Asphalt Prairies, Drug Stores, and Racism at Breakfast Time

> But look what we have built. . . . Middle-income housing projects which are truly marvels of dullness and regimentation. . . . Cultural centers that are unable to support a good bookstore. Civic centers that are avoided by everyone but bums. . . . Commercial centers that are lackluster imitations of standardized suburban chain-store shopping. Promenades that go from no place to nowhere and have no promenaders. Expressways that eviscerate great cities.
> —JANE JACOBS, *The Death and Life of Great American Cities*

> There is a significance there but I will leave it for the critics to find. It has to do to a certain extent with the early part of my life, with my making peace with certain things that happened to me during the breakfast of my life.
> —KURT VONNEGUT, May 1973 *Media and Methods* interview

In late November 1972, Vonnegut sent Jerome Klinkowitz a gift "Only a college prof could love" in celebration of *The Vonnegut Statement*, the first edited scholarly collection of essays on Kurt's writing and career.[230] The gift was three beginnings of a novel called *Upstairs and Downstairs*, which Vonnegut described as a book "intended to give my personal reactions to the Great Depression."

Started around 1957, the three short drafts totaled twenty-four pages and switched from prose to poetry. While varying in intended audience, the first-person narratives involved a character named Fred T. Barry moving into the family house, painting the front door and his upstairs apartment "garish colors, and having long conversations with the narrator" when he "was a kid—life lessons starting with mundane details."[231] As Vonnegut explained to Klinkowitz, "the book thus begun so long ago eventually evolved into *Breakfast of Champions*," but "there is virtually no trace of these pages in the finished book."[232]

Perhaps prompted by his father's death in October 1957 or deeply personal reflections on home and family in drafts of "A Hoosier Symphony," Vonnegut returned to Fred T. Barry and his shocking pink door in numerous drafts titled *Goodbye, Blue Monday* between 1957 and the mid-1960s. Varying wildly in plot, scope, and even genre, the drafts continued the story of Fred T. Barry's arrival at the Pilgrim[233] household and the impacts of the Great Depression on the family. A central thread of the drafts is the father's emasculation first by job loss and then by Barry's rent money, his larger-than-life presence in the family, and, finally, his job offer to Mrs. Pilgrim. As he suggested to Klinkowitz, the drafts are filled with Vonnegut's thinly fictionalized childhood memories from the 1930s, such as his father's retreat to an upstairs arts studio once architectural jobs dried up, his mother's struggles with sodium amytal addiction, loss of the Lieber brewing business, family ties to Germany, his father's gun collection, Indianapolis's racial segregation, and the Depression's broader social, cultural, and economic impacts. From these and other childhood memories, Vonnegut created the foundational traces of both *Breakfast of Champions* and *Deadeye Dick*—the Robo-Magic washing machine, the Hoover and Waltz families, and the countless people and ghosts that inhabit Midland City.

By the mid-1960s, the *Goodbye, Blue Monday* drafts evolved into the famous coupling of *Slaughterhouse-Five* and *Breakfast of Champions* that Vonnegut wrote during his two-year residency at the Iowa Writers' Workshop. As its subtitle indicates, that manuscript was "the autobiography of a Pontiac Dealer in the American West, as told to Kurt Vonnegut, Jr.," and it merged the stories of Fred Barry, the Robo-Magic corporation, and the background of the earlier Pilgrim family with key portions of *Slaughterhouse-Five*: the overly equipped Roland Weary, the Three Musketeers, Billy's capture after the Battle of the Bulge, Billy's coat and general "filthy flamingo" appearance, the Cinderella play in the British POW camp, Wild Bill from Cody, Wyoming, and an unconventional sense of "time as pendulum."[234] The transformation of that draft into Vonnegut's 1969 masterpiece might be the most important textual process of Vonnegut's career. The personal prologue, unconventional storytelling, and creative blending of science fiction, history, and postmodern elements profoundly reshaped American war literature, and the novel's incredible commercial and critical success launched Vonnegut's meteoric rise as a celebrity and cultural icon.

But the parts of *Goodbye, Blue Monday* that *didn't* make their way into *Slaughterhouse-Five*, which wound up in his two Midland City novels, meant far more to Vonnegut personally. As he told Terry Gross in a March 1987 interview, "It's the things that happened when I was six years old that explain far more thoroughly what I am than Dresden."[235] Perhaps that was why Vonnegut concluded the interview with some reflective comments about his 1982 Midland City novel. While noting his fondness for all his novels, he explained that *Deadeye Dick* was "more literary and deeper" than some of his more critically acclaimed works. "I was dealing with things that mattered to me in depth in *Deadeye Dick*, and I think I dealt with them quite well. That book wasn't that popular, but I think it's a good book. I'm particularly fond of it, for personal reasons," he said.[236]

Those personal, multigenerational connections are what make Midland City a key site within Vonnegut's literary planetary citizenship. Originally based on his home city of Indianapolis, place at its most intimate level, Midland City is where Vonnegut best models the idea of thinking globally but acting locally. In Vonnegut's case, these actions are largely ones of mourning and outrage—grieving the loss of a vibrant city while exploring the political, social, racial, and pharmaceutical toxins that poisoned it. These strong emotions make Midland City the bittersweet, paradoxical center of his fictional cosmos, blending the universal and provincial to offer some of Vonnegut's most important environmental and social justice critiques.

Midland City is both an everyplace and a non-place, the "asshole of the universe" and location for celebrating our unwavering bands of light, a locale steeped in both violence and artistic redemption. Having witnessed Vonnegut family businesses and buildings give way to parking lots and having confronted the realities of racial segregation in Indianapolis, Vonnegut poses critiques of urban renewal, environmental pollution, and racial injustice in *Breakfast of Champions* that are heartfelt. Likewise, growing up in the shadow of pharmaceutical giant Eli Lilly and living with a gun-collecting father and a mother struggling with barbiturate dependency undoubtedly sharpened treatments of the prescription drug and weapons industries in *Deadeye Dick*. But Midland City is not just a "thinly-veiled surrogate for Vonnegut's Indianapolis."[237]

While inspired by and still very much about Vonnegut's Indianapolis, Midland City is also one of the most carefully constructed places in the Vonnegut fictional cosmos. As he revised *Goodbye, Blue Monday* drafts both prior to and after the University of Iowa manuscript, Vonnegut universalized his setting, sometimes emphasizing its place in "the Corn Belt" or the "dead-center of the United States." Other times he noted its status as a manufacturing city, changing its population from 200,000 to 100,000, but usually noting its flatness and location "in the American Middle West." Vonnegut took pains to differentiate Midland City from Indianapolis by including characters from his home city, while simultaneously adding national chains such as Howard Johnsons, Holiday Inns, and Tastee-Freeze stands.[238] By the late 1960s and early 1970s, Vonnegut located his more fully fictionalized Midland

City and neighboring Shepherdstown off the interstate, exactly "midway between two poisoned seas."[239]

This shift from the provincial to a broader, more universal portrait of America's changing urban and suburban landscapes is what gives his Midland City novels their enduring appeal and power as environmental works. More than just a story about Indianapolis's early and mid-twentieth-century transformations, Vonnegut's Midland City explores much larger tales of homogenization, suburbanization, and environmental degradation that accompanied urban renewal and post–World War II development. Greatly expanded from their shared *Goodbye, Blue Monday* origins, *Breakfast of Champions* and *Deadeye Dick* comment on the slow poisoning of the natural environment that accompanied the loss of community as towns became "interchangeable parts in the American machine . . . another someplace where automobiles lived."[240] While Vonnegut uses Midland City to tell broader national and global environmental stories about pollution, radiation, racism, and the plasticization of culture, his remedy for addressing these spiritual and physical poisonings harkens back to some of the earliest scenes in *Goodbye, Blue Monday*: the redemptive power of the arts.[241] To explore the Midland City stories born from Vonnegut's planetary citizenship, we need to begin with another road trip.

A PLAGUE ON WHEELS:
DWAYNE HOOVER'S
EXIT 11 PONTIAC VILLAGE

As he told Charles Reilly in a 1980 interview, cars played a key role in the decoupling of *Slaughterhouse-Five* and *Breakfast of Champions* drafts. "As I was working on the novel," Vonnegut explained, "I realized the automobile business was so damned interesting, especially in a car crazy country like America, that it would take over *Slaughterhouse-Five* sooner or later."[242] Thus Billy Pilgrim became an introspective optometrist instead, and Vonnegut "deferred the automobile business to *Breakfast of Champions.*"

Manuscript drafts of *Slaughterhouse-Five* clearly bear this out. Mid-1960s drafts not only expanded the descriptions of the road trip Vonnegut took with his daughter Nanette and her best friend Allison Mitchell, but also have more details about the Ford and General Motors exhibits at the 1964 New York World's Fair.[243] Quite late in *Slaughterhouse-Five*'s compositional process, Vonnegut was still siphoning off automobile details. In a near-final draft, Vonnegut included a very different depiction of the adult film star character Montana Wildhack and her arrival on Tralfamadore, which addressed American car culture and other topics found in *Breakfast of Champions.*[244]

More in keeping with characters from the 1973 novel, this version of Montana felt that her body "was an impersonal piece of foolishness and ostentation . . . manufactured by adolescent, girl-crazy engineers in some busy city she would never see like Flint, Michigan." Complementing this more mechanistic vision of her body, which "wasn't going to last much longer than [a] damned Continental," is the idea that people frequently want to photograph her and her car, "a Lincoln Continental covered with rabbit fur" chosen by her press agent. This deleted scene anticipates the contrast between "dead machinery" and human awareness that artist Rabo Karabekian explains during the climactic Holiday Inn scene in *Breakfast of Champions.* Montana, who "was spookily intelligent . . . much smarter than Billy" doesn't appreciate her beautiful, "engineered" body at all: "What she treasured was the soul that rode around in all her topographically exaggerated meat. She believed it was sacred and eternal, full of electricity and love, and about the size of a golfball."[245]

Given Vonnegut's deliberate efforts to channel automobile-related elements into his 1973 novel, I'd like to offer the peculiar travel suggestion that we put cars "at the heart of the book."[246] After all, the key plot point of protagonists Kilgore Trout and

dive into an icy stream that has just jumped off a mountain.
I scream when I dive, and I scream again when I come up for air,
and I bloody my shins, scrambling up rocks to get out of the water.
And I laugh, and I try to think of something amazing to ~~say~~ yell. The
Creator never knows what I'm going to say.   After my icy dip today
I yelled this: "Cheese!"

And there's an angel who visits me occasionally, in the form of
a cinnamon bear. He's a robot, too, and he was programmed to ask
me today, "Why did you yell Cheese?"

"Because I felt like it," I said, which was true. What will
I yell tomorrow? Not even the Creator knows.

****

The Creator made the planet Earth and all its robots just for
me, for good old Dwayne Hoover. He aged it for billions of years
before I was introduced onto it from between my mother's robot
legs. When I got there at last, it was a stinking cheese that
crawled with robots, who were programmed to be happy and affable
for only very short periods of time.

Cheese.

Earth was a poisoned ball that bubbled and stank with garbage
from robot picnics and crusades and cities and factories and in-
sect-control projects and scientific farming and high-speed transportation and so on. I was born in Midland City, in the American
Middle West, on October 12, 1922. The population of the city
in those days was 96,661 robots and me.

One robot in three in Midland City was a black one.
Black.

****

5.1 *   As he experimented with different openings in a ca. 1971
draft of *Breakfast of Champions,* Vonnegut increasingly emphasized
various forms of pollution poisoning both the Earth and Midland
City. Archival image by Kurt Vonnegut, courtesy of the Lilly Library,
Indiana University, Bloomington. Copyright © Kurt Vonnegut LLC,
used by permission of The Wylie Agency LLC.

Dwayne Hoover's meeting occurs after a road trip—a journey that allows Trout to comment on the poverty, drug use, environmental exploitation, commercialization, and other social justice issues found across America.[247] The lead-up to Trout's encounter with Dwayne, Pontiac dealer extraordinaire, also offers a more localized glimpse into the "asphalt prairie" and car-focused culture that pervades Midland City. These two intertwined characters and plotlines unite to expose the consequences of America's "new highway culture," the postwar US landscape that environmentalists and other critics were calling "the geography of nowhere."[248]

Along with Vonnegut's felt-pen drawings, Trout's road trip added the anthropological and science fiction perspectives so central to Vonnegut's literary planetary citizenship. Like the images throughout *Breakfast of Champions*, Trout's embedded stories and observations defamiliarize American history and culture, forcing readers to look at the novel's larger narrative and critiques in unexpected ways. It's significant, then, that Vonnegut chose *Plague on Wheels* as the first Kilgore Trout–authored book mentioned in the novel. Clearly a parable about US automobile culture, *Plague on Wheels* imagines not just an individual civilization, but an entire world of cars. It chronicles "a dying planet named *Lingo-Three*" populated by creatures that "resembled American automobiles."[249] Threatened with extinction because they destroyed their natural resources and atmosphere, the wheeled, fossil-fuel-eating creatures try to send to Earth one of their eggs, containing a baby automobile, with an alien name Kago. Because of the egg's great weight, the tiny Kago can only carry the story of *Lingo-Three*'s civilization with him to Earth. Thus the "rusting junkers who were out of gas . . . 'will be gone, but not forgotten.'" Rather than heed the warning of *Lingo-Three*, Earthlings build and worship cars, polluting their planet until "every form of life on that once peaceful and moist and nourishing blue-green ball was dying or dead."

This heavy-handed parable, which ends with Kago being killed by a Detroit autoworker by mistake, might seem hyperbolic. But many environmentalists in the late 1960s and early 1970s perceived automobiles as a major national and planetary destructive force. As Vonnegut knew from his own involvement in the first Earth Day, numerous events featured symbolic funerals for vehicles or banned car traffic to highlight their colossal environmental impacts.[250] Joseph Myler, senior editor for United Press International, tallied these toxic effects, observing that automobile exhaust put "more than 90 million tons of pollutants into the air each year" and accounted for "at least 60 percent of total U.S. air pollution, 85 percent of pollution in big urban areas, and 90 per cent of all carbon monoxide pollution." With an estimated 10 to 30 million junked cars lying around the country, Myler predicted that by 1975 "the car discard rate [would] reach eight million a year."[251]

Building on *Plague on Wheels*, Vonnegut reinforced these impacts through Trout's firsthand observations and conversations during his journey. Kago's fictional warnings become more urgent as Trout passes through "the poisoned marshes and meadows of New Jersey," hitchhiking aboard a truck with a "General Motors-Astro-95 Diesel tractor." While talking to the truck driver, Trout alludes to the 1969 Cuyahoga River fire and Santa Barbara oil spill, key events that prompted the first Earth Day, and notes the localized pollution of the trip itself.[252] The truck driver even realizes "that his truck was turning the atmosphere into poison gas, and that the planet was being turned into pavement so his truck could go anywhere."

Infusing more dark humor, Vonnegut caps off the exchange with Trout's embedded "anti-conservation story" called "Gilgongo!" The story celebrates extinction events because "people were doing their best to cut down on the number of species, so that life could be more predictable." In a reversal of expectations, "nature was too creative" for people's extinction efforts, and "all life on the planet was suffocated at last by a living blanket one hundred feet thick." Clarifying the irony of Trout's earlier renunciation of conservation, Vonnegut selects extinct and endangered species for the living "blanket." He notes that it "was composed of passenger pigeons and eagles and Bermuda Erns and whooping cranes." The intended irony in "Gilgongo!" and lessons of *Lingo-Three*'s civilization manifest themselves in the landscapes Trout encounters on his journey westward. Whether noting the litter and smoke enveloping the Walt Whitman bridge in Philadelphia, the strip-mined "surface of West Virginia, with its coal and trees and topsoil gone," or a car- and appliance-strewn gully, the interstate environs are choked by pollution and debris, not a "living blanket."

From his brief time working as a Saab Dealer on Cape Cod in the early 1960s, Vonnegut recognized that cars were not just modes of transportation or agents of pollution.[253] He knew that automobiles were important symbols of identity, wealth, and status, so he broadened his study of America's car culture by associating characters in *Breakfast of Champions* with the cars they drive or own. As he imagined earlier in the deleted Montana Wildhack scenes, associations between people and their vehicles could reduce people to machines. This type of mechanization and loss of humanity is perhaps best illustrated in Dwayne's view of Patty Keene, the seventeen-year-old white waitress he encounters at a Burger Chef. Although the reader learns of Patty's enormous parental health care and economic challenges, Dwayne can only appreciate her "brand-newness" and regard her "like a new automobile, which hadn't even had its radio turned on yet."

The vast inventory of cars in *Breakfast of Champions* also allowed Vonnegut to create an ethnographic snapshot of Americans and their vehicles. From the mid-1960s onward, Vonnegut chose to associate his protagonist with General Motors, the largest and most powerful automaker of the time. But *Breakfast of Champions* also offers a Kago-inspired portrait of car ownership, representing a great cross-section of the big three carmakers' general types and models. From the full-size Buick Skylark and Ford Galaxie to the midsize Chrysler Plymouth Fury to the more compact Pontiac LeMans and two-door Plymouth Barracuda and Duster, the cars in the novel vary almost as much as the anatomical features of

He told Trout about people he'd heard of in the area
who grabbed live copperheads and rattlesnakes during church
services, to show how much they believed that Jesus would protect them.

"Takes all kinds of people to make up a world," said Trout.

2 li#

Trout marveled at how recently white men ▬▬▬▬▬
had arrived in West Virginia, and how quickly they had demolished
it ⎯ for heat.

Now the heat was all gone, too ⎯ into outer space,
Trout supposed. It had boiled water, and the steam had made
steel windmills whiz around and around. The windmills had
made rotors in generators around and around, jazzing America
with electricity for a little while. Coal also had powered old-fashioned
steamboats and choo-choo trains. A choo-choo train looked like
this.

5.2 ✳ The deleted train illustration and corrections on this ca. 1972
draft page of *Breakfast of Champions* reveal Vonnegut's efforts to
present coal and energy consumption in a new light. Archival image
by Kurt Vonnegut, courtesy of the Lilly Library, Indiana University,
Bloomington. Copyright © Kurt Vonnegut LLC, used by permission
of The Wylie Agency LLC.

Midland City residents. In keeping with the novel's running joke about male penis sizes, Vonnegut includes cars marketed to suggest class status or masculine identity. The roads to and around Midland City sport the Pontiac GTO, one of the original "muscle" cars of the 1960s and 1970s and personal luxury vehicles such as the Oldsmobile Toronado and the Cadillac Eldorado.

More than just the character who reveals what the breakfast of champions really is, Bonnie MacMahon demonstrates how automobile purchases shaped the priorities and aspirations of American consumers. The Holiday Inn cocktail waitress, most famous for her signature way of serving martinis, puts up with her skimpy uniform and customers' demeaning comments because of car-related financial decisions.[254] Although she works principally because her husband "lost all their money by investing it in a car wash in Shepherdstown," we learn that Bonnie and her husband seem particularly enamored with the status that comes with new automobile purchases. Not only have she and her husband purchased nine Pontiacs from Dwayne "over the past sixteen years," but one of Bonnie's two "goals in life" is "to have steel-belted radial tires for the front wheels of her automobile." With mention of the MacMahons' purchases, Vonnegut emphasizes the continued escalation of car sales that accompanied the suburbanization and consumer culture of postwar America. In 1972, the year of Dwayne Hoover and Kilgore Trout's fateful meeting, US car sales neared eleven million, with the number of automobiles owned by Americans exceeding the number of licensed drivers.[255]

To explore how advertising fueled those incredible auto sales, Vonnegut litters *Breakfast of Champions* with signs, slogans, advertising campaigns, and hilarious glimpses into the inner workings and promotions of Dwayne's Pontiac dealership. As manuscript drafts reveal, Vonnegut's investigations of automobile advertising inspired the novel's signature felt-tipped pen drawings. Well before Dwayne Hoover came down with echolalia and began to repeat words from radio ads and stories, Vonnegut punctuated

large portions of mid-1960s drafts with repeated words, emphasizing products and brands such as "Burger Chef," "Drano," or
"Wishbone." Taking the idea to the next level in a ninety-five-page,
ca. 1969 draft, Vonnegut played with the idea of using different
typeface to highlight key words, slogans, and signs such as the
one imploring people to "VISIT SACRED MIRACLE CAVE!
86 MILES."[256] Still not used to his fame as the best-selling author
of *Slaughterhouse-Five*, Vonnegut mused in a note, "It would be
lovely to have headlines in different colors, but that would be
far too expensive, I suppose." From this idea, it was only a short
leap to asking the book designer to insert an actual 1949 Pontiac
advertisement and to turning slogans into illustrations by drawing arrows around text about visiting Sacred Miracle Cave. In
fact, one of Vonnegut's earliest hand-drawn illustrations, a tourist
sign for the cave, appeared in the text Dwayne read in a lavatory
"wallpapered with Pontiac advertisements."

While his hand-drawn illustrations help readers cut through
the visual clutter and trash choking America's roads, communities,
and airwaves, Vonnegut didn't want them to hide the "uglification"
of Midland City. A key part of Vonnegut's critique of America's
car culture is tied to Midland City becoming an "asphalt prairie"
or, as visiting artist Rabo Karabekian calls it, "the asshole of the
universe." Vonnegut examined this "uglification" both spiritually
and aesthetically, cataloging the ways suburbanization, urban
renewal, and corporate homogenization was turning Midland City
into an everyplace and non-place. Like many environmentalists
of his day, Vonnegut took aim at the suburban American dream,
specifically targeting Dwayne's enormous house in "Fairchild
Heights." Dwayne's four-acre-plus lot and tall fence isolate him
both literally and metaphorically from neighbors and community,
allowing him to plunge deeper into mental illness and loneliness.
When he contemplates suicide, shoots up one of his expensive tiled
bathrooms, and then plays nighttime basketball on the asphalt apron
outside his five-car garage, no one hears the shots or the cries for

help because of the space-age "miracle" insulation and high-tech building materials protecting him from human contact.

In addition to the huge environmental footprint of Dwayne's suburban dream home, Vonnegut reveals that Fairchild Heights was built at the expense of the cultural and economic vitality of the city itself. Although *Breakfast of Champions* offers no direct allusions to Jane Jacobs's landmark study, Vonnegut comes to many of the same conclusions as *The Death and Life of Great American Cities*. Sitting amid vacant parking lots, factories, and warehouses, waiting for Kilgore Trout, the character Kurt Vonnegut reflects on the "ghost" of another Fairchild structure: "There was no traffic on Fairchild Boulevard, which had once been the aorta of the town. The life had all been drained out of it by the Interstate and the Robert F. Kennedy Inner Belt Expressway."

This draining of the city's lifeblood, as planners designed for cars instead of people, coincides with a literal loss of human lives. As Vonnegut discusses Bunny Hoover's apartment building in the neglected inner-city section of "skid row," we hear that there have been fifty-six murders in the nearby Fairchild Park over the last two years.[257] We also learn that Bunny's window looks out on the remnants of one of Midland City's former cultural centers: the former Keedsler Opera House, once home to the "Midland City Symphony Orchestra." Vonnegut includes poignant autobiographical reflections about this loss. The old Keedsler mansion prompts him to think about his paternal grandfather Bernard and some of the "dream houses" he had designed for "Hoosier millionaires": "They were mortuaries and guitar schools and cellar holes and parking lots now."

Complementing the pairing of wealthy suburban "Fairchild Heights" and the neglected, impoverished, crime-ridden area near "Fairchild Park," *Breakfast of Champions* also chronicles how Midland City and neighboring Shepherdstown have become "populated" with auto-related and other corporate franchises. Instead of small businesses, the twin cities are home to the new Holiday Inn next to Dwayne's Pontiac dealership, the Burger Chef where Patty Keene works, and the Quality Motor Court near the Adult Correctional Institution on Route 103. Dwayne takes comfort in the predictability and uniformity of these chains, preferring the hospitality of the Holiday Inn over his own home. It's clear from Vonnegut's descriptions of the "asphalt deserts" surrounding these properties that he saw little promise, beauty, or culture in the standardized structures springing up all over the contemporary American landscape.

In *Deadeye Dick*, Vonnegut shifted from cars to weapons, pharmaceuticals, and other elements poisoning American culture, but he still returned to suburbanization, urban renewal, and architectural homogenization in his later Midland City novel. Thanks to broad sweeps in time that precede and follow the "present" of *Breakfast of Champions*, *Deadeye Dick* offers glimpses into Midland City's prewar landscape and its ultimate "asphalt prairie" fate. Narrator Rudy Waltz's retrospective lens helps us see the archaeological layers of the city's development. We learn, for instance, how John Fortune's dairy farm became a proving ground for tanks during World War II and then finally the suburban "shitboxes" of the Avondale neighborhood. Rudy's broader perspective also firmly situates Midland City in southwestern Ohio, placing it on an interstate (most likely Route 71) between Columbus and Cincinnati. It also continues the story of cultural loss, as Rudy notes the exodus of his extended family and the local "Waltz Brothers Drug Company" chain.

Midland City's most disturbing progression toward becoming a true asphalt prairie, of course, is the mass grave constructed for the city's former inhabitants after the "accidental" detonation of a neutron bomb along the interstate. With all its buildings and roads still intact, the depopulated Midland City gains its final parking lot. To dispose of the dead, Army engineers bury the bodies "under the block-square municipal parking lot across the street from police headquarters, where the old courthouse stood."[258] Since the city no longer needs justice or people, the engineers decide to serve cars. Rudy notes that they "repaved the lot, and put the dwarf arboretum of parking meters back in place." It seems that Kago's tale and prophecy in *Plague on Wheels* was finally able to find just the right ending.

BARRYTRON AND
RADIOACTIVE MANTELPIECES

As Vonnegut contemplated the plastic molecule polluting Sugar Creek in *Breakfast of Champions*, he presciently saw an Earth covered with plastic and exclaimed, "It's all like cellophane." As we turn to the many personal, cultural, and environmental poisonings within *Deadeye Dick*, Vonnegut's manuscript drafts make me say, "It's all Barrytron!" All along, the fictional company seems to have been the wellspring for multiple destructive, toxic forces in Midland City and beyond. In *Breakfast of Champions*, we discover that Barrytron is unintentionally polluting the water with plastic waste from manufacturing a new "anti-personnel bomb." In *Deadeye Dick*, Barrytron's connections to the military-industrial complex prove to be a far deadlier, immediate threat to people and the planet.

The destructive, polluting aspects of Barrytron originated in what ultimately became *Slaughterhouse-Five* drafts as Vonnegut wrestled with the still-intertwined novels in mid- to late 1960s drafts of *Goodbye, Blue Monday*. As he repeatedly drafted versions of his trip with daughter Nanette and her friend Allison to visit Bernard O'Hare, Vonnegut experimented with fictionalized accounts of the journey, imagining a stopover in Schenectady and Alplaus.[259] There the girls go to a creek to look for eels, but instead find only "raw sewage, a rainbow scum of petroleum products, and carp the size of Polaris submarines." The carp "as big as atomic submarines" made their way into *Slaughterhouse-Five*, but the detailed depiction of the area surrounding the river and brook did not. The trees and thickets near the water are "big and weak and sick, and short-lived" because of their proximity to "a top-secret military research installation." Vonnegut further associated the polluted environment with weapons tests, which produce "a frightful, voracious roar of death in life."

That *Slaughterhouse-Five* draft and another composed around the same time look to the "accidental" erasure of American city populations that would become a central component of *Deadeye Dick*. During the stopover, the narrator discusses the 1964 Cold War film *Fail Safe*, which is "about the accidental beginning of World War Three." The error and "misunderstanding" that leads to the bombing of Moscow in the film is countered when "an American plane drop[s] a hydrogen bomb on New York City while all the people are still in it." While processing his own experiences after the firebombing in Dresden, the idea of vanishing *American* cities was unmistakably on Vonnegut's mind. In another version of the trip with Nanny and Allison, the narrator contemplates the disappearance first of Albany and then of Schenectady, asking, "how would you feel if you read in a paper some night that Albany had blown up, and everybody was dead?"[260]

Deadeye Dick allowed Vonnegut to address that question along with other specific critiques of the military-industrial complex. In contrast to the wide-scale planetary or species-level destruction imagined in *Cat's Cradle* or *Galápagos*, *Deadeye Dick* enabled Vonnegut to examine more localized casualties via guns and other military technologies in sensitive and profound ways. *Deadeye Dick* places a pair of two seemingly disconnected accidents at its center—Rudy's shooting of Eloise Metzger and her unborn child and the detonation of a neutron bomb near interstate Exit 11 that depopulates the entire city. Rudy's response to the accidental murders is to become a "perfect neuter," "a perfectly uninvolved person," who cuts himself off from most human contact to avoid injuring other human beings. Vonnegut contrasts Rudy's incredible guilt and penance after the fateful 1944 Mother's Day shooting with the US government's utterly inadequate response to killing more than a hundred thousand people with a neutron bomb.

Like *Fail Safe*, *Deadeye Dick* doesn't show the explosion. Instead, Vonnegut tells the story through Rudy, who had moved to Haiti to run the hotel he co-owns with his brother. The former pharmacist and failed playwright can't provide the reader with definitive information about why or how the neutron bomb explodes, but he can offer rich portraits of Midland City residents and their pasts. Although he saves Rudy's speculations on the blast for the epilogue, it's clear that Vonnegut is scrutinizing the concept of "acceptable casualties." In *Deadeye Dick*, people become as disposable as the goods that litter the roads to and environs of Midland City. Discussing a leaflet printed by "farmers on the fringe of the flash area," Rudy summarizes their argument: "The United States of America was now ruled, evidently, by a small clique of power brokers who believed that most Americans were so boring and ungifted and small time that they could be slain by the tens of thousands without inspiring any long-term regrets on the part of anyone." Rudy continues: "They have now proved this with Midland City, and who is to say that Terre Haute or Schenectady will not be next."

In a 1982 interview with Peter Reed shortly after the publication of *Deadeye Dick*, Vonnegut confirmed that his fictional neutron bombing of Midland City spoke to a sense of human disposability rooted both in the recessions of the late 1970s and early 1980s and the Cold War. Using Terre Haute as an example, Vonnegut mentioned that what he "showed happening in Midland City [was] like the indifference of our government to the closing down of these towns."[261] He then went on to compare the government's indifference to people's economic woes and feelings of uselessness to the same mindset that allowed for "manageable casualties in war," likely alluding to Ronald Reagan's 1981 reauthorization of the production of neutron warheads.

Once again, the disposability of people economically and militarily can be traced back to Barrytron and its shift from manufacturing appliances to weapons systems during World War II. The transition is made possible when the electronic "brain" of its Robo-Magic washing machine becomes the "nerve center" of the BLINC (Blast Interval Normalization Computer) system, which guides bomb release patterns. The BLINC system removes the "human element" both in the release and impacts of bombs, and it sets Barrytron on its Cold War path of developing "much more sophisticated weapons systems" for the US government and polluting Midland City with chemical and other wastes.

Rudy's accidental shooting of the pregnant Eloise Metzger, however, reveals the "human element" can claim lives as well. Although Rudy's father, Otto Waltz, dramatically claims responsibility for the bullet that kills Metzger, Rudy acknowledges the stupidity, carelessness, and cockiness of his actions as a twelve-year-old boy. To emphasize these all-too-human traits, Vonnegut adds personal details to the shooting, choosing the date of his own mother's death for Eloise Metzger's and adding details reminiscent of his own reckless firing of a rifle over Indianapolis as a boy.[262]

With another shift from the provincial to universal, Vonnegut ties the shooting to broader cultural commentary. He uses Rudy's reflections on the symbolism of the bullet to mark a broader "farewell to childhood and a confirmation of . . . manhood." That violence-prone model of manhood, which Vonnegut explicitly critiques in *Happy Birthday, Wanda June* and elsewhere, is precisely what enables cycles of war. Vonnegut takes pains to mention that the Springfield rifle Rudy shoots was a former "standard American infantry weapon," and that the collection of three hundred guns from which it came "encompassed almost the entire history of firearms up until 1914 or so." The accidental shooting also occurs on the day Eleanor Roosevelt visits a local "tank-assembly line" and Rudy's older brother, Felix, departs for his military service.

Rudy's initiation into manhood, which comes with access to Otto's gun collection, is further merged with a "great wartime fraternity" as the bang from his shot blends in with the roaring sounds of tanks traveling from the factory to the proving grounds. To complete the connections between Rudy's localized shooting and the nation's war machine, the "wrecked guns, including the fatal Springfield" are donated to a scrap drive, which enables them to potentially kill "a lot more people when they were melted up and made into shells or bombs or hand grenades or whatever." Ultimately, *Deadeye Dick* suggests the only way to end weapons-based violence is to stop producing deadly technologies. Vonnegut sums up the idea pithily in widower George Metzger's editorial: "I give you a holy word: DISARM."

As *Deadeye Dick* shows, shifting from weapons manufacturing back to consumer goods is not a guarantee of safety—especially in the age of the military-industrial complex. Rudy and his family discover firsthand that the products created as America's factories shifted from building weapons to cars, appliances, and new disposable items can also be dangerous. In *Deadeye Dick*, the dangerous impacts come from nuclear technologies and radiation—a topic that became increasingly important to Vonnegut and other environmentalists during the 1970s.

Deadeye Dick's layered examination of the radioactive mantelpiece in Rudy and his mother's suburban Avondale home underscores the dangerous by-products of nuclear weapons technology. One of the first things Rudy tells readers about the mantelpiece is that it "had been made with radioactive cement left over from the Manhattan project, from the atomic bomb project in World War Two." When the builders, Gino and Marco Maritimo, procure and place the mantelpiece in a model suburban home, everything seems fine; Gino finds the mantelpiece in the scrap heap of "an ornamental concrete company outside of Cincinnati." Despite the Maritimo brothers' kind intentions of selling the model home to Rudy and Emma cheaply after Otto's death, the backstory and disposal of the mantelpiece are laden with criminal and negligent decisions. Through careful research, Rudy locates the cement's origins in Oak Ridge, Tennessee, "where pure uranium 235 was produced for the bomb they dropped on Hiroshima in 1945." The disposability of enemy lives shifts to a disregard for Americans' health and safety as we learn that the "government somehow allowed that cement to be sold off as war surplus, even though many people had known how hot it was." And, lest readers miss the connections between that action and the broader web of harmful military technologies, Rudy adds, "In this case, the government was about as careless as a half-wit boy up in a cupola with a loaded Springfield rifle—on Mother's Day."

Even more sinister than the initial sale of radioactive cement is the reaction of the Nuclear Regulatory Commission (NRC) when it learns of the contamination from Lowell Ulm, the county civil defense director who investigates the mantelpiece. Although knowing that it was "hotter than a Hiroshima baby carriage," NRC officials swear to secrecy the workmen who remove the mantelpiece and invent a cover story to prevent panic "in the name of patriotism, of national security." Like "good citizens," Rudy and his mother don't panic. But after Emma dies from radiation-related brain tumors, the Waltz sons begin a quest for information that results in lawsuits against the construction companies and the NRC. The settlement allows them to purchase their hotel in Haiti, allowing Rudy to escape both the radioactive mantelpiece and the later neutron bomb.

Just as *Breakfast of Champions* confronted pressing environmental issues of its moment, the Midland City of *Deadeye Dick* gave Vonnegut a chance to address recent anti-nuclear and environmental justice concerns. In the mid-1970s, anti-nuclear groups gained momentum as environmental coalitions like the Clamshell Alliance and the Abalone Alliance protested the construction of new nuclear plants, such as Seabrook in New Hampshire and Diablo Canyon in California. But the anti-nuclear movement took center stage after the March 28, 1979, accident at Three Mile Island released some "2.5 million curies of radioactive noble gases" into the area near the plant.[263] Immediately following the partial meltdown, anti-nuclear rallies took place in dozens of US cities and even in Tokyo, as survivors of the bombing at Hiroshima protested the continued use of nuclear energy after the accident. Just over a month later, on May 6, 1979, approximately 125,000 environmental activists, celebrities, and citizens alike gathered in Washington, DC, for what was then the largest anti-nuclear rally in US history.[264] Once again, Kurt Vonnegut was there.

Speaking alongside other activists and celebrities such as Jane Fonda, Ralph Nader, Joni Mitchell, Barry Commoner, and Jackson Browne, Kurt Vonnegut gave a brief but scathing speech that captured many of the sentiments that would appear in *Deadeye Dick*.[265] After noting his "embarrassment" over the way "Americans have guided our destinies so clumsily," Vonnegut opened the address with the lament "that we now must protect ourselves against our own government and our own industries." Much of the speech focused on the irresponsibility of creating weapons and generating electricity from "the most unstable substances and most persistent poisons to be found anywhere in the universe." Vonnegut's main point was that citizens needed to take action and refuse to believe "the lies we have been fed about nuclear energy" by lawyers, government spokespersons and "public relations people." Failure to do so, he suggested, might result in killing "everything on this lovely blue-green planet."

Deadeye Dick captures these concerns, pairing the neutron bomb explosion and the radioactive mantelpiece constructed from cement left over from the Manhattan Project. The novel also questions the NRC's ability to realize its mission of ensuring "the safe use of radioactive materials for beneficial civilian purposes while protecting people and the environment."[266] The depopulated Midland City, with its empty buildings and government occupation, also conjures up another major environmental story of the late 1970s—the numerous poisoned sites such as Love Canal, Niagara Falls, and "Valley of the Drums" in Bullitt County, Kentucky, that prompted the passage of the Superfund Act of 1980.[267] Nevertheless, it was another slow poisoning from his childhood that Vonnegut chose to return to *Deadeye Dick*—his mother's barbiturate addiction and the broader dangers of the pharmaceutical industry.

ALL-NIGHT DRUG STORES

Although many of the biographical details of his mother's struggles with prescription drug addiction from early *Goodbye, Blue Monday* did not make it into his published Midland City novels, Vonnegut drew some parallels between Edith Lieber Vonnegut and Celia Hoover's character in *Breakfast of Champions*. He noted their shared beauty and love of music, along with a common hatred of having their photograph taken, struggles with depression, manic episodes, and respective suicides.[268] While Celia remained an absent presence haunting Dwayne in *Breakfast of Champions*, in the later Midland City novel, she emerges as a central, tragic character in her own right.

Celia's character also allowed Vonnegut to explore gendered dimensions of America's growing drug industry. Her addiction to amphetamines, specifically the widely prescribed Pennwalt Biphetamine, or "black beauties," mirrors the habits of many middle-class women during the 1960s and 1970s, who turned to diet drugs like Dexedrine or "pep" pills to control their weight, lift their moods, and maintain the appearance of happy, productive homemakers.[269] Although we never get direct access to Celia's inner thoughts and desires, it's clear from her barefoot departure from the Waltz house on prom night that she loathes being valued only for her beauty, which "had nothing to do with what she was like inside." The few glimpses we get of Celia reaching for spiritual and creative fulfillment—compassionately volunteering for twenty-four hours straight as a hospital receptionist during a blizzard, attending night classes at the YMCA, and giving a stellar performance as the female lead in Midland City's production of *Katmandu*—are overshadowed by her amphetamine-inspired scenes at Will Fairchild Memorial Airport or Schramm's Drug Store. Tragically, her addiction to Biphetamine succeeds in destroying the face Celia lamented on prom night. When Rudy encounters her in the drugstore after she's been cut off at all the other pharmacies in town, he sees "the raddled, snaggletoothed ruins of the face of Celia Hoover, once the most beautiful girl in town."

Although Celia's amphetamine addiction is the central drug abuse story in *Deadeye Dick*, Rudy, as a pharmacist by profession and neutered observer, takes pains to place Celia's decline within the broader fabric of Midland City's quiet desperation. In keeping with patterns of women's amphetamine abuse, Celia's addiction and eventual destruction begins innocently enough with a doctor prescribing the pills for her and other affluent suburban residents. As Rudy explains,

> Dr. Mitchell was building a big practice on the principle that nobody in modern times should ever be the least uncomfortable or dissatisfied, since there were now pills for everything. And he would buy himself a great big house in Fairchild Heights, right next door to Dwayne and Celia Hoover, and he would encourage Celia and his own wife, and God only knows who else, to destroy their minds and spirits with amphetamines.

Adding to the depiction of Dwayne's isolation and loneliness in his suburban dream house in *Breakfast of Champions*, Dr. Mitchell's profit-driven prescriptions describe another layer of dangerous postwar products poisoning Midland City. It's no surprise that a later description of Celia's roaming the airport runway at night ends with her being returned to a dark house, with no one home except for Dwayne's neglected dog, Sparky. Tragically, Celia and Dwayne's estranged homosexual son, Bunny, also turns to drugs to cope with his own lonely existence at the Fairchild Hotel; instead of using transcendental meditation as he does in *Breakfast of Champions*, Bunny is "heavily into cocaine."

Deadeye Dick weaves the Hoover family's encounters with "bad chemicals" into a much larger epidemic of substances destroying individuals, communities, the nation, and the planet. Shortly after Rudy's embedded mini play about Celia's visit to Schramm's Drug Store and his conjecture that amphetamines caused her suicide by Drano, we learn of Rudy's own brother's prescription drug abuse. Characters like Dr.

Mitchell seemingly abound as we discover that Felix "came home from New York City—bombed on Darvon and Ritalin and methaqualone and Valium and God only knows what all. He had prescriptions for every bit of it." Based on these patterns of drug use, Rudy offers the prescient prediction, "The late twentieth century will go down in history, I'm sure, as an era of pharmaceutical buffoonery." Although this remark uncannily anticipates the recent US epidemic of opioid, antidepressant, and antibiotic use, with nearly two-thirds of Americans taking prescription drugs in 2021, Vonnegut has Rudy offer the comment shortly before the descriptions of Celia's funeral at the First Methodist Church.

As symbolic as Rudy's bullet or the empty arts center, Celia's funeral encapsulates the larger tragedy and slow destruction of Midland City. Despite the large turnout of more than two hundred people, Celia is only really mourned by Dwayne, Lottie Davis, the Waltz brothers, and a stranger wearing mirrored sunglasses reminiscent of the Kurt Vonnegut character in *Breakfast of Champions*. Most attendees are there not for Celia, but for Dwayne; they are his customers, suppliers, or employees. Professional relationships have replaced familial ones, amphetamines have effaced aspirations and creativity, and Drano has completed the process of destroying the machine Celia Hoover had become. Celia's funeral, not Dwayne's breakdown in *Breakfast of Champions*, is the harbinger for Midland City's death via neutron bomb:

> The corpse was a mediocrity who had broken down after a while. The mourners were mediocrities who would break down after a while. The city itself was breaking down. Its center was already dead. Everybody shopped at the outlying malls. Heavy industry had gone bust. People were moving away. The planet itself was breaking down. It was going to blow itself up sooner or later, if it didn't poison itself. In a manner of speaking, it was already eating Drano.

This passage not only provides a "prequel" to the "planet that was dying fast" in the opening of *Breakfast of Champions*, but pulls together the various poisonings via machines, pharmaceuticals, suburbanization, urban renewal, and war that plague Midland City. To finish exploring Midland City's toxic layers, though, we need to go back to the systemic racism Vonnegut discovered during "the breakfast" of his life.

THE KKK, BRAINCASES, AND GOBLET CELLS

Although Vonnegut never got to deliver his final speech at the April 27, 2007, Clowes Hall address that would start Indianapolis's "Year of Vonnegut," he used the upcoming occasion to reflect on both inspiring and troubling aspects of his Hoosier identity.[270] He began the written address by honoring the architectural and cultural legacies of his father and paternal grandfather, but quickly noted the Ku Klux Klan's powerful presence in Indiana during his childhood in a racially segregated Indianapolis. In keeping with the juxtapositions of painful and sweet moments in the speech, Vonnegut also observed that "the most spiritually splendid American phenomenon" of his life was "how African American citizens have maintained their dignity and self-respect" despite decades of racist treatment by white Americans "both in and out of government." Near the end of the speech, he paid particular tribute to his teachers at School 43 and Shortridge High School and to Ida Young, the Black woman who worked as a cook and housekeeper for the Vonneguts from the mid-1920s to early 1930s.[271] Although he had already acknowledged his enormous personal, professional, and spiritual debts to Young in *Wampeters, Foma & Granfalloons*, he wanted his 2007 audience to appreciate her wisdom, kindness, nobility, intelligence, and honor while noting that she was a descendant of enslaved people.

While Vonnegut addressed the history, lived realities, and legacies of racism in Indianapolis at the end of his life, he also tackled the topics at midlife, as he crossed "the spine" of the "roof" of his career.[272] Although some of his most honest, personal attempts to address this history didn't make their way into the published novel,

Vonnegut explored complex layers of racism poisoning American institutions, culture, and history in *Breakfast of Champions*, channeling racial injustices that occurred during his childhood. Before turning to scenes from earlier drafts, it's useful to see how Vonnegut critiqued racism and social injustices in the published novel.

Just as the central pairing of Dwayne Hoover and Kilgore Trout raised environmental and automobile-related issues, Vonnegut utilized the "two lonesome, skinny, fairly old white men," along with drawings and narrative commentary, to probe layers of historical and contemporary racism in the United States.[273] The opening descriptions of Trout's and Hoover's nation, which weave together central American symbols and myths, exposes gaps between ideals of cultural plurality, fairness, equity, and brotherhood, and a history of racism, genocide, and current inequalities. The narrator brashly and irreverently reexamines historical dates such as 1492 and presents the "founding fathers of the nation" as white "sea pirates" who disregard the "copper-colored" Indigenous inhabitants and introduce Black slavery, sarcastically noting, "Color was everything."[274]

Trout's journey westward, meanwhile, enables the narrator and the failed science fiction writer to observe how the legacies of these foundational inequalities continue to produce "disposable" people—from the "two young black prostitutes" who can't find work after their Northern migration, to the disenfranchised Puerto Rican boys who don Pluto Gang jackets to project toughness to "defend themselves and their families," to the West Virginian so worn out by his fifty-two years of coal mining that he's "usually too tired to care" about anything. The descriptions of Trout's journey further highlight significant moments and figures in American history. Trout's Thomas Jefferson High School in Ohio is "named after a slave owner who was also one of the world's greatest theoreticians on the subject of human liberty," while the Lincoln Tunnel is "named in honor of a man who had had the courage and imagination to make human slavery against the law in the United States of America." As Vonnegut, via

persona Philboyd Studge, notes in the preface, his efforts to examine
and then purge America's historical and cultural "sidewalk strewn
with junk" are attempts to create "humane harmony" within his
head and the nation at large. Thus, it's only fitting that Vonnegut's
gift to Trout at the moment of the character's liberty is an apple, a
symbol "not poisoned by great sins our nation has committed, such
as slavery and genocide and criminal neglect."

While Trout's narrative sections offer sweeping perspectives on
racism and inequalities, the Dwayne Hoover and other Midland
City–focused sections investigate institutional and interpersonal
dimensions of racism more specifically. For example, the narrator points to neighboring Shepherdstown's Adult Correctional
Institution, "where the guards were all white and most of the prisoners were black." Harry and Grace LeSabre's coded conversation
about "the reindeer problem" or "the black problem in the city,"
meanwhile, captures their internalized racism and sets up a presciently sobering description of America's criminal justice system.
As the narrator observes, "The Midland City Police Department,
and the Midland County Sheriff's Department, were composed
mainly of white men. They had racks and racks of sub-machine
guns and twelve-gauge automatic shotguns for an open season on
reindeer, which was bound to come." The institutional racism of the
criminal justice system is supported by the wider web of attitudes,
practices, and rampant discrimination that pervades the city—from
the segregated high schools to the frequent use of the N-word.[275]

The juxtaposition of Dwayne Hoover and Wayne Hoobler further demonstrates how power and privilege are concentrated in
the hands of white men. Although both hail from the same state
and originally share the same last name, white Dwayne owns huge
swaths of Midland City and is "fabulously well-to-do" while Black
Wayne is a recently released parolee with no home, family, or job
prospects despite his excellent work ethic. Dwayne's family history
and personal backstory, meanwhile, highlights racism's multi-gen-
erational effects. Despite attempts to distance himself from his

stepfather's virulent racism by recruiting Black Boy Scouts, trying to save the life of a Black death-row inmate, and hiring African Americans "when nobody else would hire black people," Dwayne later reverts to his stepfather's views. At the start of his rampage, he plays a game of African Dodger with Wayne after recalling his father's story of a horrific lynching in Shepherdstown.[276] Although freed from normal, more socially responsible behavior by his "bad chemicals" and Trout's story *Now It Can Be Told*, the racism, sexism, and homophobia connected to Dwayne's violent attacks reveal that his father's and the sea pirates' legacy of racism is alive and well.

✻ ✻ ✻ ✻ ✻

At the risk of introducing yet more foma to the world of Vonnegut Studies, I suspect that Vonnegut assigned a C grade to *Breakfast of Champions* in *Palm Sunday* because he was dissatisfied with his ability to address racial injustice in the novel. In late manuscript drafts, he struggled intensely with diction, use of racial epithets, and material relating to his home city and state's legacies of slavery, segregation, and white supremacy. Some of the largest final edits he made were to sections that harkened back to early drafts of *Goodbye, Blue Monday*.[277] To fully understand Vonnegut's efforts to address racial injustice in *Breakfast of Champions*, we need to return to those early drafts and the painful historical episodes that happened during the breakfast of Kurt's life.

While the Anton Pilgrim/father figure in early *Goodbye, Blue Monday* drafts highlighted economic impacts of the Great Depression, Vonnegut used Mrs. Pilgrim's genealogy to investigate the KKK's strong, corrupt presence in Indianapolis during the 1920s.[278] Whether her maiden name appears as "Cooper" or "Dyer," the narrator describes her as being descended from "pioneers of English and Scotch stock who came up from the Carolinas around 1800." "They tried to bring slavery with them," he adds, noting that they "nearly made the state a slave state at its founding. This has almost been forgotten. Forgotten." With this reference to slavery in the Indiana Territory and its initial slaveholder-friendly government, Vonnegut laid the groundwork for confronting other legacies of racial violence in his home state.

To probe this history, Vonnegut loosely based the narrator Billy's maternal grandfather on David Curtis Stephenson, the Grand Dragon of Indiana's KKK, who once famously boasted, "I am the law in Indiana."[279] Although Vonnegut changed many details about Mr. Dyer/Cooper, the narrator repeatedly mentions that his grandfather was the "secret head of the State Ku Klux Klan," who yielded great political power and was brought down by an enormous scandal that involved "him and his cronies and women and the Ku Klux Klan." In the draft, Mr. Cooper commits suicide via poison, but other details allude to Stephenson's 1925 trial, when he was convicted for abducting, raping, and killing Madge Oberholtzer, who attempted to poison herself with mercuric chloride tablets after Stephenson brutally attacked her.[280] The drafts also capture Stephenson's famous admiration for Benito Mussolini. However, in truly vintage Vonnegut fashion, that detail becomes a joke. Despite the great wealth he gained from his KKK connections, Mr. Cooper dies broke because "he invested every nickel he had in a stock called 'Italian Super-Power,' which was the Italian dictator Mussolini's scheme for harnessing the energy of Italian volcanoes in order to generate cheap electricity."

That touch of humor doesn't mask the narrator's discomfort in recalling memories of a KKK rally near a covered bridge when he was about seven years old. The sheet-covered men on horseback emerge "as though from the mouth of hell" in an "apocalyptic procession" that includes a Model T truck, carrying a "wooden cross swaddled in oil-soaked rags." Oddly enough, the truck is driven by his grandfather's chauffeur, an African American man named John Barnard. Billy remarks, "It was all right for John to be along on that particular trip I guess," adding that the Klan members "were on their way to touch off the cross in the front yard of a Jew who owned McFarland's, the biggest shoe store in town."

Later in the draft we learn that Billy has married the store owner's Jewish granddaughter, and that, despite pressure from his maternal grandfather and business associates, his father steadfastly refuses to join the Klan. These relationships help balance the narrator's close familial connection to "the Grand Dragon," allowing him to discuss the ways the "Klan dominated state politics all through the twenties, even though it was a northern state." At various points in the KKK-related sections of the drafts, the narrator mentions the Klan's actions against "gangsters," Catholics, and Jews, but notes that after a while, it "became less interested in morals and races, and more enthusiastic for graft." Veering from Stephenson's real-life story and tying together his own storylines, the culmination of this political greed and corruption is the construction of the International Pavilion at the State Fairgrounds.[281] The pavilion, the "largest building in the city," is a Klan boondoggle: "Every workman and supplier and contractor and designer on the job had been a member of the Ku Klux Klan, with one exception: the architect, Billy's father, Anton Pilgrim, son-in-law of the Grand Dragon."

Billy's repeated mentions of the Klan's powerful city, state, and regional presence are borne out by historical fact. Historians Leonard Moore, William Lutholtz, Richard Tucker, and Chelsea Sutton estimate that more than a quarter million Indiana residents were members of the KKK during that early and mid-1920s, and that in 1925 alone more than 165,000 or "nearly 21 percent of native-born white Hoosier men" were active.[282] At its height, the Indiana Klan was "the epicenter of the national" movement. It produced the Klan's largest membership, its greatest political victories, and its most powerful, well-known leaders outside of Atlanta.[283]

While most likely a composite of stories and images Vonnegut encountered in his youth, the narrator's descriptions of the Klan parade capture the fact that "Blacks took second place to Catholics and Jews" in persecutions in Indiana.[284] Although ushered in on the xenophobic, anti-immigration, nativist, morality-based wave of patriotism that took root during World War I, the Indiana Klan seemed especially eager to parlay its anti-Catholic, anti-Semitic, and temperance platforms into a "highly effective pyramid scheme" and political machine.[285] Thanks to Stephenson's leadership, by 1924, the Klan "secretly govern[ed] the State," as Billy noted in his recollections. Indiana had "a closet Klansman governor" and Klan "control of the legislature, with [KKK] members entrenched in dozens of county, town, and city offices."[286] While Vonnegut used the International Pavilion (mostly likely based on the Indiana Farmers Coliseum) to connect several storylines in *Goodbye, Blue Monday*, the building's location in the State Fairgrounds evokes links to Indianapolis's political machine. Less than two miles from Vonnegut's boyhood home on North Illinois Street, the fairgrounds was a site for cross-burnings and major parades in the 1920s.[287] Ultimately, some of this history and its emotional impact *did* make its way into *Breakfast of Champions*, albeit updated for the 1970s.

Although *Breakfast of Champions* provides a multifaceted look at the institutions, power structures, historical legacies, and other systems that foster racism in America, Vonnegut confronted these elements more extensively in a deleted forty-page section of the late, collaged together, ca. 1972 draft that he shared with typists and editors.[288] In those pages, Vonnegut explicitly drew on his anthropological training to challenge the concept of race as a scientific category and to include additional, more nuanced portraits of characters of color. The explicitly anthropological section begins by examining archaeological layers beneath Dwayne's Pontiac dealership. Vonnegut first notes that the agency was "an allusion to an Indian village" and points out "the automobiles themselves were named after a chief of the Ottawa Indians, who besieged a British garrison at Detroit for five months." After invoking the conquest and genocide perpetrated by the white "sea pirates" again, Vonnegut reminds readers that this theft was "only in very recent times." Workmen, in fact, discover traces of the original inhabitants—arrowheads, pottery shards, and a skeleton—when they excavate the land for Dwayne's businesses.

Shortly after this scene, amid numerous deleted reflections in the cocktail lounge of the Holiday Inn, Vonnegut includes several references to his first anthropology thesis advisor, Dr. Sydney Slotkin, whose scholarship divided its focus "between people in modern, urban lunatic asylums and primitive men." These references further contextualize Vonnegut's discussions of schizophrenia and a very late alternative ending that depicts himself and Dwayne Hoover together in "the Midland County loony bin."[289] But they also open the door for stream-of-consciousness reflections inspired by Vonnegut's early physical and cultural anthropology course-work at Chicago. In a lengthy portion of the deleted forty-page section, Vonnegut explores the cultural "scientific" reasons behind segregated bathrooms, water fountains, and other facilities. The scene involves a flashback of Dwayne wandering into the desolated Keedsler factory, where he discovers "two white men and one black man . . . building and testing and improving the world's first fully-automatic washing machine for use in the home." Vonnegut contrasts this scene of collaboration with illustrations and descriptions of the segregated bathrooms and drinking fountains.

In keeping with the tone and strategies of defamiliarization used throughout the novel, the narrator further explains the illustrations:

These signs were left over from the First World War, but they would assume their old importance when World War II began. The thing was that white factory workers in both wars were often physically revolted by black factory workers. It was disgusting to them to touch anything of an intimate nature which black people might have touched with their mucous membranes. Mucous membranes were the lubricated tubes in human beings which gave their bodies access to the materialistic offerings of the outside world.

Vonnegut moves from these reflections to a description and image of goblet cells and the social hierarchies created by different skin characteristics, noting that "persons with oily skins were much less popular than those with dry skins."

Returning to the image of the three men working on the Robo-Magic, Vonnegut challenges the hierarchies and segregated facilities based on different skin colors and types: "The skins of all three men, incidentally, contained a dark brown pigment called melanin, which protected the deeper parts of their bodies by absorbing ultra-violet rays, which could be harmful. The black man was so much blacker than the other two simply because his skin contained so much more melanin." Invoking his physical anthropology courses, Vonnegut then explores the number of cubic centimeters in the three men's braincases, compares his own braincase to Dwayne's, pits the braincase of Ivan Turgenev against Anatole France's, and then concludes his study by observing, "The largest brains of Earth, on average, belonged to Eskimos." This conclusion and the accompanying illustration of an igloo playfully undermine the comparative studies of skulls that helped create the racial hierar-chies that supported "sea pirate" colonization and other forms of nineteenth- and twentieth-century scientific racism.

The scenes of the three men's collective efforts to bring the Robo-Magic to life further challenge the logic of segregation. Dwayne surreptitiously observes the three men cackling, guffawing, and having a "heavenly time" as they work on the washing machine in the "whites only" bathroom. Even though the two white men, Fred T. Barry and Elias Keedsler, possess the power and privilege that comes with rank and ownership, the real ingenuity and skill behind the Robo-Magic comes from John Thompson, the Black man who built the machine's "frame and gears and drive shaft and bearings from the parts of junked Keedsler automobiles." When the other two men want to stop working to break for lunch, Thompson presses on and shames them into continuing their tests of the Robo-Magic. In frame, work habits, and creativity, he's

257.

On either side of the door was a drinking fountain. Over one was a sign that said this:

Over the other was a sign that said this:

These signs were left over from the First World War, but they assumed their old importance when World War Two began. The thing was that white factory workers in both wars were often physically revolted by black factory workers. It was disgusting to them to touch anything of an intimate nature which black people might have touched with their mucous membranes. Mucous membranes were the lubricated tubes in human beings which gave their bodies access to the materialistic offerings of the outside world.

The mucous membranes, when viewed under a microscope, were composed in part of so-called goblet cells, which in cross-section looked something like this:

5.3 ❈ These deleted hand–drawn signs and reflections on racial segregation were part of Vonnegut's more in–depth critiques of racial injustice in late drafts of *Breakfast of Champions*. Archival image by Kurt Vonnegut, courtesy of the Lilly Library, Indiana University, Bloomington. Copyright © Kurt Vonnegut LLC, used by permission of The Wylie Agency LLC.

"imperial," and the narrator notes that "he knew and everybody knew that he was the best mechanic in town." Even Thompson's clothes add commentary to the scene. While Barry removes his shirt, Thompson keeps his "purple and gold track shirt" on because it's a gift from his grandson Garfield, "a quarter-miler and broad-jumper at Crispus Attucks High School." Likely alluding to Jesse Owens and the Olympian's epic challenge to myths of Aryan superiority, the narrator explains that "Garfield would go on to win two gold medals in the Olympic Games in Germany, where factories for killing unwanted human beings were just being built."

I still wonder why Vonnegut deleted John Thompson's contributions to the invention of the Robo-Magic, an Olympian who would have brought Midland City even more fame than Mary-Alice Miller, and anthropological reflections on the category of race. Perhaps these sections were embedded in scattered, deeply personal reflections that would have made the novel too chaotic. Perhaps he feared the critiques were too didactic, or maybe he wanted to excise more traces of the *Goodbye, Blue Monday* drafts. Or maybe he hadn't yet made peace with the segregation, racist institutions, and social dynamics that affected "the breakfast of his life."

ART, RUDY'S WALTZ,
AND WILL FAIRCHILD'S GHOST

A more philosophical Montana Wildhack might have first contemplated the Vonnegutian sacred, eternal human "soul," but Rabo Karabekian deserves credit for his creator's rebirth and for placing the arts squarely at the "spiritual climax" of *Breakfast of Champions.* Karabekian's reflections on his painting "The Temptation of Saint Anthony" provide an antidote to the mechanization, pollution, injustices, and isolation that turn human beings into disposable "machines." The vertical orange band on the color field painting, Karabekian explains, captures St. Anthony's "unwavering band of light," "the immaterial core of every animal—the 'I am' to which all messages are sent." Our awareness, our "unwavering band of light," Karabekian further states, "is all that is alive and maybe sacred in any of us. Everything else about us is dead machinery."

Building on this idea, Vonnegut suggests that the process of creating art is a vital way to access this sacred part of us. As Kilgore Trout's promised Nobel Prize in Medicine and the hand-drawn, felt-tip illustrations demonstrate, art has the potential to heal and reimagine the legacies left by "sea pirates," the military-industrial complex, and America's car culture. These soul-growing and soul-saving artistic acts don't take place in Midland City's fancy new arts center or schools that disconnect literature from people's everyday lives. Instead, they happen in small, unexpected venues—from Kilgore Trout's stories to Bunny Hoover's piano music to Harry LeSabre's beautiful cross-dressing to Eddie Key's role as a modern-day griot for his six hundred relatives.

Weaving the arts more overtly into its character, plot, and structure, *Deadeye Dick* reaches similar conclusions about the potential healing powers of art. As Loree Rackstraw notes in her review of *Deadeye Dick*, the novel and the arts within it help us "to cut through the glaze of false hope that blinds us to the truth of our own self-destructive history," so that "we might be able to think and act more responsibly about the future of our planet."[290] Like embedded Kilgore Trout stories, Rudy's memoir challenges the cultural institutions and values that could create a neutron-bombed city and an asphalt parking lot covering its inhabitants. On a more pragmatic level, it also provides a path of personal redemption through everyday artistic acts. Rudy turns to scat-singing "to shoo the blues away," playwriting to nurture his creative spirit and confront painful memories, and cooking to feed body, soul, and connections to Mary Hoobler, the woman who helped raise him.

Despite his intentions to cut himself off from other people, to be a perfect neuter, the arts also help Rudy become Midland City's modern-day griot. Although his play *Katmandu* is a "catastrophe" with only three performances, it's the medium that sets him on the path of discovering the "magnificence" in John Fortune's death and the stories of Midland City's other ghosts. Rudy's narrative also captures moments of profound beauty, tragedy, and humaneness in Midland City. Through his "non-artistic" vision we see Otto's true "artistic masterpiece" (their house transformed by candles into "a great beehive filled with fireflies"), Emma's ironic transformation from a "zombie" into a "hick-town Voltaire," and Celia Hoover's tragic destruction by beauty, pills, and isolation.[291] Although there "is nobody left in Midland City anymore to know or care who Mildred Barry might have been," Rudy's narrative records her vaudeville past and British Empire bird-call imitations. And it collects the stories of Gino and Marco Maritimo, August Gunther, the Waltz and Wetzel clans, Fred T. Barry, Chief Morrissey, the Metzgers, Reverend Charles Herrell, and the many other former Midland City residents who either left or were buried there.

To reinforce this idea, Vonnegut has Hippolyte Paul De Mille, the voodoo-practicing Haitian headwaiter who accompanies Rudy and Felix to Midland City, raise a single, symbolic ghost from Calvary Cemetery. After being denied the opportunity to raise Celia's ghost, De Mille remarks, "we owed it to the past and the future to raise some sort of representative ghost which would haunt the city, no matter who lived there, for generations to come." Rudy chooses Will Fairchild, a "World War One ace in the Lafayette Escadrille" who died "while stunt flying at the Midland City County Fair."

The choice is significant because Will "was the last of the Fairchilds, a pioneering family after which so much in the city was named." From Fairchild Estates to the Fairchild Hotel to the Will Fairchild Memorial Airport, his surname evokes both larger stories of Midland City's urban renewal and the small tragedies of Dwayne's, Bunny's, and Celia's slow poisonings. Rudy, the tongue-in-cheek "William Shakespeare of Midland City," and Vonnegut infuse a small dose of hope and imagination into the symbolism of Will Fairchild's ghost. As creator of this fictional universe, Vonnegut transforms the Will Fairchild of *Breakfast of*

Champions, a war hero who murdered ten people and all the animals in the Keedsler Mansion before committing suicide, into a more honorable, less violent figure in *Deadeye Dick*. Rudy's creation of a legend—that Will Fairchild is roaming Midland City looking for his parachute—further demonstrates the transformative power of stories. With its layers of Midland City stories and ghosts, Rudy's narrative reveals that even in the face of powerful machines and military technologies, the arts and humanity will endure.[292]

PART THREE

HUMANITY AND TECHNOLOGY

CHAPTER 6

M-)7 HOUSES, EPICAC, AND WOLFGANG

The trouble with automation is that it often gives us what we don't need at the cost of what we do.
—NICHOLAS CARR, *The Glass Cage*

"The main business of humanity is to do a good job being human beings," said Paul, "not to serve as appendages to machines, institutions, and systems."
—KURT VONNEGUT, *Player Piano*

I think big business is a terrible thing for the spirit of the country, as our spirit is the best thing about us.
—KURT VONNEGUT, letter to Knox Burger,
   May 29, 1952

If you blinked, you might miss it. The publisher Charles Scribner's Sons' ad for *Player Piano*, Vonnegut's first novel, appeared on page 170 of the September 1952 issue of *Scientific American*. It was buried near the end of the issue, in the lower half of the right-hand column, after the slick full-page advertisements for Bendix, Raytheon, Dow Corning, Leeds & Northrup, Taylor Instruments, Honeywell, and

General Electric. In retrospect, the ad's small size and marginal placement seems fitting. As a novel that questions the ethics, social implications, and human costs of automation, *Player Piano* unabashedly went against the grain of techno-liberationist optimism that characterized the issue, which was entirely devoted to the new "inevitable" era of automation. "The central question" about automatic control, the editors explained, "is not whether it is good or bad, but how we may best use it." Automatic control, they promised, would "liberate" humans from "the routine tasks of mere survival," offering "more time for the creative enjoyment of life and for the exploration of the universe."[293]

The ad itself, however, cleverly blended in, promising potential readers "A novel about the coming Age of Electronics that is just around the corner." Like much of the issue, the ad's copy highlighted the technical aspects of *Player Piano*'s vision for the nation's future: "An America that runs itself completely . . . an electronic 'brain' that computes how many refrigerators, how many dinner plates, how many door knobs that the economy can absorb . . . mechanized saloons . . . trains that call their own stations." The text also telegraphed the novel's dystopian elements, placing the As in the title slightly askew and using scare quotes to highlight the potential dark underside of this "scientific 'paradise.'" Perhaps more importantly, it made a subtle appeal to the issue's target audience—engineers, researchers, and industry, military, and government leaders. Placing a male professional figure next to the title and author's name, the ad suggested that the novel's action hinged on the decisions of "one of the elite class of engineers" and his challenges to "the well-oiled machinery of progress."

While the *Scientific American* ad highlights *Player Piano*'s historic and technological contexts, the simple hand-drawn dust jacket design Vonnegut sent to Scribner's editor Harry Brague in May 1952 captures the book's true subject matter. Instead of presenting a suit-clad engineer beneath wires, tubes, and a central cog, Vonnegut's simple ink drawing depicts a small person holding hands with a towering mechanical

A novel about the coming Age of Electronics that is just around the corner

An America that runs itself completely . . . an electronic "brain" that computes how many refrigerators, how many dinner plates, how many door knobs the economy can absorb . . . mechanized saloons . . . trains that call their own stations. This exciting novel gives a preview of a scientific "paradise" we may see in our lifetime — and of what happens when one of the elite class of engineers throws a monkey wrench into the well-oiled machinery of progress.

PLAYER PIANO

by Kurt Vonnegut, Jr.

$3.00

At your bookseller

CHARLES SCRIBNER'S SONS

6.1 ✳ This Charles Scribner's Sons advertisement for *Player Piano,* which appeared in the September 1952 issue of *Scientific American* subtly emphasized the dystopian and technical elements of automation in the novel.

figure. The image of humanity dwarfed and led by a large machine encapsulates the futuristic world of *Player Piano*, where people have been rendered useless via the superior productivity, decision-making, and efficiency delivered by automation and centralized computer control. Vonnegut's anthropomorphic image of the machine system, while also in keeping with cybernetics concepts of the time, reminds us that *Player Piano* isn't a novel about technology; it's an examination of humanity and its complicated relationships *with* technology.[294] Despite its prescient depictions of driverless cars, ATMs, fully automated factories, and white-collar jobs outsourced to AI, *Player Piano* spends very little time describing the machines themselves. Although critical in shaping the fictional world of *Player Piano*, machines and automated systems are primarily foils for examining paradoxical human behaviors—our efforts to speed our own obsolescence, creative pursuits that can dull our imaginations, and the invention of digital technologies that connect and disconnect us from each other. More importantly, machines provide the impetus for the novel's central question, "What people are for?"—a query of little interest to editors of *Scientific American* in September 1952, but of enormous significance to Vonnegut's writings and planetary citizenship.

These explorations of humanity and technology might seem far afield from Vonnegut's later environmental critiques. *Player Piano* offers no visions of a planet frozen in ice-nine, paved with asphalt prairies, or poisoned by Barrytron's chemicals. Although also born of the military-industrial complex, the world of *Player Piano* is one of prosperity, peace, and plenty. It's one "cleared of unnatural terrors— mass starvation, mass imprisonment, mass torture, mass murder," where the earth has turned "into an altogether pleasant and convenient place in which to sweat out Judgment Day."[295] Viewed through the more contemporary lens of environmental sustainability, *Player Piano* and Vonnegut's short stories from that period offer incisive critiques of America's emerging postwar consumer culture. These early 1950s works presciently question the ways automation helped foster a culture that valued consumerism over citizenship, things over

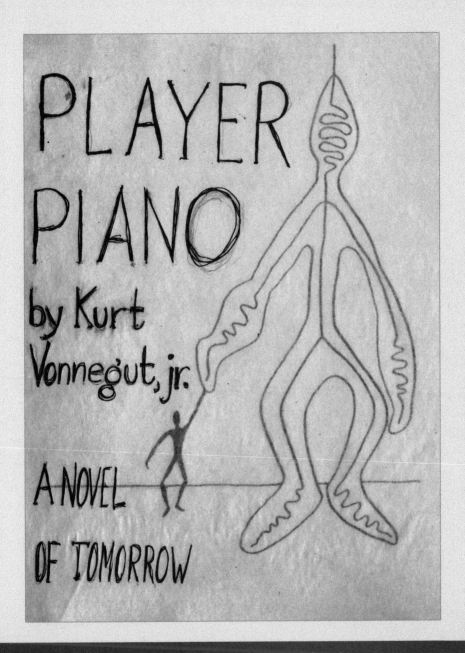

6.2 ✻ Vonnegut's proposed dust jacket design for *Player Piano* illustrates his fears about humanity being dwarfed and led by auto-mated systems. Archival image by Kurt Vonnegut, Charles Scrib-ner's Sons, Department of Rare Books and Special Collections, Princeton University Library. Copyright © Kurt Vonnegut LLC, used by permission of The Wylie Agency LLC.

people, and economic growthmanship at all costs. While concerns about the impacts of digital technologies and automation pervade Vonnegut's entire canon, his first and final novels explicitly capture his insightful, sometimes caustic, but always entertaining views on our increasingly automated, networked lives.

Although best appreciated in their specific technological and historical moments, *Player Piano*, selected early 1950s short stories, and *Timequake* still offer key ethical questions as we enter new frontiers driven by increasingly advanced algorithms, machine learning, automation, big data, robotic technologies, and smart networks. As we co-evolve with our machines, changing ourselves and the planet, at ever-accelerating rates, Vonnegut's prescient pleas to join "Team Human" just might be one of his greatest legacies.[296] Whether tackling the existential threats caused by climate change or automation, any type of planetary citizenship will need to value people, collective human wisdom, and new ways of thinking about what people are for.

AUTOMATION, GE, AND
A NEW AMERICAN TRINITY

The tale of Vonnegut's inspiration for *Player Piano* is a story familiar to many Vonnegut fans. In his 1973 *Playboy* interview with David Standish, Vonnegut recalled the time when he saw a computer-operated milling machine that replaced the "expensive" labor of a skilled machinist. Vonnegut explained that even during this 1949 moment, "the guys who were working on it were foreseeing all sorts of machines being run by little boxes and punched cards." "*Player Piano,*" Vonnegut continued, was his "response to the implications of having everything run by little boxes." He turned to science fiction because there "was no avoiding it, since the General Electric Company *was* science fiction." Wrapping up the novel's origin tale, Vonnegut added that he "cheerfully ripped off the plot of *Brave New World*, whose plot had been cheerfully ripped off from Eugene Zamiatin's [*sic*] *We.*"[297]

As Ginger Strand reveals in *The Brothers Vonnegut*, the GE origins and satirical references of *Player Piano* were far more complex than Vonnegut's comments suggested. From its allusions to "GE's first celebrity scientist: Charles Proteus Steinmetz," to the weekly "unabashedly pro-America and antilabor" workplace posters, to the skits, songbook, teams, and activities that shaped "Camp GE" at Association Island, Strand meticulously traces numerous other GE origins for key elements in the novel.[298] *Player Piano* was so deeply rooted in GE culture and technologies that Vonnegut took pains to make sure Scribner's distanced the novel from GE in its marketing.

In the November 1951 letter to Harry Brague that accompanied the finished draft of the novel with its revised "last third" and "new ending," Vonnegut was clear about protecting Bernard's career at GE.[299] "If you decide to publish it," he wrote, "I would like one thing understood: that this is not to be billed, by implication, as a satire on General Electric, and that my relationship with that industrial behemoth not be mentioned. G-E has a hostage, my brother, and I would hate to see his career jeopardized on account of our relationship."[300] While Vonnegut's insistence at dissociating *Player Piano* from GE stemmed from brotherly concern, his request to Brague also captures the widening scope of the novel's subject matter and critical commentary as he sought to tell a national story.

Vonnegut's intentions to investigate the broader social implications of automation appear in his early notes and the two-page "Outline for Science Fiction Novel" he sent to his agent Kenneth Littauer during the summer of 1950.[301] Vonnegut assured Littauer that the book "would be important science fiction, about machines taking over more and more human activities." "This trend," he explained, "will have a more profound effect on society and culture than peacetime uses of atomic energy." To support this claim, Vonnegut included a long block quote from Norbert Wiener's *Cybernetics* about the respective industrial revolutions (first and modern) devaluating human muscle and routine brain work, and cited the famous MIT mathematician's claim that "chess-play-ing robots can now be built."[302] Vonnegut also noted the Hoover Commission's efforts "to replace human mail sorters with machines" and recounted "'electronic brains,' infinitely superior to human brains in limited applications, such as plotting rocket trajectories" and other wartime applications. Vonnegut imagined a near-futur-istic setting, "no more than fifty years" from then because, he felt, "the revolution Wiener talks about is well underway now." The rest of the outline, in keeping with Vonnegut's earliest notes and drafts, focused on the automated system and hierarchies that shape the world of *Player Piano* along with descriptions of the complex and tormented protagonist whose conflicts would anchor the novel.

As notes and outlines gave shape to the novel, Vonnegut remained steadfast in using his hero, now named Paul Proteus, and his position as Manager of the Ilium Works to offer readers an insider's view of the system shaping the near-future America of *Player Piano*. However, it was Vonnegut's return to his anthropology studies that broadened the novel's focus to explore the spiritual, cultural, and national dimensions of these structures. Because he was still trying to finish his master's thesis when he first started at GE,[303] it wasn't too far a stretch from the initial plotline about tensions between Paul, his wife Anita, and his old friend Ed Finnerty, to create the characters Reverend James J. Lasher and the Shah of Bratpuhr. Lasher, a chaplain and unemployed anthropologist, gave Vonnegut a way to incorporate his research on Ghost Dance and revitalization movements and to critique the ways automation erodes human dignity and purpose. The chapters focusing on the Shah of Bratpuhr, added in the summer of 1951, meanwhile, broadened the novel's setting, offering the defamiliarizing and often comic perspective that only a foreigner could bring.[304]

Given Vonnegut's late addition of the Shah chapters, it's amazing they are so seamlessly integrated.[305] They work so well because Vonnegut sets up the shift from Paul's internal conflict and central narrative thread to the roving vignettes of the Shah's tour at the beginning of the novel. After noting Ilium's divided social structure, which places the machines and professional class of managers, engineers, and civil servants on the north side of the river and virtually everyone else on the south side, the first chapter describes the layout of Ilium Works. We meet the plant's tiny staff and original automated machine groups and learn of Paul's unease about his privileged role in the system. The first chapter ends with a description of the centralized control meter boxes, which contain buzzers to signal "a unit's complete breakdown." While this image foreshadows both the Ghost Shirt Society's attack on the Works and Paul's break with the system, it also creates a transition to the first of the Shah chapters, which survey and gradually expose the fault lines in America's key institutions. Collectively, the Shah sections transport readers all over the nation, highlighting cracks in the nation's military, industrial, political, educational, and artistic organizations.

The Shah sections also serve as a leitmotif, threading an outside curious, religious figure into the narrative to reinforce the questions about human spirituality, dignity, and worth raised by Lasher and the Ghost Shirt Rebellion. We learn at the start of chapter 2 that the Shah is the "spiritual leader of the 6,000,000 members of the Kolhouri sect, wizened and wise and dark as cocoa." Like the machines themselves, the Shah's Kolhouri faith, rites, and rituals are foils rather than foci for analysis. His faith provides a lens to challenge the spiritual dimensions of the new American system he has come to observe. Vonnegut maintains this dynamic by creating wide language and culture gaps between the Shah and the people and institutions he encounters, which must be bridged by US State Department host Ewing Halyard and the Shah's nephew and translator, Khashdrahr Miasma. These filter characters open up new subplots and provide comic relief during propagandistic presentations of the "wonders" of a largely machine-run America.

The first and perhaps most famous of these "mistranslations" occurs as the Shah's limousine stops near a "large work crew filling a small chuckhole" while an old Plymouth (driven by Paul Proteus) crosses the bridge separating the north-side elite from those living in the Homestead. The Shah inquires about the Reconstruction and Reclamation Corps (Reeks and Wrecks) workers, calling them *"Takaru,"* or slaves, and noting their prominence "all the way up [the state] from New York City." Halyard "patronizingly" laughs off the Shah's mistake and explains that the men are "citizens, employed by the government [with] free speech, freedom of worship, the right to vote." Halyard continues, "Before the war, they worked in the Ilium Works controlling the machines, but now machines control themselves much better."

With the Shah, the reader learns that anyone "who cannot support himself by doing a job better than a machine is employed by the government either in the Army" or in Reeks and Wrecks, and that taxes on the machines and personal incomes get funneled "back into the system for more products for better living." The Shah's suggestion that the government-run employment and economic system sounds like "Communism" is "vehemently" dismissed by Halyard, who explains that the "industry is privately owned and managed," though run by efficient, error-free machines that have "raised the standard of living of the average man immensely."

Despite this improved standard of living and guaranteed employment, the Reeks and Wrecks men are not contented citizens. Assigning forty men to fill a chuckhole two feet in diameter not only leads to distractions like the men tossing rocks at a squirrel a hundred feet above them, but it spurs resentment, prompting one of the workers to spit in Halyard's face. This anger is later contrasted with the immense satisfaction and pride the men feel when they fix the fuel pump in Paul's Plymouth, with the lead mechanic remarking, "First money I've earned in five years. I oughta frame that one, eh?" What Vonnegut captures here and throughout *Player Piano* is the idea that *work* rather than leisure is more satisfying. As technology author Nicholas Carr observes, this notion has been substantiated in studies on the "the paradox of work." Although people generally say that they prefer leisure time to work, Carr explains, "People were happier, felt more fulfilled by what they were doing, while they were at work than during their leisure hours." Elaborating on the findings, Carr writes:

> We're happiest when we're absorbed in a difficult task, a task that has clear goals and challenges us not only to exercise our talents but to stretch them. We become so immersed in the flow of our work ... that we tune out distractions and transcend the anxieties and worries that plague our everyday lives.[306]

Player Piano presciently predicts the sobering psychological, practical, and other human costs of twenty-first-century computer automation Carr examines in *The Glass Cage* by uncovering the deep human need to feel useful via labor. From the numerous exchanges in the Homestead saloon to Private First Class Elmo Hackett's desire to achieve "a little glory" overseas to Wanda Hagstrohm's efforts to hand-wash clothes because it "gives [her] something to do," the novel repeatedly chronicles the disquietude born of uselessness. Lest readers miss this crucial point, Vonnegut employs Paul as a mouthpiece, as he explains to his wife Anita that the system stripped Homesteaders of "what was the most important thing on earth to them—the feeling of being needed and useful, the foundation of self-respect." The idea that human happiness depends on engaging in "enterprises that make them feel useful," becomes a central tenet of the Ghost Shirt Society's manifesto.

The Shah's position as a spiritual leader also reinforces Vonnegut's critiques of how spirituality has been transferred from human-centered enterprises to a new "national holy trinity, Efficiency, Economy, and Quality." Nowhere is this contrast more apparent than in the meeting between the Shah and EPICAC XIV, the newest addition to the network of super computers that take up thirty-one subterranean chambers in Carlsbad Caverns for the important work of running the country.

The visit or "pilgrimage" is a familiar one for Halyard, who is used to bringing "foreign potentates" to the fourteen linked EPICAC computers, because "their people represented untapped markets for America's stupendous industrial output." This pilgrimage takes on added diplomatic weight because the US president, Jonathan Lynn, is there to dedicate EPICAC XIV "to a happier, more efficient tomorrow." Like most of his fellow citizens, President Lynn has little real work to do; he's an actor turned politician whose main responsibility is to "read whatever was handed to him on state occasions" and "to be suitably awed and reverent" in his performances. "EPICAC XIV and the National Industrial, Commercial, Communications, Foodstuffs, and Resources Board," Halyard makes clear, "did all the planning, did all the heavy thinking."

To reinforce the emptiness of Lynn and America's democracy, the Shah initially mistakes the president as "the spiritual leader of the American people" until Halyard corrects him. After learning from Lynn's remarks that EPICAC XIV was "the greatest individual in history," equivalent to "the wisest man that had ever lived," the Shah decides to address EPICAC instead. The spiritual Kolhouri leader drops to his knees and begins "to fill the entire cavern with his mysterious, radiant dignity . . . communing with a presence no one else could sense." The Shah's behavior is met with bewilderment, with President Lynn remarking, "The crazy bastard's talking to the machine." Through Khashdrahr's translation, we learn that the Shah asked EPICAC a poetic riddle but received no response. Khashdrahr further explains:

> "Our people believe," he said shyly, "that a great, all-wise god will come among us one day, and we shall know him, for he will be able to answer the riddle, which EPICAC could not answer. When he comes," said Khashdrahr simply, "there will be no more suffering on earth."

As the Shah exits the chambers housing EPICAC's gigantic "brain" and "nervous system," he curls "his lips at the array of electronics about them" and utters the word "*Baku!*," which Khashdrahr translates as "false god."

The Shah's rejection of EPICAC as a false god reinforces Lasher's earlier railings against a system that exorcised "the life of their spirit" and taught people instead "to worship competition and the market, productivity and economic usefulness." The subsequent displacement of people from industry, according to Lasher, stripped the average workers of their spirituality and purpose while giving the managers, engineers, and larger American system more divine status. Developing fully automated systems became a "holy war," Lasher explained, and the managers and engineers began to "believe with all their hearts the glorious things" advertisers said about them: "Yesterday's snow job becomes today's sermon."

The Shah's dismissal of EPICAC also provides a sharp critical lens for later events in the novel, such as the rituals, songs, chants, "sermons," and Meadows's keynote play designed to encourage blind faith in the national system. Calling the supercomputer a false god heightens the profundity of the Shah's later rhetorical question, "would you please ask EPICAC what people are for?" This question, which Vonnegut rescued from Scribner's editor Harry Brague's cuts, is the central paradox and critical core of the book.[307] As a machine "wholly free of reason-muddying emotions," EPICAC can never truly understand or experience what it is to be human. EPICAC has already "solved" the problem of humanity by simply assigning people to the role of consumers for the ever-expanding system of automation. Only human beings can contemplate the question, and it's the novel's readers who need to address the ethical, philosophical, and social justice issues tied to automation and machine learning.

Asking difficult questions rather than simply championing humans over machines was what Vonnegut had intended from the start. As he corresponded with Harry Brague about final edits, Vonnegut explained why he rejected his agent's suggestion that the novel "will sell better with a happy ending." Not only was Ken Littauer "wrong," but a different ending would mar his vision for the book: "I intended from the first to have the thing end pessimistically, and thought that I might be able to point out a sober problem without depressing anyone by treating the whole business lightly."[308]

Given his scientific training, research in cybernetics, and experiences at GE, Vonnegut recognized that the four Ghost Shirt Society leaders' vision of "how well and happily men could live with virtually no machines" could only be a foolish Utopian dream. Although the Ghost Shirt rebels successfully take over the Ilium Works, they fail to achieve their national objectives and lose sight of their mission. Instead of strategically destroying specific automated systems, the rioters attack virtually all of Ilium's machines. With signature Vonnegutian irony, shortly after hatching their plan for a localized pre-industrial "Renaissance" fueled by "the human mind and hand," the four Ghost Shirt leaders find a group of people repairing an Orange-O machine and inventing ways to fix the very machines they had destroyed the previous night. Paul notices the Reeks and Wrecks man who had repaired his car, noting that he was "proud and smiling because his hands were busy doing what they liked to do best . . . replacing men like himself with machines."

That situational irony and Finnerty's post-riot lament that the "earth would be an engineer's paradise" if only "it weren't for . . . the goddamned people" also speak to broader questions about humanity's complex relationships with technology. The riot's denouement illustrates key tenets about humanity in the Ghost Shirt Society manifesto. The whole enterprise is one of "brilliance followed by stupidity," rooted in the "imperfection," "frailty," and "inefficiency" of its human agents. Finnerty's and the rioters' relapsing dreams of mechanization and automation are no more ironic than the Ghost Shirt Society's own failure to recognize Paul's individuality or to ask for his unique human signature on the manifesto attributed to him.

In the wreckage of Ilium Works, Paul and Finnerty relearn another important truth that Vonnegut captured in his own hand-drawn dust jacket: machines are human creations. Sitting outside Building 58, the plant's original machine shop, Paul and Finnerty wistfully recall their early Ilium days when they recorded Rudy Hertz's movements to control fifty lathe machines. They sit with "melancholy rapport . . . amid the smashed masterpieces, the brilliantly designed and beautifully made machines." They realize that "a good part of their lives and skills had gone into making them," and they helped destroy those machines in mere hours. Their insights, and the novel's ending as a whole, are perhaps best summed up by Nicholas Carr's reflections on humanity and technology, penned some six decades later:

> Technology isn't what makes us "posthuman" or "trans human" . . . It's what makes us human. Technology is in our nature. Through our tools we give our dreams form. We bring them into the world. The practicality of technology may distinguish it from art, but both spring from a similar, distinctly human yearning.[309]

Vonnegut captures this intersection between art, technology, and creativity not only through the novel's title and Finnerty's improvisations "on the brassy, dissonant antique," but also through a broader musical motif woven throughout *Player Piano*. From Paul's mental composition of the *Building 58 Suite* based on the movements of the lathe group, to Alfy's entrepreneurial game of identifying songs played on soundless TV screens, to Meadows's songs designed to build team morale and belief in the American system, human arts collide with machines time and again. Vonnegut even foregrounds the distinctly human creative process of inventing machines in the passages recalling a barber who literally dreams the prototype for barber machines from nightmares about his own obsolescence.

Like his Ghost Shirt Society leaders, Vonnegut did not see automation itself or replacement as "necessarily bad." However, systems constructed without regard for human "pride, dignity, self-respect, [and] work worth doing" might come at too high a cost. A new "national holy trinity" of "Efficiency, Economy, and Quality," Vonnegut felt, had to be questioned if both the individual's and the nation's spirit were to survive. Perhaps Vonnegut came closest to answering the Shah's question about what people are for in Paul's testimony at his trial for sabotage: "The main business of humanity is to do a good job of being human beings . . . not to serve as appendages to machines, institutions, and systems." And in its more overt moments of planetary citizenship, *Player Piano* demonstrates that human fulfillment and purpose will not come from serving the postwar system of consumerism.

"MORE PRODUCTS FOR BETTER LIVING"

The world of *Player Piano* might lack the outrageousness of Vance Packard's futuristic "Cornucopia City," with its disposable papier-mâché buildings, wall-size TVs, and plastic cars, but Vonnegut did prophetically capture the ramped-up postwar and early-1950s consumerism that inspired Packard's landmark 1960 book *The Waste Makers*. As the Shah learned on his pilgrimage to Carlsbad Caverns, the only way to keep America's increasingly efficient automated factories running was to expand the consumption of these goods. Although it had not yet been dedicated, when the Shah encounters EPICAC XIV, it "was already at work" making these important decisions:

> How many refrigerators, how many lamps, how many turbine-generators, how many hub caps, how many dinner plates, how many door knobs, how many rubber heels, how many television sets, how many pinochle decks—how many everything America and her customers could have and how much they would cost. And it was EPICAC XIV who would decide for the coming years how many engineers and managers and research men and civil servants, and of what skills, would be needed in order to deliver the goods.[310]

As he imagined EPICAC XIV, Vonnegut didn't have to make dramatic speculative leaps from the University of Pennsylvania's

ENIAC computer or GE's own OMBIAC to systems that har-
nessed wartime computing technologies for production of industrial
consumer goods. As a May 1950 Arma Corporation ad for "Brain
Blocks" illustrates, companies were already promising electrical
components that would fulfill the "dream of automatic factories and
all that they will contribute toward better living with more things
for more people."[311] Instead of extolling these systems, Vonnegut
used the Shah's interactions with EPICAC to challenge this postwar
consumerist culture, which ultimately led the average American
citizen to purchase twice as many goods by the late 1950s as they
did just before World War II.[312]

Vonnegut also presciently anticipated the consumerist philosophy
most famously stated by marketing consultant Victor Lebow in
The Journal of Retailing during the mid-1950s:

> Our enormously productive economy ... demands that
> we make consumption our way of life, that we convert
> the buying and use of goods into rituals, that we seek our
> spiritual satisfactions, our ego satisfactions in consump-
> tion. ... We need things consumed, burned up, worn out,
> replaced, and discarded at an ever-increasing rate.[313]

While *Player Piano* focuses more on the disposability of people,
not products, it captures the infancy of a system based on rampant
consumerism, planned obsolescence, disposability, and deliberate
wastefulness, which continues to wreak environmental havoc
today. This system of epic consumption has made Americans the
largest trash producers in the world; on average, people in the
United States throw away "about 7.1 pounds per person per day"
or approximately 102 tons over the course of a lifetime.[314]

Years before Lebow's famous words, Vonnegut identified the rituals and spiritual dimensions attributed to this consumerism in the
Meadows chapters of *Player Piano*, which are remarkably close to the
actual songs, skits, and activities of "Camp GE" on Association Island.

While satirizing GE's specific morale-building and corporate-loyalty-inducing rituals, Vonnegut lambastes the broader national efforts to build a "holy trinity" of consumption-driven "Efficiency, Economy, and Quality." These critiques are evident in the keynote play, which portrays "John Averageman," the "consumer," as the "big winner" of the entire system while lionizing the noble service of engineers who keep those cheap goods flowing. Infusing patriotism into play, the keynote event closes with the sounds of rocket fire and "Stars and Stripes Forever."

Its climax is the celebratory evidence that "Civilization has reached the dizziest heights of all time!" As the music swells and then crescendos, the young engineer reports on the system's latest accomplishments:

> Thirty-one point seven times as many television sets as all the rest of the world put together! . . . Ninety-three per cent of all the world's electrostatic dust precipitators! Seventy-seven per cent of all the world's automobiles! Ninety-eight per cent of its helicopters! Eighty-one point nine per cent of its refrigerators! . . . Seventy-one point three per cent of the world's generating capacity! Eighty-five per cent of its industrial control vacuum tubes!

While the high percentages and exclamation points exude hyperbole, Vonnegut accurately captured the postwar messages that fused national identity to escalating material production and consumption.

Vonnegut undercut these glorifications of manufacturing and consumerism via the Shah's visit to a typical American home, an M-17 house in Proteus Park, Chicago. Those scenes reveal that Edgar R. B. Hagstrohm and his statistically average family are *not* enjoying better living through their material comforts. The Hagstrohms are materially flush but spiritually empty, in part because Edgar's extramarital affair has started to unravel the lies holding family life together. Those tensions only enhance the chapter's more incisive critiques of the lives

Drudgery is Disappearing

...first from washing the clothes
...Now From Doing the Dishes

Automatic washing machines did away with wash-day drudgery ... and now automatic dish washers are doing the same for the drudgery of the dish pan. The "brain" of most of these labor-saving machines of both types is the Mallory interval timer switch ... controlling the entire cycle of spraying, washing, rinsing and drying. It does much of the thinking as well as the work for the modern housewife.

The Mallory interval timer switch has become standard equipment for almost every manufacturer of automatic washers. It has earned Mallory an important place in this industry ... just as precision quality and creative engineering have gained respect for Mallory in many other fields where pioneering in electronics, electro-chemistry and metallurgy is vital.

Mallory components are contributing to a richer and more enjoyable life in a host of modern products ... where Mallory experience has helped manufacturers to solve the "unsolvable". If you have a design or production problem that falls within the scope of Mallory's activities, it will pay you to call on Mallory now!

P.R. MALLORY & CO. Inc.
MALLORY

SERVING INDUSTRY with Capacitors • Contacts • Controls • Rectifiers • Switches • Vibrators • Power Supplies • Resistance Welding Materials • Special Non-Ferrous Alloys • Mallory Dry Batteries, The Original Mercury Batteries

P. R. MALLORY & CO., Inc., INDIANAPOLIS 6, INDIANA

6.3 * The 1950 P. R. Mallory & Company advertisement, "Drudgery is Disappearing," captures the promises of technological liberation and automation Vonnegut critiqued in *Player Piano* and his early short stories. By permission of Stanley Black & Decker.

shaped by their fully automated electronic home. Modeled after the real suburban neighborhoods like Levittown that sprang up after World War II, Proteus Park is a "postwar development of three thousand dream houses for three thousand families with presumably identical dreams." Like the other prefabricated M-17 houses, the Hagstrohm home has two bedrooms, an enameled steel-walled "living room with dining alcove, bath and kitchen," with radiant heating. "The house, the furniture, and the lot are sold as a package," Proteus Park Manager Ned Dodge explains to the Shah, and the appliances cook, clean, and wash everything in either seconds or minutes.[315]

After learning of the incredible speed of "the ultrasonic dish-washer and clothes-washer" and other appliances, the Shah, in his typically pointed fashion, inquires why homemaker Wanda Hagstrohm "has to do everything so quickly—this in a matter of seconds, that in a matter of seconds." "What is it she is in such a hurry to get at?" the Shah wonders: "What is it she has to do, that she mustn't waste any time on these things?" In the setup for the chapter's final punch line, Dodge replies, "Live! Get a little fun out of life." As the reader learns, this "living" mostly takes the form of watching television, and the moment of "living" the Shah cheers from outside the picture window is one seething with tension when Edgar Jr. is forced to maintain the lie of his father's affair. To pay for the "M-17 castle" and the planned furniture, appliance, and other replacements, most of Edgar's paychecks go directly to payments on the package. In effect, the Hagstrohms are *takaru* to their home and consumer goods, just as the Shah aptly names them.

The Shah's visit to the Hagstrohms' home expands Vonnegut's examinations of human obsolescence while also satirizing adver-tising techniques GE and other manufacturers were using to boost appliance sales. Vonnegut, who regularly perused a wide range of popular magazines both for work and for his writing career, parodied the ways speed and efficiency spilled over from produc-tion lines to "liberate" housewives in many advertisements. The Indianapolis-based company P. R. Mallory, for instance, promised in a May 1950 *Fortune* ad that "Drudgery is Disappearing . . . first from washing the clothes. . . . Now from Doing the Dishes."

Strikingly similar to the washer in *Goodbye, Blue Monday* drafts, the Mallory "brain" of the washer even promised to do "much of the thinking as well as the work for the modern housewife." Although labor historian Ruth Schwartz Cowan has shown that these inventions and products actually created "more work for mother," advertisements in *Good Housekeeping, Life, Collier's, Family Circle, Ladies Home Journal,* and other periodicals promised them speedy "quick-quick" meals with Minute Rice, a forty-percent time savings with Universal "Stroke-sav-r" irons, and "instant" mixes for fast-rising cakes, breads, and other baked goods.[316] Like the washer in the Mallory ad and the Hagstrohm home, newly designed, ever more efficient appliances were sold as the best way to give housewives more time to "live!"[317]

Vonnegut didn't have to wait very long until his futuristic M-17 house became the hope and speculation for homebuilders. By the mid-1950s, Packard notes, a holy alliance between Detroit-inspired marketing, construction, and manufacturing enabled homebuilders to start "talking excitedly about the House of Tomorrow, which will come in sections, and all or part of the house can be traded in for a new model. The kitchen of tomorrow is to be bought as a unit, with annual model changes available for the discontented." Appliance companies, Packard explained, began to develop "prefabricated walls and even rooms with their appliances built in," designed to be upgraded, so consumers could "trade in a room just as they now trade in their car on a new model."[318]

Vonnegut's growing concern that the automated, electronic houses of tomorrow would be materially rich but spiritually poor led him to expand his ideas about M-17 houses into a separate short story, "The Package," which appeared in the July 26, 1952, issue of *Collier's*. Instead of bringing in a foreign dignitary to survey an average American home, "The Package" used the occasion of a retired couple's "rambling, many-leveled 'machine for living,'" built during their around-the-world vacation, to explore the "packaged good life" that was being sold as the postwar American dream. Vonnegut also expanded his critiques of postwar domestic consumerism in "More Stately Mansions," this time satirizing the keeping-up-with-the-Joneses phenomenon. Drafted quickly in May 1951, the "short short" appeared in the December 22, 1951, issue of *Collier's*, while Vonnegut was in the late editing stage of *Player Piano*. The story's somewhat ironic title "More Stately Mansions" refers not to the homes of the McClellans or the one owned by the narrator and his wife Anne, but to the dream houses featured in the magazines Grace McClellan reads obsessively—*Better House and Garden, Good Homelife, Home Beautiful*.

Grace's preoccupation with these home lifestyle magazines is apparent from the moment she enters the narrator's house and imagines repaneling their living room, changing the color of their couch, adding new curtains, upgrading the carpet, and making countless other furniture and design changes. Vonnegut, who encountered voluminous decorating wisdom during his study of women's magazines, quickly reveals that there is something "off" about Grace. Not only are her suggestions outrageous, but she seemingly has trouble separating the decorating fantasies of the magazines from the realities of the rooms she's in. First with her interactions with a "phantom cobbler's bench" in the narrator's home and then with the entire contents of her own house, we see that Grace McClellan is so devoted to her bulging cabinet drawers full of home decorating ideas that she can no longer see the material realities in front of her.

This key insight becomes apparent when her husband, the narrator, and neighbor Anne remodel the dusty, poorly furnished house during Grace's two-month hospital stay for a virus. With Anne's tireless work, the house is transformed with funds from an inheritance into the near-perfect replication of Grace's imagined dream house, pieced together from countless samples, decorating articles, and glossy advertisements. The story ends with Anne and the reader uncomfortably realizing that Grace has already been living in her imagined dream house all along. Her real illness is not the virus but the unhealthy delusions that come from crafting an existence based on lifestyle magazines.

In addition to questioning consumerism and raising broad questions about automation, Vonnegut's early works often explored technology's more intimate impacts on human relationships. Whether we look to Anita and Paul's marriage in *Player Piano* or the 1954 short story "Custom-Made Bride," Vonnegut warned of the sterility and mechanization of human relationships that might come from turning women into appendages of fashionably designed home interiors. The stories "Jenny" (ca. 1949) and "EPICAC," meanwhile, revised the classic Pygmalion and *Cyrano de Bergerac* tales to investigate human-machine romances and the possibility of computers performing profoundly "human" tasks like writing poetry.

When Vonnegut published "EPICAC" in November 1950 and *Player Piano* less than two years later, he probably didn't imagine that we'd have whole research teams teaching computers to write poetry and a website designed to put algorithm-generated poems to the Turing test.[319] By the time he published his final novel and contemplated the technological and cultural forces that ushered in his own obsolescence as a short story writer, it's clear that Vonnegut was ready, indeed eager, to address the "Third Industrial Revolution" Paul Proteus and Katherine Finch contemplated at the beginning of *Player Piano*—computers devaluing "the real brainwork" of complex, creative, highly skilled thinking.

NIM-NIM'S TWEEZERS, MORPHY, AND UNCLE ALEX'S LIBRARY

Strangely enough, Vonnegut prophetically imagined but chose not to develop speculations about computers usurping creative arts, such as painting and music, in his early notes for *Player Piano*. As he tried to flesh out Paul's character, Vonnegut conceived that his protagonist "first made his reputation by making a painting machine neurotic, and having it turn out non-objective art."[320] The not-yet-named protagonist invented "a machine for composing music" while still a child. "In twenty minutes," the engineering prodigy's machine "had composed more symphonies than had been written since Haydn introduced the form." Vonnegut discarded this idea and chose instead in *Player Piano* to critique an industrial system that cheapened culture by churning out millions of inexpensive painting reproductions and books tailored entirely to "surveys of public reading tastes, readability and appeal tests." Vonnegut's initial speculations about musical composition programs were more prophetic than worries about a society where "culture's so cheap" people could insulate their houses with art prints and books.

With *Timequake*'s release in September 1997, Vonnegut fretted about people reading print books at all and saw the novel as the final chapter of his writing career (and by extension his planetary citizenship).[321] He ended his pre-release phone interview with Nelson Taylor of *Black Book Magazine* not with a final plug for *Timequake*, but with an endorsement of Thorstein Veblen: "Tell your readers to go to the library and read the books that nobody checks out anymore. Tell them to get Thorstein Veblen's *Theory of the Leisure Class*. It'll knock their hats off!"[322] A few weeks later, in an NPR interview with Robert Siegel, Vonnegut elaborated on his fears about the potential obsolescence of printed books and the lack of human interaction that would accompany the spread of digital technologies. Responding to Siegel's observation about the degenerative effects of television in *Timequake*, Vonnegut voiced much larger concerns about our increasingly networked lives:

> What concerns me, or what interests me, is what's going to happen, what these new technologies are doing to the human nervous systems. I know there's a theory that the Roman Empire failed because the plumbing was made out of lead, and lead poisoning made everybody very stupid.
>
> And I think TV may be doing that. But the new technology is Microsoft, and all that is in fact cheating people out of

the experience of being human, which is talking to each other, touching each other, smelling each other.[323]

Vonnegut undercut some of the seriousness of these comments by suggesting that body odor would make a big comeback as people yearned for genuine human presence. However, the concerns about the impacts of computer technologies on the arts, humanities, and humanity itself that he offered in *Timequake* were heartfelt—and perhaps as prophetic as the ones he had raised forty-five years earlier in *Player Piano*.

As Vonnegut scholars have noted, the "stew" that became *Timequake*—the "fillet" remnants of earlier drafts, coupled with personal reflections from 1996 as he revised the manuscript—is innovative in technique and themes. The "autobiography of a novel" thoroughly blurs the lines between fact and fiction, art and life, past and future, and explores profound subjects from Nietzsche's ideas about eternal recurrence to Newton's and Einstein's views of time to "the special place of Earthlings in the cosmic scheme of things."[324]

Timequake is about the creative joys, imagination, healing potential, and community-making possibilities of writing and reading— and what we might lose as we shift from print culture to a world of tiny screens and faster, more automated digital networks. Fittingly, Vonnegut uses his relationship with alter ego Kilgore Trout to explore these ideas and to provide *Timequake*'s narrative framework. Instead of placing himself on par with the "creator of the universe" as he does at the end of *Breakfast of Champions*, Vonnegut interacts with Trout as a colleague, allowing him to take center stage by the novel's end. Vonnegut even channeled Trout's signature literary techniques as he revised the novel; drafts expose a process of condensing key plot devices, characters, locales, and events from more complex, rounded entities to Troutesque caricatures to develop the novel's central questions and insights.[325]

These earlier drafts and a late October 1993 interview with Peter Reed and Marc Leeds reveal that *Timequake* had two constant elements in its manuscript wanderings from 1988 to 1997: its premise and the layered parable of Trout's story "The Sisters B-36."[326] The premise, as Vonnegut explains in the prologue of *Timequake*, is "that a timequake, a sudden glitch in the time-space continuum, made everybody and everything do exactly what they'd done during a past decade, for good or ill, a second time."[327] The decade of déjà vu transports all entities in the universe from February 13, 2001, back to February 17, 1991, and then they have "to get back to 2001 the hard way" repeating every action, decision, and event with knowledge of the future but not free will.[328] It's only when the timequake ends that everything in the universe can start creating "original material" again.

For Vonnegut, the interesting "what if" is not the science fiction concept of a timequake, but what happens when the "rerun" is over and, in the words of Kilgore Trout, people can "stop running obstacle courses of their own construction." While the timequake provides the premise of the book, its emotional and critical center is Trout's story "The Sisters B-36," a parable of how imagination and the arts become obsolete after television is invented on the planet Booboo. In Trout's tale, Nim-Nim, the "bad sister," invents television and a host of other "satanic devices, which made imaginations redundant" because she's envious of her widely admired artistic sisters.

Once a peaceful, matriarchal planet with a written language similar to English, Booboo changes after its inhabitants embrace TV, entertainment technologies, and Nim-Nim's other inventions: "automobiles and computers and barbed wire and flamethrowers and land mines and machine guns and so on." "Without imaginations" and the ability to "read interesting, heartwarming stories in the faces of one another," the Booboolings become "among the most merciless creatures in the local family of galaxies."[329] As in other Trout parables, the Booboolings' planetary destructions are linked to a loss of culture, human connection, and the arts.

While Vonnegut tweaked small details of Trout's story in various drafts, Vonnegut consistently had Trout deposit "The Sisters B-36" in the garbage can outside of the vandalized, largely forgotten entrance to the American Academy of Arts and Letters. In the novel, the disposal, retrieval, and discussion of Trout's story in the Academy on Christmas Eve is spread out over multiple chapters, forcing the reader to revisit the episode many times and in different contexts. Although security guard Dudley Prince, a "figure of authority and decency," is the only character that takes the story's message seriously, Vonnegut nests "The Sisters B-36" in a series of conversations and descriptions that force the reader to ponder the larger social implications of a new digital age.

To set the stage for the story's reception inside the Academy, Vonnegut mentions the building was designed by the architectural firm McKim, Mead and White in 1923, the same year "the American inventor Lee De Forest demonstrated an apparatus that made possible the addition of sound to motion pictures." What Vonnegut doesn't mention but surely knew from his work at GE, is that De Forest's invention, the Audion, an electronic audio amplifier, helped usher in "the age of electronics" and became "the workhorse of our information age."[330] The details about the building's architects and De Forest's invention frame the conversation between Monica Pepper, the Academy's executive secretary, and her husband Zoltan just prior to receiving Trout's story. Zoltan, a musical composer, informs Monica of a new technological threat to his profession. Simultaneously laughing and crying, he mentions that the "tone-deaf kid next door" has used Wolfgang, a new computer program, to compose and orchestrate "an acceptable, if derivative quartet in the manner of Beethoven." To add insult to injury, "the father of the obnoxious kid show[ed] Zoltan the sheet music his son's printer had spit out that morning and ask[ed] him if it was any good or not."

Vonnegut deepens the tragedy by mentioning that Zoltan's "older brother Frank, an architect, had committed suicide after a nearly identical blow to his self-respect only a month earlier." In Frank's case, he's bested by a computer program called Palladio that instantly produces detailed schematics, cost estimates, and "alternative plans in the manner of Michael Graves or I. M. Pei" for "the craziest assignment he could think of." Vonnegut concludes the chapter with Zoltan's insight: "'It used to be said of a man who had suffered a catastrophic setback in his line of work that he had been handed his head on a platter. We are being handed our heads with *tweezers* now.' He was speaking, of course, of microchips."

When Vonnegut imagined painting and music composition machines in early notes for *Player Piano*, computer programs like the fictional "Wolfgang" and "Palladio" were pure science fiction. By *Timequake*'s publication in 1997, computer-aided design (CAD) programs had become commonplace, although still far from ushering in the creative human obsolescence Vonnegut imagines. Still, CAD software was changing the creative process. "After CAD programs were adapted to run on personal computers in the 1980s," Nicholas Carr observes, they "quickly became essential tools for architects, not to mention product designers, graphic artists, and civil engineers."[331]

For Vonnegut, who took great pride in his family's architectural contributions to Indianapolis and made his own architectural sketches on manuscript drafts, real-life CAD programs like Sketchpad must have seemed an affront worthy of Frank's fictional suicide. Despite taking jabs at the stodginess and exclusivity of the Academy, Vonnegut pays homage to the elegant, formal, history-rich spaces in many drafts of the novel, never failing to remind readers of the human skill behind the architecture. Vonnegut anticipated that a lot more than Frank Pepper's life and dignity would be sacrificed in the age of Palladio and other CAD programs.

Earlier drafts reveal how important the obsolescence of creative and imaginative human skills via computer technologies were to Vonnegut. In an April 1996 draft, Vonnegut linked Trout's disposal of "The Sisters B-36" explicitly to another, more prescient parable about the consequences of artificial intelligence.[332] Detailing how Trout "published" his stories by naming garbage cans after various presses and magazines such as Random House, Simon and Schuster, and the *Saturday Evening Post*, the narrator explains that before Trout became a vagabond he "used to typewrite his stories neatly, and mail them off to real publishers along with stamped self-addressed envelopes, and how he used to actually sell about one in 20."

The peak of that career, we learn, was when Trout sold a story called "Morphy" in 1949, "which was about a computer by that name which had begun as an electronic chess player, and which had ended up taking charge of everything." The narrator mentions that "the apparatus was named in honor of the nineteenth-century American chess genius Paul Morphy," who became an unofficial world champion and has been ranked by Bobby Fischer as one of the ten greatest chess players of all time. Perhaps reflecting on his own period-specific characterizations of EPICAC in Carlsbad Caverns, Vonnegut concludes the discussion of "Morphy" this way:

> Trout wrote the story when the synapses in computers were vacuum tubes, so his imaginary Morphy was ten stories high and covered ten city blocks, and had its own atomic power plant. After the development of transistors and microchips, of course, a similarly capable brain might have been carried around in a shoebox, and powered by a couple of teensy-weensy batteries designed for hearing aids.

Whether inspired by his decades-long chess-playing with his son Mark or, more likely, his own chess robot, Boris, the story "Morphy" tapped into Vonnegut's personal encounters with artificial intelligence.[333] Vonnegut likely cut "Morphy" because Monica and Zoltan's conversation about CAD programs and microchips addressed the social implications of machine learning more broadly. Or perhaps Gary Kasparov's victory over IBM's Deep Blue on February 17, 1996, indicated that humans were still capable of besting computers in matches of intellect, strategy, and creative adaptation.

By the time *Timequake* was in press, the tables had turned. On May 11, 1997, a significantly updated Deep Blue beat Kasparov in the decisive game six of their rematch. According to Jeremy Howard, a distinguished data scientist, Deep Blue's victory marked the start of a new era of machine learning.[334] From its folder of "dead" matter at the Lilly Library, "Morphy" still serves as a prescient precursor for Howard's question, "Will Artificial Intelligence Be the Last Human Invention?" With Howard's 2017 estimate that 80 percent of jobs in the developed world are based on tasks computers have already learned how to do, Trout's concerns about a new era ushered in by computer chess masters aren't so easily dismissed. While artificial intelligence and other digital technologies will be vital in tackling the epic challenges of climate change, Vonnegut's concerns as a planetary citizen remind us that we will need meaningful work, purpose, shared human connections, and creativity if we want a future worth having.

Whether fillet or chum, the Christmas Eve events in *Timequake* return to and update *Player Piano*'s initial explorations of machines devaluing human thinking and creativity, and highlight the persistence of these ideas within Vonnegut's planetary citizenship. The premise of *Timequake* itself is a metaphor for large-scale cultural automation. As Vonnegut selected key ideas from earlier drafts, he increasingly emphasized the metaphorical, automation-related dimensions of the timequake over questions about individual emotional pain. Whereas earlier drafts pondered the human suffering that came with full knowledge of a determined future or asked if timequakes hurt, the published novel examines the timequake's impacts through Kilgore Trout's memoir *My Ten Years on Automatic Pilot*.

This strategy conveniently allows Vonnegut to limit the scope of the timequake's impacts, filtering the events through Trout's perspectives. The timequake is described as an epic television "rerun," what happens when the universe is on "autopilot," and as a phenomenon that made everybody "robots" in their own past lives. Trout's memoir describes people "as though they were steering something, but they weren't steering. They couldn't steer." More than just a metaphor, this inability to steer wreaks literal havoc in the novel, as fire trucks, cars, planes, and other vehicles cause accidents after the timequake ends.

The greatest danger to society and humanity itself is *"Post-Timequake Apathy*, or *PTA*," which Trout describes as people no longer "giving a shit what was going on, or what was liable to happen next." Like the Booboolings who stop developing their imagination, PTA sufferers seem all too willing to outsource their will, creativity, and thinking to machines; they don't want to steer—literally or metaphorically. Fortunately, readers aren't forced to explore these dystopian speculations in *Timequake*. With the help of Dudley Prince, homeless shelter guests, and the Peppers' chauffeur, Jerry Rivers, the reluctant hero Trout rescues humanity with his mantra, or, as it's later known, "Kilgore's Creed: 'You were sick, but you're well again, and there's work to do.'" Not without irony, Vonnegut has Trout broadcast his humanistic message over the radio and TV. And perhaps because of rather than despite this framing, Vonnegut underscores our pervasive reliance on these information and entertainment media technologies.

As *Timequake* suggests, the appropriate response to "The Sisters B-36" and metaphors of cultural autopilot is to reinvigorate our empathy and imagination "circuits" via human exchanges and reading printed books. It's no accident that Vonnegut inserts personal prescriptions in the chapters surrounding the administration of Kilgore's Creed: proposed human-centered amendments to the Constitution, the idea of noticing and savoring life's nice moments, and his son Mark's wisdom, "We are here to help each other get through this thing, whatever it is." Given *Timequake*'s rhetorical situation—a book about a writer's struggle to rescue a manuscript primarily about technology, humanity, and writing—it's hard not to emphasize Vonnegut's pleas to keep printed books as an essential element of human experience and culture. And, of course, for Vonnegut, there would be no planetary citizenship without books.

Vonnegut doesn't just pay lip service to the importance of literature. Throughout *Timequake* he references more than fifty authors from Shakespeare, Voltaire, the Shelleys, Melville, and Hawthorne to Dos Passos, Shaw, Cather, and Miller to Wiesel, Grass, Böll, Donoso, and Kosiński. Having shared writers who "made him feel honored to be alive, no matter what else" was going on, Vonnegut's musings about the potential obsolescence of print books are as deeply layered as Trout's stories and parables. Collectively, these musings build toward an homage to his uncle Alex and the education he received via his uncle's book recommendations, colorful library, and shared magical passages:

> It now appears that books in the forms so beloved by Uncle Alex and me, hinged and unlocked boxes, packed with leaves speckled by ink, are obsolescent. My grandchildren are already doing much of this reading from words projected on the face of a video screen.
>
> Please, please, please wait just a minute!
>
> At the time of their invention, books were devices as crassly practical for storing and transmitting language, albeit fabricated from scarcely modified substances found in forest and field and animals, as the latest Silicon Valley miracles. But by accident, not by cunning calculation, books, because of their weight and texture, and because of their sweetly token resistance to manipulation, involve our hands and eyes, and then our minds and souls, in a spiritual adventure I would be very sorry for my grandchildren not to know about.

To print readers of *Timequake*, Vonnegut's urgent pleas are sermons to the proverbial choir. In the wake of Project Gutenberg's tremendous growth and rapidly developing e-book technologies and markets, Vonnegut's concerns about the potential obsolescence of printed books were not melodramatic speculation in 1997. Just a year after *Timequake*'s publication, NuvoMedia launched the first hand-held e-book readers, and by the time Amazon launched its first Kindle a decade later, the much-hyped e-reader sold out in less than six hours.[335]

Despite the seemingly gloomy predictions of Trout's stories or the central plot threads of *Timequake*, it's important to remember that Vonnegut's final novel is, as Jerome Klinkowitz reminds us, "a joyful, even festive book."[336] While Trout's stories and the narrative portions of *Timequake* warn of the dangers of technologically driven human and artistic obsolescence, Vonnegut's personal framing of these sections invite the reader to share in the experience of creating, evaluating, and enjoying the novel itself. Embedded in Vonnegut's own reflections on the composition process and artistic mission of the novel are personal stories that bring together key figures who shaped Vonnegut's career—editors, critics, models for characters, family supporters, mentors, publishers, inspiring musical artists, fellow experimenters, and artistic colleagues of every medium.

Vonnegut also puts his artistic theories into practice. Reading, like other art forms, is an extended conversation (albeit a largely silent one) between human beings. With its numerous allusions to other Vonnegut texts and memorable moments, *Timequake* directly engages readers because they "see the author constructing it, coming alive as a timequake-inspired rerun of creative action."[337] Ultimately, each reading of the novel becomes a type of timequake, and readers are invited to enter Vonnegut's own literary community, the wellspring of his planetary, artistic, and other forms of citizenship.

While silent individual readers of *Timequake* are unlikely to have the shared human experience of watching a play, an "artificial timequake," Vonnegut creates a sense of community via the novel itself. Whether revealing memories of his favorite theater audience experiences, referencing more than a hundred cultural figures to trigger readers' own intellectual connections, or sharing anecdotes celebrating human interactions in post offices, stationery stores, and other public places, Vonnegut keeps stimulating our memory, literary, and community circuits. And just in case readers have missed his efforts "to be sociable with ink on paper," Vonnegut explains why he continues to write despite the ever-increasing hold that screens of all sizes have on our attention: "Many people need desperately to receive this message: 'I feel and think much as you do, care about many of the things you care about, although most people don't care about them. You are not alone.'"

In the decade between *Timequake*'s publication and Vonnegut's death, his planetary citizenship led him to be as equally outspoken about the dangers of our fossil-fuel addiction as he was about the importance of building human communities rather than electronic ones. In late-career speeches and essays, he doubled down on the idea that computers and television primarily wanted people "to sit still and buy all kinds of junk." "A computer teaches a child what a computer can become," Vonnegut argued, while "an educated human being teaches a child what a child can become."[338]

Just over a decade later, Vonnegut's warnings again seem prescient. The COVID-19 pandemic and 2020 election exposed how deeply ingrained and corrosive our digital platforms could be, as conspiracy theories, misinformation, and divisive memes spread as rapidly as the virus. Our digital networks, of course, also enabled social connections, education, remote work, and tools for promoting social, racial, and environmental justice. As Vonnegut foretold in *Player Piano*, digital technologies are human inventions that amplify the best and worst of human behaviors. But, as he worried in *Timequake*, our screens *are* changing us in profound ways. Back in October 2018, journalist Nellie Bowles reported that Silicon Valley executives and technologists were already realizing that the "benefits of screens as a learning tool are overblown, and the risks for addiction and stunting development seem high."[339] High-level employees at Facebook (Meta), Mozilla, YouTube, Google, Microsoft, Apple, and other companies have severely limited their own children's screen time, enrolling them in low-tech schools that encourage human interaction and physical play, hands-on learning, and tactile creativity. While it's unlikely we'll slow or reverse our steady co-evolution with computers and other machines any time soon, it's worth exploring Vonnegut's wisdom on human communities as we continue to ask what people are for. The planetary future our species creates will be shaped profoundly by the kinds of answers we imagine and enact.

WHAT *ARE* PEOPLE FOR?

Communities, Pacifism, and Secular Humanism

**We are here to help each other get
through this thing, whatever it is.**
—DR. MARK VONNEGUT, epigraph to *Bluebeard*

**The choice is ours: form a global partner-
ship to care for Earth and one another or
risk the destruction of ourselves and the
diversity of life. . . . [We] must decide to
live with a sense of universal responsibility, identifying ourselves with the whole
Earth community as well as our local
communities.**
—Preamble to *The Earth Charter*

**Communities are all that's substantial
about the world. All the rest is hoop-la.**
—KURT VONNEGUT, address at Rice University,
   May 9, 1998

Still struggling to finish *Timequake*, Vonnegut's planetary citizenship took him back on the road in the spring of 1996 for a speaking
tour titled "How to Get a Job Like Mine." Instead of answering
that question, the talks largely focused on education, renewed worries about climate change and the internet, and the importance of

human communities in the digital age. His April 24, 1996, address at the University of Rochester touched on many of his signature concerns: the importance of extended families, literacy, teachers, and resisting the isolating, anti-intellectual impacts of new media technologies.[340] Unlike other speeches from the tour, the Rochester talk revisited deeply personal wartime traumas to outline his humanist, planetary-minded visions.

Vonnegut began the address with comments about Edward Reginal "Joe" Crone Jr., the quiet, awkward fellow POW who inspired the character Billy Pilgrim in *Slaughterhouse-Five*. Despite having told longtime friend Loree Rackstraw that he "finally closed out World War II" by publicly acknowledging his debt to Crone a year earlier, Vonnegut shared memories of his friend, noting that Crone was buried a short distance away in Mt. Hope Cemetery.[341] Still affected by the long shadows of his Dresden experiences, Vonnegut powerfully emphasized the importance of community as he sketched out his "humanist philosophy as a manifesto of wishes for all Americans." A forerunner to the proposed constitutional amendments and definitions of secular sainthood that would appear in *Timequake*, Vonnegut's humanist manifesto called for all Americans "to be sincerely welcome at birth," to have their entrance into adulthood marked by an appropriate ceremony, to be given meaningful work, to be "sorely missed at death," and to follow the examples of "people who behave decently in this indecent world."[342]

The manifesto, which followed his time-tested joke about discovering what women want ("a whole lot of people to talk to"), was not exactly new material. Whether prescribing artificial extended families as a type of Vitamin C or calling for puberty ceremonies, Vonnegut had, for decades, been creating schemes to remedy the ill effects of having "too few people." The importance of stable communities is a sacred leitmotif that runs through Vonnegut's writings, and much of the decay of American society in his fiction can be traced to the erosion of these human structures, to privileging things or dangerous technologies over people. Like countless other environmental activists and sustainability experts, Vonnegut recognized that vibrant communities—human and nonhuman alike—are the bedrock of planetary citizenship. As renowned environmental writer and climate activist Bill McKibben observes, in any vision of a sustainable future, community "is at the heart of it all." "The future isn't one person in an electric car, or a solitary shopper . . . buying a marginally greener product," McKibben continues, "The future is car-sharing clubs. The future is the farmers' market. . . . On a rapidly urbanizing planet, community is key."[343]

The Rochester speech also highlights the strong undercurrents of secular humanism and pacifism that run throughout Vonnegut's proposals for strong communities and more humane ways of nourishing life on this planet. In many ways, his secular humanism (being "good without God") and pacifism sustain the unwavering band of light within "St. Kurt the Vonnegut."[344] Formed under the influence of generations of Freethinkers, powerfully confirmed during his wartime experiences and anthropology studies, nurtured through his writing, and given a public platform when he became honorary president of the American Humanist Association (1992–2007), Vonnegut's secular humanism and pacifism are at the center of his planetary citizenship. They profoundly shaped his visions of community, hope for a vibrant planet, and attempts to understand what people are for.

VOLUNTEER FIREMEN AND
NEW COMMANDMENTS

When "Poor Little Rich Town" appeared in the October 25, 1952, issue of *Collier's*, Vonnegut probably didn't give it much thought. The story was among the many written for "the slicks" in order to support more serious work, like his newly published first novel. There is little to no mention of it in his letters, and he didn't include it in either of his short story collections, *Canary in a Cathouse* and *Welcome to the Monkey House*. But in retrospect, "Poor Little Rich

Town" stands out for capturing Vonnegut's personal and early fictional explorations of community. Sold and then published in the immediate shadows of *Player Piano*, the story presents one of his first attempts to affirmatively answer the question "What are people for?"

The story itself is straightforward, and it's easy to see why it would have been appealing to *Collier's* readers in small towns across America. Originally titled "Time and Motion Study," the story recounts what happens to the tiny village of Spruce Falls when Newell Cady, a wealthy, attractive middle-aged efficiency expert moves there.[345] Hired as a vice president at the "Federal Apparatus Corporation" in Ilium, New York, Cady is a modern-day Frederick Winslow Taylor. He seeks to transform every element of village life to make it as fast and efficient as the factory systems he redesigns. At first, Spruce Falls residents embrace Cady's suggestions and shower him with honors, such as electing him to "full membership in the fire department" and naming him "head judge of the annual Hobby Show." They reason that if Cady can "taste the joys of village life" that "Spruce Falls will become *the* fashionable place for Federal Apparatus executives to live" and their sagging real estate values will soar. The story's simple moral and plot resolution stem from the question longtime resident Upton Beaton raises near the start: "What is a village profited if it shall gain a real estate boom and lose its own soul?"

While its sketches of folksy shopkeepers, comic hobby show entries, and message that "a village isn't a factory" give "Poor Little Rich Town" universal appeal, the story also captures the soul of Alplaus, New York, the three-hundred-person hamlet where the Vonneguts—both Kurt's and Bernie's families—lived during the GE years. Like its fictional counterpart Spruce Falls, the Alplaus of Vonnegut's time was a walkable community, with a few small businesses, a gas station, a general store, a volunteer fire department, and a small post office at its geographical and social center.[346]

As in the story, the firehouse was next to the post office, where residents retrieved their mail from individual cubbyholes and caught up on the latest gossip, bulletin board postings, and community news. When the Vonneguts lived there, Ida Boyce Dillman was the postmaster, sorting the mail and handing Kurt dozens of rejection letters in the same 1906 building where her family once ran a grocery store. Vonnegut chose to embrace community life through the activities of Alplaus's volunteer fire department, which not only responded to fires and emergencies but sponsored the annual Fourth of July parade, picnics, clambakes, and other events featuring its drum and bugle corps.

During his tenure wearing Badge 155, Vonnegut served alongside "Mayor of Alplaus" Ted Schwarz, the fire department leader who likely influenced small details of Eliot Rosewater's character. According to longtime resident Gray Watkins, Schwarz "always bought Alplaus newborns silver cups with their names engraved on the side, appearing with the gifts the very day they returned home from the hospital."[347] Like the sincerely welcomed newborns, Vonnegut's early publishing career was also nurtured by the Alplaus community—especially Ann Cheney, who ran the general store and for a tiny fee (at Kurt's insistence that it not be free) rented him her daughter Mary Lou's bedroom to use as his first writing office.[348] From that second-floor office on Alplaus Avenue, Kurt could see his Hill Street home, the post office and firehouse, and the rest of the "downtown," observing the hamlet's daily rhythms like "the narrator in Thornton Wilder's *Our Town*."[349]

Unlike Vonnegut, who understood his newfound community's soul, Newell Cady demonstrates his ignorance of the inner workings of Spruce Falls when he rejects the fire department's plans to purchase a new engine (and later capes and hats for the band). To Cady, the "sole purpose of a fire department should be to put out fires and to do it as economically as possible." Cady's dismissal of Ted Batsford's giant ball of string at the Hobby Show raises more eyebrows, but his most unforgivable crime is suggesting that Spruce Falls replace postmaster Mrs. Dickie in favor of free rural delivery from the centralized Ilium post office. Inspired by the US Postal Service's national efforts to increase its speed and efficiency in 1951, Vonnegut used Cady's suggestion to highlight the lifeblood, compassion, and community heart that would be extinguished through the change.[350]

As one Spruce Falls resident explains at the story's climax, Mrs. Dickie's "husband died in a fire, saving some of these people around the village" that Cady has called blind. "You talk a lot about wasting time, Mr. Cady," he continues, adding, "for a really big waste of time, walk around the village someday and try to find somebody who doesn't know he can have his mail brought to his door anytime he wants to." Where Cady fails in his efforts to modernize the village, he succeeds in helping Spruce Falls to realize its true wealth: its strong communal bonds, respect for every member's unique contributions, and willingness to provide meaningful work for its members despite higher economic costs.

Strangely enough, as Vonnegut shared stories about the simple joys of interacting with people while buying envelopes and stamps during the final decade of his life, Alplaus really *was* fighting to keep its tiny post office and preserve "the smallest geographic ZIP code in the United States."[351] In *Timequake, A Man Without a Country*, and his many late-career speeches, he celebrated his "Luddite" resistance to the internet and his "crush" on a Turtle Bay area postal worker. Despite these celebrations of New York postal adventures, Alplaus remained especially dear to Vonnegut. "About six months before his death in 2007, he sent a small silk [screen] print with a Maltese cross to the Alplaus Fire Department," which presumably still hangs in the building next door to the post office.[352] Sadly, the post office finally closed its doors on January 6, 2012. So it goes.

Long after he stopped wearing Badge 155, Vonnegut continued to look to volunteer firemen and fire departments as he explored community and attempted to understand what people are for. In *God Bless You, Mr. Rosewater*, protagonist Eliot Rosewater turns to science fiction, alcohol, and visits to random volunteer fire departments across the country to assuage his guilt over killing three civilian German firemen—two old men and a boy—that he mistook for soldiers during World War II. His road trips to heal personal trauma yield to a broader quest for meaning when Eliot returns to Rosewater, Indiana, to reinvent his family's philanthropic foundation. There, he and his wife Sylvia undertake the radical experiment of loving "discarded Americans" who have no use. The novel's plot focuses on the efforts of Eliot's father Lister, an ultra-conservative US senator, and conniving lawyer Norman Mushari to have Eliot declared legally insane so the $87 million family fortune can remain under "sane" management. Eliot ultimately thwarts their plans by adopting all the children of Rosewater County, but along the way, Vonnegut's 1965 novel presents a complex web of social and economic injustices through portraits of individuals and communities nested within the larger structure of American capitalism. The materially flush but spiritually poor town of Pisquontuit has even less of a soul than impoverished Rosewater County; Norman Mushari's and Lister Rosewater's political conservatism and greed balance in tension with Eliot and Sylvia's socialist leanings and boundless generosity; the dwindling few who can slurp from the stream of the "money river" are seemingly in inverse proportion to the multitude encountering the "belly up" American dream; and the sanest, most humane actions of characters are deemed insane or diseased by the rest of society.

Despite these incisive critiques of capitalism, once Vonnegut really got going with drafts of *God Bless You, Mr. Rosewater*, the novel didn't begin with a "sum of money" as "a leading character" as it would in its published form. It began with Diana Moon Glampers, a servant employed at the Rosewater mansion. In these pivotal drafts ca. summer 1962, the tale opened with a sixty-six-year-old Glampers battling terror and loneliness during a midnight thunderstorm.[353] While much of the incident and portrait of Glampers wound up in chapter 5 of the novel, these earlier draft starts present the loveless, luckless servant with more pathos. We learn of her three separate losses to electricity: her father struck holding a pitchfork at Rosewater Dairy Farm, her mother electrocuted while working at the Rosewater Steam Laundry, and her one would-be lover, a lineman, killed on the job "near the Rosewater Golf and Country Club." Like her dead loved ones, Glampers is tied to the Rosewater family for survival—to Lister for employment and to Eliot for comfort.

While Vonnegut used these opening portraits of Glampers to contrast Eliot and his father Lister and the haves and have-nots of Rosewater County, he seemingly wanted to understand Rosewater County's "unendowed" himself. Diana Moon Glampers was just the first portrait of characters "who are without wealth, luck, good looks, or negotiable abilities of any kind." In addition to developing Glampers's character, Vonnegut dreamed up Jason Rose, the gardener who tended the Rosewater estate lawn; three generations of the twin-bearing Cruddy family; and Ed Hinkle, a troubled veteran and L. S. Ayres bridal department flasher that Sylvia tries to mentor before her collapse from "Samaritrophia" (being a good Samaritan). These deleted characters gave way to Roland Barry, Mary Moody, Lincoln Ewald, Tawny Wainright, Finnerty Noyes, and other Rosewater County notables, but, like his view above Ann Cheney's store, they helped Vonnegut discover the town's rhythms and soul.

In these exploratory drafts, Vonnegut gave the minor character Delbert Peach a larger role as part-time foundation receptionist, which allowed Eliot to spend more time in his fireman's helmet, boots, and slicker. With multiple drafts subtitled "The Volunteer," Vonnegut imagined Eliot putting out fires in multiple locations, describing Eliot "in ecstasy," with "six good men on board" a "bright red cosmic dreadnought, sirens wailing, being chased by every dog in town."[354] These additional scenes of Rosewater's volunteer firemen channeled Vonnegut's own Alplaus experiences and demonstrated the community-minded altruism Kilgore Trout expresses in the published novel. Volunteer fire departments, Trout explains, are "almost the only examples of enthusiastic unselfishness to be seen in this land. They rush to the rescue of any human being, and count not the cost."[355]

As he continued to envision Rosewater's human community and portraits of Eliot's "enthusiastic selflessness" in "The Volunteer" drafts, Vonnegut also began to explore early ideas of secular sainthood and Christ's humanism.[356] To foreground these ideas, Vonnegut used Jesus's famous line from Matthew 19:14, "Suffer the little children to come unto me," first on its own and then attributed to Eliot, as the novel's epigraph.[357] The allusions to chapter 19 of the Gospel of Matthew align nicely with the novel's experiments in uncritical love and critiques of chasing wealth and worshipping materialism. After welcoming the children and reviewing the importance of keeping the commandments, Jesus encourages his followers to "sell that thou hast, and give to the poor," reminding them, "It is easier for a camel to go through the eye of a needle, than for a rich man to enter the kingdom of heaven" (Matthew 14:21–24).

While embracing Eliot's desires to divide things up more equitably and care for the poor, Vonnegut built upon those Biblical allusions to offer new secular commandments. In the two subsequent drafts where he developed the backstory for Eliot's foray into baptisms, Vonnegut framed Eliot's decision to christen Celeste Cruddy's twins in explicit conversations about religion, love, and community.[358] The exchange about baptisms takes place after Delbert Peach shares a dream about Eliot's death and celebrated arrival in heaven.[359] Responding simultaneously to Peach's sips of morning whiskey and the discovery "that the cash drawer of his desk was empty again," Eliot proclaims, "Hope of the world, love is." Moved by Peach's dream, Rosewater half-seriously decides to put the sainthood imagined by Peach to good use. As he engages in morning lavatory "ablutions," Eliot proclaims, "I give you a new Commandment: . . . Ye shall love one another."

Despite lionizing Eliot, Peach sneers and shows with "a shrug that he felt the Eleventh Commandment was trash." "I know that's in the *Bible*," Peach tells Eliot, but says, "Some people I can't cotton to." As if on cue, Celeste Cruddy calls the Rosewater Foundation, and Peach answers, registering disgust—"something Eliot never did." What follows is Eliot's conversation with Cruddy and a brief explanation of how he made the jump from distributing laxatives and tax refunds to performing sacraments. The chapter ends with the near-final version of the novel's most famous lines: "Hello babies. Welcome to Earth. It's hot in the summer and cold in the winter. It's round and wet and crowded. At the outside, you've got about a hundred years here, babies. There's only one rule I know of babies:—'Please, God damn it, be kind.'"

This command(ment) to be kind—a precursor to Vonnegut's calls for common decency and original virtue—while shrouded in Biblical contexts, is decidedly secular. Like Vonnegut's earlier novels, the final version of *God Bless You, Mr. Rosewater* presents belief systems and rituals as *human* creations that can provide beauty, community, and comfort in an unpredictable and often harsh world. From those early draft engagements with Christian humanism, Vonnegut added invented religions as backdrops for Eliot's experiments in kindness and uncritical love. One of the first things we learn about Rosewater County in the novel is that it was previously home to the "New Ambrosia" utopian community. With a slight sideways nod to some of Vonnegut's own Freethinker ancestors, New Ambrosians are described as "Germans, communists and atheists who practiced group marriage, absolute truthfulness, absolute cleanliness, and absolute love." Their principal legacy was a brewery, famous for a lager with a label depicting "the heaven on earth the New Ambrosians had meant to build."

Eliot's attempts to build an earthly paradise of "absolute love" are further contextualized in his own creative revisions of traditional religion. We learn of Eliot's unfinished novel, which chronicles people's returns to Earth from heaven, along with his affiliation as "Two-Seed-in-the-Spirit Predestination Baptist." "That's what I generally say when people insist I must have a religion," Eliot explains, noting, "There happens to *be* such a sect, and I'm sure it's a good one. Foot-washing is practiced, and ministers draw no pay. I wash my own feet, and I draw no pay."

Ultimately, Eliot does become a "saint," a "church," and a "church group" to the people of Rosewater, and his foundation embodies central ideas from the Beatitudes. Despite being described by Lister as "the maggots on the bottom of the human garbage pail," the people of Rosewater are, in Eliot's eyes, as blessed as the meek, poor in spirit, mournful, and persecuted in the Sermon on the Mount. Vonnegut takes pains, though, not to idealize Eliot or Rosewater County's "useless" "unlovable" residents. Their flaws, crimes, and other sins are as apparent as their moments of kindness, love, and generosity. What's most critical to Eliot's humanist enterprise is his focus on making life more fair, bearable, and kind in *this* world.

With no expectation of reward in the afterlife for himself or his clients, Eliot is motivated by the simple fact Sylvia observes: "They're human." To drive home this crucial idea, Vonnegut has Kilgore Trout frame Eliot's secular humanist efforts as "quite possibly the most important social experiment of our time." In the wake of increased automation, growing global inequalities, and impending new forms of human obsolescence, the central question is "How to love people who have no use?" Whether through the "enthusiastic unselfishness" of firefighting, the welcoming waters of baptism, or the emotional, social, and economic support he provides, Eliot accomplishes the rare art of "treasuring people as people." Vonnegut (via Trout) offers Eliot's humanist experiment as a model: "If one man can do it, perhaps others can do it, too. It means that our hatred of useless human beings and the cruelties we inflict upon them for their own good need not be parts of human nature."

As critic Todd Davis observes, "Vonnegut's Gospel of Hope" in *God Bless You, Mr. Rosewater* may be his "most central" fictional "conception of postmodern humanism." The novel weaves together a "patchwork of stories" to undermine "grand narratives of American culture" and "Darwinian capitalism" while celebrating humanist enterprises that "ennoble and serve the human spirit."[360] Nonetheless,

Vonnegut felt the need to reiterate his calls for secular sainthood, service to one's community, common decency, and "original virtue" in later speeches and essays. This message was so urgent that he kept shifting metaphors and strategies—from inventing new religions to likening extended families to necessary vitamins to proposing his humanist principles as new constitutional amendments.

Although most of these discussions focused on communities for and of his fellow *Homo sapiens*, Vonnegut saw the profound recognition of dignity in other human beings as a prerequisite for valuing the rest of the Earth. As he explained in *Fates Worse Than Death*, "If you see dignity in anything, in fact—it doesn't have to be human—you will want to understand it and help it." His fellow planetary citizens, he suggested, were now "seeing dignity in the lower animals and the plant world and waterfalls and deserts—and even in the entire planet and its atmosphere. And now they are helpless not to want to understand and to help those things. Poor souls!"[361]

Vonnegut offered another powerful synthesis of humanism, environmentalism, and community-mindedness in his 1974 commencement address at Hobart and William Smith Colleges. Collected in *Palm Sunday*, the address appears immediately after Vonnegut's reflections on his Freethinker heritage and excerpts from his great-grandfather Clemens Vonnegut's *Instruction in Morals* and funeral address.[362] Like modern secular humanists who believe in "being good without God," Clemens asked people to work toward a "joyous" earth by living rationally and contributing "mutually to each other's welfare." Vonnegut invoked this intergenerational pursuit of "ideas based on Truth and Justice" to give a decidedly secular frame to his call for a new religion, a "heartfelt moral code" in the speech. Returning to the idea that fabricated religions can provide guidance, comfort, and "spiritual renewal," Vonnegut suggests the code to remedy "poisoned" knowledge and beliefs of the past. Ultimately, Vonnegut merges old frameworks of myth, religion, and morality with rationality and science as he reads a recent "portent":

What might be the meaning of the comet Kahoutek, which was to make us look upward, to impress us with the paltriness of our troubles, to cleanse our souls with cosmic awe? Kahoutek was a fizzle, and what might that fizzle mean?

I take it to mean that we can expect no spectacular miracles from heaven, that the problems of ordinary human beings will have to be solved by ordinary human beings. The message of Kahoutek is: "Help is not on the way. Repeat: Help is not on the way."

Chief among these problems, Vonnegut suggests, are loneliness, economic injustice, and the appalling "speed with which we are wrecking our topsoil, our drinking water, and our atmosphere." Leaning on Kilgore Trout, Vonnegut suggests that Americans have become "planet gobblers," ravenously and disproportionately consuming natural resources in a misguided attempt to assuage loneliness through material possessions. Thanks to "intelligence and resourcefulness," Vonnegut optimistically suggests that there is a new "willingness to say 'No thank you' to our factories" and to "have life on the planet go on for a long, long time." These earthly and Earth-minded solutions stem from a "dream of human communities which are designed to harmonize with what human beings really need and are."

While Vonnegut's optimistic prediction didn't come to fruition in American culture at large, sustainability and environmental justice advocates have long noted a correlation between vibrant human communities and healthier physical environments.[363] Whether looking to the downshifting, freecycle, or voluntary simplicity movements or to mutual aid, cohousing, real estate cooperatives, and community gardens and food systems, millions of people *are* rejecting consumerism as they seek to restore themselves, their neighborhoods, and the planet as a whole.

THE VERY LONG SHADOWS OF
SLAUGHTERHOUSE-FIVE

If we lived in Kilgore Trout's fictional universe, fans of *Slaughterhouse-Five* would have to appear before The First District Court of Thankyou to express their gratitude to Knox Burger, Harry Brague, and Annie Laurie Williams.[364] And they would also have to thank editors at *Harper's*, the *Atlantic Monthly*, *American Mercury*, *Yale Review*, *Coronet*, and the *New Republic*. All these people, along with countless others, rejected Vonnegut's attempts to tell his Dresden story in the late 1940s and 1950s. In his April 5, 1951, letter, Burger told Vonnegut, "The Dresden thing sounds very risky to me. I'm sure it could be a moving and valid story; the conflict is big time. But I know Mr. A would shy away from the notion, and I must advise you against gambling on it."[365] Burger suggested instead that Vonnegut use the idea "as an interesting aside, a (removable, if necessary) grace note" in "The Commandant's Desk," the piece he wanted for *Collier's*. Following Burger's advice, Vonnegut temporarily shelved his Dresden ideas to work on *Player Piano* and the many short stories he had in the works.

On September 30, 1952, with his first novel published, Vonnegut pitched his Dresden idea to Scribner's editor Harry Brague in a letter outlining his plans for "the second book."[366] "The thing is about World War II," he explained, and it "is divided into three books, and the middle third is a play." Vonnegut had finished the middle third, a "pretty good play" about "May 8, VE-Day with the hero an American, in Sudetenland, as the Russians approach and finally occupy the last bit of German soil." Vonnegut wavered between predicting that the book would be "a turkey commercially" and dreaming that the play portion *might* "(a million-to-one if) . . . become a Broadway success." He was clear, though, in envisioning "the first and last thirds" as "illuminating prologue and epilogue (about 150 pages apiece, I figure)," which he hoped would be "good tales in themselves to boot." Vonnegut joked about loading "the last third with sex" to help it sell, but closed by telling Brague, "This is a serious book."

Encouraged by Brague's brief reply, Vonnegut started circulating drafts of the 157-page play around Cape Cod to "the fringe-type show business people," and provided more details to Brague in a typed postcard on October 9, 1952.[367] Although it was in dramatic form, Vonnegut imagined rewriting it "in straight narrative form for presentation between hard covers." The novel would focus on "a guy named Martin Heimbeck," with the first third "about his life as a P.W., the 2nd third, the play, about May 8, 1945, and the third about his return to civilian life." Vonnegut warned Brague that the story might seem "Trite, but wait'll you see."

When he found time to respond after Christmas, Brague reported that he liked "the idea of a play," and, as someone who saw action "in the Bremen area in April and May of 1945," he was moved by some of Vonnegut's graphic descriptions.[368] Although Brague saw potential in *some* of this "powerful stuff," he, like Burger, thought the material might be too "thin" and suggested that it might be "better to use it as part of a novel rather than to attempt expanding it into a novel on its own." "I don't feel there is enough meat there," Brague concluded. Once again temporarily shelving his war novel, Vonnegut returned to his Dresden story in the mid- to late 1950s as he drafted multiple versions of a television play, alternately titled *A Dresden Goodnight, I'll Say Goodnight in Dresden, Jonah,* and *Slaughterhouse-Five* for Annie Laurie Williams, Inc.[369] While some versions focused on confrontations between two wounded Jewish American POWs and a German guard in the immediate aftermath of the Dresden firebombing, the broader vision, outlined in a seven-page synopsis, called for a three-act drama with a play within the play, performed during a meeting of the New Paradise Comedy Club.

In that version of *Slaughterhouse-Five*, protagonist Paul Marachek puts on a play about his Dresden POW experiences in the aftermath of the firebombing to "tell the truth" about his murdered friend

Lamb, whose body is about to be repatriated by the Russians thirteen years after the war. The pacifist, "extremely humane" Marachek is an alter ego for Vonnegut, and many of Vonnegut's own experiences appear in this play, where "only through art can he hope to recreate the atmosphere in which the murder took place." Like Burger, Brague, and the countless editors who received drafts of Vonnegut's ca. 1947 essays and stories, "I Shall Not Want," "Brighten Up," "Wailing Shall Be in All Streets," and "Atrocity Story," Annie Laurie Williams rejected the Dresden piece.

There are good reasons why these smart, savvy editors and producers chose not to publish early versions and pieces of Vonnegut's Dresden story. While some magazine editors thought Vonnegut's writing lacked polish, many realized that his strong critiques of the US military wouldn't fit well with the postwar "Victory Culture." His stories of wartime injustices and haunting memories of civilian deaths, severe deprivations, and other hardships ran counter to stories celebrating rehabilitation and successful readjustment.[370] With the Cold War escalating, Burger recognized that any focus on Allied civilian bombings might not sit well with the patriotism and resolve needed to defeat the Soviet Union. Brague, meanwhile, noted that "there have been so many books dealing with POW's both before and after liberation" that Vonnegut would have to do something more remarkable to make the story "come alive in a novel."[371] Vonnegut's accounts of the "harrowing privations suffered by our soldiers who were prisoners of war" would not have been news to a public already familiar with the stories of Bataan Death March survivors.[372]

What's striking about Vonnegut's early World War II–related writings is how quickly he sketched the outline for the POW and Dresden narrative threads of *Slaughterhouse-Five*, how profound his early humanist-pacifist framing was, and how many immediate sensory details he captured. His May 28, 1945, letter to his family, for instance, contains key wartime elements that appear in the published novel: defeat and surrender at the Battle of the Bulge, the long forced marches, crowded boxcars, jarring experiences at the prison camp, deprivations and forced labor, the huge death toll and utter devastation of the firebombing, post-VE-Day wanderings, and references to the haunting deaths of Michael Palaia and Joe Crone that would inspire the Edgar Derby and Billy Pilgrim characters.[373] Many of the pieces he drafted in Chicago while studying anthropology and moonlighting as a city news bureau reporter, meanwhile, describe the "perfectly legal" but absurdly unjust execution of Michael Palaia ("Atrocity Story"), the fanciful meals dreamed up and recorded by starving POWs ("I Shall Not Want"), and the grisly details of exhuming corpses from basements in the charred remains of Dresden ("Wailing Shall Be in All Streets").

Even in these early writings Vonnegut doesn't share these ghoulish details merely to report what he witnessed. "Wailing Shall Be in All Streets" never lets the reader forget that each corpse encountered was a *human being*—"men, women, and children indiscriminately killed" in an "open city." While Vonnegut would later conclude that there is "nothing intelligent to say about a massacre," he was not afraid to moralize in "Wailing": "World War II was fought for near-Holy motives. But I stand convinced that the brand of justice in which we dealt, wholesale bombings of civilian populations was blasphemous." The firebombing of Dresden, he opined, "had the earmarks of being an irrational war for war's sake."

The genius of *Slaughterhouse-Five* is that it retains the most powerful elements of Vonnegut's early accounts while expanding the scope, scale, and weight of his Dresden story. The two intervening decades presented Vonnegut with more cycles of "irrational war for war's sake" via the Cold War with its hot episodes in Korea and Vietnam, and enabled him to become more innovative as a writer. Once Vonnegut could imagine Billy Pilgrim coming "unstuck in time" and the possibilities opened up by Tralfamadorian notions of time, he didn't need the three-part structures of his 1950s drafts; he could tell the story of Billy before, during, and after the war simultaneously. He could use the Tralfamadorian scenes and concepts to explore Billy's PTSD and his coping mechanisms, along with the other memories Billy carried home from the war. Offering one of the twentieth century's most innovative and seminal portraits of a mind ravaged by war traumas, *Slaughterhouse-Five* is also boldly ambitious in its antiwar aims, despite Vonnegut's acknowledgment that his efforts will be a failure, that wars are "as easy to stop as glaciers."[374] In keeping with Kurt's promise to Mary O'Hare, the novel undercuts narrative conventions that make war appear "glamorous" or "wonderful" in an attempt to break cycles of war stories that engender other conflicts. Vonnegut offers no heroic characters, no climaxes, no thrills, no suspense, and practically no descriptions of battles or bombings.

Vonnegut extends this innovative pacifist framing to all the conflicts layered into the novel via allusion, Billy's time travel, Tralfamadorian perspectives, and other metafictional techniques.[375] Moving from the 1213 Children's Crusade to the 1760 Prussian siege of Dresden to Céline's World War I "duty dance with death" to the flaming destruction of Sodom and Gomorrah described in the Bible, the first chapter creates an intertextual web of war stories. This intertextuality invites readers to examine broader cycles of armed conflict in the rest of the novel. While finally telling a fictional version of his Dresden story, Vonnegut also addresses the Vietnam War, civil rights struggles, racial violence, and other historical events that loomed over him during the novel's major 1964–68 compositional phase.

Like a Tralfamadorian novel that brings together many moments at once, *Slaughterhouse-Five* draws on a type of "multidirectional memory" to fuse Vonnegut's war traumas, writing struggles, shared memories, and research with historical narratives, current events, and the broader cultural upheaval of the 1960s.[376] Readers go from Pope Innocent III's "Children's Crusade" to Eugene McCarthy's 1968 antiwar "Children's Crusade," but keep returning to early-1945 Germany and the mid-twentieth-century events "stuck" to it. Although its characters often seem to be "the listless playthings of enormous forces," *Slaughterhouse-Five* isn't just a text about witnessing. Despite being doomed to failure, Vonnegut attempts to challenge narrative structures and ways of seeing that foster war. Given the thousands of pages that have been written about *Slaughterhouse-Five*, it's impossible to catalog all the ways Vonnegut does this. It would be easier to move an entire beach's volume of sand one teaspoon at a time. To highlight just two of his techniques, let us turn to the novel's iconic phrase "So it goes" and the war-film-in-reverse passage.

As Susan Farrell and numerous critics have noted, "Vonnegut's most famous tagline," which appears 106 times, is often interpreted as a "resigned, fatalistic outlook . . . evening out all deaths and making them all seem relatively unimportant."[377] Filtered through Billy Pilgrim's newspaper editorials, the phrase "So it goes," we learn, is "what the Tralfamadorians say about dead people." Because of their fourth-dimensional vision and understanding of time, Tralfamadorians understand that a person "only *appears* to die" because "all moments, past, present, and future, always have existed, always will exist." Vonnegut's own grisly experiences working in Dresden's "corpse mines" infuse the phrase with gallows humor and lend credence to the sense of comfort, coping, and passive acceptance Billy attaches to it.

When read in light of Vonnegut's persistent attempts to humanize an atrocity, the repeated tagline is also a way to pause and mark each occurrence of death—whether on mass scales, such as the casualties at Dresden or Hiroshima, or on an individual scale, such as the deaths of Edgar Derby, Wild Bob, Roland Weary, or Valencia Pilgrim. Although the phrase itself is repeated exactly, Vonnegut's shifts in scale and perspective as he marks the deaths are not. The same simultaneity of Tralfamadorian perspectives helps expand the scope of war's casualties ever outward—from the deaths of the war's "real soldiers" to the victims of the Holocaust to four German POW guards and their families during the firebombing to the dead animals whose fat greases the axles of the two-wheeled food cart.

Adopting his signature planetary vision, Vonnegut shifts well beyond the realm of mammals, marking the deaths of champagne bubbles, the body lice and bacteria on the POWs' clothes, the dog Paul Lazarro killed out of cruelty, and "all the hooved animals in Germany [that] had been killed and eaten" to fuel their nation's war machine. More notably, Vonnegut draws no distinction between actual and fictional deaths, using "So it goes" to note "Private Eddie D. Slovik, 36896415, the only American soldier to be shot for cowardice since the Civil War" along with the deaths of characters in embedded Kilgore Trout stories and Roland Weary's fantasy of "the worst form of execution."[378] Although the tagline frequently marks the tens of thousands of people killed during the firebombing of Dresden, it collectively and cumulatively registers both the colossal tolls of war and the shared mortality of *all* living beings.[379]

In keeping with his humanism and Rosewater-inspired ideas of treasuring human beings as human beings, Vonnegut complements his repetition of "So it goes" with attempts to challenge the dehumanizing perspectives needed to perpetrate wars. Once again drawing on a strategy from his early Dresden writings, Vonnegut underscores how easy it is to kill when you don't grant a person dignity, humanity, or subjectivity. It's no accident that Bertram Copeland Rumfoord, "the official Air Force Historian," who unproblematically accepts mass civilian casualties to achieve military objectives, is reluctant to see Billy as a human being. Suggesting that they should "turn him over to a veterinarian or a tree surgeon" because doctors "are for human beings," Rumfoord repeatedly views Billy "as a repulsive non-person" in spite of the fact that Billy can offer him firsthand testimony about Dresden—the very topic he's researching.

Rumfoord's "military manner" of thinking and opinion that "people who were weak deserved to die," of course, are no different from those of the nameless German guards who processed prisoners headed for "an extermination camp." At both the loading and unloading of prisoners into the boxcars, Vonnegut offers readers a glimpse into the dehumanizing mindset that views them as a "general sort of freight." No longer individuals, the POWs in each car become "a single organism which ate and drank and excreted through its ventilators." Within a world where death camps and other forms of mass killing are normalized, it's perfectly logical to reduce the men to their biological processes: "It talked or sometimes yelled through its ventilators, too. In went water and loaves of blackbread and sausage and cheese, and out came shit and piss and language." Employing repetition as deliberately and powerfully as his "So it goes" refrain, Vonnegut counters this dehumanizing logic in the very next paragraph:

> *Human beings* in there were excreting into steel helmets which were passed to the people at the ventilators, who dumped them. Billy was a dumper. The *human beings* also passed canteens, which guards would fill with water. When food came in, the *human beings* were quiet and trusting and beautiful. They shared.
>
> *Human beings* in there took turns standing or lying down. [italics mine]

While this passage challenges the dehumanizing logic of Nazi racial hygiene policies, *Slaughterhouse-Five* repeatedly calls attention to the shared humanity of individuals on all sides of the battle lines. Vonnegut mentions the eight Dresden POW guards who see the Americans as "human beings, more fools like themselves," the blind innkeeper who feeds and shelters the American POWs after the Allied firebombing, and the physicians on both sides of the Atlantic "devoted to the idea that weak people should be helped as much as possible, that nobody should die."

Like Billy Pilgrim and Eliot Rosewater, who try "to re-invent themselves and their universe" with science fiction at the Lake Placid VA hospital, Vonnegut fully understands the power narratives have for either offering comfort or perpetrating violence.

Just as he challenges the desensitized visions of Nazi train guards and death camp expediters with repeated assertions of the POWs' humanity, Vonnegut's description of the late-night war film in reverse offers a beautiful if fleeting counter-narrative to the novel's immense web of war stories. Deemed "one of the loveliest passages in our [American] literature" by critic John Leonard, the imaginative vision of fighter planes sucking up bullets and exerting a "miraculous magnetism" to shrink fires is a therapeutic narrative for war survivors.[380] The pacifist dream broadens, first to scenes of American factories dismantling bombs and then to specialists cleverly hiding the munitions' minerals in the ground "so they would never hurt anybody again." With combatants on both sides made "as good as new" and buildings and landscapes restored, the backward cinematic montage inspires Billy to imagine an even grander outcome. Billy extrapolates, "Everybody turned into a baby, all humanity, without exception, conspired to produce two perfect people named Adam and Eve, he supposed." As with other Vonnegutian returns to Eden, these planetary-minded musings highlight the urgent need to create new myths—new fictions that don't end in widespread destruction.

While *Slaughterhouse-Five* is filled with Edenic and other religious allusions, Vonnegut himself chose to identify most closely with Lot's wife, who was forbidden to look at Sodom and Gomorrah as they were destroyed. "But she *did* look back," Vonnegut writes, "and I love her for that because it was so human." Whether out of compassion, curiosity, disobedience, or the simple need to witness, that gesture embodies the shared humanity Vonnegut saw in his earliest attempts to tell his Dresden story. "Wailing Shall Be in All Streets" concludes with the claim, "I would have given my life to save Dresden for the World's generations to come. That is how everyone should feel about every city on Earth." Mentioning the death of Lot's wife also foreshadows Vonnegut's own "failures" to not look back now that he had finished his "war book." Claiming that *Slaughterhouse-Five* "was written by a pillar of salt" confirmed that he *would* look back because that is the human and humane thing to do. And he did.

While Vonnegut would return to his post-VE-Day experiences in *Bluebeard*, he primarily looked to contemporary wars in his never-ending pacifist efforts. Building on the personal outrage that breaks through in chapter 10 of *Slaughterhouse-Five*, Vonnegut used his newfound celebrity to amplify his protests against the Vietnam War. In the months following the novel's publication, Vonnegut called for "humanistic physicists" that would refuse to support military research and instead engage in science that wishes people "and their planet well."[381] And on October 15, 1969, he joined with millions worldwide in the Vietnam Moratorium, delivering an impassioned plea during a local rally on Cape Cod to "Let the Killing Stop."[382] A month later, he and Jane traveled to Washington, DC, to participate in the national moratorium, which drew half a million activists, celebrities, and regular citizens for peace marches and demonstrations.

Even in his turn to comedy with *Happy Birthday, Wanda June*, a modern retelling of Odysseus's homecoming, Vonnegut felt the need to address "the current fucking war" in Vietnam and intensify its pacifist messages as he revised *Penelope*, an earlier version of the play, in 1970.[383] Although steeped in a complex ten-year history of its own, *Happy Birthday, Wanda June* is a fitting post-*Slaughterhouse-Five* work, with its efforts to reject toxic models of violent masculinity and to imagine new peaceful, planetary-minded heroes and actions. Like the war film in reverse, the character Looseleaf Harper's wish to undo the bombing of Nagasaki begins to imagine more hopeful narratives. Well before global sustainability movements articulated this central idea, Vonnegut recognized that "ending the violence of war sets the stage for bright green peace."[384]

Despite these many creative antiwar efforts, Vonnegut suggested in his 1973 PEN address that the impact of his and other writers' literary activism had "the explosive force of a very large banana-cream pie." While it might have been very tempting—and very human—to give up in the face of such discouraging results,

Vonnegut didn't. And I love *him* for that. He continued to write and speak and protest, calling attention to the shared humanity of US enemies in Panama, Libya, and Iraq, the planetary dangers of the nuclear arms race, and the tremendous social costs of investing in weapons instead of people. On January 14, 1991, he spoke out against the First Gulf War before it started, and continued to critique the results of "our great victory" long after American celebrations ended.[385] With his fellow New Yorkers in Turtle Bay, he mourned those who died on September 11—especially NYC firefighters—but he protested the invasion of Iraq every step of the way, willing to become "a man without a country" to preserve the humanist, democratic, and pacifist ideals he held most dear.

A HUMANIST'S HEAVEN

Before Vonnegut had Eliot contemplate graffiti-filled pearly gates and heaven as "the bore of bores" in *God Bless You, Mr. Rosewater,* he toyed with the idea in the brief unpublished short story "Please Omit Flowers." Vonnegut's agent Kenneth Littauer returned the story to him in April 1960 after exhausting all likely publication outlets. Robert Mills, the editor at *Fantasy and Science Fiction,* told Littauer the story "makes little sense to me," an assessment that echoed Littauer's own claim a month earlier that he didn't "know what it is about."[386] Narrated by a deceased husband (Harry) speaking to his wife (Hazel) through a Ouija board, the story is one of Vonnegut's first fictional portraits of heaven. Anticipating the playful, carnivalesque vision of the afterlife in *Happy Birthday, Wanda June,* Harry's descriptions of heaven mention transportation via trampoline jumping, roller-skating on "a flat white table that goes on forever," and riding on "tricycles with wheels ten-feet in diameter." Harry also informs Hazel that heaven is a multi-species establishment, where the souls of birds, dogs, bugs, and even broken watches mingle. The most salient part of Harry's tale, though, is that "there isn't any Hell, never was." "Hell is closed for repairs," according to a popular heavenly joke.

Although "Please Omit Flowers" was literarily dead on arrival, Vonnegut returned to the idea of a multi-species, playful afterlife a decade later as he feverishly revised *Happy Birthday, Wanda June* in advance of its fall 1970 debut at Theatre de Lys. While radically transforming the 1960 version of the play, produced as *Penelope* on Cape Cod, the addition of the characters Wanda June, Major Siegfried von Konigswald, and Mildred enhanced the play's experimental, fast-paced comedic elements. Serving as a modern Greek chorus, the characters add levity to the secularist heaven, sharing details about celestial shuffleboard games and Jesus Christ's warm-up jacket emblazoned with "Pontius Pilate Athletic Club."

Instead of merely noting the absence of hell in *Happy Birthday, Wanda June*, Vonnegut challenges the idea of eternal rewards or punishments by juxtaposing the innocent Wanda June and war criminal Siegfried von Konigswald. With music indicating "happiness, innocence and weightlessness" playing in the background, Wanda June's central monologue at first reinforces popular cultural portraits of heaven as a place for good, innocent souls.[387] Hit by a drunk driver on her birthday, the "as cute as Shirley Temple" Wanda June introduces audience members to a heaven where everyone "can just play and play and play." Her portrait of a heaven filled with Ferris wheels, golf courses, and Little League games quickly darkens as she mentions people executed in the electric chair and soldiers who love the weapons that killed them because they can play shuffleboard and drink beer.

These grimly comic images narrated by a lisping eight-year-old girl yield to a far more troubling conception of heaven as we encounter von Konigswald in his ceremonial SS uniform with the "sounds of a Nazi rally" as he appears on stage. As an SS officer in charge of medical experiments and concentration camp exterminations, von Konigswald embodies Nazi brutality and pure moral evil par excellence. The antithesis of a person deserving heavenly rewards, his character offers a provocative take on the standard humanist idea of no hell. While perhaps a bit unconventional in expression, Vonnegut's humanist stance aligns with the American Humanist Association's long-standing position on the subject. As Lloyd and Mary Morain explain in their historical overview of the organization, "Humanists recognize that unkindnesses and iniquities toward other people will not be remedied in an afterlife by a supreme being."[388] Instead, as Vonnegut shows in *Happy Birthday, Wanda June*, we need to address injustices and violence at their root causes—in this case by rejecting the toxic, vengeful models of heroic masculinity embedded in central cultural myths and modern war stories.

The added heaven scenes also strengthened the play's strong environmental messages (primarily delivered by Norbert and Penelope) by highlighting the Earth's unique splendor. Granted a planetary perspective usually reserved for astronauts, von Konigswald is deeply moved by the sight of Earth from "up here." On the day he died, he noticed "the whole planet was beautiful," and his interactions with "guys from other planets" help him realize that their "planets weren't anywhere as nice as Earth." While it might seem counterintuitive to have a Nazi war criminal deliver an environmental message, von Konigswald's character is a medium of contrasts. He counters Wanda June's innocence, mirrors Harold's combat brutality, and provides a benchmark for Looseleaf's "successful" kills in Nagasaki.

Perhaps it's *because* it comes from such an unconventional mouthpiece that von Konigswald's planetary appreciations stand out. Discussing the planets inhabited by "some really crazy-looking guys up here," von Konigswald remarks, "They had clouds all the time. They never saw a clear blue sky. They never saw snow. They never saw an ocean. They had some little lakes, but you couldn't go swimming in them. The lakes was acid. [*sic*] You go swimming, you dissolve." While highlighting the preciousness of common Earthly environments, the comments further challenge the notion of an afterlife by connecting heaven to science fiction worlds.

Although it might seem paradoxical to use heaven scenes as a way of confirming a naturalist, nontheistic world, Vonnegut long regarded religious beliefs and practices as interesting *human* creations. As *Cat's Cradle* and *God Bless You, Mr. Rosewater* reveal, Vonnegut was adept at inventing religions to emphasize this creative process and promote secular humanist ideals. In 1985, he turned to music and new artistic collaborations as he continued to challenge beliefs about an afterlife and divine judgment. This time he revised a key liturgical work, co-creating a new requiem to overhaul the "sadistic and masochistic" images of divine judgment in the Catholic mass for the dead.

As Vonnegut recounts in both *Fates Worse Than Death* and a December 1986 *North American Review* article, he decided to rewrite the lyrics to the 1570 requiem after attending the world premiere of Andrew Lloyd Webber's version on February 12, 1985.[389] After reading the Latin translation of the lyrics, Vonnegut saw a tremendous disconnect between the "enraptured" musical performance and the message of the mass. Instead of offering comforting, peaceful conceptions of death and eternal life, the lyrics, Vonnegut found, "were as humane as *Mein Kampf* by Adolf Hitler." With the aim of making the Council of Trent's *Requiem* "more sane and comforting to those with death on their minds," Vonnegut immediately began rewriting the text to remove images of judgment, torture, and hell.

After finding John Collins to translate his lyrics into church Latin and Edgar Grana to compose a new musical score, Vonnegut premiered their humanist requiem at the Unitarian Universalist Church in Buffalo on March 13, 1988. Reporter Richard Chon described the performance as "perplexing" and noted that audience members were "occasionally bewildered by the Requiem" in his *Buffalo News* review the next day.[390] While noting that musically the piece, which relied on three synthesizers, was "difficult to judge on first hearing," Chon found Vonnegut's project "baldly perverse." Although a fan of "Vonnegut's fictional reflections on eternity," Chon felt the challenge to dogma was "contradictory" and wondered, "If you're a skeptic, isn't it wiser to leave the idea of the afterlife alone completely?"

Frankly, it *is* puzzling why Vonnegut went to great lengths to undertake an ambitious side project. Considering that Vonnegut attended Lloyd Webber's premiere on the eve of the fortieth anniversary of the Dresden bombings and likely had Jane's battle with cancer on his mind, it's no wonder he turned to the key humanist virtues of "courage, cognition, and caring."[391] More than just a way to offer the dead a vision of sweet, peaceful sleep, Vonnegut's requiem blends his freethinking, scientific background with his strong pacifism to explore death within a naturalistic vision of the cosmos. Like his Freethinker ancestors, who rejected their Catholic faith after embracing the scientific ideas of Darwin and the liberal ideals of the revolutions of 1848, Vonnegut presents a nontheistic vision of the cosmos, where humans, along with "all flesh" originate from the "flying Stones" of the Big Bang. Owing our existence to "Time" and "Elements," human beings in Vonnegut's lyrics are literally stardust, indebted to deep geological time and natural forces—not a divine creator and judge.

After naturalistically framing death as peaceful sleep and noting that there will be "comical disappointment" for those expecting divine judgment, Vonnegut reimagines the "day of wrath" to highlight the immense destructive power of atomic and other modern human weapons. Harkening back to his 1946 poem about the extinction possibilities unleashed by "the new Holy Trinity" of energy, matter, and time, the second stanza of the requiem describes the day "We shall dissolve the world into glowing ashes, / as attested by our weapons for wars / in the names of gods unknowable" (ll. 13–15). In keeping with his long-standing critiques of violence performed in the service of religion, these lines become a refrain, reminding us that "when ashes sleep like ashes" countless innocent lives will be lost (l. 33). As a humanist who recognized that only humanity can solve its own problems, Vonnegut follows the image of ashes with the key rhetorical question, "What advocate shall I entreat / when even the righteous have been damned / by wars in the names of gods unknowable?" (ll. 36–38).

Not wanting to trouble the dead or the living with brutal images of fiery torture or destruction, Vonnegut only alludes to this technological destruction. The real plea, of course, is to avoid the flashes of atomic bombs and other weapons, to allow the dead to have darkness for their peaceful eternal "sleep." Channeling the type of Edenic reset presented in *Galápagos*, the penultimate stanza is a humbling "prayer" that places humans' ability to act as destructive geological agents in context:

> Merciful Time, who buries the sins of the world,
> grant them rest.
> Merciful Elements, from whom a new world can be constructed,
> moist blue-green, and fertile,
> grant them eternal rest. (ll. 99–103)

Vonnegut's wonder at the awesome forces of time and elemental change transcends these environmental and pacifist critiques. It also captures the deep sense of inspiration humanists have from contemplating human beings' place in enormously complex physical cosmic tendrils. As Vonnegut explained to Terrance Sweeney in a 1985 interview, his secular humanist equivalent of a "god" was a life stance where "spring is celebrated and where there is a feeling of something terribly important going on in the universe, something unified, and awareness of that."[392] From questioning dogma to offering a science-based vision of the cosmos to providing comfort for his fellow human beings, the entire requiem project is a humanist endeavor. These core humanist features were so prominent that composer Seymour Barab later wrote a new musical version of Vonnegut's requiem, *Cosmos Cantata*, which was "more suited to the secular concert hall" than the original piece.[393]

As his requiem strayed farther from its ecclesiastical origins, Vonnegut softened in his attitudes toward organized religion. In characteristically paradoxical fashion, Vonnegut most frequently invited people to "join a church" *after* being named the American

Humanist Association's (AHA) "Humanist of the Year" in 1992 and while serving as the AHA's honorary president for the last fifteen years of his life.[394] An old hand at embracing humanist aspects of the teachings of Jesus, Vonnegut emphasized the importance of community over nontheistic perspectives, and even lamented his friend Bernard O'Hare's lost Catholic faith in late-career works. Capturing this very public, compassionate humanism, Vonnegut explained in *Timequake*, "Humanists try to behave decently and honorably without expectation of rewards or punishment in an afterlife. The creator of the Universe has been to us unknowable so far. We serve as well as we can the highest abstraction of which we have some understanding, which is our community." In speeches, essays, and fiction, Vonnegut invited his readers to join him in these community-building efforts by embracing "original virtue," honoring new amendments, and behaving decently in an indecent society.

A great example of this late-career community-focused humanism is Vonnegut's final major creative exploration of an afterlife in his 1999 volume *God Bless You, Dr. Kevorkian*. Comprised primarily of twenty-one brief pieces originally created as ninety-second interludes for WNYC's radio fundraising drives, the book itself is a humanist, community-minded endeavor. Vonnegut foregrounds these values in the introduction to *God Bless You, Dr. Kevorkian*, where he mentions his position as honorary president of the AHA. He explains his reasons for his pro bono work for WNYC, praising the station for its efforts to enhance "the informed wit and wisdom of its community."[395] Vonnegut describes WNYC's informational and comforting mission as a form of humanism, which he equates with "good citizenship and common decency."

To explore these ideals and the "vacant lot between the far end of the blue tunnel and the Pearly Gates," Vonnegut presses himself into service as "WNYC's Reporter on the Afterlife." Imagining a fictional scenario where Dr. Jack Kevorkian facilitates controlled near-death experiences, Vonnegut interviews twenty individuals just outside heaven's gates, bringing back comments from the likes of William Shakespeare, Mary Shelley, and John Brown. At first glance, the collection of interviews seems random, mixing famous historical figures with people like Salvatore Biagini, a retired construction worker who died while rescuing "his beloved schnauzer, Teddy," from a pit bull assault. As scholar Marc Leeds observes, however, the "afterlife cavalcade" is a carefully assembled group, chosen with the same precision and spirit as Chaucer's famous *Canterbury Tales* pilgrims. "There is a mixture of evil, nobility, piety, and hypocrites," Leeds explains, "to keep one forever wondering about the reaches of human comprehension and motivation."[396]

More than a study of human nature, the afterlife procession allows Vonnegut to preserve important moments of secular sainthood, common decency, creativity, and goodness. He incorporates his signature concerns throughout the pieces: human rights activism, public service, social justice, an "Edenic" love of nature, romantic love, scientific curiosity, the joy of writing, creativity, and "resolve in the face of tragedy."[397] Interspersed within these celebrations of human potential are glimpses of human evil, captured in interviews with Adolf Hitler and James Earl Ray and highlighted in the metafictional exchange with Kilgore Trout. Like his earlier creative investigations of heaven, the latter interviews argue against notions of divine judgment, reminding readers to look to Earthly paths of environmental, social, legal, and other forms of justice.

In line with his freethinking heritage and contemporary humanist lifestance, Vonnegut doesn't want his readers to simply adopt his ethical positions. Just as he contrasts human nobility and depravity in the "afterlife cavalcade," Vonnegut juxtaposes heavenly and earthly fictional settings to encourage critical thinking. It's no accident that Vonnegut imagines his Kevorkian-assisted controlled near-death experiences taking place in Huntsville Penitentiary, Texas's oldest prison and America's most active execution chamber. From *Mother Night* to *Jailbird* to *Hocus Pocus*, Vonnegut had used imprisoned characters and jails to explore issues of war guilt, miscarriages of justice, systemic racism, capital punishment, and historical reckoning. Instead of turning to the Sacco and Vanzetti, Nuremberg, or Watergate trials as he did in those novels, Vonnegut invites readers to contemplate the ethics of two different lethal-injection systems that produce permanent one-way trips through the blue tunnel: prison executions and assisted suicides.

The titular reference to Eliot Rosewater and his comments about Kevorkian's murder charges in Michigan suggest that Vonnegut saw the controversial doctor as someone who alleviated suffering but also sparked important national debate on ideas of "death with dignity."[398] Vonnegut refers to Kevorkian as a "purported murderer" and mourns "the misery" befalling Kevorkian during his real 1999 trial. The book's interview with Karla Faye Tucker, the "born-again" double pickaxe murderer, by contrast, emphasizes the "busy" nature of the Huntsville facility and Tucker's reaction to the idea "that there was no Hell waiting for her, no Hell waiting for anyone." Tucker's response to the news is that it "was too bad because she would be glad to go to hell if only she could take the governor of Texas with her" for sanctioning capital punishment. These comments echo Vonnegut's long-standing critiques of capital punishment and the inequities within the criminal justice system.

In addition to these executions, Vonnegut, the ardent pacifist, highlights recurring and far deadlier state-sanctioned forms of mass murder in *God Bless You, Dr. Kevorkian*. Departing from his afterlife conversations, Vonnegut interviews Kilgore Trout to link the horrors of ethnic cleansing in Serbia with a broader history of genocides, ranging from the Tasmanian and Armenian genocides to the Holocaust.[399] Despite these glimpses into the depths of human evil, Vonnegut ends the collection with quotes from two of the most prolific writers he can imagine—his own fictional alter ego and his AHA predecessor, Isaac Asimov—to leave the reader with important humanist wisdom. Channeling the same humanist spirit that pervaded his earliest Dresden writings, Vonnegut via Trout abhors "Serb tyranny" but lambastes NATO bombings, because "all cities and even little towns are world assets." Asimov's crucial message, as Marc Leeds notes, is that writing itself can be a vital "refuge when faced with the inhumanity of others."[400] Ending with Asimov also allows Vonnegut to complete the joke he sets up in the introduction, that Asimov, the former AHA honorary president is "up in Heaven now," hard at work "on a six-volume set about cockamamie Earthling beliefs in an Afterlife." Offering his own form of creative secular sainthood, Vonnegut doesn't just explain the importance of community; he invites his readers, old and new alike, to experience it.

A FINAL REQUIEM—FOR THE EARTH

During the final years of his life, Vonnegut relied on his writing and artistic collaboration with artist Joe Petro III to create his own vital refuge as he struggled with depression, the deaths of countless friends and fellow artists, and the realities of post-9/11 life in the United States. With Petro, Vonnegut co-created a series of largely text-based silk-screen Confetti prints that responded to the wars and policies of the Bush administration and allowed Vonnegut to leave his fans with pearls of wisdom, reprieves of laughter, sobering critiques, and stark reflections on life in the early twenty-first century. Some of these reflections and images appeared in Vonnegut's final book, *A Man Without a Country* (2005), a collection of essays and autobiographical anecdotes edited by Dan Simon. With Confetti prints interspersed throughout its twelve chapters, *A Man Without a Country* captures Vonnegut's outrage over America's preemptive war in Iraq, addiction to fossil fuels in the wake of worsening climate change, the erosion of civil liberties and civil discourse, the dehumanization of people based on religion and race, and political tribalism. Although despairing in tone and outlook, Vonnegut encouraged readers to embrace the arts, secular sainthood, human connections and communities, and common decency as a way to persist in the face of anguish and heartbreak.

Despite these nourishing prescriptions, Vonnegut concluded *A Man Without a Country* with the despair of a planetary citizen who could no longer imagine a viable future for the Earth. Although Vonnegut had warned about pollution, resource depletion, fossil-fuel addiction, climate change, and planetary destruction for decades, he ended his final book with his 2005 poem, "Requiem."[401] Instead of revising the Catholic mass for the dead to provide secular humanist comfort, this requiem mourned the death of our planet and blamed human beings for its destruction. And unlike earlier secular epitaphs for our "Rare Earth," "Requiem" draws on traditional Christian accounts of Jesus's crucifixion to convey its message:

> The crucified planet Earth,
> should it find a voice
> and a sense of irony,
> might now well say
> of our abuse of it,
> "Forgive them, Father,
> They know not what they do."
>
> The irony would be
> that we know what
> we are doing.
>
> When the last living thing
> has died on account of us,
> how poetical it would be
> if Earth could say,
> in a voice floating up
> perhaps
> from the floor
> of the Grand Canyon
> "It is done."
> People did not like it here.

Given Vonnegut's admiration for Jesus's humanist messages—especially the Sermon on the Mount—and comments about how crucifixion is a particularly brutal form of capital punishment, the image of a crucified planet conveys tragedy, cruelty, injustice, and heartbreak all at once. Divorced from Christian frameworks in which humanity's sins are redeemed through Jesus's death, the planet's crucifixion is simply bleak, final, and tragic. The Earth's final words rising "from the floor of the Grand Canyon" are especially poignant, considering that Vonnegut's own teenaged planetary citizenship was nurtured there and at other sites during his Western adventures.

While "Requiem" likely captured Vonnegut's scientific prognosis for the Earth's future based on the climate change data and other environmental information he encountered, he never stopped giving his fans small pearls of wisdom, comfort, laughter, and hope. He added a final life-affirming author's note after "Requiem" in *A Man Without a Country* and continued creating Confetti prints and short written pieces until the very end of his life. Becoming "genuinely gloomy" from depression, new endless wars, and predicted planetary catastrophes kept him from imagining vibrant planetary futures. But it doesn't mean he didn't want to—or want others to want to.

Like Isaac Asimov, Kurt Vonnegut is up in heaven, where the music is beautiful. In between long naps he's organizing interspecies shuffleboard tournaments and clambakes, creating interstellar extended families, and asking his great-grandfather Clemens and other Freethinkers, "How the hell do you talk to God?"[402] Given Sir Isaac Newton's projected completion date for a blue-tunnel mail delivery system, Vonnegut's own six-volume set on the afterlife won't be available until 2972. It's up to us to summon our original virtue, to humanely contemplate "What are people for?," and to be better planetary citizens on this once-salubrious blue-green orb. Kurt, you are sorely missed.

Acknowledgments

Toward the end of his career, Vonnegut often said one of the things that made life worth living was all the secular saints he got to meet. Perhaps it's a Kurt thing, or maybe I'm just some extra lucky mud, but writing this book has brought numerous secular saints into my life. Following Mary Kathleen O'Looney's example in *Jailbird*, I've tried to keep track of them.

One of the greatest joys has been working with other Vonnegut scholars and artists—especially members of Kurt's own karass. Whether answering questions, sharing stories and materials, or nurturing my project, Marc Leeds, Asa Pieratt, Jerome Klinkowitz, Robert Weide, and Joe Petro III have redefined generosity and lived up to Kurt's praise in *Timequake*. Joel Cohen (aka the Sticker Dude) helped me appreciate Kurt's social justice legacies and mail art, while librarian Dan Crocker unearthed countless periodical gems. I'm indebted to M. André Eckenrode, digital wampeter extraordinaire, and my adopted uncle and literary fairy godmother, Dan Wakefield, who read chapters with patience, kindness, and wisdom. Without Dan Wakefield's saintly intercession, my project never would have found its way to Dan Simon and the extraordinary team at Seven Stories Press of Ruth Weiner, Stewart Cauley, and Lauren Hooker. I could not ask for a more gifted editor than Dan Simon, who improved this book at every stage and has been instrumental in nurturing Kurt's literary and social justice legacies.

Enormous thanks also go to a new generation of writers, scholars, and organizations that continue to make Vonnegut's words and ideas live. I'm deeply grateful to Julia Whitehead, founder and CEO of the Kurt Vonnegut Museum and Library, who championed this project from the beginning, and to the sinookas that introduced me to Max Goller, Chris Lafave, Drew DeSimone, Jennifer Tianen, Rai Peterson, Greg Sumner, and Keith Andrews. The Kurt Vonnegut Society and *The Daily Vonnegut* have also preserved Kurt's literary legacies, and I can't thank Tom Hertweck, Nicole Loman, and Chuck Augello enough for their peculiar travel suggestions. As my bibliography attests, I'm indebted to the numerous Vonnegut scholars who've preceded me and to Ginger Strand, Suzanne McConnell, and Tom Roston, whose excellent books came out while I was working on this one.

As Vonnegut increasingly lost faith in his own country, he still could find the America he loved "at the front desks of our public libraries." I'm grateful that America is still there; this book would not exist without the many libraries, archives, special collections, and funds that support archival research. Working with Vonnegut's manuscripts and other collections at the Lilly Library has been my greatest window into Kurt's extraordinary mind and process. That research was extended by an Everett Helm Visiting Fellowship and supported by the Lilly's incredible staff, especially Zach Downey, Isabel Planton, Erika Dowell, David Fraiser, and Cherry Williams. Meanwhile, Susan Sutton, Amy Vedra, and Regan Steimel expertly helped me explore Vonnegut's Hoosier roots through collections at the Indiana Historical Society Archives and Library. In Schenectady, Chris Hunter, Curator of Collections and Exhibits at the Museum of Innovation and Science, made Kurt's and Bernie's careers at General Electric come to life with an efficiency that would have made EPICAC proud, while Melissa Tacke of the Grems Doolittle Library helped put their careers in historical and place-specific contexts. And I will forever be appreciative of Lucy Loomis, Director of the Sturgis Library, and Betsy Wheeler, House

Administrator of the Barnstable Historical Society, for aiding my project and all the ways they celebrated Kurt and his family's lives during Barnstable's Vonnegutfest 2014.

As I worked with archival collections related to Kurt's publishing career, other librarians earned their angel's wings. Curtis Small Jr. helped me navigate the Seymour Lawrence, Klinkowitz, and Pierratt papers at the University of Delaware Library and Special Collections, and Brianna Cregele of Princeton University's Department of Rare Books and Special Collections assisted my explorations of the PEN, Charles Scribner's Sons, and Donoso files. Tal Nadan aided my work with the Crowell-Collier records at the New York Public Library's Manuscripts and Archives Division. Special appreciation also goes to Scott Richmond, Kerrie Fergen Wilkes, Cindy Yochym, Pat Cummings-Witter, Julie Crowell, and the staff of SUNY Fredonia's Reed Library for helping with research, student library exhibits, and Vonnegut events.

If you ever want to understand why Vonnegut was so enthusiastic about extended families, try writing a book. Kurt's own family embodied the very best of his generous, humane, and artistic ideals, and I can't thank Nanette (Nanny) Vonnegut and Scott Vonnegut enough for answering research questions via email. Mark Vonnegut also kindly fielded queries and offered key insights into his father's life during Barnstable's 2014 events, while the late Kurt Vonnegut (Bernie's son) and Richard Vonnegut Jr. shared family stories at Indy's 2015 Vonnegutfest. My deepest gratitude, though, goes to the late Jane Cox Vonnegut, patron saint of all Lilly Library archive users, whose unflagging support made Kurt's writing career possible and who was a remarkable planetary citizen in her own right.

The debts I owe to my artificial extended families are too numerous to describe here, but I hope the potluck, Bunco, Robin Street, Star Union, yoga, sports, farmers' market, and other tendrils of my karass know how important they are. In Fredonia, particular thanks go to Karen Mills-Courts and Jan McVicker for reading drafts and their ongoing encouragement; Natalie Gerber, for her always sage editing advice and friendship; and Bruce Simon and Kim Marie Cole, for allowing me to teach so many Vonnegut courses. I'm grateful to Tracy Marafiote, Sam Mason, and Courtney Wigdahl-Perry, Earth Goddesses extraordinaire, and my beloved English pod (Shannon, Ann, Saundra, David, Michael, Heather) for their cheerleading, humor, and liquid camaraderie. Bill Brown, Michelle Kuns, Jeanne Frerichs, Patrick Stokes, David Kinkela, Jon Titus, and Priscilla Titus likewise deserve praise for their amazing expertise, contributions, and support. My research trips would not have been possible without SUNY Fredonia's generous funding via Faculty Summer Research and Creativity, UUP Individual Development, and Mary Louise White awards, and I'm obliged to Diane Clark and Bill Moran of Greystone Nature Preserve for allowing me to plant Vonnegut-inspired trees to offset the mileage. And epic thanks go to the students in my Vonnegut seminars, each of which became an artificial family with inside jokes, skylarking, and humane ideas. I hope all my English 427 (SP 2012, F 2015, SP 2021), Honors 228 (SP 2014, SP 2018), and English 510 (F 2010, SP 2018, SP 2021) students know how much I treasure them and their work.

My own family members earned their sainthood by indulging my Vonnegut obsession and adding so many Uncle Alex moments to my life. I wish my mother, the first planetary citizen and Vonnegut fan in my life, had lived to see me complete this book, but I take comfort in Tralfamadorian timescapes and ways her original virtue lives on in relatives—especially Michael, Anna, Charlotte, Katie, Tom, Trish, and Donna. Like my Annear clan (Sharon, Spencer, Becky, and Steve), Althea Miller, and my father, Joseph Jarvis, they exemplify how nourishing extended families can be. As always, my most profound gratitude goes to Tom, Christopher, and Calder, for their love, unwavering support, and inspiration to imagine better planetary futures for us all.

Finally, thank you, Kurt. Your words, humor, and ability to find hope for humanity even in the darkest of times have been a life raft over the many years I've spent on this project.

All archival images by and of Kurt Vonnegut, including photographs, are copyright © Kurt Vonnegut LLC, and are used by permission of The Wylie Agency LLC.

Confetti prints are courtesy of Origami Express: kurtvonnegutprints.com.

Kurt Vonnegut manuscript draft pages are courtesy of the Lilly Library, Indiana University, Bloomington.

"Requiem" from *A Man Without a Country* is reprinted by permission of Seven Stories Press.

Hillis Howie portrait and Prairie Trek images are courtesy of Indiana Historical Society.

The July 22, 1939, *Indianapolis Times* photograph is courtesy of Hoosier State Chronicles, Indiana State Library.

"Rare Earth" sticker is courtesy of Ragged Edge Press, NYC.

"Drudgery is Disappearing," 1950 P. R. Mallory & Company advertisement, is reproduced by permission of Stanley Black & Decker.

B   Box

BHS Barnstable Historical Society, Archival Collections, Barnstable, MA

CU   Cornell University Archives, Division of Rare and Manuscript Collections, Carl A. Kroch Library, Cornell University, Ithaca, NY

DE–AP Asa Pieratt Collection, MCN 301, Special Collections, University of Delaware, Newark

DE–JK Jerome Klinkowitz Papers, MCN 300, Special Collections, University of Delaware, Newark

DE–SL Seymour Lawrence Publishing Files, MCN 259, Special Collections, University of Delaware, Newark

F   Folder

GDL Grems-Doolittle Library, Schenectady County Historical Society, Schenectady, NY

IHS–CS Charles J. Shields Research Collection, M 1155, Indiana Historical Society, Manuscript and Visual Collections Department, William Henry Smith Memorial Library, Indianapolis, IN

IHS–KV Kurt Vonnegut Collection, 1975–2011, SC1509, Indiana Historical Society, Manuscript and Visual Collections Department, William Henry Smith Memorial Library, Indianapolis, IN

IHS–PT   Prairie Trek Expedition Records, M0309, Indiana Historical Society, Manuscript and Visual Collections Department, William Henry Smith Memorial Library, Indianapolis, IN

KV   Kurt Vonnegut

KVML   Kurt Vonnegut Museum and Library, Indianapolis, IN

LL–DF   Donald C. Farber Manuscripts, LMC 2833, Lilly Library, Indiana University, Bloomington

LL–DW   Dan Wakefield Manuscripts, LMC 2715, Lilly Library, Indiana University, Bloomington

LL–KV   Kurt Vonnegut Manuscripts, LMC 1860, Lilly Library, Indiana University, Bloomington

MIS–GE   GE Archive, Museum of Innovation and Science, Schenectady, NY

NYPL–CC   Crowell-Collier Publishing Company Records, Manuscripts and Archives Division, New York Public Library, NY

PCM   Paley Center for Media, Archives and Collections, New York, NY

PU–CS   Archives of Charles Scribner's Sons, C0101, Manuscript Division, Department of Rare Books and Special Collections, Princeton University Library, NJ

PU–PEN   PEN American Center Records, Manuscript Division, Department of Rare Books and Special Collections, Princeton University Library, NJ

SL–KV   Sturgis Library, Archives and Collections, Kurt Vonnegut Articles and Correspondence, MS 82, Barnstable, MA

Notes

INTRODUCTION

1 Mayo, "Vonnegut & Earth Day." For the full text of the speech, I've relied on Mayo's quotations for passages omitted from Vonnegut, "Nixon's the One."

2 Rome, *Genius of Earth Day*, 259.

3 Lingeman, *Vonnegut by the Dozen*, 10.

4 Hayes, "The Beginning," iii. The central Environmental Action office rejected funding from Monsanto, Procter & Gamble, Ford, Celanese, Mobil Oil, and Standard Oil of New Jersey. Cotton, "Earth Day," 114. To see why Vonnegut was wise to be skeptical of anti-litter campaigns, read Dunaway, "Gas Masks, Pogo."

5 Details of the request and Vonnegut's permission are in Winifred Gallagher Polyn's letter to Vonnegut's agent Max Wilkinson, August 3, 1970, and Wilkinson's letter to Polyn, October 5, 1970, LL-KV, B 1, F 17.

6 Donald Farber shared this story during his public lecture at Tales of Cape Cod in Barnstable Village on October 10, 2014. To hear Vonnegut's February 1, 1971, lecture in Coolidge Auditorium, visit the audio recording collection at www.loc.gov. For more about the event, see William Holland, "Apologizing Novelist Applauded: Intuition Cut Vonnegut Talk?" *Evening Star*, February 2, 1971.

7 *Timequake* quotations in this paragraph, 197, 163.

8 Failey, *We Never Danced*, 145–48; "A Note From Mark Vonnegut," May 7, 2007, kurtvonnegutprints.com; Dan Wakefield email message to author, January 12, 2018. For other details about the service, including Tatum Greenblatt's participation, see LL-DF, B 10.

9 Qtd. in Scholes, "A Talk," 107.

10 Sumner, *Unstuck in Time*, 6.

11 KV, *Fates Worse Than Death*, 25.

12 KV, *Hocus Pocus*, 142.

13 For an overview of the Anthropocene and its implications, see Davies, *Birth of the Anthropocene*, *The Guardian*'s reporting on the proposed geological epoch, and websites for The Anthropocene Project and Welcome to the Anthropocene (www.anthropocene.info).

14 Rentilly, "God Bless You," 153.

15 The term "useful delusion" comes from psychologist and *Hidden Brain* host Shankar Vedantam, who reminds us how essential "foma" are: "We need hope in order to function, but the world gives us endless reasons not to be hopeful." *Useful Delusions*, xix.

CHAPTER 1: BECOMING A PLANETARY CITIZEN

16 My principal source of information on the founding, curriculum, and history of the Orchard Schools is Cregor's *Path Well Chosen*, which contains rich primary materials, interviews, photographs, and secondary sources. Although I emphasize the Vonneguts' and Hillis Howie's involvement, Indy folks will recognize the names of many prominent families in the school's early history: Clowes, Carey, Failey, Appel, Lilly, Sinclair, and so on. (And Hazel Crosby would hug them all.)

17 There is some discrepancy about the specific years that Kurt Vonnegut attended the Orchard School. Shields states that Vonnegut started kindergarten in 1928; however, that date would put his entire schooling off by a year. Failey, Vonnegut's lifelong friend, notes that Vonnegut left the school in 1930. Both biographers agree that Vonnegut attended the Orchard School from kindergarten through the end of third grade. Drawing on that shared information and adjusting accordingly for his 1940 high school graduation date, I've placed Vonnegut's time at the school from fall 1927 to spring 1931.

18 Whether Vonnegut developed his own passion for gardening here or from his father's backyard, his future prized lilies, irises, hostas, and hydrangeas no doubt benefited from his Orchard School skills. To learn more about Vonnegut's love of gardening and an amazing high school garden inspired by Kurt's hydrangeas, see Jennifer Tianen's lecture "Vonnegut's Literary Garden," available through the KVML's Vimeo page (vimeo.com/353368075).

19 Although Vonnegut widely praised his James Whitcomb Riley (School 43) and Shortridge teachers in his writings and speeches, often glossing over his privileged early private schooling, some of his most enduring relationships originated at the Orchard School. His time there may also have planted a few seeds for names and details in his later fiction. While at the Orchard School, he encountered *The Book of Knowledge* set (mentioned in *Cat's Cradle*), participated in May

Festivals (which appear in *Hocus Pocus*), and the surname Wildhack (Montana's last name in *Slaughterhouse-Five*). Cregor, 40–42.

20 Nuwer, "Skull Session," in Allen, *Conversations*, 252.

21 The unpublished letter is quoted in Cregor, 67.

22 My insights into Howie's environmental education approaches, pedagogical approaches, and environmental and social justice positions come from his own publications, manuscript drafts, professional biography, and Prairie Trek reports and records, IHS-PT. To view selected photographs of the Prairie Treks online, see Henry Hooper's "Witness Post: Hillis L. Howie," henryehooper.blog/witness-post-hillis-l-howie.

23 West, *Fourteenth Annual Report*, 45.

24 Cregor, 63–74.

25 Henley, *The Story*, 10. The entire Vonnegut family was intimately involved in the founding and later management of the museum. Described as "an indefatigable worker," Kurt Sr. eventually served as board president and organized community fundraising drives and other key developmental projects for the museum. Bernie, Allie, and young Kurt helped organize the donations, and Kurt Sr. continued his involvement with the museum long after his children left Indianapolis. In 1949, he designed the museum's addition, a new exhibition space for dinosaur bones, a mastodon skull, and skeletal casts of various prehistoric creatures. Kriplen, *Keep An Eye*, 38, 45, 27, 89–91.

26 To view Howie's woodworking skills, see Failey, 37. Kurt Sr.'s original seahorse logo appears in Kriplen, 20. For further discussion of collaborations between the Children's Museum and the Prairie Trek expeditions, see Kriplen, 40–45.

27 KV, *Fates Worse Than Death*, 25. I borrow the phrase "citizen of the Earth" from Vonnegut's own reflections in his papers. On the last page of an early draft of the 1968 short story "Welcome to the Monkey House," Vonnegut scrawled the simple message, "I am a citizen of the earth." Fittingly, in the story, Vonnegut investigates the loss of freedom and purpose that stems from rampant human population growth as well as the sterile, artificial environments that accompany a world with seventeen billion human beings. "Easy Go" and "Desire Under a Hot Tin Streetcar" drafts, LL-KV, B 12, F 43.

28 Kriplen, 45. From the majestic Bluebirds of Titan to *Slaughterhouse-Five*'s famous ending "Poo-tee-weet?" to Raymond Trout's fictional study of Bermuda Erns and Dalhousies, Vonnegut's writings are filled with bird references, imagery, sounds, and symbolism. For an overview and analyses of these elements, see Leeds, *Vonnegut Encyclopedia*, 62–65, and Olson, "Poo-tee-weet?"

29 Specific details and information about the 1937 Prairie Trek come from the *Twelfth Annual Report* and the organization's extensive records, media clippings, scrapbooks, and other papers, which are available at IHS-PT.

30 Howie, "Expedition for Older Boys," 100, IHS-PT B 10, F 5. For further discussion of automobile tourism in US national parks and wilderness areas, see Steinberg, *Down to Earth*; Sellars, *Preserving Nature*; and Dunaway, "Cultures of Nature."

31 Howie, "Prairie Trek," IHS-PT, B 10, F 5. Subsequent Howie quotations are from the published version of his 1941 *Regional Review* article unless otherwise noted. Again, specific details about the 1937 Prairie Trek come from *Twelfth Annual Report*, IHS-PT, B 11, F 14, and other records in IHS-PT.

32 Alternative forms of collecting had been in place for some time, such as the dinosaur footprint and other plaster casts that trek members brought back to the Children's Museum in 1932. Kriplen, 43. Although Vonnegut was not a member of the entomologist team, it's hard not to see Hitz's influence on future works, such as Frank Hoenikker's bug jars in *Cat's Cradle* or the careful attention to insect behavior in the short stories "The Petrified Ants" and "The Drone King."

33 *Twelfth Annual Report*, 24.

34 Nuwer, "Skull Session," in Allen, *Conversations*, 252–53. Vonnegut misremembers a few details about the trek, such as the year and the specific museum commission, but his debt to Howie and his naturalist philosophies is obvious in the interview.

35 Howie, ms. draft, "Prairie Trek," IHS-PT, B 10, F 6. Notably, Howie's critiques of Euro-American conquests of the land and Indigenous peoples were cut from or toned down in the published version.

36 Leopold delivered this speech at the American Association for the Advancement of Science annual meeting in Las Cruces, New Mexico, on May 1, 1933. Key ideas from this speech formed the basis for Leopold's famous "land ethic" in *A Sand County Almanac*.

37 Leopold qtd. in Howie, "Prairie Trek," 14.

38 *Twelfth Annual Report*, 28.

39 Howie, ms. draft, "Prairie Trek," IHS-PT, B 10, F 6.

40 Failey, 48. The Florida trip was led by Howie's friend and Orchard School colleague, Herb Sweet. For an account of the 1939 Florida expedition, including excerpts from Victor Jose's diary, see Failey, 49–52. Vonnegut also participated in another 1940 spring break Florida camping trip, this time led by Shortridge zoology teacher Jim Hall. To learn

about that adventure, see Failey, 52–53, and KV, "Shortridge Boys Are Successful on Trek," *Shortridge Daily Echo*, April 11, 1945.

41 Strand, "Vonnegut on the Road," 45.

42 Strand, "Kurt Vonnegut's Oklahoma Eden." For additional discussion of the adventure in Vonnegut's early career, see Wakefield, *Making of a Writer*.

43 Failey, 49. To read selections from Bud Gillespie's travel diary, see "Southwest Adventure," *Shortridge Daily Echo*, September 13, 1939.

44 Howie, ms. draft, "Prairie Trek," IHS-PT, B 10, F 6.

45 All quotations from and details about the rip come from KV, ms. draft, "The Rover Boys in the American Southwest," LL-KV, B 38, F "Rover Boys."

46 If fictional references are any indication, Carlsbad Caverns seem to have made an especially strong impression on Vonnegut. Carlsbad Caverns figure prominently in *Player Piano* as the home of super-computer EPICAC, and get mentioned in a variety of texts from *Slaughterhouse-Five* to *Jailbird*. See Leeds, *Vonnegut Encyclopedia*, 106–7.

47 Vonnegut scholars have noted how the events, radio shows, and economic impacts of the Great Depression affected Vonnegut's life and writings. For example, see Klinkowitz and Lawler, *Vonnegut in America*, 7–11; Failey, 14–16; Klinkowitz, *Kurt Vonnegut's America*, 3–4; and Sumner, *Unstuck in Time*, 10–13.

48 Notably, Vonnegut's account of his family here contrasts sharply with Charles Shields's biography, where Vonnegut's parents are portrayed as cold and distant and Kurt's relationship with Bernie is character-ized as jealous and strained. *And So It Goes*, 15–16. In "The Rover Boys," Vonnegut mentions numerous letters from his parents, with Edith Vonnegut writing twice as often as anyone else.

49 We can see the influence of Kurt and Jane's planetary citizenship on their two oldest children in Mark Vonnegut's back-to-the-land com-mune adventures in *The Eden Express* and Edith Vonnegut's numerous environmental (in)justice paintings, which can be view through her website (edithvonnegut.com).

50 A photo of the inscription appears on page seventeen of *Love, Kurt: The Vonnegut Love Letters, 1941-1945*, edited by Edith Vonnegut. As Edith notes in her introduction, the collection of 226 letters, virtually all from Kurt, is "a portrait of first love and early ambition." While the letters primarily chronicle Kurt's passionate, steadfast efforts to win Jane's love, they also capture Jane's unwavering faith in Kurt's nascent writing career. For letters mentioning Thoreau in the early phases of their courtship, see *Love Kurt*, 7–8, 18–19, 26.

51 Vonnegut's final Shortridge High School report card, LL-KV B 21, F 12. Information about Shortridge High School's campus, curriculum, and English reading lists comes from the 1940 *Shortridge Blue Book: Bulletin of Information* and "Reading List English Department Shortridge High School for English III, IV, V, VI, VII, VIII," IHS, Shortridge High School Collection, 1870–1981, M 482, B 6, F 2.

52 For more discussion of Vonnegut's *Shortridge Daily Echo* experiences and columns, see Reed, *Short Fiction*; Wakefield, *Making of a Writer*; and Eckenrode, "Appendix."

53 For other perspectives on Vonnegut's connections to Thoreau, see Morse, *Imagine Being an American*; Allen, *Understanding Vonnegut*; Thomas, *Reading, Learning, Teaching*; Freese, *Clown of Armageddon*; and Farrell, *Critical Companion*.

54 *Portable Thoreau Reader*, 78, 79. Subsequent quotations in this paragraph, 77 and 84.

55 Nanette Vonnegut, "My Father, the Doodler," 8.

56 *Walden*, 22.

57 *Timequake*, another novel that explicitly references Thoreau's writings, is also dedicated to Seymour Lawrence. Coincidence? If you'd like to concoct Vonnegut dedication conspiracy theories, see Leeds, *Vonnegut Encyclopedia*, xvi–xx.

58 Vonnegut apparently was working from memory. The phrasing in Jeffrey Cramer's fully annotated, scholarly edition is "I have travelled a good deal in Concord." *Walden*, 2.

59 Thoreau qtd. in Cramer, "Introduction," 2; KV, *Wampeters, Foma & Granfalloons*, xvii.

60 KV, *Palm Sunday*, 58; Allen, *Conversations*, 310.

61 At the risk of introducing more foma into Vonnegut Studies, I'd like to suggest a few other possible debts to Thoreau: his sense of planetary citizenship in quotes such as "I have lived some thirty years on this planet" and "This whole earth which we inhabit is a point in space"; the name Rumford; and his reflections on time, which seems quite Tralfamadorian. Thoreau writes, "Time is but the stream I go a-fishing in. I drink at it; but while I drink I see the sandy bottom and detect how shallow it is. Its thin current slides away, but eternity remains." *Walden* 9, 129, 30, 96. Here's Vonnegut, in the prologue to *Slaughterhouse-Five* after mentioning crossing the Delaware River that morning: "And I asked myself about the present: how wide it was, how deep it was, how much was mine to keep."

62 KV, "To Hell With Marriage," 241. Subsequent quotations, 241–42.

63 KV qtd. in McQuade, "Very Fringe Character," 236.

64 KV, graduate anthropology coursework materials, LL-KV, B 21, F 13–25.

65 See Klinkowitz, *The Vonnegut Effect,* preface; Reed, *Short Fiction,* chs. 1 & 2; and Davis, *Kurt Vonnegut's Crusade,* ch. 1.

66 In addition to Vonnegut's coursework materials, my information about Chicago's graduate anthropology program, its history, specific postwar elements, and professional contexts come from Stocking, *Anthropology at Chicago, The Ethnographer's Magic,* and *Race, Culture, and Evolution;* Patterson, *Social History of Anthropology;* and Eriksen and Nielsen, *History of Anthropology.*

67 This course sequence (later numbered 220-230-240), which started in 1945, "provided the comprehensive training in 'general anthropology'" for more than a decade and "was the hallmark of Chicago students in this period." Stocking, *Chicago* 33. The rest of my discussion of Anthropology 220 is based directly on Vonnegut's own syllabus, course packet, and other course materials. LL-KV, B 21, F 13.

68 From 1894 onward, Franz Boas questioned correlations between race and cultural development. Boas's influence on Chicago's program and American anthropology overall cannot be overstated. In addition to his reorganization of disciplinary subfields, Boas's studies of human growth and development in immigrant communities led to groundbreaking changes in concepts of race. Boas demonstrated that environment, not inherent racial types, affected growth and achievement. From these initial studies, Boas went on to challenge US Immigration Commission quotas and restrictions, to work with the NAACP toward racial equality, and to advocate for women's civil rights. Patterson, *Social History,* 49–50. For further discussion, see Stocking, *Race, Culture, and Evolution* and *Boas Reader;* Erickson and Murphy, *History of Anthropological Theory,* 93–97; Patterson, *Social History of Anthropology,* ch. 2; and Eriksen and Nielsen, *History of Anthropology,* ch. 3.

69 Lecture Notes, April 1946, LL-KV, B 21, F 13 (220).

70 LL-KV, B 21, F Anthropology 230.

71 Strand, *Brothers Vonnegut,* 30–31.

72 Robert Redfield letter to Lisa Redfield Peattie, in Stocking, *Chicago,* 30.

73 LL-KV, B 21, F 13 (220).

74 I can't resist pointing out Vonnegut's fictional allusions to some of the anthropologists he studied, such as Franz Boas (Boaz in *Sirens of*

Titan), G. H. R. von Koenigswald (Dr. Schlichter von Koenigswald in *Cat's Cradle*) and Alexander Lesser (James Lasher in *Player Piano*).

75 Entirely scrapping his earlier research, Vonnegut drafted and submitted a third thesis while teaching at the Writers' Workshop at the University of Iowa in October 1965. In *Palm Sunday*, he reprints portions of the rejected thesis, a cross-cultural comparison of narrative structures, entitled "Fluctuations Between Good and Ill Fortune in Simple Tales." Contrary to what Vonnegut claims in *Palm Sunday*, that thesis draft has not "vanished." A full copy, complete with a five-page appendix of "Simple Skeletons of 17 Tales Chosen from Sharply Diverse Sources," is in LL-KV, B 21, F 24. The thesis proposal for "Mythologies of North American Indian Nativistic Cults" along with extensive notes and his brief draft can be found LL-KV, B 21, F 23.

76 KV qtd. in McQuade, 238, 239, 242.

CHAPTER 2: VIEWS FROM TITAN, TRALFAMADORE . . .

77 I probably don't need to remind Vonnegut fans that "Greetings" is the sealed message Salo is charged with carrying to the other rim of the universe in *Sirens of Titan*. That brilliant, hilarious message was almost something else: "I love you stranger, don't ask me why." That alternate message and other *Sirens* manuscript adventures can be found in the scroll drafts, LL-KV, B 25.

78 Allen, *Conversations*, 35.

79 LL-KV, B 35, F "Sirens. Handwritten notes."

80 *Sirens of Titan* quotations in this section appear on pages 90, 7–8, 274–75, and 280 of the 1998 Delta edition.

81 Wolf, "Thru Time and Space," 64.

82 In very early outlines for and drafts of the novel, Vonnegut initially called the novel "Sirens of Triton." LL-KV, B 35, F "Novel Summary." Vonnegut's shift from an imagined planet, Triton, to one of Saturn's actual moons is significant; Vonnegut chose an astral body theoretically capable of hosting life within our solar system. As E.O. Wilson notes, "the vast aquatic oceans of Jupiter's moons Callisto, Europa, and Ganymede, as well as Titan," are all encased in shells of ice but possess "depths warm enough to hold liquid organism." *Meaning of Human Existence*, 106.

83 Vonnegut mentions that Kilgore Trout "has been [his] alter ego in several of [his] other novels" in the prologue to *Timequake*. For further discussion of Trout's many roles in Vonnegut's fiction, including that of alter ego, see Reed, "Hurting 'Til It Laughs" and "Kurt Vonnegut's

Bitter Fool," both in Leeds and Reed, *Images and Representations*, 19–38, 67–80; Allen, *Understanding Kurt Vonnegut*, 12–13; Leeds, *Vonnegut Encyclopedia*, 618–21; and Broer, "Vonnegut's Goodbye," 65–90.

84 Reed, "Bitter Fool," 67. For a description of the two writers meeting on Cape Cod and the traits of Sturgeon's that Vonnegut incorporated into Trout's characters, see Shields, *And So It Goes*, 157–58.

85 Reed, "Bitter Fool," 78.

86 *God Bless You, Mr. Rosewater* quotations appear on pages 21–22 and 18 of the 2006 Dial edition.

87 For summaries of these and other Kilgore Trout stories, see Farrell, *Critical Companion*, 505–11.

88 For further discussion of Kilgore Trout's and Vonnegut's complex relationship with and to science fiction, see Morse, "The Once and Future Satirist." As 1960s scholar Jan McVicker reminded me, Kilgore Trout was in good company in his planetary thinking and speculations on alternatives to human-caused destruction of whole stellar systems; the landmark television shows *Dr. Who* and *Star Trek* launched on BBC in 1963 and NBC in 1966, respectively.

89 Harry Reasoner, "Man on the Moon: The Epic Journey of Apollo 11," CBS News Transcript, July 20, 1969. Vonnegut, of course, was not alone in denouncing the vast sums of money spent on the moon landing and the space program. Reverend Ralph Abernathy, the leader of the Southern Christian Leadership Conference, led hundreds of Black Americans to the gates of NASA on July 14, 1969, to highlight systemic economic and racial injustices, and in 1970, Gil Scott-Heron recorded his (still timely) spoken-word song, "Whitey on the Moon."

90 The essay is reprinted in *Wampeters, Foma & Granfalloons*. Quotations in the paragraphs that follow can be found on pages 80–88 in the 1999 Delta edition.

91 In his preface to *Wampeters, Foma & Granfalloons*, Vonnegut explicitly links environmental change with imagination. He writes, "So I now believe that the only way in which Americans can rise above their ordinariness, can mature sufficiently to rescue themselves and to help rescue their planet, is through enthusiastic intimacy with works of their own imaginations."

92 See, for example, Vonnegut's comments about Voyager 2 photographs on page 109 in *Fates Worse Than Death*, which refer to "the space boondoggle" and highlight the idea that the satellite only confirmed "that there was only death and more death out there." For an archival adventure, see Vonnegut's unpublished 1985 skit for Marjorie Loggia's Peace Project, which pokes fun at the space shuttle program, LL-KV,

B 4, F 18. Because Vonnegut updates the time frame for the story to the late 1980s in its *Palm Sunday* reprinting, I've returned to the story's original publication in *Again, Dangerous Visions*. Quotations in the next few paragraphs can be found on pages 248 and 250.

93 Carson, *Silent Spring*, 119.

94 KV, *Palm Sunday*, 203, 210.

95 Vonnegut's 1985 MIT speech and "Ladies and Gentlemen of 2088 A.D." are reprinted in *Fates Worse Than Death*.

96 KV, *Fates Worse Than Death*, 185. Although despair over climate change and other political matters compelled Vonnegut to cancel the rest of his college speaking tour, he didn't shy away from environmental issues. When asked by writer Colin Hamblin what he would "want to report on today if [he] were a journalist," Vonnegut remarked, "I suppose the environment." Colin Hamblin, Interview with Kurt Vonnegut, *The Chautauqua Daily*, July 18, 1989.

97 Prior to Cohen's phone conversations with Kurt, Don Farber, Vonnegut's agent, had spoken to Cohen about another collaboration, a bound special limited edition of Vonnegut's essay "Fuh-kar-wee Indians and the Christian Year 2000." Joel Cohen, letter to Kurt Vonnegut, August 2, 1998, LL-DF, B 1, F "Misc. Business Letters." Details about Cohen-Vonnegut collaborations come from phone and email exchanges with the author on July 16, 2015, but have been expanded over a multi-year correspondence.

98 In keeping with Vonnegut's and Cohen's shared commitment to progressive politics and socially conscious artwork, no money exchanged hands and the stickers were never sold. Cohen supplied the stickers to Vonnegut free of charge, and Vonnegut, in return, gave Cohen a signed copy of *Galápagos*. Vonnegut also wrote a delightful personal letter to Cohen's mother.

99 Joe Petro III, telephone conversation with author, October 16, 2018.

100 The 1977 *Paris Review* interview is reprinted in *Palm Sunday*, which also includes a copy of Vonnegut's speech at the *Cornell Sun* banquet on May 3, 1980, in which he expands on his father's reasons for having him enroll as a chemistry major.

101 Vonnegut's February 28, 1977, letter to Carl Sagan, along with other excerpts from and details on their correspondence, can be found in Bill Sternberg, "The Sagan Files," *Cornell Alumni Magazine*, March/April 2014.

102 Vonnegut, Shortridge Hight School transcript, LL-KV, B 21, F 12.

103 Shields, *And So It Goes*, 29.

104 See his unsigned May 13, 1941, and signed May 4, 1942, *Cornell Daily Sun* columns.

105 Vonnegut, "Innocents Abroad," *Cornell Daily Sun*, April 23, 1941.

106 That letter and several others showcasing Vonnegut's college scientific studies can be found in *Love Kurt*, 9, 14–15, 20–21, 22, 27, 29, and 37.

107 Although contemporary estimates of the number of red blood cells put the number at twenty to thirty trillion, Vonnegut's rough calculations of the cells' diameter (6 to 8 micrometers) would produce a length that could circle the Earth at least three times at the equator.

108 Vonnegut mentions taking courses in quantitative analysis and bacteriology "in the summer school of Butler University" in *Timequake*, 14.

109 Shields, *And So It Goes*, 51. This introductory phase of the program preceded specialized engineering training in either civil, mechanical, chemical, sanitary, or marine transportation. Vonnegut was selected for the four-term mechanical engineering program. Keefer, *Scholars in Foxholes*, ch. 1.

110 Vonnegut makes these comments in track five of the CD *Essential Vonnegut*. Incidentally, he also stresses to interviewer Walter Miller that although he didn't do especially well in the classes, he *did* know something about calculus, chemistry, and optics. And how *did* Vonnegut do in these courses? He earned solid to high B's in shop practice (85), mechanical engineering drawing (86), and statistics and dynamics (85), but fared less well in his calculus and thermodynamics courses (68 in each). Guy Reel, "Kurt Vonnegut's Letters Recount His Days at UT," *Daily Beacon*, November 29, 1978.

111 If Vonnegut's drawing seems reminiscent of Rachel Carson's images of chemical molecules in *Silent Spring*, dear reader, you are probably on to something. Keep reading for more Vonnegut-Carson connections!

112 Dr. Sherri "Sam" Mason, email to author, July 15, 2015.

113 KV, *Breakfast of Champions*, 234.

114 The pagination for *Hocus Pocus* quotations here and in the next few paragraphs comes from the 1991 Berkley edition: 9, 198–99, 199, 200, 202, 242, 324.

115 Kilgore Trout is never explicitly named as the author, but it's clear that Vonnegut is indulging in some harmless intratextuality to reward his fans. Rather than name Trout directly, Vonnegut provides clues, citing Trout's long-standing history of having his work reprinted as textual filler in pornographic books and magazines. Narrator Eugene Debs Hartke describes the authorial circumstances that surely point to Kilgore Trout: "The story was very likely pirated from some other

publication, so the omission of the author's name may have been intentional. What sort of writer, after all, would submit a work of fiction for possible publication in *Black Garterbelt?" Hocus Pocus*, 205.

116 Wilson, *Meaning of Human Existence*, 104.

117 *Timequake* quotations here and in the next few paragraphs come from pages 49–51 of the 1998 Berkley edition.

118 Yes, superfans, September 1, 1945, is also the date of Kurt and Jane's wedding. Given the heartfelt and loving things Vonnegut says about Jane in *Timequake*, though, I don't think that event is connected to Trout's story. In the spirit of remembering Carl Barus and getting things right, I should note the actual surrender on the battleship *Missouri* took place on September 2, 1945, in Japan's time zone.

119 Once again, Vonnegut's scientific fears and principles are sound here. See, for example, public health journalist Maryn McKenna's March 2015 TED talk, "What Do We Do When Antibiotics Don't Work Anymore?" This and all future cited TED talks are available on TED's website or through the TED app.

120 According to NASA estimates, only 4.6 percent of the universe is composed of atoms. The other 24 percent and 71.4 percent is made up of dark matter and dark energy respectively. NASA, "Universe 101: Our Universe," wmap.gsfc.nasa.gov/universe/uni_matter.html.

121 Allen mentions receiving the bumper sticker in their February 1999 interview, and asks Vonnegut "Did you mean me personally, or was that the collective 'you'?" *Conversations*, 322.

122 For further discussion of his collaborations with Joe Petro III, see Vonnegut's author's note in *A Man Without a Country*.

123 That's right, superfans, this idea appeared twenty-six years earlier in Vonnegut's 1953 story "Ready to Wear," which explored body hopping as a radical solution to rampant human population growth. Quotations from *Jailbird* come from pages 99 to 101 of the 1999 Delta edition.

124 KV, ms. draft, "Mary Kathleen O'Looney or Unacceptable Air," LL-KV, B 8, F 22.

125 To read early proposals for the term, see Crutzen and Stoermer, "The Anthropocene," *International Geosphere-Biosphere Programme Newsletter* 41 (2000): 17, and Crutzen, "Geology of Mankind," *Nature*, January 3, 2002: 23.

126 Gould qtd. in Allen, *Conversations*, 252. Vonnegut also maintained a friendly correspondence with Gould. One of Vonnegut's letters, dated March 6, 1999, reveals that they continued to discuss theories of evolution and Darwinian evolution well after the publication of *Galapagos. Letters*, 383–84.

127 For big-brained readers who would like to find the *Galápagos* quotations in the rest of this chapter, here are the page numbers in order
from the 2009 Dial edition: 82, 19, 80, 81, 107, 25, 319, 157, 175–76, 319,
199, 9, 155, 202, 318, 281, 284, 106.

128 Chakrabarty, "Climate of History," 335.

129 Careful readers of *Galápagos* will recall that Leon's curiosity about
the fate of Mary Hepburn and her fellow passengers on the *Bahía de
Darwin* is only one of the reasons he refuses to enter the blue tunnel.
He is also repelled by the smoking, haggard figure of his father at the
tunnel's entrance.

130 During his conversation with his father, Leon explains that his
"research project" is a broad examination of human thought: "I had
chosen to be a ghost because the job carried with it, as a fringe benefit, license to read minds, to learn the truth of people's pasts, to see
through walls, to be many places at once, to learn in depth how this or
that situation had come to be structured as it was, and to have access
to all human knowledge." *Galápagos*, 276.

131 Qtd. in Chakrabarty, 342.

132 Flores, "Earthlings," 610. Well before the COVID-19 pandemic, virol-
ogists echoed these sentiments, calling attention to the numerous ani-
mal-to-human viral transmissions that will occur as we encroach further into remaining wilderness. See, for example, Quammen, *Spillover*.

133 In strengthening humans' sense of smell and response to pheromones,
Vonnegut also brings our imagined descendants more into harmony
with the rest of the animal kingdom. As E. O. Wilson reminds us, "We
are chemosensory idiots. By comparison most other organisms are
geniuses. More than 99 percent of the species of animals, plants, fungi,
and microbes rely exclusively or almost exclusively on a selection of
chemicals (pheromones) to communicate with members of the same
species." *Meaning*, 80–81.

134 Based on Vonnegut's famous 1982 sermon at St. John the Divine, delivered just two months after his trip to the Galápagos Islands, it's clear that
the difference between human and geological timescales was very much
on his mind as he wrote the novel. In that famous speech, he explains, "If
you go to the Galápagos Islands, and see all the strange creatures, you
are bound to think what Charles Darwin thought when he went there:
How much time Nature has in which to accomplish simply anything. If
we desolate this planet, Nature can get life going again. All it takes is a
few million years or so, the wink of an eye to Nature. Only humankind is
running out of time." *Fates Worse Than Death*, 145.

CHAPTER 3: A HOOSIER'S SYMPHONY OF PLACE

135 The synopsis, NBC submission letter, and various manuscript drafts of *The Hoosiers* or *The Hoosier Symphony* can be found in LL-KV, B 8, F 18. In an October 25, 1955, letter to Knox Burger, Vonnegut mentions that he "was all set to run a series of brilliantly brutal plays through Robert Alan Aurthur, when NBC benched him." As Dan Wakefield explains in his headnote, Aurthur was "a screenwriter, director, and TV producer who worked for some of the distinguished live television programs of the 1950s, such as *Studio One, Playhouse 90*, and *Producer's Showcase*." *Letters*, 62, 61.

136 Early notes for and drafts of *The Hoosier Symphony*, for example, contain the germ for Hazel Crosby's character in *Cat's Cradle*. In an outline titled "Paper Moon or The Hoosiers," Vonnegut sketches out a conversation between Mrs. Fisher and Mrs. Failey, in which the former recounts "her trip to South America, where they met Hoosiers everywhere." LL-KV, B 8, F 18.

137 Shields briefly discusses three of these plays and Vonnegut's unsuccessful turn to playwriting in the mid-1950s in *And So It Goes*, 130–31, 136, 139. While several cultural geographers, ecocritics, environmentalists and other scholars have influenced my perspectives on place, I am especially indebted to Buell, "Space, Place, and Imagination" and Yi-Fu Tuan, "Place/Space, Ethnicity/Cosmos."

138 Shields, 135–36.

139 Vonnegut used this exact phrase and mentioned these specific arts in a draft of *The Hoosiers*.

140 Drafts of and synopses for the unpublished play *Jonah* highlight the many issues of trauma, survivorship, war guilt, and pleas for peace that Vonnegut would eventually channel into *Slaughterhouse-Five* and other war texts. LL-KV, B 9, F 7. Mercer, Ohio, is the setting for *Emory Beck*, the play Vonnegut co-wrote with Robert B. Ruthman. LL-KV, B 5, F 8. Lincoln High School is the setting for "The Boy Who Hated Girls," originally published in the March 1956 issue of the *Saturday Evening Post*.

141 My work builds on previous examinations of place in Vonnegut's writings. Leeds and Farrell have already "mapped" the terrain of his fictional universe, cataloging many of the real and imagined locales that appear in Vonnegut's works. Klinkowitz and Sumner, meanwhile, have explicitly explored Vonnegut's Midwestern roots, regionalist characteristics, and biographical engagements with place in his fiction.

142 Vonnegut's cover letter to Wollaeger accompanies the original manuscript for "The Lake," LL-KV, B 28, F "The Lake." I have chosen to

use the current spelling of "Maxinkuckee," but Vonnegut consistently spelled it "Maxincuckee" in "The Lake" and its reprinting in *Fates Worse Than Death*. Although I quote from the published version of the essay, my insights into the essay's structure come from Vonnegut's distinctive use of asterisks for section breaks in the draft he sent Wollaeger, which originally divided the essay into five parts.

143 Buell, "Space, Place, and Imagination," 63.

144 See, for example, Tuan's chapter on childhood spaces in *Space and Place*.

145 If you don't already know the charming story of Jane receiving the quotation as a gift from Henry Goddard, one of her favorite Swarthmore professors, see Fiene, "Elements of Dostoevsky," 133–34.

146 Although Vonnegut himself doesn't label his swim across Lake Maxinkuckee as his most sacred childhood memory, Failey suggests that it is. Describing the swim, she writes, "The boy's boundless energy and sheer joy show that he is, at that precise moment, probably as happy as he will ever be." *We Never Danced*, 23.

147 Tuan, *Space and Place*, 33.

148 Qtd. in Failey, 25.

149 "Coda to My Career" appears in *Bagombo Snuff Box*, quotations, 354.

150 Rackstraw, *Love As Always*, 20.

151 Mark Vonnegut notes, "My parents were over-educated Midwestern liberals a long way from home with hopes and ambitions that would have perplexed and mystified their neighbors. Most Cape Codders had grown up on the Cape like their parents before them. They had quiet jobs and inherited a little money they didn't talk about." *Just Like Someone*, 23.

152 Yarmolinsky, *Angels Without Wings*, 141.

153 "In the Beginning with Larry Josephson," Vonnegut radio interview, April 17, 1972, PMC, Catalog ID R:11611.

154 Sumner, *Unstuck in Time*, 31.

155 Klinkowitz, *Vonnegut Effect*, 79.

156 Photos and descriptions of the church and bell's restoration, which was completed in the summer of 1958, can be found in "The West Parish Church of Barnstable," BHS, Village Hall Memorabilia Collection, MC 12, B 1. For the full range of Vonnegut's Barnstable references, see Leeds, *Vonnegut Encyclopedia*, 39–49.

157 All quotations appear on pages 1–6 of the 1968 Delta edition of *Welcome to the Monkey House*.

158 Lynne Richmond, "Sturgis Too Stodgy, Vonnegut Claims," *Cape Cod Standard Times*, August 26, 1970. The article, Vonnegut's resignation letter, and other materials relating to his time in Barnstable are available in SL-KV.

159 Handy, *Barnstable Village*, 77. For additional firsthand accounts of these marsh treks, see Ben and Jane Thompson's "K.V., Stick-in-the-Mud" tribute in Krementz, *Happy Birthday*, 58–59.

160 Vonnegut appears in a group photo and is listed in the cast in "Dress Rehearsal Held of Scene from 'Dulcy,'" *Barnstable Patriot*, November 12, 1953. This article, along with many others that detail Kurt and Jane's involvement in the Barnstable Comedy Club are available SL-KV and SL "Town and Local History Collection." Other specific Comedy Club details mentioned in this paragraph come from "Barnstable's Village Hall Purchased by Comedy Club," *The Barnstable Patriot*, 1961, and "Barnstable Comedy Club's Offering Has All Male Cast," *The Barnstable Patriot*, October 17, 1957, both in SL-KV.

161 In a July 2004 letter, Vonnegut urged Robert Weide to visit many of the sites he wrote about in his essay on Barnstable and explained why St. Mary's church was so sacred to him. Vonnegut had donated a Madonna statue, which "used to be in [their] atheistic homes in Indianapolis," to the church in memory of his sister Alice. *Letters*, 407.

162 KV, "The Cape Cod National Seashore," LL-KV, B 12, F 30. All subsequent references to and quotations come from this fourteen-page manuscript.

163 As my Hoosier colleague Jan McVicker speculates, perhaps the designation of Indiana Dunes National Lakeshore in 1966 prompted Vonnegut to write about the Cape Cod National Seashore. If you solve the mystery, please let me know.

164 US Congress, "Cape Cod National Seashore." At the risk of putting my ORD (obsessive research disorder) on full display, here's a sample of some of the documents Vonnegut quotes from in his essay: Bertram Courier's June 17, 1960, letter to Congressman Hastings; Chester Crocker's June 14, 1960, letter to Senator Murray; Norman Cook's statement on page 399; and Charles Frazier's statements on pages 168 and 378. This was no *Back to School* scenario; Vonnegut did his homework.

165 See, for example, Thoreau's descriptions of the *Franklin*: "The sea, vast and wild as it is, bears thus the waste and wrecks of human art to its remotest shore. There is no telling what it may not vomit up. It lets nothing lie; not even the giant clams which cling to its bottom." *Cape Cod*, 133.

166 Thoreau, *Cape Cod*, 318.

167 Kurt J. Adams mentions this journey along with his uncle's playful efforts to pose as a marsh monster during a summer 1962 campout in his Festschrift tribute in Krementz, *Happy Birthday*, 152–53.

168 Thoreau, *Cape Cod*, 318–19.

169 Vonnegut had already associated the bird call "poo-tee-weet" with images of mass destruction during Eliot's vision of Indianapolis consumed by firestorm in *God Bless You, Mr. Rosewater*. Even earlier, in *Cat's Cradle*, Vonnegut links a bird's "poo-tee-phweet" to the ice-nine-induced global apocalypse.

170 Solnit, "Water," 92.

171 KV, *Letters*, 383.

172 For a discussion of Vonnegut's romantic and familial relationships during this tumultuous period, see Rackstraw, *Love As Always*, 37–41; Shields, *And So It Goes*, 260–68, 274–75, 292–97; and Sumner, *Unstuck in Time*, 148–50.

173 Vonnegut letter to José Donoso, October 24, 1971. *Letters*, 174. Vonnegut also captured the city's energizing effects in the November 1972 letter he sent to Rackstraw: "I'm fine at fifty. New York jazzes me up. It's my monkey gland transplant. People speak to me on the street. I glow. I feel like a useful citizen." *Love As Always*, 45.

174 Noble, "Unstuck in Time," in Allen, *Conversations*, 59.

175 Jacobs, *Life and Death*, 443–44.

176 Sellers, "Cities and Suburbs," 470.

177 As Failey recalls in her account of the service, family and close friends gathered in the Helen Hayes room of the Algonquin, the former salon of "Sinclair Lewis, Dorothy Parker, Harold Ross, and Robert Benchley" in the 1930s. For more details about the service, see *We Never Danced*, 145–48.

178 What kind of guild member was Vonnegut? He was an active and generous one. Vonnegut's fierce defense of the First Amendment and writers' freedom of expression is well known from his testimony before Congress; famous letter to the school board of Drake, North Dakota; appearance in documentaries; and involvement with the ACLU. Perhaps less well known is the fundraising he did for PEN America and its efforts to champion writers' free speech, which included donating royalties from productions of plays or particular editions of novels to the organization. PU-PEN, S 3, B 23. The Farber Files, meanwhile, highlight Vonnegut's generosity in allowing small presses to translate and print foreign language editions of his novels. My favorite example

is when Vonnegut sold the rights for a Polish edition of *Mother Night* to a small independent press for one zloty (roughly twenty cents). He sent the Polish coin to his agent, Don Farber, with the instructions to "Take out your ten per cent and deposit the rest." See LL-DF, B 7, F Misc. Requests. Vonnegut's support of writers and literature extended well beyond New York City networks. His papers at the Lilly Library document his involvement in the National Foundation for the Arts and Humanities, the National Endowment for the Arts, and many international conferences and organizations.

CHAPTER 4: APOCALYPTIC LANDSCAPES

179 Although there are no dates on Vonnegut's early outlines and story notes, he carefully marked the day he started writing "Ice-9" on the GE folder where he kept the drafts: April 11, 1950, exactly fifty-seven years before he died. So it goes. (In the spirit of Carl Barus and getting things right, Vonnegut titled the 1950 drafts "ICE-9" and later drafts "Ice-9." I've simplified things by simply using "Ice-9" for the short story and "ice-nine" for the crystal throughout; life is confusing enough.)

180 This paragraph, along with other early handwritten notes and typed outlines, can be found in LL-KV, B 36, F "Miscellaneous Papers, *Cat's Cradle*."

181 Although the initial sales of *Cat's Cradle* were disappointing, the novel did garner a very favorable review by Terry Southern in the *New York Times* and helped widen Vonnegut's early underground readership.

182 Carson, *Silent Spring*, 3.

183 While the origins of *Silent Spring* are well known, I've drawn specifically on Linda Lear's introduction to the fortieth-anniversary edition.

184 Vogt qtd. in Wellrock, 135. For further discussion of apocalyptic rhetoric in 1960s and 1970s texts, see Heise, "The Virtual Crowds," 26.

185 Garrard, *Ecocriticism*, 93.

186 Vonnegut scholars have long noted this trend. See, for example, Goldsmith, *Fantasist of Fire and Ice* and Giannone, *Preface to His Novels*.

187 Garrard, 99.

188 The metafictional layers of *Cat's Cradle* are much more complicated. The novel takes the form of a post-apocalyptic book drafted six months after the release of ice-nine, but begins with the story of another book about the day the United States dropped the first atomic bomb on Hiroshima (fittingly titled *The Day the World Ended*). Just a few pages into the backstory of the narrator's first failed book, the reader learns about another apocalyptic text, the science fiction novel

2000 A.D., which Marvin Sharpe Holderness has sent in manuscript form to Felix Hoenikker. Felix uses the string holding the manuscript together to play cat's cradle with his younger son Newt, setting up many inter- and intratextual loops of meaning.

189 I should probably offer a few warnings here. First, there's no way I can tell *Cat's Cradle*'s entire compositional history here. The Lilly Library has more than a dozen drafts, with at least ten distinct versions composed over four major time windows. Second, based on correspondence to editors Knox Burger, Harry Brague, and Sam Stewart, it's clear that other drafts were written but are missing from the Lilly's collection. These additional drafts could turn my arguments into a pack of foma.

190 Strand, *Brothers Vonnegut*, 95–96. My discussion of Bernard's influence on and GE elements in "Ice-9" and *Cat's Cradle* comes from Strand, 95–96, 235–39.

191 Quotations from drafts of "Ice-9" come from manuscripts in LL-KV, B 36. Quotations from the draft with Dr. Macon and Dr. Dale come from the seventy-page version of the story, while quotations involving the romantic plot between David and Marion are from the fifty-two-page version.

192 On March 6, 1953, Vonnegut wrote to Harry Brague, an editor at Scribner's Sons, about several new books that he had started, and specifically mentioned "Ice-9" as one of the titles in an unpublished letter to Knox Burger a week later. Other correspondence from August 1953 specifically mention either work on "Ice-9" or the $500 advance from Scribner's for it. Writing to Brague on May 7, 1954, Vonnegut began to identify the book as *Cat's Cradle*, stating that it's "about what three brothers do when they inherit from their father a terrible thing called ice-9." The May 7, 1954, letter is available at PU-CS, B 349, F 5. Some of these 1953 and 1954 "Ice-9" drafts can be found in LL-KV, B 36, B 12.

193 Vonnegut put quite a few autobiographical details into Bud's character. Let's see . . . Bud hated his publicity-writing job in a corporate news bureau, moved to Cape Cod to work with his hands and invent things, bought a rambling old house in need of repairs, was married to an incredibly supportive intelligent wife, and just happened to have been a POW in Saxony, Germany, who encountered people collecting war loot, including a clock shaped like an Eiffel Tower. Coincidence?

194 As Schweitzer explained in his best-selling autobiography, "Only by the means of reverence for life can we establish a spiritual and humane relationship with both people and all living creatures within our reach." *Civilization and Ethics*, 57.

195 Howard Harkel, "Dr. Schweitzer, a Renowned Medical Missionary with a Complicated History," *PBS NewsHour*, January 14, 2016.

196 *Cat's Cradle* quotations in this paragraph come from pages 166, 169, and 171 of the 1998 Delta edition. Vonnegut would go on to celebrate Schweitzer's pacifism and reverence for life "as a foundation for all honorable, beautiful human lifetimes" more explicitly in his 1973 essay "What One Person Can Do."

197 KV letter to Harry Brague (HB), May 7, 1954, PU-CS, B 349, F 5.

198 My hunch is that all of these drafts postdate the manuscript of *Cat's Cradle* that Vonnegut sent to Charles Scribner's Sons; however, the seventy-page, five-chapter draft *could* be a close version of one section of that manuscript. According to a May 18, 1959, letter from Scribner's editorial department, the manuscript in question "was originally submitted in two parts, one running to 190 pages and the other consisting of 75 pages." The 1957 and 1959 correspondence pertaining to Vonnegut's requests to have the manuscript returned is accessible at PU-CS, B 349, F 5.

199 Although there is only one copy of the draft "CAT'S CRADLE: A True Science Adventure," it's likely that there were multiple versions at some point. The draft has alternative pages (2, 2A, 6, 6A, etc.), with sections stapled and taped in, along with Jane's handwritten edits. It's impossible to definitively date the draft, but references to Castro suggest a post-1959 date, and the image of Newt, John, and Mona straining to pull Papa's golden boat with a rope likely places the draft within a similar period to the 289-page draft Vonnegut sent to Stewart. LL-KV, B 37, F Photocopy typescript (35 pages).

200 Reader, she didn't marry him (Frank), but she wanted to. Although it's not entirely clear, Vonnegut suggests that Bernice Mergendeiler is none other than Jack's wife (from Jack's Hobby Shop). Wait! It gets better. In this outline draft for the novel, Franklin, "in a gesture at least equal to that of Vincent Astor on the sinking Titanic . . . leaps across the widening gap" of the Monzano's destructing castle into Bernice's arms so they can perish together.

201 Although he continued to revise the opening paragraphs, narrator's identity, ending, and chapter titles, those drafts are very close to the published novel.

202 LL-KV, B 37, F 3, "*Cat's Cradle* Typescript."

203 This line was obviously a key moral for Vonnegut, who also included it on the penultimate page of the 289-page draft that ends with Bokonon's impending rule and predictions.

204 Gopnik, "Voltaire's Garden," 9.

205 Garrard, *Ecocriticism*, 107.

206 While many Vonnegut scholars have told the tale of *Slapstick*'s review saga, Peter Freese offers one of the best, most comprehensive discussions of the novel's reception and Vonnegut's response to the reviews. See *Clown of Armageddon*, 407–17.

207 In an interview with Ira Berkow, Vonnegut indicated that he was "wobbled" by "the bludgeoning reviews" of *Slapstick*. He told Berkow, "I was so roundly embarrassed. I thought the book was good when I finished it. But a writer can't be sure. I did believe that there was a feeling of wholeness to it." Ira Berkow, "Vonnegut Wobbled Over Novel's Unpopularity," *Advance News*, Jan 9, 1977.

208 Klinkowitz, *Vonnegut Effect*, 115. For further discussion of *Slapstick*'s place within the broader "novel of ideas" phase of Vonnegut's career, see Klinkowitz, *Vonnegut Effect*, 112–15.

209 If you'd like to find the *Slapstick* quotations for the rest of this chapter, here are the page numbers in order from the 2006 Dial edition: 23, 50, 117, 37, 24, 92, 117, 24, 90, 265, 70, 189, 190, 214, 255, 52, 185, 189–190, 203, 217, 251, 258, 25, 254, 249–50, 245–46, 57, 40, 162, 34, 254–55, 274.

210 Vonnegut's use of the term "slave" to describe this voluntary agrarian system is not intended to minimize or whitewash the brutal, horrific institution of slavery. On the contrary, the references to Thomas Jefferson's identity as a slaveholder are part of Vonnegut's critiques of the wide gap between American ideals of democracy and freedom and actual practices.

211 Wellrock, *Preserving the Nation*, 197.

212 Benson, "Raspberry 14 Calling," 12–13.

213 Allen, *Conversations*, 210–11.

214 Ehrlich, *Population Bomb*, 45–46, 47.

215 See Edward Cowan's *New York Times* articles, "Nixon Sets Voluntary Curbs in Oil and Gas Shortage," May 11, 1973, and "Sunday Sales and Holiday Lights to Be Forbidden," November 26, 1973.

216 Wellrock, *Preserving the Nation*, 194.

217 Qtd. in Kevin Bezner, "A Conversation with Kurt Vonnegut," *The Washington Book Review*, Oct./Nov. 1979.

218 Vonnegut mentioned these alternative sources for new middle names in his 1973 *Playboy* interview.

219 Vonnegut, *If This Isn't Nice*, 153.

220 Vonnegut, review of *Nashville*, in *Vogue*, June 1975, 103.

221 Vonnegut does suggest a few of these directions. By highlighting Dorothy's agency and efficacy, the novel's extended families critique

and revise some of the legacies of slavery—especially the practices of selling enslaved children and separating Black families.

222 This quotation and much of my information about Mott comes from Douglas Martin, "Stewart R. Mott, 70, Offbeat Philanthropist, Dies," *New York Times*, June 14, 2008. Vonnegut also knew Mott well enough to invite him to Delacorte Press's October 6, 1976, publication party for *Slapstick*. The guest list and other party information can be found at DE-SL, B 3, F 165.

223 For another equally optimistic reading of *Slapstick* that offers comparisons to Wendell Berry's environmental restoration farming projects, see Davis, *Kurt Vonnegut's Crusade*, 91–97.

224 *Galápagos*, 297. Subsequent *Galápagos* quotations in this chapter use the pagination from the 2009 Dial edition, and appear in this order: 319, 86, 140, 5, 248, 107, 117, 184–85, 51, 118, 235, 274, 140, 197, 63, 303, 166, 168, 164, 299, 100, 106, 281.

225 Mustazza, *Forever Pursuing Genesis*, 168, 172.

226 Mustazza, 173.

227 This alternative version of the chapter is available LL-KV, B 8, F 16.

228 Mustazza, 170.

229 This is the question Vonnegut asked listeners during his sermon at St. John the Divine shortly after he returned from his trip to the Galápagos Islands. Vonnegut told his audience "If we desolate this planet, Nature can get life going again. All it takes is a few million years or so, the wink of an eye to Nature. Only humankind is running out of time." Vonnegut's pacifism and sarcasm are pretty direct: "perhaps we should be adoring instead of loathing our hydrogen bombs. They could be the eggs for new galaxies." *Fates Worse Than Death*, 145.

CHAPTER 5: MIDLAND CITY

230 This quotation appears in a letter Vonnegut wrote to Jerome Klinkowitz from his temporary apartment on Fifty-Fourth Street on November 29, 1972. I am grateful to Professor Klinkowitz for sharing the unpublished letter and additional information about drafts of *Breakfast of Champions* with me.

231 Jerome Klinkowitz letter to the author, October 31, 2015.

232 KV to Klinkowitz letter, November 29, 1972, personal collection of Jerome Klinkowitz.

233 Until Vonnegut firmly sundered the *Slaughterhouse-Five* and *Breakfast of Champions* storylines after the Iowa Writers' Workshop draft, he used the surname Pilgrim fairly consistently for his protagonist.

References to the Pilgrim family over the next several pages refer to the one in *Goodbye, Blue Monday* drafts—not Billy Pilgrim's family in the published version of *Slaughterhouse-Five*.

234 Vonnegut divided the manuscript into two main parts: "Robo-Magic" and "Slaughterhouse Five." The former is grouped with *Breakfast of Champions* drafts, LL-KV, B 4, F 1, the latter with *Slaughterhouse-Five*, LL-KV, B 11, F 2. For more detailed discussion of *Slaughterhouse-Five*'s composition, see Roston, *The Writer's Crusade*.

235 Gross, "Interview: Kurt Vonnegut, Jr.," 19.

236 Gross, 21.

237 Sumner, *Unstuck in Time*, 213.

238 LL-KV, B 3, F 31.

239 This quotation comes from the draft of *Breakfast of Champions* that Vonnegut read from during his lecture at Coolidge Auditorium on February 1, 1971. An audio file of the speech is available through the Library of Congress, www.loc.gov/item/94838609.

240 Vonnegut's comment about the homogenization of his home city appears in the prologue to *Slapstick*, but it applies perfectly to his Midland City novels.

241 Even in the earliest drafts of *Goodbye, Blue Monday*, Vonnegut imagined the arts as a redemptive counter to mechanical threats via the imagined origins of the Robo-Magic washing machine. A gift from Fred Barry after he moved into the Pilgrim home in 1936, the fully automatic Robo-Magic would "walk" from its place in the kitchen during the "ferocious sloshing of the deep-cleaning cycle," shaking the house at its foundation and rattling dishes a block away. "Built like a tank" with a two-cycle gasoline engine, the Robo-Magic was a menace to the entire family as it spewed oily smoke, "ate" a chair, and threatened to squash anything in its path. Saving the family is the narrator's younger sister Ellen, who learns to "dance" the machine back to its place in the kitchen. LL-KV, B 3, F 29. Other early *Goodbye, Blue Monday* drafts can also be found at B 3, F 30, F 31.

242 Allen, *Conversations*, 202.

243 LL-KV, B 10, F 21.

244 KV, ms. draft, *Slaughterhouse-Five*, LL-KV, B 10, F 25.

245 Ready for another Easter egg? This more complex Montana Wildhack also immediately grasps the Tralfamadorian vision of time. In the same deleted scene, Billy isn't "very good" at paraphrasing Tralfamadorian conceptions of time, but "Montana was marvelous again." She invents her own metaphor, explaining, "Life is a series of

telegrams which can be read over and over again in any order at all."
LL-KV, B 10, F 25.

246 In his 1973 *Playboy* interview with David Standish, Vonnegut
remarked that "suicide is at the heart" of *Breakfast of Champions.*
Vonnegut went on to describe not his mother's death from an overdose
of sleeping pills, but rather all the "uselessness" people felt during
the Great Depression when "the machines fired everybody." Allen,
Conversations, 108.

247 Kilgore Trout fans might be interested to know that he first made his
appearance in the novel at the end of the first extant draft specifically
titled "Breakfast of Champions," which Vonnegut wrote ca. 1969 as
he was developing the automobile-focused elements of the novel. In
addition to including a twenty-seven-car pileup on the interstate,
explicit comments about the highway beautification program, and
several driving tours of Midland City and Shepherdson, the ninety-
five-page manuscript also includes additional characters and storylines that focus on the arts festival and modern-day race relations.
As Vonnegut swooped away, working out details of the arts festival,
he added Trout on page ninety-three, imagining him riding on a
Greyhound bus writing the story *Now It Can Be Told.* The ninety-five-
page draft and others from the same period were collected in a folder,
presumably labeled by Jane, "Breakfast of Champions, early versions
(70–71)," LL-KV, B 38, F 3 & 4. For the record, Vonnegut had not
introduced himself as a character yet.

248 Steinberg, *Down to Earth*, 203.

249 *Breakfast of Champions* quotations in this section can be found on the
following pages of the 2006 Dial edition: 26–29, 86–89, 105, 123–24,
139–40, 199, 216, 86, 201, 292, 187, 295, 231.

250 Vonnegut commented on some of these car-related events in his
pre–Earth Day interview for the *Village Voice.* In a near-final draft
of *Breakfast of Champions*, Vonnegut also included details about Trout
fans objecting to the pornographic images included in *Plague on
Wheels*, suggesting instead the book should have "pictures of junk-
yards and wrecks and cloverleaf intersections from the air and people
wearing gas masks and things like that." LL-KV, B 4, F 3.

251 Myler, "The Dirty Animal," 126, 136. The human health impacts of
automobile emissions also received a lot of attention in the early 1970s.
Thanks to EPA regulations in 1973–74, unleaded gasoline was introduced to reduce exposure to lead—especially in children.

252 In addition to the landmark environmental events that remained in the
novel, Vonnegut included specific explorations of Great Lakes pollution

in ca. 1970–71 drafts. Written in the shadow of Earth Day, those drafts set the stage for the opening of the published novel. In some drafts Dwayne, the only creature with free will in the universe, is on another planet because Earth has been so poisoned. LL-KV, B 38, F 1.

253 For the story of Vonnegut's Saab dealership, see Nash, "The Story Behind."

254 And now it should be told: the original "Breakfast of Champions" drink was not a martini. In the ninety-five-page, ca. 1969 draft, two manufacturers' representatives named Ben and Horace order Boilermakers with Wild Turkey Bourbon and Schlitz Beer, which the latter dubs "Breakfast of Champions." Wouldn't Hazel Crosby be proud? The official Purdue University drink!

255 According to Autodata statistics, car sales by unit were 10,940,000 in the United States in 1972, more than double what they were in 1951. My source for the number of licensed drivers is the US Department of Transportation Federal Highway Administration. For more in-depth history of the automotive industry during this period, see Mantle, *Car Wars*.

256 LL-KV, B 38, F 3.

257 For Vonnegut fans wishing to identify Indianapolis elements, "Skid Row" is likely based on the commercially decimated Massachusetts Avenue of the 1960s. Today this lifeblood street is alive and well, and guess which Hoosier has a thirty-seven-foot-tall mural there?

258 *Deadeye Dick* quotations here and in the next two sections can be found on the following pages of the 1985 Laurel edition: 227, 176, 232, 64, 53, 23, 58, 63–64, 167, 87, 58, 213–19, 49, 179, 165, 185, 191, 197.

259 The purpose of the stopover is to visit Mrs. Martin McSwan, the mother of a soldier executed for "plundering" after the firebombing in Dresden. The character David McSwan, partially based on Vonnegut's fellow POW Michael Palaia, is a precursor of Edgar Derby in the published novel.

260 LL-KV, B 10, F 15. Vonnegut imagined but then crossed out a cause for the explosion: "an unsuspected natural gas deposit under" the city.

261 The economic and cultural devastation that accompanied the closing of Columbia Records' plant, Vonnegut explained, transformed the city in such a way that "it might as well have been neutron bombed." Reed and Leeds, "A Conversation with Kurt Vonnegut," in *Vonnegut Chronicles*, 9.

262 In a 1989 interview with Zoltán Abádi-Nagy, Vonnegut commented on Rudy's shooting in *Deadeye Dick*: "You know, I did that. I didn't kill anybody. But I fired a rifle, out over Indianapolis. I didn't hit anybody

as far as I know. . . . I never told anybody about it until I was an adult. I cleaned that gun and put it away." *Vonnegut Chronicles*, 21, 22.

263 Swarthmore College's Global Nonviolent Action Database, "U.S. Anti-nuclear Activists Campaign," nvdatabase.swarthmore.edu.

264 Attendance figures for the event have ranged from 65,000 to 125,000, but more recent sources tend to use the higher number. For firsthand reporting on and information about the rally on May 6, 1979, see Pacifica Radio's online archives.

265 Vonnegut reprints a slightly revised version of the speech in *Palm Sunday*. To best capture the immediacy of his remarks, I quote from the original copy of the speech, DE-SL, B 4, F 188.

266 This quotation comes from the "About NRC" section of the US Nuclear Regulatory Commission's website.

267 Although the toxic dumping in communities of color didn't gain national attention until the September 1982 protests in Warren County, North Carolina, environmental racism has a deep history in the United States. To begin exploring this history and the birth of the environmental justice movement, see Robert Bullard's landmark book *Dumping in Dixie* and the extensive bibliography and resources on his website, drrobertbullard.com.

268 Although Edith Lieber Vonnegut's death was officially attributed to an accidental overdose from sleeping pills, Kurt consistently called it a suicide in his writings. Not all family members agree, and several have offered more complicated portraits of Edith than her son did. For example, see Mark Vonnegut's chapter "A Brief Family History" in his memoir *Just Like Someone* and Nanette Vonnegut's comments about the impact of Edith's childhood traumas in her 2012 interview with Jennifer Bowen Hicks for *The Rumpus*.

269 For more discussion of women's 1960s addictions to amphetamine diet pills and a broader history of postwar amphetamine use in the United States, see Moon, "The Amphetamine Years." These addictions were also captured in the Rolling Stones' 1966 hit song "Mother's Little Helper," Jacqueline Susann's best-selling 1966 novel *Valley of the Dolls*, and the 1967 film based on Susann's book. Vonnegut was clearly aware of *Valley of the Dolls*; it's the only novel Billy Pilgrim has to read on his journey from Earth to Tralfamadore in *Slaughterhouse-Five*.

270 The speech, delivered posthumously by Mark Vonnegut, is included with an introduction in *Armageddon in Retrospect*. In addition to the specific reflections on his Hoosier roots, Vonnegut addressed other

career-long concerns such as the dangers of military technology, environmental destruction, the death penalty, and the need for humor, humanism, and extended families.

271 For more information about Ida Young and her relationship with Kurt, see Wakefield, *Making of a Writer*, ch. 1 and Shields, *And So It Goes*, 16–18. To read transcripts of Shields's interviews with Young's grandsons, see IHS-CS, B 11, F 18–19.

272 KKK activities in Indianapolis during Vonnegut's childhood were clearly on Vonnegut's mind in the weeks before his death. In his final interview with Heather Augustyn for *In These Times*, Vonnegut mentions both the Klan's Indianapolis headquarters and the fact that "the last lynching to take place north of the Mason-Dixon line was in Marion in 1930." McCartan, *The Last Interview*, 165. While the violent racism of his home city and state seemed to weigh heavily on Vonnegut at the end of his life, he had addressed the topic earlier; see, for example his passing comment about the KKK's national headquarters on pages 126–27 of *Fates Worse Than Death*.

273 *Breakfast of Champions* quotations for the rest of chapter 5 can be found on the following pages of the 2006 Dial edition: 7, 10–11, 73, 78, 129, 34, 85, 301, 158, 167–68, 268, 226.

274 Vonnegut's caustic critiques of European colonization, slavery, and genocide in the novel are toned down from the final typescript manuscript. At the eleventh hour, Vonnegut cut passages and illustrations relating to the roles Christianity, diseases, and alcohol played in wiping out Indigenous cultures and people. See the typescript draft, September 29, 1972, in clamshell boxes, LL-KV.

275 This is my conjecture; I don't think Vonnegut ever commented explicitly on his repeated use of the caustic racial epithet. In the ninety-five-page ca. 1969 draft, however, Vonnegut introduced two white characters that vocally challenged racism in its institutional and interpersonal forms—Beatrice Keedsler, who teaches French at the all-Black Crispus Attucks High School and Dr. Peloro, who serves as Chairman of the local chapter of the NAACP. Peloro specifically challenges racist comments of his fellow Midland City residents during conversations in the cocktail lounge of the Holiday Inn. While it's problematic to conflate an author's and a character's ideas, Vonnegut's comments about Dr. Peloro on page thirty-four offer insight into his own use of the dehumanizing term: "This man was programmed to be brave and warm-hearted about race relations in Midland City. His use of the word 'N°°°er' was ironic, a quietly reproachful echo of the heartless opinions others around him often held of blacks." (asterisks mine) LL-KV, B 38, F 3.

276 For more information about the history of African Dodger games
at fairs, carnivals, and circuses in the United States from the late
nineteenth century until the mid-1940s, see the article on human zoos
from Ferris State University's online Jim Crow Museum of Racist
Memorabilia.

Once Vonnegut shifted from Billy Pilgrim to Dwayne Hoover, he consistently imagined his protagonist's stepfather as a virulently racist,
abusive figure—even more violent in drafts than in the finished novel.
Rather than focus on Dwayne's stepfather's individual actions, the
published novel includes broader references to the lynching of African
Americans, sundown signs, and other terror tactics.

277 Once again, I will be examining the late 1950s and early 1960s drafts
of *Goodbye, Blue Monday*, LL-KV, B 3, F 29.

278 Although capturing some of Edith's struggles with barbiturates and
economic-related depressions, Mrs. Pilgrim's character in the drafts has
no Germanic heritage and distinctly incorporates many purely fictional
elements. All ties to the Klan are purely fictional ones. In fact, given the
Indiana and national Klan's unwavering support for prohibition, it's
possible that the Lieber family could have been a target of Klan scorn.

279 Tucker, *Dragon and the Cross*, 1. The history of the KKK in Indiana is
obviously far more complex that I can describe here. For more detail,
please see Moore, *Citizen Klansmen*; Lutholtz, *Grand Dragon*; Tucker,
Dragon and the Cross; and Sutton, "Klan Records."

280 Moore, 181.

281 Given the inclusion of bribes and other corruption mentioned here, it's
possible that Vonnegut was incorporating references to Indianapolis
mayor John Duvall and the Klan-run city council and school board
from the mid-1920s. Vonnegut might have been old enough to remember that throughout 1927 and 1928 "the *Indianapolis News* kept up a
steady campaign against the Klan school board, charging its members
with misuse of public funds, corrupt practices in the awarding of construction contracts, and a number of other offenses." Moore, 182.

282 Sutton, "Klan Records," 27. I've used Sutton's figures because they
are the most recent. Moore places membership at higher percentages;
he suggests that during the 1920s, between "one-quarter and one-third
of all native-born white men in the state paid ten dollars to become
Klansmen." *Citizen Klansmen*, 7.

283 Moore, 7.

284 Tucker, *Dragon and the Cross*, 5.

285 Sutton, 28.

286 Tucker, 10.

287 Indiana Historical Society photos record the especially large May 6, 1924, voting primary event "in which Klan-backed candidates won by a landslide." After the ceremony, "which attracted an estimated 25,000 men, women, and children, approximately 7,000 robed Klansmen and Klanswomen marched from the fairgrounds to downtown through African American neighborhoods." Sutton, "Klan Records," 35. Obviously Vonnegut would have been too young to remember this event, but it's likely that Ida Young, relatives, and family friends would have.

288 Specifically, I am referring to the pages marked "SHARON: EVERYTHING FROM 242 UNTIL 281 IS CUT" in LL-KV, B 4, F 11 (part 11).

289 On page 111 of *The Vonnegut Effect*, Klinkowitz tells the story of how a courier "taking pages from the author to the office of Seymour Lawrence at Delacorte Press complained that he did not think the novel's ending fit." Vonnegut responded by writing his way out of the Midland City insane asylum, producing the final ending of *Breakfast of Champions*.

290 Rackstraw, "Vonnegut Cosmos," 54.

291 *Deadeye Dick* quotations here and in the next two paragraphs can be found on the following pages of the 1985 Laurel edition: 44, 94, 150, 236–39.

292 In honor of Rudy Waltz, Midland City's griot, here are some characters and ideas that never made their way into the published novels: Monica Steel, Gwen Boomer, Dr. George Peloro, Floyd Hoover, Loretta Tallman, Horace and Ben, a talking cinnamon bear, Eddie Schoeffler, Fred T. Barry's nipples, morphine molecules, barn swallows, vitamin D, Oscar Schoeffler's three operas, goblet cells, John Thompson, Naomi Fike, Lily Hoover, Milos Foreman, Jody Clarke, Elias Keedsler, Gilbert Wheeler, a maroon, boat-tailed Auburn, Garvey Wheeler Sterling, the Wallfahrts and Wallfahrers, extra-telepathic butterflies, Sylvia Dyer, and so on. And wouldn't Kurt just beam up there in heaven if you gave one of these characters life through some artistic soul growth?

CHAPTER 6: M-17 HOUSES, EPICAC, AND WOLFGANG

293 Dennis Flanagan, editor, "Preface." *Scientific American* 187.3 (September 1952): 43.

294 Vonnegut's image may have been inspired by the illustration of the human nervous system that appeared in Wiener's November 1948 *Scientific American* article "Cybernetics." The illustration depicts the

nervous system as a brain linked to a central frame (the spine) with radiating smaller nerve networks that form the outline of the human figure.

295 *Player Piano* quotations in this section can be found on the following pages of the 1999 Delta edition: 7, 18–24, 71, 67, 165, 175, 302, 115–23, 91–92, 320, 117, 332–38, 301, 315.

296 I borrow the phrase "team human" from Douglas Rushkoff's September 2018 TED Talk, "How to be 'Team Human' in the Digital Future," which argues for the importance of reclaiming human values and connections in the wake of digital networks that primarily value people for their data.

297 *Wampeters, Foma & Granfalloons*, 262–63. First published in English in 1924, Yevgeny Zamyatin's *We* presents a futuristic dystopian world in which a totalitarian state has stripped all its citizens of their privacy, identities, and relationships with nature. As Vonnegut notes, *We* not only influenced Orwell's *1984* and Huxley's *Brave New World*, but also provided inspiration for some key elements in *Player Piano*: an engineer protagonist, a symbolic resistance movement, a futuristic postwar setting, centralized mathematical control, numerical assignments, and the erasure of human individuality and self-worth.

298 Strand, *Brothers Vonnegut*, 44, 99, 96–99.

299 Ready for another Easter egg? In the initial "completed" 405-page draft of the novel, Vonnegut included two full chapters that chronicled what happened after Paul, Finnerty, Lasher, and Von Neumann handed themselves over to the authorities. The first, labeled chapter 37, provided some initial resolution of key character arcs via newspaper headlines and a brief scene at the airport, where the Shah refuses the "modernization package" and implores Halyard to "ask EPICAC what people are for?" The final chapter, which served as an epilogue, detailed Paul's return to Ilium after serving a seventeen-year prison sentence for his role in the revolution. In that chapter, we learn that the other three leaders were killed, EPICAC XXI has taken full command of the entire system, Ilium has been rebuilt into "the most up-to-date city in the East," Fred Garth has escaped to Chile, Bud Calhoun and Katherine Finch have married, and Edmund Harrison has escaped to the Everglades to live with Seminole Indians. Paul returns to his farm and cottage, where an eighty-year-old Kroner welcomes him and extols the promise of "mass space travel for the common man." Paul, whose only regret is not having children, offers the novel's final lines in response to Kroner's excitement about new space frontiers for industry: "Maybe, maybe. But if I had children, I think I'd rather have them try to make a better earth of this one than the same earth out of Mars. Besides, who says they have

spring days as nice as this one on Mars?" These discarded chapters,
along with another brief deleted chapter that would have followed chapter 18, are available at LL-KV, B 35, F 4 of 4 (405-page typescript draft).

300 KV letter to HB, November 30, 1951, PU-CS, B 349, F 5.

301 Although the outline (LL-KV, B 10, F 4) is undated, Strand places it
in the early summer of 1950, *Brothers Vonnegut*, 166.

302 The Wiener quote Vonnegut selected appears in the introduction to
Cybernetics. During his conversation with Katherine Finch, Paul cred-
its Wiener as he discusses the first and second industrial revolutions.

303 Vonnegut mentions his upcoming master's examinations and plans to
continue research for his thesis in a letter to his father, dated October
15, 1947. *Letters*, 22–23.

304 As Strand reveals, Vonnegut got the initial inspiration for the Shah's
character from the Prime Minister Liaquat Ali Khan's grand tour of the
United States, which made a stop at the GE plant in Schenectady in May
1950. *Brothers Vonnegut*, 164–65. For additional discussion of the Shah
sections and excellent synthesis of other reviews, articles, and scholarly
treatments of the novel, see Peter Freese's chapter on *Player Piano* in *Clown
of Armageddon*.

305 Vonnegut's drafts demonstrate that he worked out most of the main
storyline of *Player Piano* prior to adding the Shah sections. LL-KV, B
35, F "Typescripts to Insert," F "Setting Copy."

306 Carr, *Glass Cage*, 14, 16.

307 Vonnegut felt so strongly about the question that he wrote to Harry
Brague on Christmas Eve about it: "There's only one line I really hate
to see cut out of PLAYER PIANO in the discarding of chapters 37 and
38: it's the Shah's suggestion that someone ask EPICAC What people
are for." KV letter to HB, December 24, 1951, PU-CS, B 349, F 5.

308 KV letter to HB, January 10, 1952, PU-CS, B 349, F 5.

309 Carr, *Glass Cage*, 215. While I continue to put Vonnegut and his writings in the secular humanist camp, Andrew John Hicks thoughtfully
challenges this approach in *Posthumanism in the Novels of Kurt Vonnegut*.

310 *Player Piano* quotations in this section and the start of the next one
can be found on the following pages of the 1999 Delta edition: 118, 218,
160–64, 243.

311 Arma Corporation, "Here Comes Your Future, Mr. Machine Tools
Manufacturer," *Fortune*, June 1950, 151.

312 Packard, *Waste Makers*, 9.

313 Qtd. in Packard, 21. Readers already familiar with the excellent scholarship on consumerism and overconsumption by Durning, Schor, Leonard, Wann, de Graaf, and Naylor probably know the Lebow quote well. Those interested in the full text of Lebow's comments should see his *Journal of Retailing* essays, Spring 1955, p. 7, and Winter 1955–56, p. 166.

314 Humes, *Garbology*, 5.

315 Although Vonnegut does not explore the racism and de facto racial segregation associated with these standardized, white suburban neighborhoods as he does in his Midland City novels, it's worth noting that Chicago, home to fictional Proteus Park, was one of many US cities that used restrictive covenants, redlining, and other discriminatory practices to keep Black Americans out of white neighborhoods during this period. For more on the history of redlining in Chicago, see Ta-Nehisi Coates's landmark June 2014 *Atlantic* article, "The Case for Reparations."

316 The specific Minute Rice and Universal Iron ads can be found in the August 21, 1950, issue of *Life*. This focus on speed and "instant" gratification was part of a much broader advertising strategy, which Vance Packard describes: "Hedonism was also actively promoted by campaigns to persuade the American people that they deserved to enjoy the pleasures of enriched living *instantly* and without lifting a finger. 'Instant' and 'ready' became the magic words in marketing everything from soda pop, whipped cream, and cherry pies to headache remedies." *Waste Makers*, 143.

317 To state the obvious, these ads were primarily targeted toward white, middle-class women and an ideal that was far from the reality of most women's lives—especially Black, Indigenous, and other women of color. For a more historically grounded analysis of women's lived experiences in the postwar period, see Meyerowitz, *Not June Cleaver* and Coontz, *The Way We Never Were*.

318 Packard, 103, 104. Even food manufacturers bought into the "instant" home of tomorrow. General Foods Chairman of the Board, Charles Mortimer lectured businessmen, "Just about everything we buy today must be ready to use, ready to wear, ready to plug in, ready to turn on, ready to take home." The home of tomorrow, he predicted, "would be pre-packaged and sold 'almost ready for a family to move in and start living!'" Qtd. in Packard, 143–44.

319 To explore the Turing test for poetry, visit botpoet.com or view Oscar Schwartz's May 2015 TED talk "Can a Computer Write Poetry?"

320 LL-KV, B 35, F 2.

321 As Rackstraw notes, Vonnegut didn't see *Timequake* "as a freestanding novel, but as the last chapter in one long book." *Love As Always*, 197.

322 Nelson Taylor, "*Timequake*: Vonnegut Punches the Clock for the Last Time." *Black Book* Magazine, Autumn 1997, 166–68.

323 Robert Siegel, "Interview with Kurt Vonnegut." *All Things Considered*, NPR, September 22, 1997. Transcript # 97092210-212.

324 *Timequake*, xvii. For analysis of *Timequake's* literary innovations and reflections on art, writing, and storytelling, see Klinkowitz, *Vonnegut Effect*, 151–74 and Farrell, *Critical Companion*, 357–81. For analyses of *Timequake* in biographical context, including significant events not mentioned in the novel, see Shields, *And So It Goes*, 384–401 and Sumner, *Unstuck in Time*, 311–21. To explore *Timequake's* engagements with Nietzsche's idea of the eternal return and other philosophical concepts, see Taylor, "Fictional Humans" and Tally, *American Novel*, 153–58.

325 While it's impossible to summarize the many false starts and discarded drafts of the novel, the portions Vonnegut cut largely focused on characters from and relationships within the Pembroke Mask and Wig Club. He also deemed most of the Xanadu scenes to be unworthy "chum." As he salvaged material for the novel, he sometimes combined characters such as Monica Schramm and Sylvia Pepper, originally two Academy employees, to produce a single character. Vonnegut also condensed Trout's artistic residency at Xanadu and excerpts from his alter ego's memoir, *My Ten Years On Autopilot*. These and other stories can be found in the more than twenty folders of drafts, LL-KV, B 27–28.

326 The 1988 start date is based on Vonnegut's comment that he had already spent five years on the novel at the time of the 1993 interview with Reed and Leeds. It's striking how similar Vonnegut's overview of the timequake and description of "The Sisters B-36" in the interview are to the versions in the published novel. See *Vonnegut Chronicles*, 36.

327 *Timequake* quotations for the rest of this chapter can be found on the following pages in the 1998 Berkley edition: xv, 18, 21, 64, 35–38, 110, 113, 196, 78, 182–83, 221.

328 The February 13 date of the timequake is ripe with personal, historical, and literary significance. Transforming the date of the initial firebombing of Dresden, an event filled with tragedy and trauma, into the start date of Kilgore's Creed captures Vonnegut's extraordinary ability to layer hope into despair. God bless you, Mr. Vonnegut, for hope in dark times.

329 The story's ending further underscores the connections between
the sisters' family name and real B-36 bombers, which were dubbed
"Peacemakers" because of/despite their capability to deliver nuclear
weapons. The largest piston-engine aircraft ever mass produced, the
B-36 was itself an example of rapid technological obsolescence; too
large to fit in most hangars, it was soon replaced by its svelter sister,
the B-52.

330 Carr, *Shallows*, 178–79.

331 Carr, *Glass Cage*, 138.

332 LL-KV, B 27, F 4.

333 Vonnegut's November 16, 1978, letter to Annie and Don Farber,
thanking them for giving him Boris as a birthday present, captures
Vonnegut's lifelong love of chess and marvel at technological advance-
ments. *Letters*, 261–62.

334 Jeremy Howard, "Will Artificial Intelligence Be the Last Human
Invention?" TED Radio Hour, NPR, April 21, 2017.

335 Marie Lebert, "eBooks: 1998—The First eBook Readers," *Project
Gutenberg News*, July 16, 2011; Michael Kozlowski, "The Evolution of the
Kindle e-Reader," May 11, 2014, Goodreader.com. Vonnegut's concerns about the marginalization of print reading were well warranted.
Christopher Ingraham reported in a June 29, 2018, *Washington Post* article that leisure reading hit an all-time low in the United States in 2017,
with only 19 percent of Americans reading for pleasure on a given day.
For more discussion of the ways our neural pathways are being rewired
by our increased time online, see Carr, *Shallows*, 64–77, 116, 138.

336 Klinkowitz, *Vonnegut Effect*, 157.

337 Klinkowitz, 164.

338 Vonnegut's graduation address at Agnes Scott College on May 15,
1999 is reprinted in *If This Isn't Nice, What Is?*

339 Nellie Bowles, "A Dark Consensus About Screens and Kids Begins
to Emerge in Silicon Valley." *New York Times*, October 26, 2018.

CHAPTER 7: WHAT *ARE* PEOPLE FOR?

340 For an overview of Vonnegut's University of Rochester address, see
Rachel Dickler, "Vonnegut Reflects on Education, Society," *Campus
Times*, April 25, 1996.

341 Rackstraw, *Love As Always*, 182–83.

342 Qtd. in Dickler, "Vonnegut Reflects."

343 McKibben, "Introduction," 14.

344 The phrase being "good without God" comes from Greg Epstein, not Vonnegut. We'll be exploring Vonnegut's own definitions and practice of secular humanism throughout the chapter. Epstein's book by that title and the American Humanist Association's (AHA) website offer wonderful introductions to secular humanism for the curious. Vonnegut's 1992 AHA address, when he was named Humanist of the Year, is reprinted in *If This Isn't Nice, What Is?*

345 The story is reprinted in *Complete Stories* and *Bagombo Snuff Box*. In the latter, quotations can be found on pages 93–106.

346 I am indebted to archivist and librarian Melissa Tacke for most of my information about Alplaus and its especially rich post office history. She pointed me toward the many *Daily Gazette* and Spotlight newspaper articles in GDL, "Schenectady County: Glenville/Alplaus" Files.

347 In *God Bless You, Mr. Rosewater*, Eliot adopts the tradition of gifting a share of International Business Machines stock to every newborn in Rosewater County. Gray Watkins, "Theodore G. 'Ted' Schwarz." *Home Town News* [Alplaus], 139.8 (October 2014): 4. For more information about Alplaus's Volunteer Fire Department and its social gatherings, see Cliff Hayes, "Parades at Alplaus," in the same issue of *Home Town News*.

348 According to Shields, "Mrs. Cheney liked Kurt and admired him for striking out on his own as a writer. . . . Her daughter Mary Lou was away at college, and he could have it rent-free. Kurt insisted he pay something—a few dollars every week, anyway. He wouldn't accept charity. She agreed rather than hurt his pride." *And So It Goes*, 115.

349 Shields, 115.

350 In 1951, the US Post Office Department began to outsource a significant portion of its short distance mail transportation to the trucking industry.

351 Michael Goot, "Applause for Alplaus: Residents Love its Sense of Community, Rich History," *Daily Gazette*, October 14, 2012.

352 Goot, "Applause for Alplaus." Touchingly, Vonnegut kept his Alplaus Volunteer Fireman belt buckle and card for the rest of his life. Those items are on display at the KVML in Indianapolis.

353 Typical of the "swooping," exploratory phase of his creative process, Vonnegut had many brief false starts, with elements that ranged from Eliot Rosewater's political campaign headquarters to Manny Pena's early morning fishing to the Pisquontuit drug store. These details appear in the 45-page, 47-page, and 52-page drafts written ca. summer 1962, LL-KV, B 37, B 38.

354 KV, ms. draft, "The Rosewater Foundation," LL-KV, B 37. Vonnegut originally spelled Eliot's name "Elliot" in this draft, but I have used the novel's final spelling to avoid confusion. Interestingly, Vonnegut initially planned to explore segregation and layers of discrimination within Rosewater County here as well.

355 *God Bless You, Mr. Rosewater* quotations for the rest of this chapter can be found on the following pages in the 2006 Dial edition: 266, 46, 103, 58, 68, 264–69.

356 To reward you, careful endnote reader, let me share two other significant changes in the manuscript drafts. Slightly later versions include an ending where Indianapolis is actually consumed by flames (173-page draft) and alternative versions of embedded Trout stories (303-page draft). LL-KV, B 38.

357 Vonnegut is paraphrasing or using a shortened version of the line, which in the King James translation reads "Suffer little children, and forbid them not, to come unto me." This epigraph appears in the 45-page, 47-page, and 52-page drafts ca. summer 1962, LL-KV, B 37, B 38.

358 LL-KV, B 38, F 1.

359 *God Bless You, Mr. Rosewater* fans will recognize that Vonnegut ultimately incorporated Peach's dream about Eliot's death and angelic transport to a seat "next to Sweet Jesus Himself" in chapter 12 of the finished novel.

360 Davis, *Kurt Vonnegut's Crusade*, 74.

361 *Fates Worse Than Death*, 214.

362 The *Palm Sunday* quotations that follow can be found on pages 193–210. Vonnegut consistently claimed his great-grandfather Clemens Vonnegut as the wellspring of his humanism. Inspired by the scientific ideas of Darwin and the liberal ideals of the revolutions of 1848, Clemens Vonnegut rejected his Catholic faith to become a Freethinker. Like modern humanists, Clemens was also committed to social justice and universal human rights; he served as the first President of Indianapolis's Freethinker Society, from 1870 to 1890, and was a strong supporter of public education, abolition, and women's suffrage. Many of Vonnegut's other ancestors were Freethinkers (and Turners), but the anti-German sentiment of World War I ultimately caused them to stop using the term and to identify as Unitarians. For additional background on Vonnegut's Freethinking heritage, see *Palm Sunday*, 22–31,192–94; Lee Little's 2011 essay, "'I Left Indianapolis because the Money was Gone': Kurt

Vonnegut, Jr.'s Roots," IHS-KV; and John Rauch's "An Account of the Ancestry of Kurt Vonnegut, Jr. by an Ancient Friend of His Family," LL-KV, B 21, F 1. For broader historical contextualization, see Jacoby, *Freethinkers*.

363 See Wann, *Simple Prosperity*; Leonard, *Story of Stuff*; Schor, *Overspent American*; and Van Jones's 2010 TED Talk, "The Economic Injustice of Plastic." To explore some inspiring recent examples of communi-ty-led environmental, social, and economic justice projects, check out Baratunde Thurston's website and podcast, "How to Citizen," the Majora Carter Group, the Center for Health, Environment & Justice, Mia Birdsong's Good Life Project, and Winona LaDuke's Center for Humans and Nature.

364 *Slaughterhouse-Five* fans would quickly point out, though, that this Kilgore Trout story appears in chapter 13 of *God Bless You, Mr. Rosewater*, not Vonnegut's 1969 novel.

365 NYPL-CC, B 707, F Misc Correspondence Operation Eggnog.

366 KV letter to Harry Brague (HB), September 30, 1952, PU-CS, B 349, F 5.

367 KV postcard to HB, October 9, 1952, PU-CS, B 349, F 5.

368 HB letter to KV, December 29, 1952, PU-CS, B 349, F 5.

369 LL-KV, B 12, F 45; typescript summary, B 38, F Carbon TV Synopsis.

370 See Jarvis, "'If He Comes Home Nervous.'"

371 HB letter to KV December 29, 1952, PU-CS, B 349, F 5.

372 KV, ms. draft, "I Shall Not Want," LL-KV, B 13. According to Jane's notes, Kurt entered the story in the *New Republic* essay contest in 1946 and sent it to *Coronet* on August 16, 1947. Vonnegut used the pseud-onym "Paul W. Martin" with both submissions. The essay is perhaps Vonnegut's most important unpublished early war piece.

373 The letter is reprinted in *Armageddon in Retrospect* and is widely avail-able online. Thanks to M. André Eckenrode's careful research, we can place the earliest publication of the letter to June 28, 1945, in the *Elizabethtown Post*. With its sprinkles of dark humor, careful refrain of "but not me," compressed emotion, and short, biting sentences, the letter's "literary" qualities are evident and no doubt the reason Kurt's sister-in-law Bow Vonnegut decided to share it with the newspaper. Perhaps the most prescient part of the letter is its penultimate line— "I've too damned much to say, the rest will have to wait."

374 *Slaughterhouse-Five* quotations for the rest of this chapter can be

found on the following pages in the 2009 Dial edition: 4, 34, 203, 194, 57, 46, 236, 243, 247, 102, 90, 191, 274, 128, 94–95, 28.

375 Given the incredible volume of *Slaughterhouse-Five* criticism, it would be a Sisyphean task to cite all the relevant titles. Fortunately, Tom Roston's *The Writer's Crusade* offers wonderful analysis of the novel, its compositional history, Vonnegut's wartime experiences, war trauma, other veterans' perspectives, and the novel's literary and cultural legacies. In addition to Roston's rich bibliography, Bloom's and Mustazza's essay collections on the novel offer good starting points.

376 See Rothberg, *Multidirectional Memory*.

377 Farrell, *Critical Companion*, 361.

378 Vonnegut returned to the story of Eddie Slovik in his 1993 libretto for Stravinsky's *L'Histoire du Soldat*, and published the lyrics in the fall 1998 issue of the *Paris Review*. To read about Vonnegut's desire to keep Slovik's story alive, see Alicia Zuckerman, "Life During Wartime," *New York Magazine*, March 23, 2006, nymag.com.

379 Historians continue to debate the death toll and other aspects of the Allied bombings of Dresden, and some recent studies suggest that roughly 25,000 people were killed. Although this number is drastically lower than the 135,000 estimate Vonnegut mentions in *Slaughterhouse-Five*, no one disputes that the city was destroyed and that thousands of civilians died during the firebombing. For more discussion of these debates and details about the bombings, see Taylor, *Dresden* and De Bruhl, *Firestorm*. Readers primarily interested in American POW perspectives should consult Szpek and Idzikowski, *Shadows of Slaughterhouse Five*.

380 Leonard, "God Bless You, Mr. Vonnegut."

381 Vonnegut, *Wampeters, Foma & Granfalloons*, 97.

382 Vonnegut's powerful Vietnam War moratorium speech, "Let the Killing Stop," first appeared in *The Register* on October 23, 1969, and is reprinted in *If This Isn't Nice, What Is?* The Sturgis Library also has coverage of Vonnegut's May 1970 remarks at a peace rally at Cape Cod Community College. In contrast to other speakers at the event, Vonnegut made an urgent plea for nonviolent student demonstrations in the wake of the Kent State shootings earlier that month. See Ellis Morris, "Conflicting Advice Given at Peace Rally," *The Register*, May 21, 1970, SL-KV.

383 KV letter to Don Farber, May 12, 1970, *Letters*, 159.

384 Steffen, "Ending Violence," *WorldChanging*, 434. As Steffen notes, "War undermines every aspect of sustainability: it destroys the

environment; it upends the lives of those caught within it; it impover-
ishes whole nations." "If we are to create a more stable world," Steffen
further explains, "we need to do a better job heading off conflict (or
negotiating its end), of stopping genocides, and of bringing killers to
justice." 439, 434.

385 This phrase comes from one of several drafts for antiwar speeches ca.
1991/1992. Vonnegut noted, "Our great victory in the Persian Gulf was
perhaps the most stupid, expensive, wasteful, destructive murderous
enterprise in all our history." LL-KV, B 16, F 9. For a firsthand account
of Vonnegut's January 1991 antiwar speech at All Souls Unitarian
Church in Lexington Avenue, NYC, see Wakefield, *Making of a Writer*.

386 Littauer letter to Vonnegut, April 6, 1960; Robert Mills, note, March
25, 1960; Littauer letter to Vonnegut, March 1, 1960, LL-KV, B 14, F
"Please Omit Flowers."

387 *Happy Birthday, Wanda June* quotations can be found on pages 53–54
and 76–78 in the 1971 Delta edition.

388 Morain and Morain, *Humanism as the Next Step*, 111.

389 Vonnegut, Collins, and Landau, "Requiem: The Hocus Pocus
Laundromat." I have drawn on and quote from the original publica-
tion, but Vonnegut reprints and introduces "Requiem" in *Fates Worse
Than Death*.

390 Richard Chon, "Premiere of Vonnegut-Grana Requiem Proves
Perplexing," *The Buffalo News*, March 14, 1988. More extensive media
coverage, DE-AP, B 2, F 4.

391 Shields makes a connection between Vonnegut's composition and
Jane's final battle with cancer, noting, "it can be fairly assumed that he
was thinking about the end of her life." *And So It Goes*, 376. For more on
these humanist virtues, see Kurtz, *What Is Secular Humanism?*, 41.

392 Sweeney, "Kurt Vonnegut," 86.

393 Barab, composer's note, *Cosmos Cantana*.

394 On page 84 of *Timequake*, Vonnegut further explains why he rec-
ommends joining a church: "I couldn't recommend Humanism for
such a person. I wouldn't do so for the great majority of the planet's
population. The German philosopher Friedrich Wilhelm Nietzsche,
who had syphilis, said that only a person of deep faith could afford
the luxury of religious skepticism. Humanists, by and large educated, comfortably middle-class persons with rewarding lives like
mine, find rapture enough in secular knowledge and hope. Most
people can't."

395 *God Bless You, Dr. Kevorkian* quotations come from pages 16–17, 11–13, 31, 84–89, 15, and 91 of the 2010 Seven Stories edition.

396 Leeds, *Vonnegut Encyclopedia*, 268.

397 Leeds, 268–70. This summary only begins to scratch the surface of Leeds's especially thoughtful analysis of *God Bless You, Dr. Kevorkian*.

398 For more information about Kevorkian's long and complicated history with physician-assisted suicide, see Keith Schneider, "Dr. Jack Kevorkian Dies at 83; A Doctor Who Helped End Lives," *New York Times*, June 3, 2011.

399 Vonnegut fans familiar with the original WNYC "On the Media" broadcast on April 18, 1999, will recognize that the interview comments attributed to Trout were originally spoken by Vonnegut without the guise of a character. God bless André Eckenrode for this information.

400 Leeds, *Vonnegut Encyclopedia*, 270.

401 "Requiem" appeared in both the *Spokesman* and *In These Times* before its October 2005 publication in *A Man Without a Country*.

402 I'm taking slight liberties with a statement Vonnegut made in an interview with Christopher Blazejewski for *The Harvard Crimson* on May 12, 2000. When asked what question he would ask God in the afterlife, Vonnegut replied: "Well, if I really do take a railroad train to the afterlife, I would have no idea how to speak directly to him. It would be like talking to Shakespeare. How could I compete with God or him? I guess I would turn to Ben Franklin and ask him 'How do you fucking talk to God?'" thecrimson.harvard.edu/arts.

Abádi-Nagy, Zoltán. "Serenity, Courage, Wisdom: A Talk with Kurt Vonnegut, 1989." In Reed and Leeds, *Vonnegut Chronicles*, 15–34.

Alaimo, Stacy. *Exposed: Environmental Politics and Pleasures in Posthuman Times*. Minneapolis: Univ. of Minnesota Press, 2016.

Allen, William Rodney, ed. *Conversations with Kurt Vonnegut*. Jackson: Univ. Press of Mississippi, 1999.

———. *Understanding Kurt Vonnegut*. Columbia: Univ. of South Carolina Press, 1991.

Almond, Steve. "Why I Crush on Vonnegut." *(Not that You Asked): Rants, Exploits, and Obsessions*, 15–67. New York: Random House, 2007.

Augé, Marc. *Non-Places: An Introduction to Supermodernity*. Translated by John Howe. New York: Verso, 2008.

Barab, Seymour. *Cosmos Cantata: Music of Seymour Barab*. Text by Kurt Vonnegut. Manhattan Chamber Orchestra, conducted by Richard Auldon Clark. Helicon Records, 2001, compact disk.

Benson, Phillippa Day. "Raspberry 14 Calling His Cousins." *The Australian Women's Weekly*, January 31, 1976.

Bezner, Kevin. "A Conversation with Kurt Vonnegut." *The Washington Book Review*, Oct./Nov. 1979.

Bloom, Harold, ed. *Bloom's Modern Critical Views: Kurt Vonnegut, New Edition*. New York: Infobase, 2009.

———. *Bloom's Modern Critical Interpretations: Kurt Vonnegut's Slaughterhouse-Five, New Edition*. New York: Infobase, 2009.

Boas, Franz. *A Franz Boas Reader: The Shaping of American Anthropology, 1883–1911*. Edited by George W. Stocking, Jr. Chicago: Chicago Univ. Press, 1989.

Boon, Kevin Alexander, ed. *At Millennium's End: New Essays on the Work of Kurt Vonnegut*. Foreword by Kurt Vonnegut. Albany: SUNY Press, 2001.

Broer, Lawrence R. *Vonnegut and Hemingway: Writers at War*. Columbia: Univ. Press of South Carolina, 2011.

———. "Vonnegut's Goodbye: Kurt Senior, Hemingway, and Kilgore Trout." In Boon, *At Millennium's End*, 65–90.

Buell, Lawrence. *The Future of Environmental Criticism: Environmental Crisis and Literary Imagination*. Malden, MA: Blackwell, 2005.

Bullard, Robert. *Dumping in Dixie: Race, Class, And Environmental Quality, Third Edition*. New York: Routledge, 2018.

Carr, Nicholas. *The Glass Cage: Automation and Us*. New York: W. W. Norton, 2014.

———. *The Shallows: What the Internet Is Doing to Our Brains*. New York: W. W. Norton, 2010.

Carson, Rachel. *Silent Spring: Fortieth Anniversary Edition*. Introduction by Linda Lear. New York: Houghton Mifflin, 2002.

Chakrabarty, Dipesh. "The Climate of History: Four Theses." In Hiltner, *Ecocriticism*, 335–52.

Christoff, Peter, and Robyn Eckersley. *Globalization and the Environment*. New York: Rowman & Littlefield, 2013.

Clark, Timothy. *The Cambridge Introduction to Literature and the Environment*. New York: Cambridge Univ. Press, 2011.

Collins, Robert M. *More: The Politics of Economic Growth in Postwar America*. New York: Oxford Univ. Press, 2000.

Coontz, Stephanie. *The Way We Never Were: American Families and the Nostalgia Trap*. New York: Basic Books, 1992.

Cotton, Steve. "Earth Day—What Happened." *Audubon*, July 1970.

Cregor, Caterina. *The Path Well Chosen: History of the Orchard School, 1922–1984*. Indianapolis: Orchard School Foundation, 1984.

Cresswell, Tim. *Place: An Introduction*. 2nd ed. Malden, MA: Wiley Blackwell, 2015.

Davies, Jeremy. *The Birth of the Anthropocene*. Oakland: Univ. of California Press, 2016.

Davies, Tony. *Humanism*. 2nd ed. New York: Routledge, 2008.

Davis, Harry M. "Mathematical Machines." *Scientific American* 180, no. 4 (1949): 28–39.

Davis, Todd F. *Kurt Vonnegut's Crusade: Or, How a Postmodern Harlequin Preached a New Kind of Humanism*. Albany: SUNY Press, 2006.

De Bell, Garrett. *The Environmental Handbook: Prepared for the First National Environmental Teach-in, April 20, 1970*. New York: Ballantine, 1970.

De Bruhl, Marshall. *Firestorm: Allied Airpower and the Destruction of Dresden*. New York: Random House, 2006.

de Graaf et al. *Affluenza: The All-Consuming Epidemic*. 2nd ed. San Francisco: Berrett-Koehler, 2005.

Dostoyevsky, Fyodor. *The Brothers Karamazov: A Novel in Four Parts and an Epilogue.* 1880. Translated by David McDuff. New York: Penguin, 2003.

Dunaway, Finis. "Cultures of Nature: Twentieth Century." In Sackman, *Companion,* 266–84.

———. "Gas Masks, Pogo, and the Ecological Indian: Earth Day and the Visual Politics of American Environmentalism." *American Quarterly* 60, no. 1 (2008): 67–99.

Durning, Alan. *How Much Is Enough?: The Consumer Society and the Future of the Earth.* New York: W. W. Norton, 1992.

Eckenrode, M. André Z. "Appendix: Contributions to the *Shortridge Daily Echo* and the *Cornell Sun.*" In Reed, *Short Fiction,* 157–64.

Edwards, Andres R. *The Sustainability Revolution: Portrait of a Paradigm Shift.* 2005. Gabriola Island: New Society, 2007.

Ehrlich, Paul R. "Eco-Catastrophe!" In *Ramparts, Eco-Catastrophe,* 1–14.

———. *The Population Bomb (Revised).* 1968. New York: Ballantine, 1978.

Epstein, Greg M. *Good Without God: What a Billion Nonreligious People Do Believe.* New York: Harper, 2010.

Erickson, Paul A., and Liam D. Murphy. *A History of Anthropological Theory.* 3rd ed. Toronto: Univ. of Toronto Press, 2008.

Eriksen, Thomas Hylland, and Finn Sivert Nielsen. *A History of Anthropology.* Sterling, VA: Pluto, 2001.

Essential Vonnegut: Interviews Conducted by Walter Miller. Caedmon Essentials. Harper Collins, 2006, compact disk.

Failey, Majie Alford. *We Never Danced Cheek to Cheek: The Young Kurt Vonnegut in Indianapolis and Beyond.* Carmel, IN: Hawthorne, 2010.

Farrell, Susan. *Critical Companion to Kurt Vonnegut: A Literary Reference to His Life and Work.* New York: Facts on File, 2008.

Fiedler, Leslie. "The Divine Stupidity of Kurt Vonnegut: Portrait of the Novelist as Bridge over Troubled Water." In Leeds and Reed, *Images and Representations,* 5–18.

Fiene, Donald M. "Elements of Dostoevsky in the Novels of Kurt Vonnegut." *Dostoevsky Studies,* 2 (1981): 129–42.

Flores, Dan. "Earthlings: Evolution and Place in Environmental History." In Sackman, *Companion,* 595–614.

Freese, Peter. *The Clown of Armageddon: The Novels of Kurt Vonnegut.* Heidelberg: Universitätsverlag Winter, 2009.

Fuchs, Anne. *After the Dresden Bombing: Pathways of Memory, 1945 to the Present*. New York: Palgrave Macmillan, 2012.

Gabel, J. C., "The Melancholia of Everything Completed: The *Stop Smiling* Interview with Kurt Vonnegut." Photography by Edie Vonnegut and Buck Squibb. *Stop Smiling*, August 2006.

Gannon, Matthew. "A Second Noah's Ark." *The Vonnegut Review*, Summer 2013. vonnegutreview.com.

Garrard, Greg. *Ecocriticism*. 2nd ed. New York: Routledge, 2011.

Giannone, Richard. *Vonnegut: A Preface to His Novels*. Port Washington, NY: Kennikat, 1977.

Glotfelty, Cheryll and Harold Fromm. *The Ecocriticism Reader: Landmarks in Literary Ecology*. Athens: Georgia Univ. Press, 1996.

Godwin, Gail. *Publishing: A Writer's Memoir*. New York: Bloomsbury, 2015.

Goldsmith, David H. *Kurt Vonnegut: Fantasist of Fire and Ice*. Bowling Green, OH: Bowling Green Univ. Press, 1972.

Goodell, Jeff. *The Water Will Come: Rising Seas, Sinking Cities, and the Remaking of the Civilized World*. New York: Little, Brown, 2017.

Gopnik, Adam. "Voltaire's Garden: The Philosopher as a Campaigner for Human Rights." *New Yorker*, March 7, 2005.

Gross, Terry. "Interview: Kurt Vonnegut, Jr." *Applause*, March 1987.

Handy, Edward O. *Images of America: Barnstable Village, West Barnstable, and Sandy Neck*. Charleston, SC: Arcadia, 2003.

Hatch, Gardner, and W. Curtiss Musten, eds. *American Ex-Prisoners of War: Non Solum Armis*. Paducah, KY: Turner Publishing, 1988.

Haviland, William A. *Cultural Anthropology*. 9th ed. Toronto: Harcourt Brace, 1999.

Hawken, Paul. *Blessed Unrest: How the Largest Social Movement in History is Restoring Grace, Justice, and Beauty to the World*. New York: Penguin, 2008.

Hayes, Denis. "The Beginning." In *Earth Day—The Beginning: A Guide for Survival*, edited by National Environmental Action Staff, i–iii. New York: Bantam, 1970.

Heise, Ursula K. *Sense of Place and Sense of Planet: The Environmental Imagination of the Global*. Oxford: Oxford Univ. Press, 2008.

———. "The Virtual Crowds: Overpopulation, Space and Speciesism." *Interdisciplinary Studies in Literature and Environment* 8, no. 1 (2001): 1–29.

Henley, Faye. *The Story of the Children's Museum of Indianapolis*. Indianapolis: Children's Museum, 1940.

Heyn, Marnie. "Vonnegut's Latest: Healing a Dying Planet." *Michigan Daily*, October 7, 1973.

Hicks, Andrew John. *Posthumanism in the Novels of Kurt Vonnegut: Matter That Complains So*. New York: Routledge, 2021.

Hicks, Jennifer Bowen. "The Rumpus Interview with Nanette Vonnegut." November 12, 2012. therumpus.net

Hillman, Tony. "Hooked." *Summary* 1, no. 2 (1971): 69–72.

Hiltner, Ken, ed. *Ecocriticism: The Essential Reader*. New York: Routledge, 2015.

Howie, Hillis L. "An Expedition for Older Boys." *Ford News*, April 1941.

———."The Prairie Trek." *The Regional Review*, 1941.

Humes, Edward. *Garbology: Our Dirty Love Affair with Trash*. New York: Avery, 2013.

Irving, John. "Kurt Vonnegut and His Critics: The Aesthetics of Accessibility." *New Republic*, September 22, 1979.

Jacobs, Jane. *The Life and Death of Great American Cities*. New York: Random House, 1961.

Jacoby, Susan. *Freethinkers: A History of American Secularism*. New York: Metropolitan Books, 2004.

Jarvis, Christina. "'If He Comes Home Nervous': U.S. World War II Neuropsychiatric Casualties and Postwar Masculinities." *Journal of Men's Studies: A Scholarly Journal About Men and Masculinities* 17, no. 2 (2009): 97–115.

———. "The Vietnamization of World War II in *Slaughterhouse-Five* and *Gravity's Rainbow*." In Bloom, *Kurt Vonnegut's Slaughterhouse-Five*, 61–83.

Johnson, Cecil E., ed. *Eco-Crisis*. New York: John Wiley & Sons, 1970.

Keefer, Louis E. *Scholars in Foxholes: The Story of the Army Specialized Training Program in World War II*. Reston, VA: COTU, 1998.

Kinkela, David. *DDT and the American Century: Global Health, Environmental Politics, and the Pesticide that Changed the World*. Chapel Hill: North Carolina Univ. Press, 2011.

Klein, Naomi. *No Is Not Enough: Resisting Trump's Shock Politics and Winning the World We Need*. Chicago: Haymarket, 2017.

———. *On Fire: The (Burning) Case for a Green New Deal*. New York: Simon & Schuster, 2019.

———. *This Changes Everything: Capitalism vs. The Climate*. New York: Simon & Schuster, 2014.

Kline, Benjamin. *First Along the River: A Brief History of the U.S. Environmental Movement.* 4th ed. New York: Rowman & Littlefield, 2011.

Klinkowitz, Jerome. *Kurt Vonnegut's America.* Columbia: Univ. Press of South Carolina, 2010.

——. *Slaughterhouse-Five: Reforming the Novel and the World.* Boston: Twayne, 1990.

——. *The Vonnegut Effect.* Columbia: Univ. Press of South Carolina, 2004.

——. *Vonnegut in Fact: The Public Spokesmanship of Personal Fiction.* Columbia: Univ. Press of South Carolina, 1998.

Klinkowitz, Jerome, and Donald L. Lawler, eds. *Vonnegut in America: An Introduction to the Life and Work of Kurt Vonnegut.* New York: Delacorte/ Seymour Lawrence, 1977.

Klinkowitz, Jerome, and John Somer, eds. *The Vonnegut Statement: Original Essays on the Life and Work of Kurt Vonnegut, Jr. with a Bibliography.* New York: Delacorte/Seymour Lawrence, 1973.

Kolbert, Elizabeth. *Field Notes from a Catastrophe: Man, Nature, and Climate Change.* Rev. ed. New York: Bloomsbury, 2015.

——. *The Sixth Extinction: An Unnatural History.* New York: Henry Holt, 2014.

Krementz, Jill, ed. *Happy Birthday, Kurt Vonnegut: A Festschrift for Kurt Vonnegut on his Sixtieth Birthday.* New York: Delacorte, 1982.

——. *The Writer's Image.* Preface by Kurt Vonnegut. Boston: David R. Godine, 1980.

Kriplen, Nancy. *Keep an Eye on That Mummy: A History of the Children's Museum of Indianapolis.* Indianapolis: Children's Museum, 1982.

Kurtz, Paul. *What Is Secular Humanism?* Amherst, NY: Prometheus Books, 2007.

Lamont, Corliss. *The Philosophy of Humanism.* 7th ed, rev. New York: Continuum, 1990.

Langfeldt, Gabriel. *Albert Schweitzer: A Study of His Philosophy of Life.* Translated by Maurice Michael. London: George Allen & Unwin, 1960.

Lawrence, Seymour. "A Publisher's Dream." *Summary* 1, no. 2 (1971): 73–75.

Lawson, Evelyn. *Yesterday's Cape Cod.* Foreword by Kurt Vonnegut, Jr. Miami: E. A. Seamann, 1975.

Layton, Robert. *An Introduction to Theory in Anthropology.* Cambridge: Cambridge Univ. Press, 2006.

Leeds, Marc. *The Vonnegut Encyclopedia, Revised and Updated Edition.* New York: Delacorte, 2016.

Leeds, Marc, and Peter Reed, eds. *Kurt Vonnegut: Images and Representations.* Westport, CT: Greenwood, 2000.

Leonard, Annie. *The Story of Stuff: The Impact of Overconsumption on the Planet, Our Communities, and Our Health.* New York: Free Press, 2011.

Leonard, John. "God Bless You, Mr. Vonnegut." *Nation*, April 13, 2007.

Leopold, Aldo. *A Sand County Almanac and Sketches Here and There.* 1949. Introduction by Robert Finch. New York: Oxford Univ. Press, 1989.

Lovegrove, James. "The World of the End of the World: Apocalyptic and Post-Apocalyptic Science Fiction." In *Strange Divisions and Alien Territories: The Sub-genres of Science Fiction*, edited by Keith Brooke, 97–111. New York: Palgrave Macmillan, 2012.

Lutholtz, M. William. *Grand Dragon: D.C. Stephenson and the Ku Klux Klan in Indiana.* West Lafayette, IN: Purdue Univ. Press, 1991.

McCartan, Tom, ed. *Kurt Vonnegut: The Last Interview and Other Conversations.* Brooklyn: Melville House, 2011.

McClay, Wilfred, and Ted McAllister, eds. *Why Place Matters: Geography, Identity, and Civic Life in Modern America.* New York: New Atlantis, 2014.

McInnis, Gilbert. *Evolutionary Mythology in the Writings of Kurt Vonnegut: Darwin, Vonnegut and the Construction of an American Culture.* Palo Alto, CA: Academica, 2011.

McKee, Alexander. *Dresden 1945: The Devil's Tinderbox.* New York: Dutton, 1984.

McKibben, Bill, ed. *American Earth: Environmental Writing Since Thoreau.* New York: Penguin Putnam, 2008.

———. *Eaarth: Making a Life on a Tough New Planet.* New York: Henry Holt, 2010.

———. "Introduction." In Steffen, *WorldChanging*, 13–15.

McMahon, Gary. *Kurt Vonnegut and the Centrifugal Force of Fate.* Jefferson, NC: McFarland, 2009.

McNeill, J. R. *Something New Under the Sun: An Environmental History of the Twentieth-Century World.* New York: W. W. Norton, 2000.

McQuade, Molly. "Kurt Vonnegut: A Very Fringe Character." In *An Unsentimental Education: Writers and Chicago*, edited by Molly McQuade, 235–42. Chicago: Univ. of Chicago Press, 1995.

Marvin, Thomas F. *Kurt Vonnegut: A Critical Companion.* Westport, CT: Greenwood, 2002.

Mayo, Anna. "Vonnegut & Earth Day: Can a Granfalloon Save the Planet?" *Village Voice*, April 30, 1970.

Melville, Herman. *Moby Dick: A Norton Critical Edition*. 2nd ed. Edited by Hershel Parker and Harrison Hayford. New York: W. W. Norton, 2002.

Mentak, Said. "Humane Harmony: Environmentalism and Culture in Vonnegut's Writings." In Tally, *Critical Insights*, 269–93.

——. *A (Mis)reading of Kurt Vonnegut*. New York: Nova Science, 2010.

Merrill, Robert, ed. *Critical Essays on Kurt Vonnegut*. Boston: G. K. Hall, 1990.

Meyerowitz, Joanne, ed. *Not June Cleaver: Women and Gender in Postwar America, 1945-1960*. Philadelphia: Temple Univ. Press, 1994.

Mickey, Sam. *Whole Earth Thinking and Planetary Coexistence: Ecological Wisdom at the Intersection of Religion, Ecology, and Philosophy*. New York: Routledge, 2016.

Moon, Nathan. "The Amphetamine Years: A Study of the Medical Applications and Extramedical Consumption of Psychostimulant Drugs in the Postwar United States, 1945–1980." PhD diss., Georgia Institute of Technology, 2009.

Moore, Leonard. *Citizen Klansmen: The Ku Klux Klan in Indiana, 1921-1928*. Chapel Hill: Univ. of North Carolina Press, 1997.

Morain, Lloyd, and Mary Morain. *Humanism as the Next Step*. Rev. ed. Amherst, NY: Humanist Press, 1998.

Morse, Donald E. "The Curious Reception of Kurt Vonnegut." In Tally, *Critical Insights*, 42–59.

——. "Kurt Vonnegut: The Once and Future Satirist." In *The Dark Fantastic: Selected Essays from the Ninth International Conference on the Fantastic in the Arts*, edited by C. W. Sullivan, 161–72. Westport, CT: Greenwood, 1997.

——. *The Novels of Kurt Vonnegut: Imagining Being an American*. Westport, CT: Praeger, 2003.

Mustazza, Leonard. *Forever Pursuing Genesis: The Myth of Eden in the Novels of Kurt Vonnegut*. Lewisburg, PA: Bucknell Univ. Press, 1990.

Myler, Joseph. "The Dirty Animal—Man." In Johnson, *Eco-Crisis*, 116–141.

Nash, Tom. "Kurt Vonnegut: The Story Behind the Legendary Author's Cape Cod Dealership." *Massachusetts Auto Dealer*, August 2011.

National Staff of Environmental Action, ed. *Earth Day—The Beginning: A Guide for Survival*. New York: Bantam, 1970.

O'Loughlin, Jim, ed. *Kurt Vonnegut Remembered*. Tuscaloosa: Univ. of Alabama Press, 2019.

Olson, Lynn. "Poo-tee-weet?" *Draftings in Vonnegut*. Univ. of Northern Iowa (1988): 21–32.

Packard, Vance. *The Waste Makers*. New York: Giant Cardinal, 1963.

Pardee, Shiela Ellen. "Anthropology across the Universe: Folk Societies in the Early Novels of Kurt Vonnegut." In Tally, *Critical Insights*, 185–205.

Patterson, Thomas. *A Social History of Anthropology in the United States*. New York: Berg, 2001.

Perlstein, Rick. *The Invisible Bridge: The Fall of Nixon and the Rise of Reagan*. New York: Simon & Schuster, 2014.

Pieratt, Asa B., Julie Huffman-Klinkowitz, and Jerome Klinkowitz. *Kurt Vonnegut: A Comprehensive Bibliography*. Hamden, CT: Archon Books, 1987.

Pinn, Anthony B., ed. *What Is Humanism, and Why Does It Matter?* Durham, UK: Acumen Publishing, 2013.

Quammen, David. *Spillover: Animal Infections and the Next Human Pandemic*. New York: W. W. Norton, 2013.

Rackstraw, Loree. "Dancing with the Muse in Vonnegut's Later Novels." In Reed and Leeds, *Vonnegut Chronicles*, 123–43.

———. *Love as Always, Kurt: Vonnegut as I Knew Him*. Cambridge, MA: Da Capo, 2009.

———. "The Vonnegut Cosmos." In Merrill, *Critical Essays*, 53–61.

Ramparts editors, *Eco-Catastrophe*. New York: Harper & Row, 1970.

Redfield, Robert. "The Folk Society." *The American Journal of Sociology* 52, no. 4 (1947): 293–308.

Reed, Peter J. *Kurt Vonnegut, Jr*. Writers for the Seventies Series. New York: Warner, 1972.

———. "The Remarkable Artwork of Kurt Vonnegut." In *Kurt Vonnegut: Drawings*, 12–20.

———. *The Short Fiction of Kurt Vonnegut*. Westport, CT: Greenwood, 1997.

Reed, Peter J., and Marc Leeds. *The Vonnegut Chronicles: Interviews and Essays*. Westport, CT: Greenwood, 1996.

Rentilly, J. "God Bless You, Mr. Vonnegut." In McCartan, *The Last Interview*, 153–61.

Reynolds, Alastair. "Space Opera: This Galaxy Ain't Big Enough for the Both of Us." In *Strange Divisions and Alien Territories: The Sub-genres of Science Fiction*, edited by Keith Brooke, 12–25. New York: Palgrave Macmillan, 2012.

Rome, Adam. *The Genius of Earth Day: How a 1970 Teach-In Unexpectedly Made the First Green Generation*. New York: Hill & Wang, 2013.

Roston, Tom. *The Writer's Crusade: Kurt Vonnegut and the Many Lives of Slaughterhouse-Five*. New York: Abrams, 2021.

Rothberg, Michael. *Multidirectional Memory: Remembering the Holocaust in the Age of Decolonization*. Redwood City, CA: Stanford Univ. Press, 2009.

Sackman, Douglas, ed. *A Companion to American Environmental History*. Malden, MA: Wiley Blackwell, 2014.

Said, Edward W. *Humanism and Democratic Criticism*. New York: Columbia Univ. Press, 2004.

Samuels, Charles T. "Age of Vonnegut." *New Republic*, June 12, 1971.

Scholes, Robert. "Chasing a Lone Eagle: Vonnegut's College Writing" and "A Talk with Kurt Vonnegut, Jr." In Klinkowitz and Somer, *Vonnegut Statement*, 45–54, 90–118.

Schweitzer, Albert. *Civilization and Ethics*. 3rd ed. Translated by C. T. Campion. London: Adam & Charles Black, 1955.

———. *Reverence for Life: An Anthology of Selected Writings*. Edited by Thomas Kiernan. New York: Philosophical Library, 1965.

———. *The Teaching of Reverence for Life*. Translated by Richard and Clara Winston. New York: Holt, Rinehart & Winston, 1965.

Sellars, Richard West. *Preserving Nature in the National Parks: A History*. New Haven, CT: Yale Univ. Press, 1997.

Sellers, Chris. "Cities and Suburbs." In Sackman, *Companion*, 462–81.

Shields, Charles J. *And So It Goes: Kurt Vonnegut: A Life*. New York: Henry Holt, 2011.

Simmons, David, ed. *New Critical Essays on Kurt Vonnegut*. New York: Palgrave Macmillan, 2009.

Solnit, Rebecca. "Water." In Sackman, *Companion*, 92–95.

Steffen, Alex. *WorldChanging: A User's Guide for the 21st Century, Revised and Updated*. New York: Abrams, 2011.

Steinberg, Ted. *Down to Earth: Nature's Role in American History*. 2nd ed. New York: Oxford Univ. Press, 2009.

Stocking, George W., Jr. *Anthropology at Chicago: An Exhibit Marking the Fiftieth Anniversary of the Department of Anthropology*. Chicago: Joseph Regenstein Library, Univ. of Chicago, 1979.

———. *The Ethnographer's Magic and Other Essays in the History of Anthropology*. Madison: Univ. of Wisconsin Press, 1992.

———. *Race, Culture, and Evolution: Essays in the History of Anthropology, New Phoenix Edition*. Chicago Univ. Press, 1982.

Stradling, David, ed. *The Environmental Movement, 1968–1972*. Seattle: Univ. of Washington Press, 2012.

Strand, Ginger. *The Brothers Vonnegut: Science Fiction in the House of Magic*. New York: Farrar, Straus & Giroux, 2015.

———. "How Jane Vonnegut Made Kurt Vonnegut a Writer." *New Yorker*, December 3, 2015.

———. "Kurt Vonnegut's Oklahoma Eden." *This Land*, May 3, 2016. thislandpress.com

———. "Vonnegut on the Road: A Fair Use Affair." *Tin House* 17, no. 1 (2015): 41–52.

Sumner, Gregory D. *Unstuck in Time: A Journey Through Kurt Vonnegut's Life and Novels*. New York: Seven Stories, 2011.

Sutton, Chelsea. "Klan Records: Wayne County KKK Records Paint Picture of Klan Life in 1920s Indiana and Offer Data about Our Ancestors." *Connections: The Hoosier Genealogist* 55, no. 1 (2015): 27–36.

Sutton, Mark, and E. N. Anderson. *Introduction to Cultural Ecology*. 3rd ed. New York: AltaMira, 2014.

Sweeney, Terrance. "Kurt Vonnegut, Jr." In *God &*, 86–89. Minneapolis: Winston, 1985.

Szpek, Ervin, and Frank Idzikowski. Edited by Heidi Szpek. *Shadows of Slaughterhouse Five: Reflections and Recollections of the American Ex-POWs of Schlachthof Fünf, Dresden, Germany*. Bloomington, IN: iUniverse, 2008.

Tally, Robert, Jr., ed. *Critical Insights: Kurt Vonnegut*. Ipswich, MA: Salem, 2013.

———. *Kurt Vonnegut and the American Novel: A Postmodern Iconography*. New York: Continuum, 2011.

Taylor, Frederick. *Dresden: Tuesday, February 13, 1945*. New York: Harper Collins, 2004.

Thomas, Charlotte. "The Cape Cod National Seashore: A Case Study of Federal Administrative Control Over Traditionally Local Land Use Decisions." *Boston College Environmental Affairs Law Review* 12, no. 2 (1985): 225–72. lawdigitalcommons.bc.edu. 20 September 2015.

Thomas, P. L. *Reading, Learning, Teaching Vonnegut*. New York: Peter Lang, 2006.

Thoreau, Henry David. *Cape Cod*. Edited by Dudley C. Lunt. Introduction by Henry Beston. New York: Bramhall House, 1951.

———. *The Portable Thoreau*. Edited and introduced by Jeffrey Cramer. New York: Penguin, 2012.

———. *Walden: A Fully Annotated Edition*. Edited and introduced by Jeffrey Cramer. New Haven, CT: Yale Univ. Press, 2004.

Tuan, Yi-Fu. "Place/Space, Ethnicity/Cosmos: Hot to Be More Fully Human." In *Why Place Matters: Geography, Identity, and Civic Life in Modern America*, edited by Wilfred McClay and Ted McAllister, 102–19. New York: New Atlantis, 2014.

———. *Space and Place: The Perspective of Experience*. Minneapolis: Univ. of Minnesota Press, 2008.

Tucker, Richard K. *The Dragon and the Cross: The Rise and Fall of the Ku Klux Klan in Middle America*. Hamden, CT: Archon Books, 1991.

Turkle, Sherry. *Alone Together: Why We Expect More from Technology and Less from Each Other*. New York: Basic Books, 2011.

Updike, John. "All's Well in Skyscraper National Park." In Merrill, *Critical Essays*, 40–47.

U.S. Congress, Eighty-Sixth. "Cape Cod National Seashore Park: Hearing Before the Subcommittee on Public Lands of the Committee on Interior and Insular Affairs." Parts 1 and 2. Washington: Government Printing Office, 1960. archive.org/details.capecodnationals02unit.

Vedantam, Shankar, and Bill Mesler. *Useful Delusions: The Power and Paradox of the Self-Deceiving Brain*. New York: W. W. Norton, 2021.

Vinal, William Gould. "Life, Liberty, and the Pursuit of Nature." *Nature Magazine*, April 1940.

Vonnegut, Kurt. *Armageddon in Retrospect: And Other New and Unpublished Writings on War and Peace*. Introduction by Mark Vonnegut. New York: G.P. Putnam's Sons, 2008.

———. *Bagombo Snuff Box: Uncollected Short Fiction*. 1999. New York: Berkley, 2000.

———. *Between Time and Timbuktu, or Prometheus 5: A Space Fantasy Based on Materials by Kurt Vonnegut, Jr.* Photographs by Jill Krementz. New York: Delta, 1972.

———. "The Big Space Fuck." In *Again, Dangerous Visions: 46 Original Stories*, edited by Harlan Ellison, 246–50. New York: Doubleday, 1972.

———. *Bluebeard*. 1987. New York: Laurel, 1988.

———. *Breakfast of Champions, or Goodbye Blue Monday!* 1973. New York: Dial, 2006.

———. *Canary in a Cat House*. 1961. Cutchogue, NY: Buccaneer, 1976.

———. *Cat's Cradle*. 1963. New York: Delta, 1998.

———. *Deadeye Dick*. 1982. New York: Laurel, 1985.

———. *Fates Worse Than Death: An Autobiographical Collage*. 1991. New York: Berkley, 1992.

———. "Foreword." In *A Saucer of Loneliness, Volume VII: The Complete Stories of Theodore Sturgeon*, edited by Paul Williams, ix. Berkeley, CA: North Atlantic, 2000.

———. *Galápagos: A Novel.* 1985. New York: Dial, 2009.

———. *God Bless You, Dr. Kevorkian.* 1999. Foreword by Neil Gaiman. New York: Seven Stories, 2010.

———. *God Bless You, Mr. Rosewater, or Pearls Before Swine.* 1965. New York: Dial, 2006.

———. *Happy Birthday, Wanda June.* 1970. Photographs by Jill Krementz. New York: Delta, 1971.

———. *Hocus Pocus.* 1990. New York: Berkley, 1991.

———. *If This Isn't Nice, What Is?: The Graduation Speeches and Other Words to Live By, (even more) expanded third edition.* Introduced and edited by Dan Wakefield. New York: Seven Stories, 2020.

———. *Jailbird.* 1979. New York: Delta, 1999.

———. *Kurt Vonnegut Complete Stories.* Collected and introduced by Jerome Klinkowitz and Dan Wakefield. Foreword by Dave Eggers. New York: Seven Stories, 2017.

———. *Kurt Vonnegut: Drawings.* New York: Monacelli, 2014.

———. *Kurt Vonnegut Letters.* Edited and introduced by Dan Wakefield. New York: Delacorte, 2012.

———. "The Lake." *Architectural Digest*, 45 (June 1988): 27, 30, 33, 35.

———. *Look at the Birdie: Unpublished Short Fiction.* Foreword by Sidney Offit. New York: Dial, 2010.

———. *Love, Kurt: The Vonnegut Love Letters, 1941–1945.* Edited by Edith Vonnegut. New York: Random House, 2020.

———. *A Man Without a Country.* 2005. Edited by Daniel Simon. New York: Random House, 2007.

———. *Mother Night.* 1961. New York: Avon, 1970.

———. "Nixon's the One." In *Earth Day—The Beginning: A Guide for Survival*, edited by National Environmental Action Staff, 64–65. New York: Bantam, 1970.

———. *Palm Sunday: An Autobiographical Collage.* 1981. New York: Dell, 1982.

———. *Player Piano.* 1952. New York: Delta, 1999.

———. *The Sirens of Titan.* 1959. New York: Delta, 1998.

———. "Skyscraper National Park." *Architectural Digest*, 44 (November 1987): 76, 78, 86.

———. *Slapstick, or Lonesome No More!* 1976. New York: Dial, 2006.

———. *Slaughterhouse-Five, or The Children's Crusade: A Duty-Dance with Death.* 1969. New York: Dial, 2009.

———. *Sucker's Portfolio.* Las Vegas: Amazon, 2012.

———. *Timequake.* 1997. New York: Berkley, 1998.

———. "To Hell with Marriage." In *Heaven Is Under Our Feet,* edited by Don Henley and Dave Marsh, 240–42. Stamford, CT: Longmeadow, 1991.

———. *Vonnegut by the Dozen.* Edited and introduced by Richard Lingeman. Book Mobile Printing. *The Nation,* 2013.

———. *Wampeters, Foma & Granfalloons (Opinions).* 1974. New York: Delta, 1999.

———. *We Are What We Pretend to Be: The First and Last Works.* Foreword by Nanette Vonnegut. Philadelphia: Vanguard, 2012.

———. *Welcome to the Monkey House: A Collection of Short Works by Kurt Vonnegut, Jr.* New York: Delta, 1968.

———. "What One Person Can Do." *World* 2, no. 5 (February 1973): 12.

———. *While Mortals Sleep: Unpublished Short Fiction.* Foreword by Dave Eggers. New York: Dial, 2012.

Vonnegut, Kurt, and Ivan Chermayeff. *Sun, Moon, Star.* New York: Harper & Row, 1980.

Vonnegut, Kurt, John F. Collins, and Jacob Landau, "Requiem: The Hocus Pocus Laundromat." *The North American Review* 271, no. 4 (1986): 29–35.

Vonnegut, Kurt, and Suzanne McConnell. *Pity the Reader: On Writing with Style.* New York: Seven Stories, 2019.

Vonnegut, Kurt, and Lee Stringer. *Like Shaking Hands with God: A Conversation about Writing.* 1999. Foreword by Daniel Simon. New York: Seven Stories, 2010.

Vonnegut, Mark. *The Eden Express: A Memoir of Insanity.* Foreword by Kurt Vonnegut. 1975. New York: Seven Stories Press, 2002.

———. *Just Like Someone Without Mental Illness Only More So: A Memoir.* New York: Delacorte, 2010.

Vonnegut, Nanette. "My Father, the Doodler." In *Kurt Vonnegut: Drawings,* 6–11.

Wakefield, Dan. "In Vonnegut's Karass." In Klinkowitz and Somer, *Vonnegut Statement,* 55–70.

———. "Kurt Vonnegut: Christ-Loving Atheist." *Image: Art, Faith, Mystery* 82 (2014). imagejournal.org.

———. *Kurt Vonnegut: The Making of a Writer.* New York: Seven Stories, 2022.

Waldron, Karen, and Rob Friedman, eds. *Toward a Literary Ecology: Places and Spaces in American Literature*. Toronto: Scarecrow, 2013.

Wann, David. *Simple Prosperity: Finding Real Wealth in a Sustainable Lifestyle*. New York: St. Martin's Griffin, 2007.

Warren, Louis S., ed. *American Environmental History*. Malden, MA: Blackwell, 2003.

Weide, Robert, and Don Argott, directors. *Kurt Vonnegut: Unstuck in Time*. IFC Films, 2021.

Wellock, Thomas. *Preserving the Nation: The Conservation and Environmental Movements, 1870–2000*. Wheeling, IL: Harlan Davidson, 2007.

West, James E., Chief Scout Executive, *Fourteenth Annual Report of the Boy Scouts of America*. In 68th Congress, House of Representatives, Document 354, June 4, 1924. Washington: Government Printing Office.

Whitlark, James. "Vonnegut's Anthropology Thesis." In *Literature and Anthropology*, edited by Philip A. Dennis and Wendell Aycock, 77–86. Lubbock: Texas Tech Univ. Press, 1989.

Wiener, Norbert. "Cybernetics." *Scientific American* 197, no. 5 (1948): 14–19.

———. *Cybernetics: Or Control and Communication in the Animal and the Machine*. 2nd ed. Cambridge, MA: MIT Press, 1961.

———. *The Human Use of Human Beings: Cybernetics and Society*. 2nd ed. New York: Doubleday, 1954.

Wilson, Edward O. *The Meaning of Human Existence*. New York: Liveright, 2014.

———. *The Social Conquest of Earth*. New York: Liveright, 2012.

Wilson, Edwin H. *The Genesis of a Humanist Manifesto*. Edited by Teresa Maciocha. Amherst, NY: Humanist Press, 1995.

Wolf, William. "Thru Time and Space with Kurt Vonnegut, Jr." *Chicago Tribune Magazine*, March 12, 1972.

A Writer's Roots: Kurt Vonnegut's Indianapolis. DVD. Produced by Kevin Finch, edited by Jim Hall. WFYI Indianapolis, 2015.

Yarmolinsky, Jane Vonnegut. *Angels Without Wings: How Tragedy Created a Remarkable Family*. Boston: Houghton Mifflin, 1987.

Index